RESEARCH HANDBOOK ON ACCOUNTING AND INFORMATION SYSTEMS

RESEARCH HANDBOOKS ON ACCOUNTING

This new and exciting series brings together authoritative and thought-provoking contributions on the most pressing topics and issues in accounting. *Research Handbooks* in the series feature specially commissioned chapters from eminent academics, and are each overseen by an editor internationally recognized as a leading name within the field. Chapters within the *Research Handbooks* feature comprehensive and cutting-edge research, and are written with a global readership in mind. Equally useful as reference tools or high-level introductions to specific topics, issues, methods and debates, these *Research Handbooks* will be an essential resource for academic researchers and postgraduate students.

For a full list of Edward Elgar published titles, including the titles in this series, visit our website at www.e-elgar.com.

Research Handbook on Accounting and Information Systems

Edited by

Julia A. Smith

Reader in Accounting & Finance, Strathclyde Business School, University of Strathclyde, Glasgow, UK

RESEARCH HANDBOOKS ON ACCOUNTING

Edward Elgar
PUBLISHING

Cheltenham, UK • Northampton, MA, USA

Published by
Edward Elgar Publishing Limited
The Lypiatts
15 Lansdown Road
Cheltenham
Glos GL50 2JA
UK

Edward Elgar Publishing, Inc.
William Pratt House
9 Dewey Court
Northampton
Massachusetts 01060
USA

A catalogue record for this book
is available from the British Library

Library of Congress Control Number: 2023951215

This book is available electronically in the **Elgar**online
Business subject collection
http://dx.doi.org/10.4337/9781802200621

ISBN 978 1 80220 061 4 (cased)
ISBN 978 1 80220 062 1 (eBook)

Printed and bound by CPI Group (UK) Ltd, Croydon, CR0 4YY

'A daughter is the happy memories of the past, the joyful moments of the present, and the hope and promise of the future' (Author unknown)

To my joyful inspirations, Shelagh and Ishbel

Contents

Contributors

Tibah Al Harbi, Doctoral student, School of Business, University of Dundee, Scotland, UK and Lecturer, Business Administration College, Jazan University, Saudi Arabia.

Tiago Cardão-Pito, Assistant Professor, ISEG, Universidade de Lisboa [University of Lisbon], Portugal.

Sung Hwan Chai, Lecturer in Accounting, University of Manchester, UK.

Christopher S. Chapman, Professor of Management Accounting, University of Bristol, UK.

Renzo Cordina, Senior Lecturer, School of Business, University of Dundee, Scotland, UK.

Catherine Deffains-Crapsky, Professor of Corporate Finance, Faculty of Law, Economics and Management, University of Angers, France.

David Derichs, Senior University Lecturer, Department of Accounting, Aalto University School of Business, Aalto, Finland.

Janne Järvinen, Professor and Dean, Oulu Business School, University of Oulu, Finland.

Matt Kaufman, Assistant Professor, School of Business, Portland State University, Portland, Oregon, USA.

Anja Kern, Professor of Business Administration, Baden-Wuerttemberg Cooperative State University, Mosbach, Germany.

Jiafan Li, Lecturer in Accounting, Huddersfield Business School, University of Huddersfield, UK.

Teemu Malmi, Professor of Accounting, Department of Accounting, Aalto University School of Business, Aalto, Finland.

Danielle McConville, Senior Lecturer, Queen's Business School, Belfast, UK.

Victoria McKinlay, BA Accounting & Finance, Strathclyde Business School, University of Strathclyde, Glasgow, UK.

Ana Novak, Assistant Professor, Department of Accounting, University of Zagreb Faculty of Economics and Business, Croatia.

Abdel Malik Ola, Lecturer/Researcher, Institute of Business Enterprise, University of Tours, France.

David Power, Professor of Business Finance, School of Business, University of Dundee, Scotland, UK.

Sharinah Binti Puasa, Senior Lecturer in Accounting, Labuan Faculty of International Finance, Universiti Malaysia Sabah, Malaysia.

Martin Quinn, Professor of Accounting, Queen's Business School, Belfast, UK.

Gavin C. Reid, Honorary Professor, Department of Economics, University of St Andrews Business School, Scotland and Senior Research Associate, Centre for Business Research, Cambridge Judge Business School, University of Cambridge, UK.

Ana Rep, Postdoctoral Researcher, Department of Accounting, University of Zagreb Faculty of Economics and Business, Croatia.

Vikash Kumar Sinha, Assistant Professor, Department of Accounting, Aalto University School of Business, Aalto, Finland.

Andrew Skidmore, MSc in International Accounting & Finance, Strathclyde Business School, University of Strathclyde, Glasgow, UK.

Julia A. Smith, Reader in Accounting & Finance, Strathclyde Business School, University of Strathclyde, Glasgow, UK.

Dusica Stevcevska Srbinoska, Assistant Professor, University American College Skopje, School of Business Economics and Management, North Macedonia.

Marjo Väisänen, Postdoctoral Researcher in Management Accounting & Control, Oulu Business School, University of Oulu, Finland.

Erica Wagner, Professor of Management, School of Business, Portland State University, Portland, Oregon, USA.

Katarina Žager, Department of Accounting, University of Zagreb Faculty of Economics and Business, Croatia.

Acknowledgements

There are numerous parties to whom my thanks are due for their support in the completion of this volume. First, the DEA Programme of the Fondation Maison des Sciences de l'Homme, in Paris, which sponsored my research leave in France in 2022, allowing me to spend dedicated time on this *Research Handbook*; and the Global Engagements Programme of the University of Strathclyde, Glasgow, which provided additional financial assistance. I am hugely grateful for your sponsorship of my work.

Many thanks also are due to colleagues at ESSCA School of Management, Angers for their generous welcome and for hosting me as a Visiting Professor (2022); in particular to Matthieu Ballandonne for going above and beyond expectations in the provision of help, facilities and friendship; and additionally to the University of Angers for their invitation to be a Visiting Researcher (2022). The 'Entente Cordiale' remains very strong.

For their valuable contributions to this book, and without whom it would not exist, to all authors who have responded dutifully to my requests for drafts, submissions, reviews and revisions, I thank you all. Your willingness to participate and helpful inputs along the way are very much appreciated.

And finally, for helping me to keep my sense of humour, and for always providing inspiration and support, to my husband Gavin. Your encouragement is forever valued.

Abbreviations

ABC	Activity-Based Costing
ACCA	Association of Chartered Certified Accountants
AGD	Accountant General's Department
AI	Artificial Intelligence
AICPA	Association of International Professional Accountants
AIS	Accounting Information System
ANT	Actor–Network Theory/Theorist
ASX	Australian Stock Exchange
AWS	Amazon Web Services
B2B	Business-to-Business
BA	Business Angel
BDDA	Big Data & Data Analytics
BI&A	Business Intelligence and Analytics
BVCA	British Venture Capital Association
CGMA	Chartered Global Management Accountant
CHESS	Clearing House Electronic Subregister System
CIAM	Customer Identity and Access Management
CIMA	Chartered Institute of Management Accountants
CRM	Customer Relationship Management
D&M IS Success Model	The DeLone and McLean Information Systems Success Model
DA	Discretionary Accruals
DESI	Digital Economy and Society Index
DLT	Distributed Ledger Technologies
DSS	Decision Support System
ECF	Equity Crowdfunding
eID	Electronic ID
ERP	Enterprise Resource Planning
EUCS	End-User Computing Satisfaction
EuroSCORE	European System for Cardiac Operative Risk Evaluation
EVA	Economic Value Added
FAAS	Fully Autonomous Accounting System

GCAO	Going Concern Audit Opinion
GDPR	General Data Protection Regulation
GRCIS	Governance, Risk Management, and Compliance Information Systems
HCM	Human Capital Management
HR	Human Resources
IaaS	Infrastructure as a Service
IBT	Internet-Based Technologies
IFAC	International Federation of Accountants
IFRS	International Financial Reporting Standards
IMA	Institute of Management Accountants
IoT	Internet of Things
ISA	International Standard on Auditing
IT	Information Technology
KMO	Kaiser-Meyer-Olkin
KPI	Key Performance Indicator
M&A	Mergers and Acquisitions
MAC	Management Accounting Change
MADA	Management Accounting Data Analytics
MAP	Management of an Accounting Practice
MCS	Management Control System/s
MENA	Middle East/North Africa
MIA	Malaysian Institute of Accountants
ML	Machine Learning
MRP	Material Resource Planning
MSE	Macedonian Stock Exchange
NAICS	North American Industry Classification System
NPM	New Public Management
OECD	Organisation for Economic Cooperation and Development
OCR	Optical Character Recognition
PaaS	Platform as a Service
PC	Personal Computer
PCA	Principal Components Analysis
PCAOB	Public Company Accounting Oversight Board
PLICS	Patient Level Information and Costing Systems
PMM	Performance Measurement and Management
PMS	Profitability Management Software
PMS	Performance Measurement System

PSF	Professional Service Firm
R&D	Research & Development
RGI	Revenue Generated Index
RPA	Robotic Process Automation
RPI	Relative Performance Information
SaaS	Software as a Service
SCM	Supply Chain Management
SEC	US Securities and Exchange Commission
SIC	Standard Industrial Classification
SME	Small-to-Medium-Sized Enterprise
SOX	Sarbanes–Oxley Act
SSC	Shared Services Centre
TAM	Technology of Acceptance Model
TCP/IP	Transmission Control Protocol/Internet Protocol
UAE	United Arab Emirates
VC	Venture Capital/Venture Capitalist
VP	Vice President
WoS	Web of Science
XBRL	eXtensible Business Reporting Language

PART I

INTRODUCTION

1. Accounting and information systems

Julia A. Smith

1.1   INTRODUCTION

This research handbook brings together an eclectic mix of research output from a widely dispersed authorship, drawing on work from around the globe, including authors from across Europe, the United States and Asia. It draws upon existing literature, new empirical research and developing theories, to present the reader with insights into the world of accounting and information systems in a fast-moving and technologically challenging era. There are extensive reviews of recent and relevant literature, alongside fieldwork evidence from a diverse range of countries which, it is hoped, will provide the reader with views of geographical and research areas with which they were previously unfamiliar. Hopefully, the range of work presented here will prompt ideas for new research alongside future pathways for the accounting profession.

The book is structured in six parts, the first of which includes this introduction. The title of the handbook deliberately separates the terms 'Accounting' and 'Information Systems' to show that these are two separate concepts, albeit which are often intertwined. As Jans et al. (2022, p.62) point out, 'accounting and AIS cannot be studied separately as they both form an integrated whole'. Accounting, here, is treated as the process of measuring and communicating multiple forms of information, or data, including that which is both quantitative and qualitative. Therefore this book takes a broad view of information, both of an accounting and non-accounting nature, and the way in which it is processed, managed and used in organisations. The information system is then taken to incorporate the processes within an organisation which allow that information to be effectively used for multiple purposes, with a variety of stakeholders in mind. The chapters presented in this handbook are illustrative of the nature of research in this area, and they have been chosen to show the variety of work that exists, from a worldwide trawl of experts in the field; therefore they provide both a useful introduction to the topic for the tyro who is unfamiliar with the field, whilst also highlighting a possible research agenda and emerging ideas for the expert.

Recent published research on accounting contains numerous reviews of the extant literature. In exploring digitalisation in accounting, Jans et al. (2022) find that topics related to AIS (Accounting Information System) in accounting journals tend to focus on 'information disclosure', 'network technologies' and 'audit and control', whilst neglecting other relevant topics. Therefore, they suggest that there is a need to bring the disciplines of accounting and AIS closer together, and they conclude by actively encouraging researchers to 'bridge the gap between the AIS and accounting literature and to actively integrate AIS topics in established accounting research' (Jans et al., 2022, p.82). Agostino et al. (2022) conduct a review of the literature on digitalisation, accountability and accounting in public services, highlighting, in particular, issues relating to the roles and boundaries of accountability, an increasing need for and importance of translation services, and a requirement for greater emphasis on social equity and inclusivity. And Alsalmi et al.'s (2023) paper on accounting for digital currencies explores the classification of digital currencies, alongside the necessary accounting practices and standards, suggesting that there is a need for an accounting standard to provide specific guidance on the identification, classification, measurement and presentation of digital currencies.

We cannot refer to information systems without consideration of the fast-paced technological developments that are being undertaken around the world. In June 2023 the European Parliament approved the EU AI Act (EU, 2023), a landmark in anticipating the formal regulation of Artificial Intelligence (AI) in the West. This Act provides the first comprehensive set of legal rules for the management of AI in the world. Whilst AI can provide many benefits to businesses, academics, researchers and students alike, in terms of the ease of information gathering, assessment and use, it has also given rise to concerns about job security, misinformation and bias. In voting in favour of the proposed legislation, members of the European Parliament have agreed to place further restrictions on AI tools such as ChatGPT,[1] including the requirement for formal reviews of such new products before commercial release.

This chapter now continues by introducing the various parts of the handbook and a discussion of the topics discussed therein. By their nature, some chapters will have relevance to more than one part, so they have been categorised to provide insight into a specific area, whilst also touching on topics that are covered elsewhere. Part II, which follows directly below, provides some examples of papers that explore aspects of planning and design in information system research, and includes reviews of the literature on management accounting change, alongside some specific exploration of work on enterprise resource planning systems (ERPs). Part III is about the use of information in supporting managerial decisions. This provides chapters on the use of accounting information, as well as on non-accounting patenting activity information, both within the setting of Venture Capital (VC) investment and decision-making in another investment setting, that of Equity Crowdfunding (ECF).

Part IV moves on to evidential work providing illustrations of the use of information for controlling and managing behaviour in different settings. These include healthcare in the UK, merger and acquisitions in Finland, and the Central Government AIS in Malaysia. Part V then explores practical applications of AIS research with four chapters that provide new empirical research. The first addresses a gap in the literature by exploring the use of information in auditing in the emerging economy of North Macedonia. This is followed by a chapter which considers the use of information gathered from a digital platform as part of a hotel's performance and management system. Then we present a chapter on the relationship between digital public services and AIS in Croatia. The final chapter in this part is an empirical study of the flow of information, and its use for accountability, within a small entrepreneurial firm in China.

Part VI of this handbook draws together three chapters which focus on technological developments and their impact, observed and potential, on accounting and information systems. Together, they suggest that there is much to be learned about potential threats and opportunities from advances in technology, and that there are diverse opportunities for future research projects in this area. First, there is a discussion of the role of AI and what impact might be anticipated from the literature. This is developed in the subsequent chapter by an exploration of, specifically, Internet-Based Technologies (IBT). And the final chapter concludes with a consideration of the future of accounting, using empirical evidence and questioning whether technology will negate the need for a human workforce. We move now to a discussion of each of these parts in turn.

1.2   PLANNING AND DESIGN IN INFORMATION SYSTEM RESEARCH

Part II of this handbook focuses on the considerations that organisations make when planning or designing an information system. This can include reflection on the nature and quality of the data, or information that will be fed into the system, and the predicted outputs from that process. It might also discuss potential changes in management accounting, for example in response to changes in manufacturing processes, and the impact that they might have on the information system. Further, there are clear implications for the impact of technology on accounting and information systems, and these can be built into the system from an early planning stage.

Pigatto et al. (2023) explore management accounting change theory by developing a framework to identify how 'searching, sagacity and chance' are essential tools for making positive, yet unexpected discoveries. This enables them to understand how various management accounting practices are translated and adopted in their case study of an organisation. They argue that their 'serendipitous drift framework' can facilitate the discovery of unique opportunities, through networking and experimentation. Weerasekara and Gooneratne (2023) discuss the implementation of ERP systems in a manufacturing firm. Again, they use a case study firm to explore the motives for adopting ERP, investigating both its benefits and the challenges it poses. They argue that it has implications for organisational structure, decision-making processes and communications systems. Acknowledging a dearth of extant literature that explores the implementation of ERPs in practice, they use case study evidence from a manufacturing firm in Sri Lanka to uncover the motivations for its use, through a framework of institutional theory. And Papiorek and Hiebl (2023) produce a paper that finds the quality of information has a positive effect on the effectiveness of management control. They further find that this relationship is stronger if the firm features a higher degree of process automation.

Chapter 2 explores key themes arising from the literature on management accounting change and information systems, and provides a useful conspectus of the research themes discussed throughout this handbook. It starts with a review of change in management accounting, and how this has been perceived and studied by numerous researchers, highlighting how information systems and technologies have driven much of this change. It further reviews the accounting and AIS literature to explore contemporary technologies that are relevant to management accounting and the role of management accountants. The chapter adds weight to existing calls for specific research in the area, emphasising the limited body of extant work that examines contemporary technologies as a driver of management accounting change.

Al-Dmour et al. (2023) research the use of information systems in planning systems and solving database problems. Their focus is primarily on ERP systems and the fact that their effects and characteristics make them a primary software tool with transferability benefits, which means they can be used by businesses across the world. This is the case whether they are large or small firms. Arredondo-Soto et al. (2022) also discuss the use of information systems for ERP. They explore the multifaced nature of ERP systems, which are used to manage day-to-day business activities such as accounting, procurement, project management, compliance and risk management, and supply chain operations. And Christiansen et al. (2022) further evaluate the factors that affect cloud ERP adoption decisions in organisations. Their paper looks at evidence from literature on both large and smaller enterprises. As a literature review, it identifies a gap in the work on larger enterprises, as well as a lack of differentiation between small and medium-size organisations, which they hope may be filled by future research.

Chapter 3 here therefore explores the literature on how ERP systems are employed for integrating organisational business processes through software, infrastructures and digital platforms. Typically, these systems integrate accounting alongside other business processes. Their impact has been revolutionary, through their ability to enhance 'business intelligence', but published accounting research has yet to fully appreciate and embrace these systems. This chapter therefore explains key research topics relevant to ERP systems, describing their historical evolution and integration into accounting and other organisational business processes. It further explores the requirements for success in implementing and managing these systems. Beyond that, it introduces transformations in ERP systems that have come about from recent Industry 4.0 and 5.0 technological developments, including the cloud, machine learning (AI) and the Internet of Things (IoT).

Through their exploration of multi-criteria decision-making methods in ERP selection, Hansen et al. (2023) provide one of a number of qualitative papers on ERP systems. They find that the literature agrees that one of the most critical success factors in the ERP adoption life cycle is in choosing the correct system to start with, but that very few studies focus on the selection stage. They address this gap by treating ERP selection as a multi-criteria decision-making problem, with various methods and techniques that can be utilised for such problems, using the influence of contingent factors to explain the assimilation of the cloud enterprises resources plan in a public sector setting. Alsharari (2022) addresses this too, in looking at cloud computing and ERP assimilation in the public sector, again using qualitative methods and an interpretive approach. They find that organisational culture has led to a radical change by implementing the cloud ERP system and institutionalising its usage. And Trigueiros and Alves (2022) show how AIS are adopted in multisite organisations. Using data collected through observations, in-depth interviews and document analysis they find that the majority of daily basis tasks depend on the AIS, which is integrated into the ERP system, in order to function.

In Chapter 4 we see how ERP systems can be employed as a tool to facilitate standardisation, centralisation and control. The chapter analyses thirty years' worth of qualitative research to examine fieldwork undertaken between 1993 and 2018. It highlights the transition of ERP within the qualitative accounting literature from an organisational problem to a data platform with influence beyond corporate reporting. This review of qualitative accounting studies on ERP highlights a persistent tension between central and peripheral organisational actors as a central theme. The chapter uses findings from numerous studies to illustrate the implications for several accounting topics; and emerging examples of potential areas for application are identified, including analytics, blockchain and cybersecurity.

1.3   USING INFORMATION TO SUPPORT DECISIONS

Part III moves on to discuss one of the key roles of the management accountant, that of making decisions, and using the information system to produce evidence that will support the decisions to be made. Essential to this is managing the information to ensure that it is of the best quality (whether that be timely, relevant, specific etc) to facilitate optimal decision-making. Again, technology can have a role to play in this process. Some of the chapters here rely upon empirical evidence to illustrate how, in practice, information flows can be manipulated or managed to improve decision-making, for example in corporate governance, or in making ethical choices.

The moderating role of accounting information quality is the focus of Zuo and Lin's (2022) exploration of R&D (Research & Development) subsidies and firm innovation performance. They observe that, although the quality of accounting information helps investors to make efficient decisions on investments, what has been less investigated is the specific role of corporate accounting information in assessing the *ex post* effectiveness of R&D subsidies. Wright and Robbie (2022) further explore the role of accounting information in VC settings. They show that venture capitalists (VCs) use a wide range of accounting and non-accounting information and techniques, relating to the specific factors concerning a particular investment. Of particular interest is the fact that unpublished accounting information and subjective information are both important. And Lei et al. (2022) look at accounting information quality, financing constraints and company innovation investment efficiency by big data analysis, taking listed companies in China as their sample. Their paper provides confirmation that the quality of accounting information can alleviate financing constraints and agency conflicts.

The use of accounting information is discussed in Chapter 5, where it is observed that the role of accounting and a company's information system in the assessments and valuations of investee firms by VC investors remains poorly understood. This is particularly true for investors in developing nations. The chapter therefore examines the importance placed on accounting data and an investee's information system by Saudi VCs who operate throughout the Middle East. The analysis is based on interviews with investors and entrepreneurs, and results suggest that, in the Saudi context, accounting information can play a crucial role in the VC decision to invest in a company.

Beyond the accounting data that VCs use to assess potential investments, there is additional valuable information on innovation, which might be embodied within patents. Therefore a body of literature exists which looks at this supplementary information available to investors, in discerning amongst the best investment opportunities. On this theme, Dushnitsky and Yu (2022) provide an example of why incumbents fund start-ups in China, finding that innovative entrepreneurs 'serve as a vehicle to leverage the global innovation frontier'. Dai et al. (2022) explore VC and firm performance, again in China, and focus specifically on innovation and financial performance. They show that late-stage VC improves investee firms' financial performance, although it also reduces their innovation performance. Further exploring the impact of innovation on VC investment, Shuwaikh and Dubocage (2022) look at the 'complementary resources' available to investors in biotech companies. They use patenting information to determine that companies that have achieved VC backing tend to be higher innovators.

Further exploring the use of patent data, Chapter 6 examines the role of non-accounting information in attracting more VC funding in the UK. It uses a novel data set, which covers various non-accounting measures related to patenting and VC deals. Whilst prior literature has often focused on transactional data relating to VC deals in the United States, this chapter extends a simplistic 'count' of patent activity to more complex patent measures, in order to examine whether patenting has an effect on the size of the investment made by the VC firm. For the UK, the study finds that patenting appears to attract more VC funding, particularly in investee companies which are not operating in the IT sector.

Exploring the investment decision further, a relatively recent form of investment is ECF. Ndou et al. (2022) use this as their theme in analysing fundraising activities and digitalisation, looking specifically at the risk indicators for evaluating ECF campaigns. They find that quantitative evaluations of risk used to decide upon investments can also be used *ex ante* to assess the degree of riskiness of the investment in the ECF campaign, thus reducing information asymmetry for 'crowd' investors. Cade et al. (2023) use an experimental design, in a securities-based crowdfunding setting, to investigate whether some investors avoid accounting information for psychological reasons, even when they understand the information is useful in their decision-making. Their results suggest that investors who experience relatively more psychological discomfort when working with quantitative information are relatively less likely to acquire the financial statements of a potential crowdfunding investment. This expands our understanding of a 'theory of information avoidance', and provides a behavioural explanation for investors' underuse of accounting information. Further, Mazzocchini and Lucarelli (2023) provide a literature review on the success or failure in ECF, giving an integrated understanding of the reasons for success or failure. In particular, they find that the outcome of an ECF campaign relies upon information which is both hard (firm characteristics, finances, business characteristics and project description) and soft (intellectual, human, social capital and social media network).

In Chapter 7, therefore, we have a study of the use of information in investment decision-making, as it relates specifically to ECF. Such platforms are now seen to provide a serious alternative or complementary source of funding for the entrepreneurial firm. The evolution of European regulation is a demonstration of this. If the ECF platform allows the democratisation of VC for both providers and seekers of capital, the question of the capacity of platforms to better manage the strong asymmetry of information in order to improve the decision-making of investors remains open. The ECF literature advocates that the strength of platforms not only significantly increases information but also diversifies its nature by further legitimising the importance of soft or qualitative information. Therefore improvements related to the decision-making process remain an important challenge for ECF platforms.

1.4   USING INFORMATION TO CONTROL AND MANAGE BEHAVIOUR

Once decisions have been made and implemented, the management accountant needs to ensure that there is a flow of information for controlling the outcome of these decisions. The chapters in Part IV therefore explore the use of accounting information for effective control. This can incorporate costing systems, and their role in corporate governance. It might equally relate to behavioural issues that can arise when AIS are used for management control. For example, employees may be reluctant to follow decisions made purely on the basis of a financial information system. It is therefore important to ensure that systems of control are put in place and clearly communicated to encourage goal congruence, through the alignment of individual motivations in the best interests of the organisation.

Saleh et al. (2023) produce a literature review on the quality of cost accounting systems, specifically in manufacturing firms. They summarise the paper with the view that implementing a cost accounting system will lead to enhanced performance, and will also naturally assist in decision-making and financial reporting. They further suggest that recent technological innovations will impact upon the future role of the accountant, and that this will need to be incorporated into accounting training. Pavlatos and Kostakis (2023) explicitly examine the moderating role of the quality of cost accounting information in public hospitals, exploring in more detail the use of budgeting during the COVID-19 pandemic. According to their results, the organisations that were most affected by the pandemic increased their use of budgets for planning, resource allocation and control, compared to those that were less affected, highlighting the relationship between crises and use of accounting information. Further exploring the use of costing in the public sector, Alqudah et al. (2022) undertake an empirical study in Jordan to examine the effectiveness of government services and the role of accounting in increasing budget realism, savings and openness in public spending. They find that multiple aspects play a role in calculating the cost and effectiveness of services.

Developing this theme, Chapter 8 looks at the management of data, decisions and cost system accuracy, through a field study in UK healthcare. It points out that developing accurate cost systems is not only a technical but also an organisational challenge, as it requires the participation of non-accountants who might not understand the technical contents of AIS. Given the lack of available evidence on how costing systems are improved in practice, this study sheds important light on the results from a field study undertaken in a UK hospital. The chapter suggests that healthcare organisations, such as hospitals, might not necessarily achieve an 'optimal' costing system, and highlights that there are opportunities for clinical efficiency and effectiveness that can trigger process redesign, thereby leading to further improvements to the costing system.

Moving on to another area of research, mergers & acquisitions (M&A) involve activities that require access to detailed accounting information. Gal-Or et al. (2022) look specifically at the literature on an auditor's task-specific expertise by examining the role of auditor experience in M&A. They find that firms with an acquisitive strategy who engage with expert auditors experience improved M&A-related audit outcomes. Stewart (2023) explores the theme further by looking at appraisal rights and corporate disclosure during M&A. Explicitly, it examines 'target shareholders' who have the right to ask for a higher merger price if good news emerges after a merger agreement. The paper leads to suggestions of agency problems and collusion on the part of target managers, which might be mitigated by enhanced AIS. And an analysis of the literature, by Cumming et al. (2023), finds that, in the accounting area, major themes addressed by researchers include corporate governance and accounting outcomes, predicting takeovers and their outcomes, valuation, financial reporting and takeover decisions, and financial reporting and performance. However, there remain gaps in the literature which should be addressed by future and ongoing work.

Chapter 9 contributes to this body of literature by addressing the role played by AIS in M&A. The important role which AIS play in these situations has often been underestimated or neglected altogether in the literature. While fast and efficient AIS integration is necessary, acquirers must ensure that the value-creating capabilities or qualities of the acquired subsidiaries, such as a creative workforce or customer contacts, are maintained. The chapter argues that successful AIS implementation requires the establishment of vertical and horizontal networks in a way that supports both flexibility and efficiency. Furthermore, AIS can enable control at a distance, supporting the emergence of new organisational forms, such as virtual teams cooperating efficiently in different locations. In the M&A context, careful planning and execution are found to be the key elements of successful AIS integration.

In order to understand how AIS can be effective to management, it is useful to re-visit the development of accounting through the ages, as presented in Edwards (2023, p.40), who reports that 'beginning in the second decade of the 19th century, recurrent proposals for the replacement of cash accounting by accruals accounting were founded on the conviction that "commercial" accounting practices provided a more effective basis for performance measurement, financial control and public accountability'. His paper explores the development of new public management (NPM) and the ultimate acceptance of private sector practices. On a more contemporary level, Duan et al. (2023) suggest that government AIS might be made more efficient by the use of social media information, to support accountability to stakeholders and managerial decision-making. Their work suggests that information from social media platforms can be linked to government AIS 'to evaluate costs and provide a better understanding of the efficiency and effectiveness of operations'. For a further consideration of the use of AIS within government organisations see also Setyani et al. (2022), who examine the use of budgeting and performance.

In measuring the effectiveness of the AIS in the Malaysian Federal Government, Chapter 10 addresses an area that has been only inadequately explained through prior literature. This chapter investigates the criteria, develops a model and proposes an instrument to measure AIS effectiveness within a unique setting. It uses both qualitative and quantitative fieldwork evidence, derived from interviews with accounting staff who use the system in the Malaysian Federal Government. It finds, from analysis, that there are ten identifiable items that can be used to represent system quality, information quality and the benefit or usefulness of AIS; and that these are reliable and valid for measuring AIS effectiveness, from a 'user satisfaction' standpoint.

1.5   PRACTICAL APPLICATIONS OF ACCOUNTING INFORMATION SYSTEM RESEARCH

Part V considers some empirical evidence and other practical implications that arise from extant research on AIS. For example, there are a couple of chapters which consider the more qualitative aspects, including a look at ERP. Another looks at how information systems can be used to facilitate the auditing process. Different settings have different requirements, for example central government might require very different information to a small private company. Likewise, healthcare systems require accounting information flows about very specific objects, such as the cost of patient care or medical treatment, and cost-benefit analysis of alternating treatment plans.

Starting with a study of going concern issues in auditing, Grosse and Scott (2022) explore whether auditing statements have 'information content'. Overall, they find that there are benefits to having mandatory interim assurance. Further, the going concern conclusions that are contained in interim financial statements provide investors with new and relevant information, which can be used to assess investments. Chi and Shen (2022) take a quantitative approach, and use hybrid AI and machine learning technologies to assess going-concern prediction, arguing that a failure to predict bankruptcy, for example, can contribute to losses for corporate stakeholders. Their discussion considers that the Big4 accounting firms[2] have embraced AI for auditing purposes with the aim of achieving greater accuracy. And Yang et al. (2022) provide an empirical investigation into the accuracy of going-concern audits in charities, exploring the link between these opinions and any subsequent revocation of organisations' charitable status.

This issue is explored, for the case of a developing country, in Chapter 11, treating the going-concern audit as having the role of reducing information asymmetry. As management and stakeholder decisions are shaped upon information obtained from accounting, assurance is vital for ensuring the reliability of economic information systems. Here, auditing is considered to be a governance mechanism. Prior literature gives little evidence on accounting behaviour in emerging economies and empirical findings indicate that the Big4 are more incentivised to issue accurate audit reports compared to local auditors. This chapter controls for both auditor and auditee features, exploring the relationship between earnings management and going-concern modifications. It concludes that there is a lower information asymmetry for non-Big4 auditors, from the perspective of entities with elevated bankruptcy scores.

With the proliferation of digital platforms now providing information on performance, from a more qualitative standpoint, there is a growing body of evidence, alongside financial information, on which to base rewards and incentives in organisations. With that in mind, Manthei et al. (2022) undertake a field experiment on performance reviews and incentives. They provide evidence to show that performance pay changes the nature of conversations, leading to a stronger self-reliance of store managers, and subsequently undermining the value of performance reviews. Boccali et al. (2022) further investigate 'data-rich environments', discussing how to leverage online review analytics through data envelopment analysis to empower managers and entrepreneurs. They find that online review analytics can be suitably embedded into analytical models to assess prices, citing the benefits of having access to widely available information from the Internet. Watson and Wu (2022) also explore the impact of online reviews on the information flows and outcomes of marketing systems, observing (p.146) that 'online reviews are changing the way that consumers shop and firms respond to consumer feedback … [and] are an information flow with the potential to change well-being outcomes for all stakeholders, rather than just a tool to be exploited by firms or consumers'. They suggest future research to explore how online reviews and information flows may impact the efficiency and effectiveness of a marketing system.

In Chapter 12 we have a contribution to the empirical literature on the use of digital platforms in the performance measurement and management of a hotel. The chapter explores how Tripadvisor[3] interacts with hotel performance measurement and management practices. The primary data for this study is collected from a case study of a luxury hotel resort located in Vietnam. The chapter examines the relationship between Tripadvisor and performance measurement and management through a sociomateriality perspective. Despite the resistance and distrust from different groups of users in the case organisation, the study finds that user-generated information from Tripadvisor is integrated into existing performance measurement and management practice, giving rise to alternative ways of interacting with the guests.

Also focusing on the opportunities offered by new technologies, but with regard to public sector services, Mariani et al. (2022) explore accessibility through natural language processing, suggesting that AI provides significant benefits from the standpoint of efficiency and effectiveness. The paper concludes with a consideration of the lessons learnt about the readiness to fully exploit the potential benefits from the adoption of AI solutions. Polzer and Goncharenko (2022) discuss a failed public service, in the form of the UK COVID-19 app.[4] Their study analyses social media evidence to understand the production of a digital public service in an emergency situation, using Twitter[5] 'netnography'[6] and discourse analysis to examine citizens' perceptions of the contact tracing app. They reflect upon the lack of governmental accountability and the difficulties experienced in mitigating societal concerns, which together led to resistance by the public to engage in and support the introduction of the app. In a Brazilian case, Saldanha et al. (2022) explore transparency and accountability in digital public services, showing that there is a need to inform the user of such systems that there may be bias and damage arising, which are not readily observed.

Chapter 13 explores the relationship between AIS and digital public services in Croatia. It acknowledges that the use of digital technologies impacts upon traditional accounting tasks that were previously done manually. The purpose of this chapter is to investigate the effects of digital technologies on AIS and public services, with a focus on financial and other administrative reporting. Therefore, the specific forms of digitalisation in accounting, their combination with the digitalisation of public services and the impact of digital technology on the IT skills of professional accountants are analysed. Digital technologies influence the development of new products and services that enable new means of interaction between companies and accounting information users, primarily regulatory stakeholders. In order to investigate the current state of development of Croatian digital public services and their interaction with AIS, the chapter also provides a content analysis of selected digital public services.

Whilst accounting and information flows may be observed, as above, in the public sector, they are also relevant to private sector organisations. Mbeche et al. (2022), for example, investigate the extent of downward accountability from the Kenya Tea Development Agency to smallholder farmers who are both owners and users of agricultural services. While the setting provides opportunities for increased accountability and empowerment of smallholder farmers, downward accountability is found to be limited by, for example, the presence of multiple accountabilities, the existence of a strong top-down governance structure, and stronger incentives for upward accountability. Reinking and Resch (2023) explore accounting management control systems within a Small-to-Medium-Sized Enterprise (SME) setting, to determine why some firms can transition more successfully than others to sophisticated systems. They find that having controls such as basic human resources and systematic communication routines enhance employee cooperation, through accountability, participation and information-sharing. Without these, firms fail to transition successfully to sophisticated control systems. Gyamera et al. (2023) use an agency theory to frame their research on the use of financial accounting services by SMEs. They conclude that both information technology and the use of financial services have a positive effect on the financial performance of SMEs, providing a basis for emerging nations to focus on financial accounting in order to improve business performance.

Chapter 14 presents qualitative empirical evidence on the use of accountability within a small entrepreneurial firm in China. It uses the ethnographic approach of participant-observation to become fully immersed in the business, and the chapter explores how accountability issues that have been commonly acknowledged in Western literature can be addressed and overcome in a developing economy. In doing so, the chapter highlights the tensions and issues that are confronted by a strong owner-manager, with a global perspective and international education. Overall the study shows that accountability exists in China, but that cultural tensions can lead to difficulties in its implementation. Educating SMEs in developing economies about the advantages of transparent communication is a lesson to be learned from the findings of this chapter.

1.6   TECHNOLOGICAL DEVELOPMENTS

We have touched above on technological developments and their relevance to the field of accounting. The final part develops this further by considering the impact of technology on

AIS, and the obvious implications for the format and processing of data and information. AI is one pathway that opens up potential for a new research agenda, for example in developing the nature of the auditing process. Further, intelligent systems can have an impact upon decision-making. In manufacturing, there are opportunities for real-time feedback on industrial processes, to enhance control in organisations. When it comes to assessing the plethora of information that now exists, technology can also assist in handling big data. Associated with this, there are developments in cloud computing and using this to develop new ways of handling accounting information and systems. These suggest novel paths forward for future research.

From an ethical standpoint, there are additional issues to be explored, as highlighted through the literature review of Ashok et al. (2022). They argue that the use of AI in digital technologies has given rise to numerous ethical considerations, with repercussions for intelligibility, accountability, fairness, autonomy and privacy. There are additional ethical implications for the governance of organisations, all of which have academic and professional consequences. Gonçalves et al. (2022) note that digital transformation has redefined industrial structures and reinvented business models, posing threats and challenges as well as opportunities. Their empirical work in Portugal highlights opportunities being provided by Industry 4.0 technologies, Optical Character Recognition (OCR), AI, robotics and ERP in the cloud. On the other hand, they identified threats to digital technologies as coming from a resistance to change, organisational culture and price. Fülöp et al. (2022), in their study of Fintech accounting and Industry 4.0, find that trust, too, is important in embracing digitisation.

Extending the issues above, Chapter 15 has been motivated by calls for further research into the impact of AI on accounting, and the chapter therefore provides a review of the existing literature on this area. The review considers how AI is impacting accounting processes and benefiting firms in the accounting sector, how it is changing the roles and skills of accountants, and the challenges it creates for accounting. Through this, gaps in the literature are identified and possible avenues for future research are highlighted. Furthermore, an analysis and summary of the existing literature is presented followed by a research plan that could be carried out by future research.

AI offers opportunities for new software and web-based technology development. Atanasovski and Tocev (2022) explore trends in research in disruptive technologies, such as big data, data analytics, cloud, AI, and blockchain, identifying implications for the future of accounting. Deng (2022) proposes a cloud computing-based accounting system, primarily for SMEs. He uses experiments to show that the accuracy of data monitoring by an accounting system based on sensor monitoring and cloud computing is more efficient than traditional accounting systems. And Al-Okaily et al. (2023) discuss the use of cloud-based AIS in a sample of Jordanian SMEs. They find that users of these systems were significantly influenced by factors such as expected performance, social motivation, COVID-19 risk and trust.

Specifically related to management control systems, therefore, Chapter 16 IBT and accounting processes. It covers five potentially disruptive IBT (cloud computing, big data and data analytics, AI, IoT and blockchain), which offer opportunities to enhance Management Control Systems (MCSs) through data-driven control. The latter enables the effective guidance of employees' efforts by incorporating nonfinancial indicators (for example, customer sentiment) during goal setting. It also enables timely effort and goal adjustment, by facilitating real-time monitoring and feedback, as well as effective goal congruence, through transparent sharing of information amongst employees. On the other hand, it is seen that IBT-enabled data-driven control presents several challenges for MCS, such as demotivation of employees due to perceived 'surveillance'. Further challenges include issues with data governance, quality and security, as well as biases and comprehension-related issues with control models. Legal and ethical liability concerns also arise over autonomous task execution, as discussed elsewhere in this handbook.

All of the developments discussed previously lead to concerns about the future role of the professional accountant. How will accounting and accountants change to meet the varying demands of the new technologies? Coman et al. (2022) consider this question, with the aim of highlighting 'the impact of the digitalization of accounting on the business environment, the work style, and the role of professional accountants'. They suggest that digitisation concerns both technology and people, equally, and that the 'role of professional accountants is evolving from "transaction logger" to analyst and consultant for entrepreneurs'. Qasim et al. (2022) consider the impact this will have on the education of accountants, in response to concerns about whether or not existing accounting curricula are well suited to preparing accounting graduates for emerging IT needs. Moore and Felo (2022) also examine the evolution of accounting technology education, through a survey of accounting professionals, who found generally that data analytics were thought to add value and should therefore form part of accounting education.

Finally, Chapter 17 of this book uses empirical evidence to reach an understanding of the impact of advancing technologies on the requirement for a human workforce in accounting. As we have seen, the development of technology over recent years has created concern surrounding the future need for a human workforce. This chapter therefore explores the impact AI has had on the accountancy profession. The awareness of individuals within the industry is assessed empirically, using an interpretive approach, in order to gain a better understanding of the future for accounting professionals. The study uses a questionnaire to gain insight into the opinions of professionals within the industry and their thoughts on AI and advancing technologies. It utilises narrative analysis to conclude that the leading factor of the adoption of technology and AI within the industry is thought to be increased efficiency. While automation can work longer and faster than humans, it does not yet have the capabilities to make fair and justified judgements and, for this reason, the chapter concludes that, currently, the human workforce still has the advantage.

1.7   CONCLUSION

This chapter has outlined this research handbook on accounting and information systems by taking a path through the developments of accounting, from its initial role, up to and including the recent developments in technology that have emerged and are relevant to the industry. The discussion is framed and supported by reference to selected and recent literature in the relevant area. It starts by explaining the role of accounting in planning and design noting, where relevant, implications for AIS. It then considers how information, both quantitative and qualitative, is used to support decisions and to control and manage behaviour. Beyond that, the chapter moves on to a consideration of the practical applications of research in the accounting and information systems area, extending to technological developments brought about through stratospheric improvements in AI. It is hoped that this handbook will, therefore, provide the reader with a wider view of accounting, and its use in managing organisations, than they might have had previously, and will provoke novel insights and new ideas for future research possibilities.

NOTES

1. Commercially available software that interacts in a conversational way, making it possible to 'answer follow-up questions, admit its mistakes, challenge incorrect premises, and reject inappropriate requests' (OpenAI, 2023).
2. Deloitte; PricewaterhouseCoopers (PwC); Ernst & Young; KPMG.
3. The world's largest travel guidance platform [https://www.tripadvisor.com].
4. A contact tracing app.
5. Online social media and social networking platform [https://twitter.com; now 'X'].
6. A specific type of qualitative social media research.

REFERENCES

Agostino, D., Saliterer, I., & Steccolini, I. (2022). Digitalization, accounting and accountability: A literature review and reflections on future research in public services. *Financial Accountability & Management*, 38, 152–176. https://doi.org/10.1111/faam.12301

Al-Dmour, N.A., Ali, L., Salahat, M., Alzoubi, H.M., Alshurideh, M., & Chabani, Z. (2023). Information systems solutions for the database problems. In *The Effect of information technology on business and marketing intelligence systems* (pp. 703–715). Cham: Springer International Publishing.

Al-Okaily, M., Alkhwaldi, A.F., Abdulmuhsin, A.A., Alqudah, H., & Al-Okaily, A. (2023). Cloud-based accounting information systems usage and its impact on Jordanian SMEs' performance: The post-COVID-19 perspective. *Journal of Financial Reporting and Accounting*, 21(1), 126–155. https://doi.org/10.1108/JFRA-12-2021-0476

Alqudah, M.A., Mansor, N., and Salleh, S.I.M. (2022). Difficulties in accounting system implementation for service costs in the public sector. *Cogent Business & Management*, 9(1), https://doi.org/10.1080/23311975.2022.2150119

Alsalmi, N., Ullah, S., & Rafique, M. (2023). Accounting for digital currencies. *Research in International Business and Finance*, 64, 101897. https://doi.org/10.1016/j.ribaf.2023.101897

Alsharari, N.M. (2022). Cloud computing and ERP assimilation in the public sector: Institutional perspectives. *Transforming Government: People, Process and Policy*, 16(1), 97–109. https://doi.org/10.1108/TG-04-2021-0069

Arredondo-Soto, K.C., Hernández-Escobedo, G., Realyvásquez-Vargas, A., & Miranda-Ackerman, M.A. (2022). Information systems for enterprise resource planning. In *Algorithms and Computational Techniques Applied to Industry* (pp. 3–28). Cham: Springer International Publishing.

Ashok, M., Madan, R., Joha, A., & Sivarajah, U. (2022). Ethical framework for artificial intelligence and digital technologies. *International Journal of Information Management*, 62, 102433. https://doi.org/10.1016/j.ijinfomgt.2021.102433

Atanasovski, A., & Tocev, T. (2022). Research trends in disruptive technologies for accounting of the future – A bibliometric analysis 21(2), 270–288. *Journal of Accounting and Management Information Systems*. http://dx.doi.org/10.24818%2Fjamis.2022.02006

Boccali, F., Mariani, M.M., Visani, F., & Mora-Cruz, A. (2022). Innovative value-based price assessment in data-rich environments: Leveraging online review analytics through Data Envelopment Analysis to empower managers and entrepreneurs. *Technological Forecasting and Social Change*, 182, 121807. https://doi.org/10.1016/j.techfore.2022.121807

Cade, N.L. Garavaglia, S., & Hoffman, V.B. (2023). Why some investors avoid accounting information: Identifying a psychological cost of information acquisition using the securities-based crowdfunding setting (February 27). Available at SSRN: https://ssrn.com/abstract=4130407 or http://dx.doi.org/10.2139/ssrn.4130407

Chi, D-J., & Shen, Z-D. (2022). Using hybrid artificial intelligence and machine learning technologies for sustainability in going-concern prediction. *Sustainability* 14(3), 1810. https://doi.org/10.3390/su14031810

Christiansen, V., Haddara, M., & Langseth, M. (2022). Factors affecting cloud ERP adoption decisions in organizations. *Procedia Computer Science*, 196, 255–262. https://doi.org/10.1016/j.procs.2021.12.012

Coman, D.M., Ionescu, C.A., Duică, A., Coman, M.D., Uzlau, M.C., Stanescu, S.G., & State. V. (2022). Digitization of accounting: The premise of the paradigm shift of role of the professional accountant. *Applied Sciences*, 12(7), 3359. https://doi.org/10.3390/app12073359

Cumming, D., Jindal, V., Kumar, S., & Pandey, N. (2023). Mergers and acquisitions research in finance and accounting: Past, present, and future. *European Financial Management*, 1–41. https://doi.org/10.1111/eufm.12417

Dai, X., Chapman, G., & Shen, H. (2022). Late-stage venture capital and firm performance: Evidence from small and medium-sized enterprises in China. *Applied Economics*, 54(20), 2356–2372. https://doi.org/10.1080/00036846.2021.1989370

Duan, H.K., Vasarhelyi, M.A., Codesso, M., & Alzamil, Z. (2023). Enhancing the government accounting information systems using social media information: An application of text mining and machine learning. *International Journal of Accounting Information Systems*, 48, 100600. https://doi.org/10.1016/j.accinf.2022.100600

Deng, J. (2022). The informatization of small and medium-sized enterprises accounting system based on sensor monitoring and cloud computing, *Mobile Information Systems*, 5007837. https://doi.org/10.1155/2022/5007837

Dushnitsky, G., & Yu, L. (2022). Why do incumbents fund startups? A study of the antecedents of corporate venture capital in China. *Research Policy*, 51(3), 104463. https://doi.org/10.1016/j.respol.2021.104463

Edwards, J.R. (2023). Cash to accruals accounting in British central government: A journey through time. *Financial Accountability & Management* 39, 40–59. https://doi.org/10.1111/faam.12295

EU (2023) *Artificial Intelligence Act*, European Union: https://artificialintelligenceact.eu/

Fülöp, M.T., Topor, D.I., Ionescu, C.A., Căpuşneanu, S., Breaz, T.O., & Stanescu, S.G. (2022). Fintech accounting and Industry 4.0: Future-proofing or threats to the accounting profession? *Journal of Business Economics and Management*, 23(5), 997–1015. https://doi.org/10.3846/jbem.2022.17695

Gal-Or, R., Hoitash, R., & Hoitash, U. (2022). Auditor expertise in mergers and acquisitions. *AUDITING: A Journal of Practice & Theory 1*, 41(4): 135–162. https://doi.org/10.2308/AJPT-2019-120

Gonçalves, M.J.A., da Silva, A.C.F., & Ferreira, C.G. (2022). The future of accounting: How will digital transformation impact the sector? *Informatics*, 9(1), 19. https://doi.org/10.3390/informatics9010019

Grosse, M., & Scott, T. (2022). Disclosure of interim review reports: Do interim going concern conclusions have information content? *AUDITING: A Journal of Practice & Theory 1*, 41(3), 121–147. https://doi.org/10.2308/AJPT-19-041

Gyamera, E., Atuilik,W.A., Eklemet, I., Adu-Twumwaah, D., Baba Issah, A., Tetteh, L.A., & Gagakuma, L. (2023). Examining the effect of financial accounting services on the financial performance of SME: The function of information technology as a moderator. *Cogent Business & Management*, 10(2) https://www.org/10.1080/23311975.2023.2207880

Hansen, K., Haddara, M., & Langseth, M. (2023). Exploring multi-criteria decision-making methods in ERP selection. *Procedia Computer Science*, 219, 879–888. https://doi.org/10.1016/j.procs.2023.01.363

Jans, M., Aysolmaz, B., Corten, M., Joshi, A., & van Peteghem, M. (2022). Digitalization in accounting – warmly embraced or coldly ignored? *Accounting, Auditing & Accountability Journal*, 36(9), 61–85.

Lei, Z., Gong, G., Wang, T., & Li, W. (2022). Accounting information quality, financing constraints, and company innovation investment efficiency by big data analysis. *Journal of Organizational and End User Computing*, 34(3), 1–21.

Manthei, K., Sliwka, D., & Vogelsang, T. (2022). Talking about performance or paying for it? A field experiment on performance reviews and incentives. *Management Science* 69(4), 2198–2216. https://doi.org/10.1287/mnsc.2022.4431

Mariani, I., Karimi, M., Concilio, G., Rizzo, G., & Benincasa, A. (2022). Improving public services accessibility through natural language processing: Challenges, opportunities and obstacles. In

Intelligent Systems and Applications: Proceedings of the 2022 Intelligent Systems Conference (IntelliSys) 3, 272–289. Cham: Springer International Publishing.

Mazzocchini, F.J., & Lucarelli, C. (2023). Success or failure in equity crowdfunding? A systematic literature review and research perspectives. *Management Research Review*, 46(6), 790–831.

Mbeche, R., Mose, G.N., & Ateka, J.N. (2022). The influence of privatised agricultural extension on downward accountability to smallholder tea farmers, *The Journal of Agricultural Education and Extension*, 28(3), 341–362. https://doi.org/10.1080/1389224X.2021.1932538

Moore, W.B., & Felo, A. (2022). The evolution of accounting technology education: Analytics to STEM. *Journal of Education for Business*, 97(2), 105–111. https://www.org/10.1080/08832323.2021.1895045

Ndou, V., Scorrano, P., Mele, G., & Stefanizzi, P. (2022). Fundraising activities and digitalization: Defining risk indicators for evaluating equity crowdfunding campaigns. *Meditari Accountancy Research*, 30(4), 1169–1190.

OpenAI (2023). 'Introducing ChatGPT': https://openai.com/blog/chatgpt

Papiorek, K.L., & Hiebl, M.R.W. (2023). Information systems quality in management accounting and management control effectiveness. *Journal of Accounting & Organizational Change*, Vol. ahead-of-print No. ahead-of-print. https://doi.org/10.1108/JAOC-09-2022-0148

Pavlatos, O., & Kostakis, H. (2023). Moderating role of cost accounting information quality on the relationship between the COVID-19 pandemic and budgeting in public hospitals. *Australian Accounting Review*, 33(1), 14–30. https://doi.org/10.1111/auar.12393

Pigatto, G., Cinquini, L., Tenucci, A., & Dumay, J. (2023). Serendipity and management accounting change. *Meditari Accountancy Research*, 31(7), 88–115.

Polzer, T., & Goncharenko, G. (2022). The UK COVID-19 app: The failed co-production of a digital public service. *Financial Accountability & Management*, 38, 281–298. https://doi.org/10.1111/faam.12307

Qasim, A., El Refae, G.A., & Shorouq, E. (2022). Embracing emerging technologies and artificial intelligence into the undergraduate accounting curriculum: Reflections from the UAE. *Journal of Emerging Technologies in Accounting*, 19(2): 155–169. https://doi.org/10.2308/JETA-2020-090

Reinking, J., & Resch, P. (2023). Gaining traction: How SMEs succeed in making management control systems stick. *Qualitative Research in Accounting & Management*, 20(3), 372–397. https://doi.org/10.1108/QRAM-01-2022-0011

Saldanha, D.M.F., Dias, C.N., & Guillaumon, S. (2022). Transparency and accountability in digital public services: Learning from the Brazilian cases. *Government Information Quarterly*, 39(2), 101680. https://doi.org/10.1016/j.giq.2022.101680

Saleh, Q.Y., Barakat AL-Nimer, M., & Abbadi, S.S. (2023). The quality of cost accounting systems in manufacturing firms: A literature review. *Cogent Business & Management*, 10(1), http://doi.org/10.1080/23311975.2023.2209980

Setyani, S., Abu Hanifah, I., & Ismawati, I.I. (2022). The role of budget decision making as a mediation of accounting information systems and organizational culture on the performance of government agencies. *Journal of Applied Business, Taxation and Economics Research*, 1(3), 311–324. https://doi.org/10.54408/jabter.v1i3.59

Shuwaikh, F., & Dubocage, E. (2022). Access to the corporate investors' complementary resources: A leverage for innovation in biotech venture capital-backed companies. *Technological Forecasting and Social Change*, 175, 121374. https://doi.org/10.1016/j.techfore.2021.121374

Stewart, C.R. (2023). Appraisal rights and corporate disclosure during mergers and acquisitions. *Journal of Accounting and Economics*, 75(1), 101527. https://doi.org/10.1016/j.jacceco.2022.101527

Trigueiros, E.V.D.C., & Alves, M.C.G. (2022). Accounting information system adoption in multi-site organisations. *International Journal of Business Information Systems*, 41(2), 236–257. https://doi.org/10.1504/IJBIS.2022.126133

Watson, F., & Wu, Y. (2022). The impact of online reviews on the information flows and outcomes of marketing systems. *Journal of Macromarketing*, 42(1), 146–164. DOI. https://doi.org/10.1177/02761467211042552

Weerasekara, U., & Gooneratne, T. (2023). Enterprise resource planning (ERP) system implementation in a manufacturing firm: Rationales, benefits, challenges and management accounting ramifications. *Accounting and Management Information Systems*, 22(1), 86–110.

Wright, M., & Robbie, K. (2022). Venture capitalists, unquoted equity investment appraisal and the role of accounting information. In *Venture capital* (pp. 159–174). Abingdon, Oxfordshire, UK: Routledge.

Yang, Y., Simnett, R. & Carson, E. (2022). Auditors' propensity and accuracy in issuing going-concern modified audit opinions for charities. *Accounting & Finance*, 62, 1273–1306. https://doi.org/10.1111/acfi.12823

Zuo, Z., & Lin, Z. (2022). Government R&D subsidies and firm innovation performance: The moderating role of accounting information quality. *Journal of Innovation & Knowledge*, 7(2), 100176. https://doi.org/10.1016/j.jik.2022.100176

PART II

PLANNING AND DESIGN IN INFORMATION SYSTEM RESEARCH

2. Management accounting change and information systems: key themes from the literature

Martin Quinn and Danielle McConville

2.1 INTRODUCTION

The pace of technological change seems unrelenting, having increased exponentially in the past two decades or so. Accounting Information Systems (AIS) experience such changes too, and this is noticeable in the literature. It is useful at the outset of this chapter to define an AIS. An AIS is a technology-based system which collects, stores and processes accounting-related data (financial and nonfinancial) and provides information to support decision-making (Bodnar and Hopwood, 2004[1]). This assumes that the definition of an information system is understood. In other words, an AIS has hardware, software and networking capabilities. Thus, as this chapter progresses, both information technology and information systems are considered.

The list of technologies which have developed in the past two decades or so is a long one, and some will be explored later. Technologies such as cloud computing have brought storage, processing capabilities and service to firms who previously could not have had access or indeed could not afford the space or processing power. This, coupled with ever-increasing Internet access and data transmission speeds, has opened up vast data sources (big data) and provided management accountants with analytical tools to harvest and analyse data in ways not previously possible. Other technologies such as Robotic Process Automation (RPA), Artificial Intelligence (AI) and Blockchain which are more commonly a feature of organisational systems are also affecting the AIS and the work of a management accountant.

Management accounting has been particularly affected by technology developments (Lawson, 2019). Management accounting is that part of the accounting discipline which works to provide managers with information to make decisions. It is thus more oriented toward the information needs of internal users than the external recipients of accounting such as shareholders. This chapter provides a review of literature to tease out key issues and identify (potential) Management Accounting Change (MAC) brought about by changes in technology and information systems. More importantly, we aim to identify what areas remain under-researched. This is particularly important, given a lack of studies on the impact of technological change, in contrast to anecdotal/practitioner evidence that contemporary technologies will change the roles and practices of management accounting in ways not previously seen.

The chapter continues as follows. In the next section we review how MAC has been studied, before focussing on specific studies of MAC and technological change up to the early 2000s. The chapter then discusses four contemporary technologies – data analytics, RPA, AI and Blockchain – and their potential implications for management accounting and MAC. We conclude with a call for more research into the implications of contemporary technologies for management accounting and MAC.

2.2   STUDYING MANAGEMENT ACCOUNTING CHANGE

The phrase 'if we want things to stay as they are, then they must change' is often cited by practitioners as a way to contextualise the fact that change and stability go hand in hand. This is also acknowledged in academic studies (for example, Burns and Scapens, 2000a). Organisational change has been subject to many volumes of academic research and has used contingency (for example, Donaldson, 1987), consultancy (for example, Kanter, 1983) and processual (for example, Pettigrew, 1987; Dawson, 2003) theoretical lenses (among others) to study it.

The management accounting literature too has reported on change (and stability) in and around management accounting practices and the roles of management accountants. Interest in studying MAC increased with the release of Johnson and Kaplan's (1987) text *Relevance Lost*. In it, Johnson and Kaplan argued that management accounting had not changed much since the 1920s and had lost its relevance. By the year 2000, Burns and Scapens wrote 'whether management accounting has not changed, has changed, or should change have all been discussed' (2000a, p.3). One of the discussion points in the management accounting literature at this time was what drives MAC. The literature at that time identified three drivers of MAC, namely: (1) increasing globalisation, (2) improved technologies and (3) improved methods of production (Scapens et al., 2003; Burns et al., 1999) – technology being the most relevant here. Lower cost and more widespread computing power, more integrated networks (including the Internet) had implied that the nature of information technology-based tasks and associated outputs had changed dramatically (Scapens et al., 2003). Enterprise Resource Planning (ERP) systems were becoming a common feature of globally connected organisations (Davenport, 1998). The literature noted how management accountants in such organisations could draw on these technologies to produce more detailed relevant management information and make it more readily available to users throughout the organisation (Dechow et al., 2007). The kind of MAC witnessed as a result of this era of technology change will be discussed later. Of course, much technology change has occurred since the turn of the new millennium. Researchers such as Bhimani and Willcocks (2014) and Bhimani (2020a) have noted that technology has (or will) disrupt management accounting in the new 'digital era'. MAC brought about, or potentially being brought about, by increased digitalisation will also be discussed later.

Following the work of Burns and Scapens (2000a), researchers of MAC have followed in their footsteps and taken on various non-accounting theoretical lenses to study change. Burns and Scapens (2000a) used concepts from institutional theory – namely rules and routines – to explain MAC, or the stability of management accounting in practice. Burns and Scapens (2000a) noted how external shocks can bring about change in embedded practices. One such shock could be rapid technological change – for example, how the world moved to online meeting and collaboration tools during the COVID-19 pandemic. Others such as Siti-Nabiha and Scapens (2005), Ribeiro and Scapens (2006), Lukka (2007), Quinn (2011) and Bertz and Quinn (2022) similarly drew on institutional concepts like rules and routines in their studies of MAC. Others have used another branch of institutional theory to study MAC, namely New Institutional Sociology. This approach has helped explain MAC in response to external influences such as political pressures, regulatory changes and cultural factors and includes studies by Tsamenyi et al. (2006) and Nor-Aziah and Scapens (2007). Structuration Theory has also been used to analyse change and stability in accounting systems (for example, Coad and Herbert, 2009). Another approach used is Actor Network Theory, although it is less used (for example, Dechow and Mouritsen, 2005).

As mentioned, Burns and Scapens (2000a) introduced the concept of organisational routines to the literature on MAC. Briefly a routine per Burns and Scapens (2000a) describes 'the way things are done' (2000, p. 5). Some authors (for example, Quinn, 2011) have proposed this description of a routine is not clear. Looking to the economics literature, Pentland (2011) collated much previous research and defined organisational routines as having four features: (1) routines are repetitive, (2) a recognisable pattern of action occurs, (3) actions are interdependent, indicating several interrelated 'steps' in the performance of a routine and (4) multiple actors are involved. This definition of routines highlights several interesting points relevant to MAC and information systems/technology. Pentland (2011, p.287) noted 'in typical routines, many actants are not human'. In other words, systems and technologies can be components of routines. To give an AIS-related example, Pentland et al. (2010) noted the percentage of actions undertaken by humans in an invoice processing routine ranged from 15 to 89 per cent. Similar to Pentland (2011), Volkoff et al. (2007) mentioned the concept of a material routine, or a routine embedded within technology. They noted how such routines are 'hard-coded into the system, it is the same for everyone, and individual interpretations do not affect how transactions are performed' (Volkoff et al., 2007, p.840). Quinn and Hiebl (2018) highlighted how such material routines likely affect the foundation of management accounting routines, noting also that even the smallest firms are typically computerised in some way today.

In summary, MAC has been studied using several theoretical approaches, with all studies recognising information technology and systems as a change driver. The literature also recognises that management accounting is a routinised practice, thus taking on board a fundamental concept from the organisational literature (i.e. routines). Routines are also embedded in technology, and thus technology change may imply change to routine management accounting practices. Alternatively, management accounting practices may be so routinised that they are replicated and embedded within an organisation's AIS. To this end, the following two sections present a review of the literature on information systems change and MAC. In this review, the concept of management accounting as a routinised practice should be retained, although MAC may be brought about by broader information systems/technology changes.

2.3 'TRADITIONAL' ACCOUNTING INFORMATION SYSTEMS AND MAC

Rosati and Paulsson (2022) provide a useful overview of the evolution of AIS, describing several phases. The first phase they term 'the information age', which spans the 1950s to the 1980s; the second phase is 'the integration phase' of the 1990s; the third is termed 'AIS 2.0' and spans from 2000 to the present day. This section focusses on the first two phases mainly, outlining key AIS concepts and linking to MAC as relevant. The next section explores the 'AIS 2.0' phase.

It can be argued that prior to the year 2000, AIS was less prevalent in the minds of practitioners and academic researchers. The Y2K issue focussed the minds of the former. Academic interest in AIS similarly increased as journals, such as the *International Journal of Accounting Information Systems*, emerged as successors to *Advances in Accounting Information Systems*. The 'information age' phase noted above (1950s–1980s) can be divided into two phases – the mainframe phase (1950s–1960s), and the personal computer (PCs)/decision support system (DSS) phase (1970s–1980s) (Rosati and Paulsson, 2022). The mainframe phase saw AIS moving from a manual-based system to a computerised one for data processing activities – at least in larger organisations. The mainframe phase affected management accounting in two main ways. First, the role of the management accountant now included duties around the running of the AIS (Anandarajan et al., 2004). Second, the number of bookkeeping clerks was dramatically reduced as automation took over (Rosati and Paulsson, 2022).

From the 1970s, PCs and accounting software became available. Comparatively, PCs were much lower in cost than mainframe systems and thus were adopted by more organisations – about $5,000–8,000 compared to $4 million plus per Rosati and Paulsson (2022). The increased availability of desktop technology saw the emergence of a new role for management accountants – 'business partner' – as 1980s technology automated more tasks (see for example, Järvenpää, 2007). As this role emerged, it was supported by the emergence of DSS (Baldvinsdottir et al., 2009). As noted by Rosati and Paulsson (2022), the business partner role was supported further as ERP systems emerged. As hinted above, the literature took more notice of AIS in general post-2000. This may have been due to the increased use of ERP systems, with more detailed whole-organisation data and information (Dechow et al., 2007), which offered an interesting environment to study MAC. Some key themes of such literature are now detailed.

Granlund and Malmi (2002) suggested ERP systems have direct and indirect effects on management accounting and thus are a driver of MAC. Direct effects may present in the form of change in reporting practices, i.e. differing layouts, depth of analysis, etc. Indirect effects may result from changes in business processes, practices and organisational structure resulting from ERP implementation. They also suggested change from such indirect effects is one-way, as ERP modification is less likely than organisation modification (also Davenport, 1998). Granlund and Malmi (2002) also mentioned two impacts on the work of management accountants – (1) new roles and challenges and (2) the organisation of the accounting function. These changes were attributed to the automation or elimination of many internal transactions and traditional number-crunching tasks from management accountants. However, they did note that the accounting function initially served as a mediation centre, as poor data or errors became apparent in accounting data and reports.

Scapens and Jazayeri (2003) explored the effect of ERP on routine management accounting work. They noted a higher level of direct effect on the work of management accountants than Granlund and Malmi (2002). More centralisation of functions such as accounts receivable/payable reduced the number of accounting staff and caused a reorganisation of the accounting function. They also noted how the ERP in their case study calculated many standard costs and collected actual costs, reducing the input of the management accountant. Additionally, responsibility for cost management was devolved to cost centre managers, reducing the need for some monthly management reports typically produced by the management accountant. Scapens and Jazayeri (2003) did also note that despite losing work to ERPs, the management accountant's role became one of an internal consultant, with the ability to analyse data from the ERP to provide decision-making information.

Literature such as that just mentioned points to the changing role of the management accountant. In this vein, Burns and Scapens (2000b) referred to the concept of a hybrid accountant – one with management accounting skills and additional skills oriented toward a business unit or process. They suggest the hybrid role evolved from the early 1990s and mention database systems, organisational change, operational forecasting and strategic focus as reasons for the emergence of this hybrid role. No reference is made to ERP in their study, and it confirms the effect of AIS on management accounting was seen prior to ERP. Caglio (2003) also suggested accountants as 'hybrids' in the aftermath of ERPs specifically. Caglio (2003) suggested that as many of the traditional management accountants' tasks were performed by ERP, more time was available for 'business planning ... [and] ... the design and management of IT systems' (Caglio, 2003, p. 124). Caglio (2003) specifically noted three areas of change affecting management accountants following ERP implementation – (1) a standardisation of accounting activities, (2) a need for integration and collaboration across business functions and (3) a prominent role of the accountant in the management and configuration of the ERP. Newman and Westrup described ERP as allowing what they termed 'lights off financial processing' (2005, p. 258). This means removing the skills of management accountants in financial reporting. They also suggested that management accountants could adapt and increase skills or lose power and position to other organisational members. They supported the notion of a hybrid accountant, suggesting such a role preserved the expertise of management accountants.

In summary, while the above is not an exhaustive list of literature, it reflects how AIS (and broader IS) can affect management accounting. This is before what might be termed the technology explosion from the mid-2000s, which brought about more societal and organisational change than any previous era. The next section explores literature from this more recent period, and highlights how MAC driven by AIS has continued and developed.

2.4 CONTEMPORARY INFORMATION SYSTEMS AND CHANGE

Subsequently, and into the AIS 2.0 phase (Rosati and Paulsson, 2022), literature exploring the impact of contemporary technologies on MAC is limited. Presently, much of the related literature suggests possible uses of these technologies, challenges and expected changes to the management accountant role, rather than reporting from empirical settings. This section summarises some present literature, focussing on key technologies adopted/available to management accountants.

2.4.1 Data Analytics

One of the key drivers of technological change is the explosion of data available to organisations – often referred to as 'big data'. Big data is often described by characteristics known as the four V's: Volume ,Velocity, Variety and Veracity (Laney, 2001; Zhang et al. 2015). This data can be derived from internal (for example, ERP) and external sources, and includes ever-increasing quantities of data from sensors and social media. This has important implications for the organisation's underlying infrastructure to store and process such data, but also, critically, to verify and analyse such data. Warren et al. (2015) describe big data sets as those that cannot be stored/processed/analysed easily using traditional systems or software. With the accountant's traditional tools such as spreadsheets less able to analyse such data, data analytics is increasingly presented as essential. Data analytics is defined as 'the process of using structured and unstructured data through the applications of various analytic techniques such as statistical and quantitative analysis and explanatory and predictive models to provide useful information to decision-makers' (Schneider et al., 2015, p.720). Data analytics typically includes collection of data, cleansing or transformation of data, detailed analysis and finally communication of insights, often including tools for visualisation.

For the management accountant, data analytics is expected to be transformative (Warren et al., 2015; Möller et al., 2020). As in previous changes, this is suggested as moving the accountant from the role of analyst to interpreter or communicator. Appelbaum et al. (2017) highlight a change from working with historical, internally generated data to real-time data from internal and external sources. Data processing is also enhanced and reporting can be interactive, for example using dashboards with drill-down capabilities or user-friendly visual-isations. Schneider et al. (2015) argue that the increase in breadth of data and tools available permits much faster, real-time (or near real-time) insights vs. human analysis. Such change to the management accountant role, perhaps reflecting similar changes following ERP imple-mentations, points toward the potential for similar MAC.

These changes impact on various management accounting activities, including performance management and management control systems. Nielsen (2015) proposed that analytics creates new possibilities for management accountants, with the potential to integrate accounting tools such as Activity-based Costing or Lean Management into the Balanced Scorecard, creating a holistic framework for performance management. He argued that this would 'develop a com-prehensive, data-driven approach to dynamic performance management relevant for decision making' (p.1). Appelbaum et al. (2017) proposed a detailed Management Accounting Data Analytics (MADA) framework which integrated three types of analytics (descriptive, predic-tive and prescriptive) into the four performance measurement perspectives of the Balanced Scorecard, and highlighted critical success factors for implementation of this. Relatedly, Warren et al. (2015) suggest that big data can play a significant role in the operation of man-agement control systems, with big data allowing organisations to identify which behaviours are correlated with specific goal outcomes. Organisations could then create corresponding performance measures and track performance against these.

Only a few empirical studies have addressed the use of analytics for performance manage-ment, with mixed results. Vuksic et al.'s (2013) case study identified the use of analytics in providing performance information to knowledge workers to support their decision-making. However, they found multiple issues with this, including misalignment between performance measurement processes and the use of analytics, user needs and capabilities. Bronzo et al.'s (2013) survey explored the impact of analytics use on organisational performance (measured across dimensions including financial, customer, process and learning and growth). Survey respondents identified the use of analytics in a range of management accounting processes including product and customer profitability analysis and cost forecasting, and argued that use of these tools improved their organisational performance. Rikhardsson and Yigitbasioglu (2018) identified a number of papers that used experiments to assess the usefulness of various means of displaying displaying findings, with mixed results on the usefulness of graphical displays (for example, Yigitbasioglu and Velcu, 2012), allowing end-users to control the presentation of data (for example, Locke et al., 2015) and how users' knowledge and abilities impact their use of data (for example, Dilla et al., 2013).

Data analytics may also improve support for decision-making. Appelbaum et al. (2017) suggest that prescriptive analytics has a particular role – taking in a range of types of data to prescribe and revise prescriptions that optimise business outcomes and mitigate relevant risks.

They give the example of using social media data to project the optimal marketing budget with the aim of reducing the risk of misdirecting resources. However, they caution that this will become 'unmanageable' unless systems are 're-engineered to accommodate the new complexities presented by different data streams and advanced business analytics' (2017, p.34). Other examples include the use of data analytics to detect operational inefficiencies within organisations, such as the identification of bottlenecks with the production process (Dai and Vaserhelyi, 2017). Empirically examining this suggested role for analytics, Kowalczyk and Buxmann's (2015) case study highlighted use of analytics in routine and nonroutine decisions including on product mix and product pricing. They identified tensions in implementation such as trade-offs between breadth and focus, complexity and understandability, or flexibility and stability of data sources and methods.

Rikhardsson and Yigitbasioglu (2018) completed a structured literature review of data analysis in management accounting research. Focussing on journals from both accounting and IS disciplines up to 2015, they identified relatively few papers, despite their assertion that 'management accounting would have much to gain from successfully integrating BI&A [business intelligence and analytics] techniques into managerial accounting tasks' (p.37). They comment that much of the research to that date was conceptual and lacked critical research perspectives. All of the papers mentioned in this chapter and by Rikhardsson and Yigitbasioglu (2018) suggest that data analytics can improve management accounting, indicating a potential for future MAC. For example, data analytics can enable much faster and more regular analysis of huge data sets (Schneider et al., 2015). What will that mean for how, and how regularly, budgets and variance analyses are prepared? Do traditional methods of cost estimation become obsolete? However, most recent papers also note the need for caution in application (see also Bhimani, 2020a) and empirical papers note a range of challenges in implementation. Similar sentiments are expressed in publications from professional bodies (for example, ACCA, 2020a and ICAEW, 2019). If organisations continue to face such challenges, these may reduce use of data analytics, and the impact on MAC might be less than have been suggested by other authors. Alternatively, the methods to work around such challenges may themselves lead to MAC.

2.4.2   Robotic Process Automation

RPA is an umbrella term that describes the use of software programs (or bots) to perform specified tasks by following structured commands to perform if, then, else statements on structured data (Cooper et al., 2019). Processes that suit this type of automation are therefore generally highly structured, repetitive, simple and routine (van der Aalst et al., 2018; Cooper et al., 2019). Examples include communicating with other digital systems and humans, sending email notifications, capturing data, manipulating data, retrieving information, structured decision-making, processing transactions and more. Returning to the key concept in management accounting literature of routines (Burns and Scapens, 2000a), this would go beyond Pentland's (2011) non-human actants within a routine, or even Volkoff et al.'s (2007) material routines, in that the entire routine would be automated.

Some authors' comments on the impact of RPA on the underlying information systems indicate that the potential implications for MAC are likely to vary depending on how RPA is implemented. Van der Aalst et al. (2018) suggest that where the RPA is simply acting as an agent in place of a human, the existing information system remains unchanged: indicating little MAC. However, McCann (2018) suggests that the process of implementing RPA encourages organisations to reconsider and redesign their processes or routines, for example, to improve the logic, to skip steps that humans might take or to bring in more data to improve decision-making. This points to a significant potential for MAC from RPA that would bear empirical investigation.

In contrast to data analytics, there is very limited literature on RPA in management accounting specifically, including a lack of empirical studies on implementation. Nothing has connected RPA to MAC. However, some studies have explored the suggested impact of RPA on accounting more broadly, highlighting possible impacts of RPA on MA and potential for MAC. Moffitt et al. (2018) highlight repetitive tasks such as payroll, accounts payable and accounts receivable as ripe for automation. McCann (2018) identifies the potential for increasing automation of core finance functions including financial closing and consolidation, cash-flow statement preparation and tax reporting. They suggest similar benefits in various applications, primarily that RPA can more accurately and efficiently complete process tasks as the potential for human error in completion is removed (see also Cooper et al., 2019). As above, if RPA is implemented and these benefits are seen, then this may point to a potential for significant MAC.

Cooper et al. (2019) studied the implementation of RPA in Big4 accounting firms, identifying implementation across all service lines, but that this was most developed in tax compliance followed by audit and advisory. Relevant to this chapter, Cooper et al. (2019) highlight that many of these firms began with automation of their internal manual processes and compliance checking in their own operations: examples include bank reconciliations (also McCann, 2018), expense processing, inventory tracking, timesheet administration and supplier and purchase order validations. Finding benefits in efficiency and effectiveness, they offered such services to clients and across service lines. They highlighted the importance of accountants having a clear understanding of RPA: to identify opportunities for RPA, implement RPA and for control of these. They noted that change was often driven by lower-level employees, contrary to the often top-down applications of new technologies. Beyond this, Kokina et al. (2021) suggest that accountants are well positioned to take up to five roles in implementing RPA – from identifying processes suitable for automation, to providing analysis of results. Identifying relevant skills and competencies for each role, the substantial change in role they envisage points to the potential for MAC. For example, when simple transaction recording can be automated, how might costing and cost estimation change? Do IT specialists control such processes in place of accountants, and what might that mean for the controls enacted?

However, these studies also suggest challenges with RPA that might stymie its application, or potential impact on MAC. For example, trying to apply RPA where processes are less structured and where human judgement is needed will be problematic (Cooper et al., 2019; McCann, 2018). Gotthardt et al. (2020) highlight the importance of understanding the risks introduced by RPA and the need to ensure controls are well designed and effective to mitigate these. McCann (2018) notes ongoing implications for IT resources to ensure that RPA continue to function as designed. For individuals, Kokina et al. (2021) identified skills gaps and a tendency for accountants to restrict themselves in practice, ceding these roles to IT professionals. Cooper et al.'s (2019) survey of accountants engaged with RPA strongly indicated that they saw RPA 'as a stepping-stone to more sophisticated automation' (p.16), expecting RPA to be combined with AI and specifically machine learning (ML) (discussed further below) (see also McCann, 2018). Again, this points to the shifting role of the (human) management accountant in the affected processes, and to the potential for MAC.

2.4.3 Artificial Intelligence

AI is a broad term, colloquially used to describe the use of technology for tasks that traditionally require human input. More formally, AI has been defined as: 'the theory and development of computer systems able to perform tasks normally requiring human intelligence, such as visual perception, speech recognition, decision-making, and translation between languages' (Petkov, 2020, p.100). In its broadest definitions, AI includes a range of technologies, including data mining, ML, speech and image recognition and semantic analysis (Gotthardt et al., 2020). ML is often discussed synonymously with AI (Cho et al., 2020), and describes a computer automatically learning patterns and trends from a data set and iteratively improving its learning performance.

Studies suggest that AI has not yet had widespread impact on the accounting function – in a survey of 700 global finance executives in 2019, only 11 per cent have implemented AI in finance functions (Oracle, 2019). Bakarich and O'Brien (2021) explored implementation and training of accountants in practice on RPA and AI, and their research found limited implementation or training, but a very wide-scale expectation that this will change substantially over the following five years. As noted by Hasan (2022) in his literature review of AI in accounting and auditing, this is still a relatively new field, and much of the research to date has focussed on understanding the concepts and suggesting potential implementations and impact. Where studies have been completed these often focus on specific areas such as auditing (for example, Zemánková, 2019) or tax (for example, Huang, 2018). Few have explored implementation in management accounting settings, but two early examples are Chukwudi et al. (2018) and Lee and Tajudeen (2020). Chukwudi et al. (2018) explored the use of AI to support back-office functions of accounting firms in Nigeria – as for RPA, accounting firms have used their back-office functions as a sort of sandbox for early AI projects – and found increases in efficiency and effectiveness of these functions. Lee and Tajudeen (2020) explored the use of AI-based accounting software in Malaysian organisations and found evidence of AI adoption in a range of organisation sizes, with benefits in automating information capture and storing invoice images. Neither of these studies looked in detail at the likely implications of such uses for MAC.

Other literature around AI and accounting suggests, but does not empirically explore, the potential for AI to assist in common management accounting tasks. Petkov (2020) suggests examples including recording expense accruals by training AI to analyse historical data or bank statements to make relevant journal entries. He contrasts the time delays associated with manual estimation vs. almost instantaneous ML estimation, and points to potentially reduced manual internal control processes. There are suggestions (Cho et al., 2020) and some limited empirical evidence (Ding et al., 2020) that ML can also improve the accuracy of accounting estimates, not least by potentially reducing some forms of bias in decision-making, including confirmation and availability bias (ICAEW, 2018). Others suggest a role for AI in budgeting and forecasting – ICAEW (2018) suggest using ML-based predictive models to forecast revenues, facilitating analysis of very large data sets that might not otherwise be possible. Moreover, as ML adapts to new data over time, forecasting will improve with experience (Cho et al., 2020). Yook (2019) identifies further uses in revenue prediction and in setting target costs plus monitoring variances, while Cho et al. (2020) suggest uses in control processes to predict accounting fraud or to automate stocktaking. Zhang et al. (2020) note that EY already uses drones equipped with optical character recognition for stocktaking. The potential breadth of possible uses, and the fundamental changes suggested (particularly, for example, around estimation and forecasting) point to very substantive potential changes in processes and the role of the management accountant – which may have significant bearing on future MAC.

AI also presents challenges for management accountants. Effective AI requires sufficient data of the right quality to act as training data (ICAEW, 2018) and AI based on incomplete or corrupted data is very likely to be misleading or inaccurate (ACCA, 2020b). AI can learn biases that are present in the underlying data sets (ICAEW, 2018) and replicate these biases in their rules – for example, applying excessive prudence in estimations. AI often becomes extremely complex, which can cause issues in applying professional scepticism and enacting controls (ACCA, 2020b). Cost is also a major factor which may impede development: Petkov (2020) highlights the initial costs associated with creating, planning and implementing new AI systems, but also cautions the need for continued investment in monitoring and improving the system over time. As before, such challenges may impact on the potential of MAC.

2.4.4   Blockchain

Blockchain refers to the use of distributed ledger technology secured by cryptography (Schmitz and Leoni, 2019). It enables transactions between parties in a network (peer-to-peer) without the need for a third authoritative body or arbiter. Participants in the network work together to create and approve transactions, creating a shared ledger and recording accounting entries for both transacting parties (Schmitz and Leoni, 2019). Dai and Vaserhelyi (2017) point to the need for consensus between parties to update the chain as enhancing authenticity and reliability of recorded transactions, while Fullana and Ruiz (2021) talk of Blockchain being immutable and transparent (by virtue of the distributed ledger).

Literature on the (potential) impacts of Blockchain on accounting is less developed than in other areas discussed above. Recent literature reviews point to the lack of academic research to date but highlight reports by professional bodies and (notably Big4) accounting firms (Schmitz and Leoni, 2019; Zhang et al., 2020). Moreover, literature to date has tended to be conceptual rather than empirical, and focussed on potential implications for transaction recording, external reporting and auditing. Notwithstanding the lack of reference to traditional management accounting activities such as budgeting, costing and performance management, suggestions that Blockchain will fundamentally alter the recording, control and audit of accounting transactions (Coyne and McMickle, 2017; Schmitz and Leoni, 2019) indicate that if even some of the proposed impact is seen, then there may be implications for management accountants and for MAC. For example, increased transparency between external partners is a benefit of Blockchain (Dai and Vaserhelyi, 2017). Could this increased visibility extend within organisations and threaten the management accountant's traditional role of gathering and reporting data for control and performance management purposes? Or could Blockchain's automated recording of transactions, like other technologies discussed in this chapter, change the management accountant's role toward analysis and strategic advice (Schmitz and Leoni, 2019)?

2.4.5   Summary

The technologies discussed here are key enabling tools for the transformation of the role of the management accountant, from a focus on recording transactions to support of decision-making across the organisation (ACCA, 2020b; Rosati and Paulsson, 2022). Technologies including RPA, AI and Blockchain will have a role in reducing time spent in transaction recording, while analytics and AI will facilitate in-depth analysis and advice. Some studies indicate the role is already changing. For example, Wadan et al. (2019) explored the changing role and competencies required of German management accountants through literature reviews, expert interviews and analysis of job descriptions. They confirm the automation and standardisation of technical management accounting tasks, with more working time now spent in data analysis, particularly using statistical analysis methods. This causes a shift in the role toward stronger business partnering, interpreting and exchanging information within the company. It also changes the skills profile of the management accountant – they highlight the importance of comfort with technologies such as spreadsheets, VBA, SAP and SQL, but also softer skills including communication and project management. Other studies discussed here have highlighted that management accountants will increasingly need to understand logistical issues, including technical compatibility with existing systems (Appelbaum et al., 2017), internal IT resource requirements and availability (Bakarich and O'Brien, 2021) and be mindful of data and security concerns to ensure regulatory obligations are met (ACCA, 2020a).

As noted, implementation of some of these technologies remains at an early stage, and academic research on all is limited. There is much we do not know about how these will work in practice and therefore the implications for MAC. However, the studies discussed here reflect our understanding that change is coming for the management accountant's role.

2.5   RESEARCH GAPS AND SUGGESTIONS FOR FUTURE RESEARCH

As highlighted earlier, research suggesting that one driver of MAC is information systems and technologies has been available since around the turn of the century. Research in and around this time tended to focus on the implementation of ERP systems and how such systems may have driven MAC. Since this time, as highlighted in the previous section, the AIS field has benefitted from leaps in technological advancement. Technologies such as AI, RPA and the trends in data analytics capabilities open many opportunities for management accountants in practice, and of course for academic research.

Our review, which we will not claim as extensive, reveals relatively little recent research on the impact of contemporary technologies on management accounting. Data analytics is the most researched, but this largely consists of speculative research on how it may change management accounting practices and/or roles. There is limited empirical work on how this is used and challenges faced, and relatively fewer studies on how analytics may drive MAC, or why or why not this may be the case. Earlier, several studies were mentioned which adopted institutional approaches. The claimed transformative effects of data analytics on management accounting practices, roles and even education represent a new (and possibly stronger than previous) driver of MAC. Yet few, if any, studies use institutional or similar framings to study if, how or why MAC due to data analytics happens (or does not). There would thus seem to be an opening for much more research on management accounting practices and roles in this space, addressing questions such as how, why and if data analytics is affecting institutionalised management accounting practices. Bhimani (2020b), referring to digitalisation of research methods in management accounting, suggested that digital research may reveal answers to questions we did not even know we had. In a similar vein, while it is important to use sound theoretical bases and draw on prior literature, we could encourage researchers to consider new approaches and methods as they research contemporary technologies as a driver of MAC. For example, to research the effects of data analytics on what management accountants do, perhaps researchers could consider including social media data, similar to Suddaby et al.'s (2015) work on accountants in practice. Indeed, their study used an institutional work framing, which may be useful to analyse how management accountants engage in work to promote or resist technology-driven change.

Research on RPA and AI is also scarce in a management accounting context. The research cited here does suggest management accounting has/will have a supporting or oversight role to ensure that automated processes are efficiently and effectively used, with consideration given to controls and reliability of outputs. This suggests role changes for management accountants, and possibly new skill sets. We would suggest more research is needed to understand the skills management accountants need in this new policing role. While management accountants have historically been referred to as having a policing role, among other roles (see for example, Yazdifar and Tsamenyi, 2005) the nature of what is policed, and how, is changing with technology. A further aspect of this role development is more a move toward more 'value-added' work, with basic, routine tasks increasingly automated away. Indeed, what exactly this new role is has not been widely researched and it would seem to be somewhere between a business partner role and a controlling role as identified by Järvenpää (2007) and others. The hybridisation of the management accounting role previously discussed by Burns and Scapens (2000b) and Caglio (2003) is being discussed again (ACCA 2020a, Lawson, 2019) with the important difference that this is no longer a hybrid of accounting and business skills, but also of skills formerly associated with IT or data specialists. Thus, research to tease out new roles of management accountants in the context of technologies like RPA and AI is to be encouraged. Can management accounting effectively claim this role, or is it left to the IT and data specialists? Does the role change for all, or will some specialise within management accounting? Arguably, without a clear understanding of what the role is, it is difficult to ensure university courses or professional qualifications provide relevant content and skills development. Indeed, there is a specific gap in research in management accounting education research, as highlighted by Rikhardsson and Yigitbasioglu (2018) – further research could explore whether such technologies should be included in accounting curricula, and how these are or could be taught.

As noted above, literature on how and why (or not) Blockchain may bring about MAC is conceptual at this point. How Blockchain will develop in organisations is not fully certain, but it has been compared to TCP/IP by practitioners in that it is an open and distributed technology. TCP/IP gave us the Internet as we know it today, and if Blockchain were to follow a similar path, it could have dramatic effects on how business is done – at least in terms of how transactional data is recorded and verified. This in turn has the potential to bring about MAC, or at least a change in the roles of management accountants as suggested by Schmitz and Leoni (2019). There is a great opportunity for researchers to actively follow Blockchain initiatives in organisations as they emerge.

To conclude, while some research has been undertaken on contemporary technologies as drivers of MAC, we would suggest much more can and should be done. This has the potential to support the development of the management accounting role in practice. In contrast to the early 2000s when ERP and MAC was a popular topic of research, today there are some specific AIS-focussed journals which offer more outlets for such research than previously. Research into these technologies has the potential to contribute to the general management accounting literature, re-examining traditional management accounting roles, management accounting skill sets and other topics, to defend the relevance of this important role.

NOTE

1.   See David et al. (1999) for a comprehensive definition of AIS.

REFERENCES

ACCA. (2020a) *Professional insight report: Analytics in finance and accountancy*, https://www.accaglobal.com/in/en/professional-insights/technology/analytics_finance_accountancy.html

ACCA. (2020b) *Explainable AI: Putting the user at the core*, https://www.accaglobal.com/in/en/professional-insights/technology/Explainable_AI.html

Anandarajan, A., Srinivasan, C.A., and Anandarajan, M. (2004) Historical overview of accounting information systems in *Business intelligence techniques*, eds M. Anandarajan, A. Anandarajan, and C.A. Srinivasan, Berlin: Springer, pp. 1–19.

Appelbaum, D., Kogan, A., Vasarhelyi, M.A., and Yan, Z. (2017) Impact of business analytics and enterprise systems on managerial accounting, *International Journal of Accounting Information Systems*, 25, pp. 29–44.

Baldvinsdottir, G., Burns, J., Nørreklit, H., and Scapens, R. (2009) The image of accountants: From bean counters to extreme accountants, *Accounting, Auditing & Accountability Journal*, 22(6), pp. 858–882.

Bakarich, K.M. and O'Brien, P.E. (2021) The robots are coming … but aren't here yet: The use of artificial intelligence technologies in the public accounting profession, *Journal of Emerging Technologies in Accounting*, 18(1), pp. 27–43.

Bertz, J. and Quinn, M. (2022) Situated rationalities and management control change – an empirical note on key actors, situated rationalities and generalised practices, *Qualitative Research in Accounting & Management*, 19(1), pp. 77–100.

Bhimani, A. (2020a) *Accounting disrupted: The reshaping of financial intelligence in the new digital era*, New York: Wiley.

Bhimani A. (2020b) Digital data and management accounting: Why we need to rethink research methods, *Journal of Management Control*, 31, pp. 9–23.

Bhimani A. and Willcocks L. (2014) Digitisation, Big Data and the transformation of accounting information, *Accounting and Business Research*, 44(4), pp. 469–490.

Bodnar, G.H. and Hopwood, W.S. (2004) *Accounting information systems*, New Jersey: Pearson Prentice Hall.

Bronzo, M., de Resende, P.T.V, de Oliviera, M.P.V., McCormack, K.P., de Sousa, P.R., and Ferreira, R.I. (2013) Improving performance, aligning business analytics with process orientation, *International Journal of Information Management*, 33(2), pp. 300–307.

Burns, J. and Scapens, R. (2000a) Conceptualising management accounting change: An institutional framework, *Management Accounting Research*, 11(1), pp. 3–25.

Burns, J. and Scapens, R. (2000b) *The changing nature of management accountants and the emergence of 'hybrid' accountants,* New York: IFAC.

Burns, J., Ezzamel, M., and Scapens, R. (1999) Management accounting change in the UK, *Management Accounting*, 77(3), pp. 28–30.

Caglio, A. (2003) Enterprise resource planning systems and accountants: Towards hybridisation, *European Accounting Review*, 12(1), pp. 123–153.

Cho, S., Vasarhelyi, M.A., Sun, T., and Zhang, C. (2020) Editorial: Learning from machine learning in accounting and assurance, *Journal of Emerging Technologies in Accounting*, 17(1), pp. 1–10.

Chukwudi, O., Echefu, S., Boniface, U., and Victoria, C. (2018) Effect of artificial intelligence on the performance of accounting operations among accounting firms in South East Nigeria, *Asian Journal of Economics, Business and Accounting*, 7, pp.1–11.

Coad, A. and Herbert, I. (2009) Back to the future: New potential for structuration theory in management accounting research?, *Management Accounting Research*, 20(3), pp.177–192.

Cooper, L.A., Holderness, D.K., Sun, T., and Wood, D.A. (2019) Robotic process automation in public accounting, *Accounting Horizons*, 33(4), pp. 15–35.

Coyne, J. and McMickle, P. (2017) Can Blockchains serve an accounting purpose?, *Journal of Emerging Technologies in Accounting*, 14(2), pp. 101–111.

Dai, J. and Vasarhelyi, M.A. (2017) Toward blockchain-based accounting and assurance, *Journal of Information Systems*, 31(3), pp. 5–21.

Davenport, T.H. (1998) Putting the enterprise into the enterprise system, *Harvard Business Review*, July–August, pp. 121–131.

David, J.S., Dunn, C.L., McCarthy, W.E., and Poston, R.S. (1999) The research pyramid: A framework for accounting information systems research, *Journal of Information Systems*, 13(1), pp. 7–30.

Dilla, W., Janvrin, D.J., and Jeffrey, C. (2013) The impact of graphical displays of pro forma earnings information on professional and nonprofessional investors' earnings judgements, *Behavioural Research in Accounting*, 25(1), pp. 37–60.

Ding, K., Lev, B., Peng, X., Sun, T., and Vasarhelyi, M.A. (2020) Machine learning improves accounting estimates, *Review of Accounting Studies*, 25(3), pp. 1098–1134.

Dawson, P. (2003) *Reshaping change: A processual perspective,* London: Routledge.

Dechow, N. and Mouritsen, J. (2005) Enterprise resource planning systems, management control and the quest for integration, *Accounting, Organizations and Society,* 30(7–8), pp. 691–733.

Dechow, N., Granlund, M., and Mouritsen, J. (2007) Interactions between information technology and management control in *Issues in management accounting*, pp. 45–64.

Donaldson, L. (1987) Strategy and structural adjustment to regain fit and performance: In defence of contingency theory, *Journal of Management Studies,* 24(1), pp. 1–24.

Fullana, O. and Ruiz, J. (2021) Accounting information systems in the blockchain era, *International Journal of Intellectual Property Management*, 11(1), pp. 63–80.

Gotthardt, M., Koivulaakso, D., Paksoy, O., Saramo, C., Martikainen, M., and Lehner, O. (2020) Current state and challenges in the implementation of smart robotic process automation in accounting and auditing, A*CRN Journal of Financial and Risk Perspectives*, 9, pp. 90–102.

Granlund, M. and Malmi, T. (2002) Moderate impact of ERPS on management accounting: A lag or permanent outcome?, *Management Accounting Research*, 13(3), pp. 299–321.

Hasan, A.R. (2022) Artificial intelligence in accounting & auditing: A literature review, *Open Journal of Business and Management,* 10(1), pp. 440–465.

Huang, Z. (2018) Discussion on the development of artificial intelligence in taxation, *American Journal of Industrial and Business Management*, 8, pp. 1817–1824.

ICAEW. (2018) *Artificial intelligence and the future of the accountancy profession*, https://www.icaew .com/-/media/corporate/files/technical/technology/thought-leadership/artificial-intelligence-report .ashx?la=en

ICAEW. (2019) *Big data and analytics: The impact on the accountancy profession*, https://www.icaew .com/-/media/corporate/files/technical/technology/thought-leadership/big-data-and-analytics.ashx

Järvenpää, M. (2007) Making business partners: A case study on how management accounting culture was changed, *European Accounting Review*, 16(1), pp. 99–142.

Johnson, H. and Kaplan, R. (1987) *Relevance lost: The rise and fall of management accounting*, Boston: Harvard University Press.

Kanter, R.M. (1983) *The change masters: Corporate entrepreneurs at work,* London: Routledge.

Kokina, J., Gilleran, R., Blanchette, S., and Stoddard, D. (2021) Accountant as digital innovator: Roles and competencies in the age of automation, *Accounting Horizons*, 35 (1), pp. 153–184.

Kowalczyk, M and Buxmann, P. (2015) An ambidextrous perspective on business intelligence and analytics support in decision processes: Insights from a multiple case study, *Decision Support Systems*, 80, pp. 1–13.

Laney, D. (2001) 3D data management, controlling data volume, velocity and variety. In *META Group Research Note*, 6, p. 70.

Lawson, R. (2019) *Management accounting competencies: Fit for purpose in a digital Age?* https://www.imanet.org/-/media/4cab087f40b54bac878cae99c892d9a4.ashx

Lee, C.S. and Tajudeen, F.P. (2020) Usage and impact of artificial intelligence on accounting: Evidence from Malaysian organisations, *Asian Journal of Business and Accounting*, 13, pp. 213–240.

Locke, J., Lowe, A. and Lymer, A. (2015) Interactive data and retail investor decision making: An experimental study, *Accounting and Finance*, 55(1), pp. 213–240.

Lukka, K. (2007) Management accounting change and stability: Loosely coupled rules and routines in action, *Management Accounting Research*, 18(1), pp. 76–101.

McCann, D. (2018) Special Report: Robotic Process Automation. The New Digital Workforce, CFO. https://www.cfo.com/applications/2018/09/special-report-the-new-digital-workforce/

Moffitt, K.C., Rozario, A., and Vasarhelyi, M.A. (2018) Robotic process automation for auditing, *Journal of Emerging Technologies in Accounting*, 15(1), pp.1–10.

Möller, K., Schäffer, U., and Verbeeten, F. (2020) Digitalization in management accounting and control: An editorial, *Journal of Management Control*, 31(1), pp. 1–8.

Newman, M. and Westrup, C. (2005) Making ERP's work: Accountants and the introduction of ERP systems, *European Journal of Information Systems*, 14(3), pp. 258–272.

Nielsen, S. (2015) *The impact of business analytics on management accounting*, http://dx.doi.org/10.2139/ssrn.2616363

Nor-Aziah, A.K. and Scapens, R. (2007) Corporatisation and accounting change: The role of accountants in a Malaysian public utility, *Management Accounting Research*, 18(2), pp. 209–247.

Oracle. (2019) *Agile finance unleashed: The key traits of digital finance leaders*, https://go.oracle.com/LP=79114?elqCampaignId=169045

Pentland, B. (2011) The foundation is solid, if you know where to look: Comment on Felin and Foss, *Journal of Institutional Economics*, 7(2), pp. 279–293.

Pentland, B., Haerem, T., and Hillison, D. (2010) Comparing organizational routines as recurrent patterns of action, *Organization Studies*, 31(7), pp. 917–940.

Petkov, R. (2020) Artificial Intelligence (AI) and the accounting function – a revisit and a new perspective for developing framework, *Journal of Emerging Technologies in Accounting*, 17(1), pp. 99–105.

Pettigrew, A. (1987) Context and action in the transformation of the firm, *Journal of Management Studies*, 24(6), pp. 649–670.

Quinn, M. (2011) Routines in management accounting research: Further exploration, *Journal of Accounting and Organizational Change*, 7(4), pp. 337–357.

Quinn, M. and Hiebl, M.R.W. (2018) Management accounting routines: A framework on their foundations, *Qualitative Research in Accounting & Management*, 15(4), pp. 535–562.

Ribeiro, J. and Scapens, R. (2006) Institutional theories in management accounting change: Contributions, issues and paths for development, *Qualitative Research in Accounting & Management*, 3(2), pp. 94–111.

Rikhardsson, P. and Yigitbasioglu, O. (2018) Business intelligence and analytics in management accounting research: Status and future focus, *International Journal of Accounting Information Systems*, 29(C), pp. 37–58.

Rosati, P. and Paulsson, V. (2022) The evolution of accounting information systems in *Routledge handbook of accounting information systems*, pp. 21–32

Scapens, R. and Jazayeri, M. (2003) ERP systems and management accounting change: Opportunities or impacts? A research note, *European Accounting Review*, 12(1), pp. 201–233.

Scapens, R., Ezzamel, M., Burns, J., and Baldvinsdottir, G. (2003) *The future direction of UK management accounting*, London: CIMA.

Schmitz, J. and Leoni, G. (2019) Accounting and auditing at the time of blockchain technology: A research agenda, *Australian Accounting Review*, 29, pp. 331–342.

Schneider, G.P., Dai, J., Janvrin, D.J., Ajayi, K., and Raschke, R.L. (2015) Infer, predict, and assure: Accounting opportunities in data analytics, *Accounting Horizons*, 29(3), pp. 719–742.

Siti-Nabiha, A.K. and Scapens, R. (2005) Stability and change: An institutionalist study of management accounting change, *Accounting, Auditing & Accountability Journal*, 18(1), pp. 44–73.

Suddaby, R., Saxton, G.D., and Gunz, S. (2015) Twittering change: The institutional work of domain change in accounting expertise, *Accounting, Organizations and Society*, 45(C), pp. 52–68.

Tsamenyi, M., Cullen, J., and Gonzalez, J. (2006) Changes in accounting and financial information systems in a Spanish electricity company: A new institutional theory analysis, *Management Accounting Research,* 17(4), pp. 389–408.

van der Aalst, W.M.P., Bichler, M., and Heinzl, A. (2018) Robotic Process Automation, *Business Information Systems Engineering*, 60(4), pp. 269–272.

Volkoff, O., Strong, D.M., and Elmes, M.B. (2007) Technological embeddedness and organizational change, *Organization Science*, 18(5), pp. 832–848.

Vuksic, V.B., Bach, M.P. and Popovic, A. (2013) Supporting performance management with business process management and business intelligence: A case analysis of integration and orchestration, *International Journal of Information Management*, 33(4), pp. 613–619.

Wadan, R., Teuteberg, F., Bensberg, F., and Buscher, G. (2019) Understanding the changing role of the management accountant in the age of Industry 4.0 in Germany. In Proceedings of the 52nd Hawaii international conference on system sciences. https://hdl.handle.net/10125/60017

Warren, J.D., Moffitt, K.C., and Byrnes, P. (2015) How Big Data will change accounting, *Accounting Horizons,* 29(2), pp. 397–407.

Yazdifar, H. and Tsamenyi, M. (2005) Management accounting change and the changing roles of management accountants: A comparative analysis between dependent and independent organizations, *Journal of Accounting and Organizational Change*, 1(2), pp. 180–198.

Yigitbasioglu, O.M. and Velcu, O. (2012) A review of dashboards in performance management: Implications for design and research, *International Journal of Accounting Information Systems*, 13(1), pp. 41–59.

Yook, K.H. (2019) Challenges and prospects for management accounting in Industry 4.0, *Korean Journal of Management Accounting Research*, 19, pp. 33–57.

Zemánková, A. (2019) Artificial Intelligence and Blockchain in audit and accounting: Literature review, *WSEAS Transactions on Business and Economics,* 16, pp. 568–581.

Zhang, J., Yang, X., and Appelbaum, D. (2015) Toward effective big data analysis in continuous auditing, *Accounting Horizons*, 29(2), pp. 469–476.

Zhang, Y., Feng, X., Xie, Y., and Xu, A.H. (2020) The impact of Artificial Intelligence and Blockchain on the accounting profession, *IEEE Access*, 8, 110461–11047, https://ieeexplore.ieee.org/stamp/stamp.jsp?arnumber=9110603

3. Enterprise resource planning systems[1]
Tiago Cardão-Pito

3.1 INTRODUCTION

Enterprise Resource Planning (ERP) systems enable the integration of different organisations' business processes through digital information technologies and Internet-based technologies. Originally, these systems were defined by the type of software that they rely on (Monk & Wagner, 2009; Sumner, 2007), or by leading companies that launched and sold ERP software, as SAP, Oracle, Sage, Syspro, or Microsoft Dynamics (Magal & Word, 2012; Koksalmis & Damar, 2021; Malinić & Todorović, 2012). Indeed, software is a critical component of every ERP system and it has evolved substantially and cannot be dissociated from the company that created it. Nevertheless, ERP systems must not be seen as being limited to their software (Amani & Fadlalla, 2016; Katuu, 2021; Wallace & Kremzar, 2001), for at their core is the integration of different organisational components on the same digital platform. Many business processes from different areas can be integrated through an ERP system, as, for instance, accounting and finance, supply chain management (SCM), marketing and sales, people management, inventory, production, shipping, maintenance, and supplier interactions (Ali & Miller, 2017; Katuu, 2021; Borisova et al., 2019; Kale, 2016; Jagoda & Samaranayake, 2017; Wareham, Fox & Giner, 2014). ERP systems have thus brought about considerable transformations for organisations. Accounting and financial information does not need to be produced in isolation because it can be obtained from a platform which is constantly updating information from the business processes of many other organisational areas (Ali & Miller, 2017; Appelbaum et al., 2017; Kanellou & Spathis, 2013; Maas, van Fenema & Soeters, 2016; Martins & Santos, 2021).

There is another important reason why there is no advantage in reducing the concept of the ERP system to just that of software: it would not be possible to fully capture the substantial transformations these systems have experienced in recent years, particularly regarding the hardware connected to their infrastructure and platforms. Earlier enterprise systems traditionally required advanced computer mainframes to run them, which were installed within the organisation. These early systems required significant investments and maintenance costs connected with the in-house mainframes (Monk & Wagner, 2009; Sumner, 2007; Magal & Word, 2012; Koksalmis & Damar, 2021; Malinić & Todorović, 2012). However, in recent years many systems have been transferred to the cloud, that is, to mainframes operated by third-party service providers that host substantial constituents of these systems' hardware and software (Hustad et al., 2020; Gupta et al., 2019; Bjelland & Haddara, 2018). Although cloud-based enterprise systems still require a significant level of investment and costs, the associated financial burden has been reduced for those companies that adopt them. Several firms, including start-ups that previously could not adopt advanced ERP systems, now find that it is within their financial capabilities to possess such systems (Aremu, Shahzad & Hassan, 2019; Ghobakhloo & Fathi, 2020).

In addition, developments in hardware technology have brought about several other transformations to these systems. For as computing and processing power has significantly increased, including via cloud-based systems, the possibilities concerning the quantity, velocity, and reliability of real-time data have much improved (Ghobakhloo & Fathi, 2020; Holsapple, Sena & Wagner, 2019). To position itself for the global marketplace, nowadays a small firm can even adopt an advanced enterprise system via cloud services, which is something that was unimaginable 30 years ago. Furthermore, additional services via machine learning (or artificial intelligence) can now render such enterprise systems much more effective and productive (Zdravković, Panetto & Weichhart, 2022; Bjelland & Haddara, 2018; Gupta et al., 2019; Greasley & Wang, 2017). Recently, smart sensors and the Internet of Things technology have introduced many more options regarding equipment, machines, robots or facilities for communicating directly with the enterprise systems, without the requirement to always require the intervention of human beings (Manavalan & Jayakrishna, 2019; Tavana, Hajipour & Oveisi, 2020).

In this chapter, we introduce ERP systems as key accounting and information systems. Furthermore, we address the extensive technological transformations that they have experienced in recent years. The next section describes the historical evolution of these systems and the third section explains how ERP systems enable the integration of accounting, along with many other organisational business processes. The fourth section discusses the success (and failure) factors for the implementation and management of ERP systems. The fifth section explores the transformations in ERP systems that have resulted from recent technologies and the sixth and final section concludes this chapter.

3.2   THE EVOLUTION OF ERP SYSTEMS INTO INDUSTRY 4.0

Resources, information, and processes have always been crucial elements for human activity. ERP systems address these elements in organisational contexts and accordingly the heritage of these systems can be connected to the dawn of business activity. Nevertheless, many scholars still place the origins of ERP systems' current versions in the 1960s, alongside the possibilities that have been enhanced by the scientific revolution created through computation and connected automation (Caserio & Trucco, 2018; Jacobs & Weston, 2007; Katuu, 2021; Monk & Wagner, 2009). That is, in the case of Industry 3.0, which is a term used to describe the third industrial revolution counting from the first one whose origins were in steam power, coal and mechanised factory systems in the 18th and 19th centuries. Nevertheless, according to many scholars, we are now witnessing a fourth industrial revolution, or Industry 4.0 (Xu, Xu & Li, 2018; Olsen & Tomlin, 2020). Contemporary enterprise systems have been enhanced with technologies that often include Industry 4.0, as cloud computing, machine learning (artificial intelligence), smart sensors or the Internet of Things (Ghobakhloo & Fathi, 2020; Holsapple, Sena & Wagner, 2019; Manavalan & Jayakrishna, 2019; Hustad et al., 2020; Gupta et al., 2019; Bjelland & Haddara, 2018; Tavana, Hajipour & Oveisi, 2020; Majstorovic et al., 2020; Zdravković, Panetto & Weichhart, 2022; Greasley & Wang, 2017).

The systems often credited with being the starting point for contemporary ERP systems are the computerised inventory control and reorder point systems of the 1960s (Caserio & Trucco, 2018; Jacobs & Weston, 2007; Katuu, 2021; Monk & Wagner, 2009). The latter helped organisations that handle goods and/or raw materials as well as the management of their storage and production. The major aim of these early ERP systems was to reduce costs and save time. Indeed, they addressed basic needs in manufacturing/retailing planning and control (Caserio & Trucco, 2018; Jacobs & Weston, 2007; Katuu, 2021; Monk & Wagner, 2009) and were to evolve into what became known as Material Resource Planning (or MRP) (Caserio & Trucco, 2018; Jacobs & Weston, 2007; Katuu, 2021; Monk & Wagner, 2009). IBM was the leading firm developing these systems in the 1960s and 1970s. However, many other firms were also formed in the 1970s that would later become key vendors of ERP systems for many years, namely, SAP, Oracle, J.D. Edwards and Baan. Another key vendor of ERP systems, PeopleSoft, was created in the 1980s. All these firms employed advanced innovative proposals (Caserio & Trucco, 2018; Jacobs & Weston, 2007; Katuu, 2021).

The fast pace of the evolution of software and hardware soon rendered MRP systems obsolete in comparison with the new systems that emerged in the 1970s, specifically, the Material Resource Planning systems (known as MRP II). The latter were dominant during the 1980s, being characterised by lower costs, much higher data processing capacity, and the ability to integrate more areas and organisational business processes. The new integrated areas included, for example, marketing, shipping or management. Furthermore, MRP II systems also became available to small and medium companies. MRP II systems were thus responsible for bringing about a substantial transformation to the sector (Caserio & Trucco, 2018; Jacobs and Weston, 2007; Katuu, 2021).

The next stage was the development of ERP systems, which is often associated with the 1990s (Caserio & Trucco, 2018; Jacobs & Weston, 2007; Koksalmis & Damar, 2021; Katuu, 2021; Malinić & Todorović, 2012; Monk & Wagner, 2009; Sumner, 2007). According to Jacobs and Weston (2007, p. 361), the term Enterprise Resource Planning (ERP) was coined by the Gartner Group, a consultancy and research firm, in Wylie (1990). The search was for software that could be integrated both across and within the various functional organisational areas, and thus avoid the formation of traditional organisational silos. That is to say, software that could integrate the entire enterprise, and not just some of its functional areas. It was during the 1990s, when IBM was losing its worldwide dominance, that other firms, namely, SAP, Oracle, J.D. Edwards, PeopleSoft and Baan developed solutions for the worldwide market. These proposals attempted to match the integration predicted in the definition of ERP systems (Caserio & Trucco, 2018; Jacobs & Weston, 2007; Koksalmis & Damar, 2021; Katuu, 2021; Malinić & Todorović, 2012; Monk & Wagner, 2009; Sumner, 2007).

Two important developments in ERP systems occurred during the 2000s, namely the consolidation of vendor firms and the development of further modules that could be integrated with previous ERP systems through the Internet (Caserio & Trucco, 2018; Jacobs & Weston, 2007; Koksalmis & Damar, 2021; Katuu, 2021; Malinić & Todorović, 2012; Monk & Wagner, 2009). In addition, after being launched in the previous decades, the basis for large-scale cloud computing was being built, which was to revolutionise ERP systems over the following decade (Ghobakhloo & Fathi, 2020; Holsapple, Sena & Wagner, 2019).

Oracle later acquired J.D. Edwards and PeopleSoft (which themselves had merged beforehand) and by the end of the 2000s there were two leading firms in the ERP market: SAP and Oracle (Caserio & Trucco, 2018; Katuu, 2021). Furthermore, the growth of the Internet in the 2000s has facilitated the integration of several modules created in the previous decade, including modules such as customer relationship management (CRM), human capital management (HCM), enterprise asset management, product lifecycle management, product information management, product data management, quality assurance, manufacturing execution systems, transportation management systems, warehouse management, and business-to-business (B2B) systems (Caserio & Trucco, 2018; Katuu, 2021; Kale, 2016; Appelbaum et al., 2017; Sasidharan, 2019). While the initial ERP systems were focussed on SCM, the objective of the new modules was to capture the entire organisation's business processes. Some writers no longer call these new module-based systems ERP systems, but rather they merely call them enterprise systems, or business intelligence (for example, Kale, 2016; Appelbaum et al., 2017; Sasidharan, 2019). Other writers refer to them as Extended ERP or ERP II (for example, Haddara & Constantini, 2020; Caserio & Trucco, 2018). We will keep referring to them as ERP systems (which is still a widespread practice in research), albeit bearing in mind that such modules can be implemented in an organisation either connected or disconnected to the SCM systems, and consequently the traditional ERP systems (Haddara & Constantini, 2020; Tenhiälä, Rungtusanatham & Miller, 2018).

Firms such as Amazon, Salesforce, or Google started selling cloud-based services before the 2010s. However, the great expansion of cloud-based ERP services took place in the 2010s (Caserio & Trucco, 2018; Katuu, 2021 Ghobakhloo & Fathi, 2020; Holsapple, Sena & Wagner, 2019). This ushered in three innovative types of services, namely: Infrastructure as a Service (IaaS), Platform as a Service (PaaS), and Software as a Service (SaaS). In other words, ERP service providers were able to offer not only the software to their customers, but also the platform and the infrastructure. Although many firms have continued to develop their own in-house or hybrid ERP systems (Caserio & Trucco, 2018; Elragal & Kommos, 2012; Greasley & Wang, 2017), many no longer need to buy their own expensive computer mainframes, because they can simply hire them as services (Caserio & Trucco, 2018; Katuu, 2021; Hustad et al., 2020; Gupta et al., 2019; Bjelland & Haddara, 2018; Elragal & Kommos, 2012). Furthermore, in direct competition with SAP and Oracle, a range of new service providers based on the cloud were to gain market share in the ERP market, such as, for instance, Microsoft, Workday, Sage, Infor, and Syspro. More recently, other Industry 4.0-related technologies such as machine learning (artificial intelligence), smart sensors, and the Internet of Things have been impacting ERP systems (Ghobakhloo & Fathi, 2020; Holsapple, Sena & Wagner, 2019; Manavalan & Jayakrishna, 2019; Tavana, Hajipour & Oveisi, 2020; Zdravković, Panetto & Weichhart, 2022; Greasley & Wang, 2017). Some scholars are already referring to some of these technologies as Industry 5.0, to depart from 4.0. A closer look at these transformations will be made at the end of the chapter.

After observing the historical evolution of the ERP systems, we will now study how the ERP systems can be used to integrate accounting and many other organisational business processes.

3.3　INTEGRATING ACCOUNTING WITH OTHER ORGANISATIONAL BUSINESS PROCESSES THROUGH ERP SYSTEMS

As mentioned above, ERP systems have brought about great transformations for organisations. Accounting information can now be produced from a platform that integrates different modules comprising the organisation's different business activities. For instance, CRM modules allow managing the interactions with clients. Other modules are designed for the management of supplier relationships (for instance, B2B modules). Other models are for the management of personnel, while others are for the management of an organisation's assets. Specific modules exist for managing products and their life cycles, while many other modules are available for managing quality, manufacturing, transportation, warehouse management, and other business processes (Caserio & Trucco, 2018; Katuu, 2021; Kale, 2016; Appelbaum et al., 2017; Sasidharan, 2019). Indeed, some firms prefer to manage these modules independently, while others fail to achieve full module integration, but rather use different software for different modules (Tenhiälä, Rungtusanatham & Miller, 2018; van Roekel and van der Steen, 2019). Similarily, some firms have not yet adhered to the cloud as they prefer on-site systems (Katuu, 2021; Chang, 2020; Bjelland & Haddara, 2018). A technological ecosystem faces several tensions, such as the standardisation of processes versus its variability, the control of process versus their autonomy, or the emphasis on the collective versus the individual (Wareham, Fox & Giner, 2014). Nevertheless, there is a clear tendency for module integration and the adoption of recent technologies.

Either way, either integrated or dispersed, ERP modules follow an accounting logic where data is received, processed, and analysed after specific procedures. For instance, Heinzelmann (2017) investigated the implementation of SAP software in a manufacturing firm. SAP software is also a reference for many other ERP vendors. In his qualitative research study, Heinzelmann concluded that the implementation of SAP software brought with it a German accounting logic for the entire organisation. Rather than merely impacting the financial and accounting departments, this specific accounting logic was replicated to different areas of the firm under study by the different modules in the ERP software (Heinzelmann, 2017; see also Soh and Sia, 2004). The expansion of the accounting logic to other organisational areas represents a challenge for accountants (Heinzelmann, 2017; Youssef & Mahama, 2021; Kale, 2016; Malinić & Todorović, 2012).

Additionally, the implementation of ERP systems has caused subtle changes for the role of accountants in organisations (Appelbaum et al., 2017; Jagoda & Samaranayake, 2017; Malinić & Todorović 2012; Youssef & Mahama, 2021, Kale, 2016). Emanating from both internal and external sources, ERP systems have provided accountants with expanded data storage power and enhanced computational power (Appelbaum et al., 2017; Malinić & Todorović 2012), which have grown even faster with the advent of cloud-based systems (Caserio & Trucco, 2018; Katuu, 2021; Hustad et al., 2020; Gupta et al., 2019; Bjelland & Haddara, 2018; Elragal & Kommos, 2012). Accordingly, accountants can thus apply less of their time to traditional data gathering activities and rather apply more time to activities involving the analysis, interpretation, and reporting of the obtained data (Appelbaum et al., 2017; Malinić & Todorović, 2012). Accountants' advice regarding strategic analysis and predictive analytics, which is often described as 'business intelligence', has thus become much more influential in the higher ranks of organisations (Youssef & Mahama, 2021; Kale, 2016; Appelbaum et al., 2017; Sasidharan, 2019). There is a risk, however, of the illusion of control, as a larger quantity of data does not necessarily imply that it has been analysed, interpreted, and reported well. Several intangible parts of the organisation may well still not appear in the quantitative data (Cardão-Pito, 2021, 2017; Beaubien, 2013). Nevertheless, ERP systems have provided accountants with important tools that were not previously available.

Furthermore, the activities of external and internal auditing have also been profoundly transformed, as they can now be conducted throughout the organisational ERP systems with assistance from artificial intelligence (Elbardan, Ali & Ghoneim, 2015; Zdravković, Panetto & Weichhart, 2022; Appelbaum et al., 2017; Katuu, 2021; Thottoli, Ahmed & Thomas, 2022). Nevertheless, ERP systems do not appear to imply a loss of jobs for accountants, but, on the contrary, ERP systems have made accountants even more necessary for the operation of contemporary organisations (Appelbaum et al., 2017; Jagoda & Samaranayake, 2017; Malinić & Todorović 2012; Youssef & Mahama, 2021, Kale, 2016). Accountants are required to perform the various tasks related to the possibilities enhanced by ERP systems and, accordingly, organisations' accounting departments are becoming ever closer intertwined with their IT departments (Al-Sabri, Al-Mashari & Chikh, 2018; Appelbaum et al., 2017; Borisova et al., 2019; Jagoda & Samaranayake, 2017; Kanellou & Spathis, 2013; Martins & Santos, 2021; Malinić & Todorović, 2012; Youssef & Mahama, 2021; Kale, 2016)

Despite these rapid transformations, there is nevertheless an underlying concern that vast sectors of accounting academia and theory might not have kept pace with these developments. Several universities still fail to anchor ERP expertise in their academic environment (De Villiers, 2021; Youssef & Mahama, 2021; Gollner & Baumane-Vitolina, 2016; Barkhi & Kozlowski, 2017; Blount et al., 2016). For instance, the traditional balanced scorecard that is lectured to students in management accounting classes only has four areas, namely: financial, the customer, internal processes, and learning and growth (Kaplan & Norton, 1992, 2006; Free & Qu, 2011). Appelbaum et al. (2017) have notably tried to link the balanced scorecard model with ERP-based business intelligence systems. However, in comparison with the technological possibilities for business intelligence brought about by ERP systems, which can be tailor-made for each organisation, the balanced scorecard is but a simplistic and outdated model, which does not clearly explain how to obtain, process, analyse, interpret, and report the respective data. Compared with ERP systems, the balanced scorecard mainly consists of a few ambiguous and remotely scientific graphs (Free & Qu, 2011). Given the high importance that ERP systems have for the future professional lives of accountants, ERP systems need to be taught to accounting students in the lecture room (De Villiers, 2021; Youssef & Mahama, 2021; Barkhi & Kozlowski, 2017; Blount et al., 2016).

After studying how the ERP systems can be used to integrate many organisational business processes, we will now observe the success (and failure) factors in the implementation and management of ERP systems.

3.4   SUCCESS (AND 'FAILURE') FACTORS FOR THE IMPLEMENTATION AND MANAGEMENT OF ERP SYSTEMS

A substantial portion of the research literature on ERP systems concerns accomplishment and failure in implementing and managing these systems. Besides its importance for academic studies regarding accounting and information systems, this research effort can also be quite helpful for both practitioners and real-life organisations (if adequately communicated). Decades ago, it was not clear whether every organisation should adopt an MRP system, or even an initial ERP system to integrate their business processes and manage data in real time (Jakobs & Weston, 2007; Lepistö, 2015). However, after the advent of the Internet and Industry 4.0, it has become unimaginable to think that an organisation could run its day-to-day operations without some form of ERP system, or, as also called, 'business intelligence' (see above). Nonetheless, although cloud computing has reduced IT infrastructure costs, these systems still demand a substantial financial investment by organisations (Caserio & Trucco, 2018; Katuu, 2021; Ghobakhloo & Fathi, 2020; Holsapple, Sena & Wagner, 2019). Furthermore, a sizeable number of ERP system implementations fail (Janssens et al., 2020; Jagoda & Samaranayake, 2017; Ali & Miller, 2017; Gollner & Baumane-Vitolina, 2016; Katuu, 2021) and even when an ERP system is implemented, the adopting organisation might not necessarily achieve its full potential (Ali & Miller, 2017; van Roekel & van der Steen, 2019; Costa, Aparicio & Raposo, 2020).

Besides cost-related issues, there are many other motives for this type of research to be of relevance for the world of practice. Undeniably, ERP systems exercise a large impact on organisations, as these systems enable the processing of a larger quantity of data, more rapidly, and more efficiently. Kang and Suh (2022) have shown that these systems have impacted firms' spatial organisation. In addition, ERP systems imply less internal coordination costs, and therefore organisations can reallocate diverse types of work and workers themselves across establishments in separate locations. Firms' headquarters now have much faster and easier real-time access to non-headquarter locations through data, communication, and inter-actions. Furthermore, ERP systems are now an integral part of many jobs and accordingly they affect employees' productivity and motivation (Rossi, Nandhakumar & Mattila, 2020; Yen et al., 2015; Liang et al., 2015; Maas, van Fenema & Soeters, 2014).

Contemporary organisations must adapt to the potentialities and implications arising from ERP systems. There has been a drastic transformation in the tools available to support decision-making (Caserio & Trucco, 2018; Kale, 2016; Appelbaum et al., 2017; Sasidharan, 2019; Haddara & Constantini, 2020) and risk management (Tian & Xu, 2015; Janssens, Kusters & Martin, 2020; Lai, Lai & Lowry, 2016; Shao et al., 2022). Nevertheless, ERP systems alone do not concede a competitive advantage to those organisations that adopt them. For it is rather the effective use of these systems that can lead to competitive advantages over other organisations (Alomari et al., 2018; Hsu, 2013; van Lieshout et al., 2021). Accordingly, there is both a theoretical and practical need for a better understanding of what could be the critical success factors for implementing and managing ERP systems.

Several important questions thus arise regarding what these critical success factors indeed are, how they should be identified, and how they can be recognised and/or measured. The research has studied a panoply of topics, methods, and proposals to address these questions which present a wide-ranging diversity of perspectives. For instance, studies have researched the implementation and management of ERP systems in large corporations (for example, Ali and Miller, 2017; Kang and Suh, 2022), small and medium firms (for example, Aremu, Shahzad & Hassan, 2019; Holsapple, Sena & Wagner, 2019), and governmental organisa-tions and not-for-profit organisations (for example, Alves & Matos, 2013; Gavidia, 2017; Carlsson-Wall et al., 2022). Apart from the design of the necessary computational methods for ERP software, a broad range of research methodologies have also been employed, such as case studies (for example, Costa, Aparicio & Raposo, 2020; Maas, van Fenema & Soeters, 2014), surveys (for example, Hiebl, Gärtner & Duller, 2017; Alves & Matos, 2013), obser-vation and interviews (for example, Drummond, Araujo & Borges, 2017; Andersson, 2016; Maas, van Fenema & Soeters, 2016), educated user perspectives (for example, Reitsma & Hilletofth, 2018; Wallace & Kremzar, 2001), and reflexive analysis (for example, Lepistö, 2015; Spraakman et al., 2018).

Nevertheless, as is to be expected, there is no unanimous agreement regarding what success or failure in implementing and managing ERP systems actually means. Success can be a broad term, which is more overarching than other factors, such as usefulness or effectiveness (Holsapple, Sena & Wagner, 2019, p. 2; DeLone & McLean, 1992, 2003). Given the constant innovation and uploading of ERP systems, even the separation between implementation and management can be fuzzy to a certain degree. Researchers must be careful when defining their research methods, as their methods may affect the findings (Spraakman et al., 2018). Furthermore, those who are responsible for implementing these systems might have different perspectives of what success is for those who manage them (Drummond, Araujo & Borges, 2017).

Two research approaches have been conventional in attempting to infer success in managing and implementing an ERP system. The first involves the direct use of technology-adoption models, such as the task-technology fit model or the technology acceptance model. The task-technology fit model suggests a method for assessing the relationship between the technology and tasks that technology aims to support (Dishaw & Strong, 1998; Spies, Grobbelaar & Botha, 2020). In turn, the technology acceptance model is derived from a theory about how users of a certain technology come to perceive its usefulness and ease of use (Davis, 1989; Hwang, 2005). Several researchers have used models such as these to investigate the implementation and management of specific ERP systems in real organisations (for example, Borisova et al., 2019; Gollner & Baumane-Vitolina, 2016; De Toni, Fornasier & Nonino, 2015; Koksalmis & Damar, 2021; Holsapple, Sena & Wagner, 2019). The second research approach, which is in effect more indirect, has been to investigate outcomes resulting from implementing and managing ERP systems. For instance, to investigate what effects these systems have had on a range of issues, including productivity (for example, Reitsma & Hilletofth, 2018; Jagoda & Samaranayake, 2017; Agarwal & Dhar, 2014), competitive advantage (for example, Alomari et al., 2018; Hsu, 2013), improving business analytics (for example, Holsapple, Sena & Wagner, 2019; Appelbaum et al., 2017; Kale, 2016), employee and customer loyalty (for example, Yen et al., 2015; Liang et al., 2015; Maas, van Fenema & Soeters, 2014), and so forth.

The implementation and management of ERP systems can be rather complex activities (Janssens, Kusters & Martin, 2020; Kang & Suh 2022; van Roekel & van der Steen, 2019; Abbasi & Varga 2022). Research has found that many factors can affect and/or be affected by ERP systems. These include, for instance, the organisation's environment (Aremu, Shahzad & Hassan, 2019; Dezdar & Ainin, 2011; Reitsma & Hilletofth, 2018), the software producer and vendor (Borisova et al., 2019; Katuu, 2021), adequate management (Aremu, Shahzad & Hassan, 2019; Elbanna & Newman, 2022; Tanriverdi & Du, 2020), the characteristics of the Chief Financial Officer (Hiebl, Gärtner & Duller, 2017), the centralisation and decentralisation of power (Nandi & Kumar, 2016; Hassan & Mouakket, 2018), the communication process (Andersson, 2016), the knowledge management carried out by the organisation (Costa, Aparicio & Raposo, 2020; Tsai et al., 2021; Maas, van Fenema & Soeters, 2016), organisational characteristics (Aremu, Shahzad & Hassan, 2019; Dezdar & Ainin, 2011; Reitsma & Hilletofth, 2018), and employee motivation (Yen et al., 2015; Liang et al., 2015; Maas, van Fenema & Soeters, 2014). The implementation and management of ERP systems are not fully understood and these systems are constantly evolving. Accordingly, many research opportunities exist to expand our knowledge in these areas.

As we will observe in the next section, recent technologies associated to Industry 4.0 and 5.0 have enabled many recent transformations in the ERP systems.

3.5 ERP SYSTEMS MOVE AHEAD: THE CLOUD, MACHINE LEARNING, THE INTERNET OF THINGS, AND OTHER TECHNOLOGIES

ERP systems are at the forefront of Industry 4.0 (and 5.0) and they are thus extensively shaped by emerging technologies, such as the cloud, machine learning (artificial intelligence), the Internet of Things, and others. Additionally, these systems also play an active role in enabling the adoption, implementation, and management of new technologies related with Industry 4.0 (Ghobakhloo & Fathi, 2020; Holsapple, Sena & Wagner, 2019; Manavalan & Jayakrishna, 2019; Hustad et al., 2020; Gupta et al., 2019; Bjelland & Haddara, 2018; Tavana, Hajipour & Oveisi, 2020; Majstorovic et al., 2020; Zdravković, Panetto & Weichhart, 2022; Greasley & Wang, 2017).

As mentioned above, the cloud must not be understood as being the mere transfer of software and data from in-house mainframes to those of third-party service providers. Indeed, such a transfer is better known as Software, or as a Service (SaaS), both of which are quite an important part of cloud computing. Nevertheless, business proposals by cloud service providers involve at least two other relevant activities, namely, IaaS and PaaS. These offer third-party infrastructures that can replace on-site hardware and cloud-based platforms through which organisations interact and collect data, such as data from actual or potential customers, suppliers, workers, and many other stakeholders (Hong et al., 2022; Zdravković, Panetto & Weichhart 2022). These two additional services are perhaps more transformative than SaaS, because, when compared with on-site ERP systems, they both bring about additional operational effectiveness and cost reduction in obtaining and maintaining complex hardware (Caserio & Trucco, 2018; Katuu, 2021; Hustad et al., 2020; Gupta et al., 2019; Bjelland & Haddara, 2018; Elragal & Kommos 2012). Let us consider, for instance, the case of updating the ERP system. Before the advent of the cloud and Internet-ready systems, on-site ERP systems needed to be updated on the spot, which involved the direct intervention of at least one technician. In addition, technicians were eventually required to serve geographically separate sites. On the other hand, cloud-based ERP systems can be constantly updated directly through the cloud (Gupta et al., 2019; Bjelland & Haddara, 2018) and the advent of the cloud has also resulted in an important transformation in the ERP market. Several firms that were not traditional ERP software providers have entered the market as providers of IaaS and/or PaaS. Examples of these firms are Microsoft, Google, and Amazon. Nevertheless, it is not uncommon for firms such as these to have ambitions regarding developing their own successful SaaS ERP systems (Hong et al., 2022; Katuu, 2021).

Other organisations exist which, although they have adopted ERP systems, have not yet been persuaded to move their operations onto the cloud (Katuu, 2021; Chang, 2020; Bjelland & Haddara, 2018; Gao, 2020). Several studies have tried to understand what drives a firm to move their ERP system to the cloud. Generally, these studies reason in terms of costs and the benefits of switching to the cloud. Naturally, direct financial advantages/costs are one key factor in the analysis, for even though managing an ERP system through the cloud requires less initial investment and maintenance costs, there are still significant fees to be paid to the suppliers of SaaS, IaaS, and PaaS (Chang, 2020; Tavana, Hajipour & Oveisi, 2020; Link & Back, 2015). Several firms, however, do not use the cloud, owing to a concern about the security of the data being handled by a third-party service provider (Chang, 2020; Tavana, Hajipour & Oveisi, 2020; Gao, 2020), and other firms opt not to use the cloud because they are concerned with the customisation of the system to meet their specific needs (Chang, 2020; Tavana, Hajipour & Oveisi, 2020; Gao, 2020). Another reason concerns the burden of the process of implementing, operating, and maintaining the system in the cloud (Chang, 2020; Tavana, Hajipour & Oveisi, 2020; Gao, 2020). Furthermore, the perceived benefits of moving to the cloud seem to be affected by several factors, such as the system's quality, industry pressure, the perceived risk of cloud ERP systems, and the level of satisfaction with and the breadth of use of incumbent ERP systems (Chang, 2020).

The Industry 4.0 appears to be unstoppable. However, it is not limited to cloud computing. Some scholars are already identifying an Industry 5.0 based upon artificial intelligence and machine learning. For Industry 4.0 and 5.0 systems have different layers, with the cloud being one critical component which contains vital abilities regarding big data storage and processing. However, another layer exists regarding those connected devices that are detectable and receive data through smart sensors, actuators, and network stratums. Furthermore, the application layer corresponds to the software and apps that process the big data in the cloud and on the different devices (adapted from Manavalan & Jayakrishna, 2019; Tavana, Hajipour & Oveisi, 2020). These enterprise systems can now be assisted by artificial intelligence at every layer in the system (Zdravković, Panetto & Weichhart, 2022; Manavalan & Jayakrishna, 2019; Tavana, Hajipour & Oveisi, 2020; Gilchrist, 2016).

Owing to technologies such as the Internet of Things, the tendency is to evolve towards systems where several machines can be integrated, which work interdependently and manage themselves (Zdravković, Panetto & Weichhart, 2022; Manavalan & Jayakrishna, 2019; Tavana, Hajipour & Oveisi, 2020). Human interaction is only required for many tasks that are based on the Internet of Things to manage exceptions or conflicts with the forecast output (Zdravković, Panetto & Weichhart, 2022; Manavalan & Jayakrishna, 2019; Tavana, Hajipour & Oveisi, 2020; Gilchrist, 2016). These systems work in real time, are decentralised, and can redraw modules as needed (Vogel-Heuser & Hess, 2016; Tavana, Hajipour & Oveisi, 2020; Peres et al., 2017). Human intervention is still very much needed to operate ERP systems. Nevertheless, these systems demonstrate the ostensibly unstoppable march of Industry 4.0 and 5.0.

3.6   CONCLUSION

ERP systems are key information systems for contemporary organisation. They rely on software, infrastructures, and platforms to integrate organisations' multiple business processes. Furthermore, they possess an accounting logic. This chapter has described key research topics that relate these systems to accounting research. We have seen that several researchers attribute the origins of ERP systems to the 1960s, and more specifically, to the dawn of the third industrial revolution (counting from the one in the 18th and 19th centuries). However, back in the 1960s the expression ERP system did not exist. This expression only became widely known in the 1990s and subsequently they have evolved considerably over the last decades. We are now witnessing the fourth industrial revolution, where ERP systems remain quite relevant. For not only have these systems been redesigned and adapted to new technologies, such as the cloud, machine learning (artificial intelligence), or the Internet of Things, but they currently also enable many organisations to benefit from novel Industry 4.0 technologies.

Some scholars think they should be given another name to distinguish them from previous ERP systems.

To date, ERP systems do not appear to be a threat to accounting or to accountants; in fact, they reinforce the relevance of accounting for organisations. However, it appears that academic accounting has not yet entirely caught up with these systems. Nevertheless, these systems have ushered in a deep transformation in the role of real-life accountants, who currently work much closer with the IT department. In addition, accountants contribute to what has been called 'business intelligence', where there is a need for new competences in collecting, interpreting, and reporting large portions of data, better known as 'big data'. Accountants have enhanced their role in producing vital information for management decision-making, however they also require training and further skills to perform these new tasks adequately.

We have seen that a vast research literature exists which represents an attempt to identify and understand the key success factors for implementing and managing ERP systems. This research set is very diverse in terms of topics, research objectives, and research methods. We have reviewed some of its key findings and have surmised that there is no consensus regarding what those key factors are. These gaps in the research literature provide many opportunities for further research.

Last, but not least, this chapter has further investigated how ERP systems are impacted by and impact other Industry 4.0 (and 5.0) technologies, such as the cloud, machine learning (artificial intelligence), or the Internet of Things. Similar to past industrial revolutions, not all people and all organisations have adopted these new technologies: nonetheless, there is an undeniable tendency towards adopting such new technologies. This is why ERP systems (even if described under other names) are at the forefront of Industry 4.0 (and 5.0) and accounting research must not be left behind.

NOTE

1. Funding: the ADVANCE Research Centre at ISEG, and the Portuguese national funding agency for science, research and technology (FCT - Fundação para a Ciência e a Tecnologia, I.P.) under the Project UIDB/04521/2020.

REFERENCES

Abbasi, M., & Varga, L. (2022). Steering supply chains from a complex systems perspective. *European Journal of Management Studies*. Ahead-of-print.

Agarwal, R., & Dhar, V. (2014). Big data, data science, and analytics: The opportunity and challenge for IS research. *Information Systems Research*, 25(3), 443–448.

Ali, M., & Miller, L. (2017). ERP system implementation in large enterprises – a systematic literature review. *Journal of Enterprise Information Management*, 30(4), 666–692.

Alomari, I. A., Mohd Amir, A., Aziz, K. A., & Md Auzair, S. (2018). Effect of enterprise resource planning systems and forms of management control on firm's competitive advantage. *Asian Journal of Accounting and Governance*, 9, 87–98.

Al-Sabri, H. M., Al-Mashari, M., & Chikh, A. (2018). A comparative study and evaluation of ERP reference models in the context of ERP IT-driven implementation: SAP ERP as a case study. *Business Process Management Journal*, 24(4), 943–964.

Alves, M. do C., & Matos, S. I. A. (2013). ERP adoption by public and private organizations – a comparative analysis of successful implementations. *Journal of Business Economics and Management*, 14(3), 500–519.

Amani, F., & Fadlalla, A. (2016). Organizing ERP research: A knowledge-centric approach. *Journal of Enterprise Information Management*, 29(6), 919–940.

Andersson, A. (2016). Communication barriers in an interorganizational ERP-project. *International Journal of Managing Projects in Business*, 9(1), 214–233.

Appelbaum, D., Kogan, A., Vasarhelyi, M., & Yan, Z. (2017). Impact of business analytics and enterprise systems on managerial accounting. *International Journal of Accounting Information Systems*, 25(March), 29–44.

Aremu, A. Y., Shahzad, A., & Hassan, S. (2019). Factors affecting enterprise resource planning adoption on firms' performance among medium-sized enterprises. *International Journal of Supply Chain Management*, 8(1), 142–149.

Barkhi, R., & Kozlowski, S. (2017). ERP in the classroom: Three SAP exercises focused on internal controls. *Journal of Emerging Technologies in Accounting*, 14(1), 77–83.

Beaubien, L. (2013). Technology, change, and management control: A temporal perspective. *Accounting, Auditing and Accountability Journal*, 26(1), 48–74.

Bjelland, E., & Haddara, M. (2018). Evolution of ERP systems in the cloud: A study on system updates. *Systems*, 6(2), 22.

Blount, Y., Abedin, B., Vatanasakdakul, S., & Erfani, S. (2016). Integrating enterprise resource planning (SAP) in the accounting curriculum: A systematic literature review and case study. *Accounting Education*, 25(2), 185–202.

Borisova, V. V., Demkina, O. V., Mikhailova, A. V., & Zieliński, R. (2019). The enterprise management system: Evaluating the use of information technology and information systems. *Polish Journal of Management Studies*, 20(1), 103–118.

Cardão-Pito, T. (2017). Organizations as producers of operating product flows to members of society. *SAGE Open*, 7(3), July–September, 1–18.

Cardão-Pito, T. (2021). *Intangible flow theory in economics: Human participation in economic and societal production*. London. Routledge.

Carlsson-Wall, M., Goretzki, L., Hofstedt, J., Kraus, K., & Nilsson, C. J. (2022). Exploring the implications of cloud-based enterprise resource planning systems for public sector management accountants. *Financial Accountability and Management*, 38(2), 177–201.

Caserio, C. & Trucco, S. (2018). *Enterprise resource planning and business intelligence systems for information quality an empirical analysis in the Italian setting*. Cham, Switzerland. Springer.

Chang, Y. W. (2020). What drives organizations to switch to cloud ERP systems? The impacts of enablers and inhibitors. *Journal of Enterprise Information Management*, 33(3), 600–626.

Costa, C. J., Aparicio, M., & Raposo, J. (2020). Determinants of the management learning performance in ERP context. *Heliyon*, 6(4), e03689.

Davis, F. D. (1989). Perceived usefulness, perceived ease of use, and user acceptance of information technology, *MIS Quarterly*, 13(3), pp. 319–340.

DeLone, W. H., & McLean, E. R. (1992). Information systems success: The quest for the dependent variable. *Information System Research*, 3(1), 60–95.

DeLone, W. H., & McLean, E. R. (2003). The DeLone and McLean model of information systems success: A ten-year update. *Journal of Management Information Systems*, 19(4), 9–30.

De Toni, A. F., Fornasier, A., & Nonino, F. (2015). The impact of implementation process on the perception of enterprise resource planning success. *Business Process Management Journal*, 21(2), 332–352.

De Villiers, R. (2021). Seven principles to ensure future-ready accounting graduates – a model for future research and practice. *Meditari Accountancy Research*, 29(6), 1354–1380.

Dezdar, S., & Ainin, S. (2011). The influence of organizational factors on successful ERP implementation. *Management Decision*, 49(6), 911–926.

Dishaw, M. T. & Strong, D. M. (1998). Supporting software maintenance with software engineering tools: A computer task-technology fit analysis, *Journal of Systems and Software*, 44(2), pp. 107–120.

Drummond, P., Araujo, F., & Borges, R. (2017). Meeting halfway: Assessing the differences between the perceptions of ERP implementers and end-users. *Business Process Management Journal*, 23(5), 936–956.

Elbanna, A., & Newman, M. (2022). The bright side and the dark side of top management support in digital transformation – a hermeneutical reading. *Technological Forecasting and Social Change*, 175(3), 121411.

Elbardan, H., Ali, M., & Ghoneim, A. (2015). The dilemma of internal audit function adaptation: The impact of ERP and corporate governance pressures. *Journal of Enterprise Information Management*, 28(1), 93–106.

Elragal, A., & El-Kommos, M. (2012). In-house versus in-cloud ERP systems: A comparative study. *Journal of Enterprise Resource Planning Studies* 2.

Free, C., & Qu, S. Q. (2011). The use of graphics in promoting management ideas: An analysis of the Balanced Scorecard, 1992–2010. *Journal of Accounting and Organizational Change*. 7(2), pp. 158–189.

Gao, L. (2020). Exploring the data processing practices of cloud ERP – a case study. *Journal of Emerging Technologies in Accounting*, 17(1), 63–70.

Gavidia, J. V. (2017). A model for enterprise resource planning in emergency humanitarian logistics. *Journal of Humanitarian Logistics and Supply Chain Management*, 7(3), 246–265.

Ghobakhloo, M., & Fathi, M. (2020). Corporate survival in Industry 4.0 era: The enabling role of lean-digitized manufacturing. *Journal of Manufacturing Technology Management*, 31(1), 1–30.

Gilchrist, A. (2016). *Industry 4.0: The industrial Internet of Things*. Apress, Bangken, Nonthaburi, Thailand.

Gollner, J. A., & Baumane-Vitolina, I. (2016). Measurement of ERP-project success: Findings from Germany and Austria. *Engineering Economics*, 27(5), 498–508.

Greasley, A., & Wang, Y. (2017). Integrating ERP and enterprise social software. *Business Process Management Journal*, 23(1), 2–15.

Gupta, S., Qian, X., Bhushan, B., & Luo, Z. (2019). Role of cloud ERP and big data on firm performance: A dynamic capability view theory perspective. *Management Decision*, 57(8), 1857–1882.

Haddara, M., & Constantini, A. (2020). Fused or unfused? The parable of ERP II. *International Journal of Information Systems and Project Management*, 8(3), 48–64.

Hassan, M. K., & Mouakket, S. (2018). Power, trust and control: The interaction of political behaviours in accounting-based ERP system implementation processes. *Journal of Accounting in Emerging Economies*, 8(4), 476–494.

Heinzelmann, R. (2017). Accounting logics as a challenge for ERP system implementation: A field study of SAP. *Journal of Accounting and Organizational Change*, 13(2), 162–187.

Hiebl, M. R. W., Gärtner, B., & Duller, C. (2017). Chief financial officer (CFO) characteristics and ERP system adoption: An upper-echelons perspective. *Journal of Accounting and Organizational Change*, 13(1), 85–111.

Holsapple, C., Sena, M., & Wagner, W. (2019). The perceived success of ERP systems for decision support. *Information Technology and Management*, 20(1), 1–7.

Hong, P., Jiang, W., Yu, W., & Wang, C. (2022). Comparison of SaaS and IaaS in cloud ERP implementation: The lessons from the practitioners. *VINE Journal of Information and Knowledge Management Systems*. Ahead of print.

Hsu, P. F. (2013). Commodity or competitive advantage? Analysis of the ERP value paradox. *Electronic Commerce Research and Applications*, 12(6), 412–424.

Hustad, E., Sørheller, V. U., Jørgensen, E. H., & Vassilakopoulou, P. (2020). Moving Enterprise Resource Planning (ERP) systems to the cloud: The challenge of infrastructural embeddedness. *International Journal of Information Systems and Project Management*, 8(1), 5–20.

Hwang, Y. (2005). Investigating enterprise systems adoption: Uncertainty avoidance, intrinsic motivation, and the technology acceptance model, *European Journal of Information Systems*, 14(2), pp. 150–161.

Jacobs, F. R., & Weston, F. C. (2007). Enterprise Resource Planning (ERP) – A brief history. *Journal of Operations Management*, 25(2), 357–363.

Jagoda, K., & Samaranayake, P. (2017). An integrated framework for ERP system implementation. *International Journal of Accounting and Information Management*, 25(1), 91–109.

Janssens, G. L. S. G., Kusters, R. J., & Martin, H. H. (2020). Expecting the unexpected during ERP implementations: A complexity view. *International Journal of Information Systems and Project Management*, 8(4), 68–82.

Kale, V. (2016). *Enhancing enterprise intelligence: Leveraging ERP, CRM, SCM, PLM, BPM, and BI.* Florida. CRP Press.

Kanellou, A., & Spathis, C. (2013). Accounting benefits and satisfaction in an ERP environment. *International Journal of Accounting Information Systems*, 14(3), 209–234.

Kang, Y., & Suh, J. (2022). Information technology and the spatial reorganization of firms. *Journal of Economics and Management Strategy*, 31(3), 674–692.

Kaplan, R. S. & Norton, D. P. (1992). The balanced scorecard: Measures that drive performance, *Harvard Business Review,* 70(1), pp. 71–79.

Kaplan, R. S. & Norton, D. P. (2006). *Alignment: Using the balanced scorecard to create corporate synergies,* Boston, MA. Harvard Business School Press.

Katuu, S. (2021). Trends in the enterprise resource planning market landscape. *Journal of Information and Organizational Sciences,* 45(1), 55–75.

Koksalmis, G. H., & Damar, S. (2021). An empirical evaluation of a Modified Technology Acceptance Model for SAP ERP System. *Engineering Management Journal*, 00(00), 1–16.

Lai, V. S., Lai, F., & Lowry, P. B. (2016). Technology evaluation and imitation: Do they have differential or dichotomous effects on ERP adoption and assimilation in China? *Journal of Management Information Systems*, 33(4), 1209–1251.

Lepistö, L. (2015). On the use of rhetoric in promoting enterprise resource planning systems. *Baltic Journal of Management*, 10(2), 203–221.

Liang, H., Peng, Z., Xue, Y., Guo, X., & Wang, N. (2015). Employees' exploration of complex systems: An integrative view. *Journal of Management Information Systems*, 32(1), 322–357.

Link, B., & Back, A. (2015). Classifying systemic differences between software as a service-and on-premise -enterprise resource planning, *Journal of Enterprise Information Management.* 28(6), 808–837.

Maas, J. B., van Fenema, P. C., & Soeters, J. (2014). ERP system usage: The role of control and empowerment. *New Technology, Work and Employment*, 29(1), 88–103.

Maas, J. B., van Fenema, P. C., & Soeters, J. (2016). ERP as an organizational innovation: Key users and cross-boundary knowledge management. *Journal of Knowledge Management,* 20(3), 557–577.

Magal, S., & Word, J. (2012). *Integrated business processes with ERP systems.* Hoboken, NJ: Wiley.

Majstorovic, V., Stojadinovic, S., Lalic, B., & Marjanovic, U. (2020). ERP in Industry 4.0 context. In *IFIP Advances in Information and Communication Technology:* 591 IFIP (Issue August). Springer International Publishing.

Malinić, S., & Todorović, M. (2012). How does management accounting change under the influence of ERP? *Ekonomska Istraživanja*, 25(3), 722–751.

Manavalan, E., & Jayakrishna, K. (2019). A review of Internet of Things (IoT) embedded sustainable supply chain for Industry 4.0 requirements. *Computers and Industrial Engineering,* 127(November 2017), 925–953.

Martins, J. L., & Santos, C. (2021). The influence of ERP systems on organizational aspects of accounting: Case studies in Portuguese companies. *Accounting Research Journal*, 34(6), 666–682.

Monk, E., & Wagner, B. (2009). *Concepts in enterprise resource planning.* Boston, MA. Cengage Learning.

Nandi, M. L., & Kumar, A. (2016). Centralization and the success of ERP implementation. *Journal of Enterprise Information Management*, 29(5), 728–750.

Olsen, T. L., & Tomlin, B. (2020). Industry 4.0: Opportunities and challenges for operations management. *Manufacturing & Service Operations Management*, 22(1), 113–122.

Peres, R. S., Rocha, A. D., Coelho, A., & Oliveira, J. B. (2017). *A highly flexible, distributed data analysis framework for Industry 4.0 manufacturing systems. Service orientation in holonic and multi-agent manufacturing* (pp. 373–381). Cham, Switzerland: Springer.

Reitsma, E., & Hilletofth, P. (2018). Critical success factors for ERP system implementation: A user perspective. *European Business Review*: //doi.org/10.1108/EBR-04-2017-0075

Rossi, M., Nandhakumar, J., & Mattila, M. (2020). Balancing fluid and cemented routines in a digital workplace. *Journal of Strategic Information Systems*, 29(2), 101616.

Sasidharan, S. (2019). Reconceptualizing knowledge networks for enterprise systems implementation: Incorporating domain expertise of knowledge sources and knowledge flow intensity. *Information and Management*, 56(3), 364–376.

Shao, C., Chen, X., Almalki, M. A., & Zhang, L. (2022). Use and research of ERP in financial management of large enterprises using nonlinear system. *Fractals,* 30(2), 1–12.

Soh, C., & Sia, S. (2004), An institutional perspective on sources of ERP package-organization misalignment, *Journal of Strategic Information Systems*, 13(4), 275–397.

Spies, R., Grobbelaar, S., & Botha, A. (2020). *A scoping review of the application of the task-technology fit theory*. In *Conference on e-Business, e-Services and e-Society* (pp. 397–408). Cham, Switzerland. Springer.

Spraakman, G., O'Grady, W., Askarany, D., & Akroyd, C. (2018). ERP systems and management accounting: New understandings through "nudging" in qualitative research. *Journal of Accounting and Organizational Change*, 14(2), 120–137.

Sumner, M. (2007). *Enterprise resource planning*. Essex, UK: Pearson Education.

Tanriverdi, H., & Du, K. (2020). Corporate strategy changes and information technology control effectiveness in multibusiness firms. *MIS Quarterly: Management Information Systems*, 44(4), 1573–1618.

Tavana, M., Hajipour, V., & Oveisi, S. (2020). IoT-based Enterprise Resource Planning: Challenges, open issues, applications, architecture, and future research directions. *Internet of Things*, 11, 100262.

Tenhiälä, A., Rungtusanatham, M. J., & Miller, J. W. (2018). ERP system versus stand-alone enterprise applications in the mitigation of operational glitches. *Decision Sciences,* 49(3), 407–444.

Thottoli, M. M., Ahmed, E. R. & Thomas, K. V. (2022). Emerging technology and auditing practice: Analysis for future directions, *European Journal of Management Studies*, 27(1), 99–119.

Tian, F., & Xu, S. X. (2015). How do enterprise resource planning systems affect firm risk? Post-implementation impact. *MIS Quarterly*, 39(1), 39–60.

Tsai, M. T., Li, E. Y., Lee, K. W., & Tung, W. H. (2011). Beyond ERP implementation: The moderating effect of knowledge management on business performance. *Total Quality Management and Business Excellence*, 22(2), 131–144.

van Lieshout, J. W. F. C., van der Velden, J. M., Blomme, R. J. & Peters, P. (2021). The interrelatedness of organizational ambidexterity, dynamic capabilities and open innovation: A conceptual model towards a competitive advantage, *European Journal of Management Studies*, 26(2/3), pp. 39–62.

van Roekel, H. J., & van der Steen, M. (2019). Integration as unrealised ideal of ERP systems: An exploration of complexity resulting from multiple variations of integration. *Qualitative Research in Accounting and Management*, 16(1), 2–34.

Vogel-Heuser, B., & Hess, D. (2016). Guest editorial Industry 4.0 – Prerequisites and visions. *IEEE Transactions on Automation Science and Engineering*, 13(2), 411–413.

Wallace, T. F., & Kremzar, M. H. (2001). *ERP make it happen*. New York, USA: John Wiley & Sons, Inc.

Wareham, J., Fox, P. B., & Giner, J. L. C. (2014). Technology ecosystem governance. *Organization Science*, 25(4), 1195–1215.

Wylie, L. (1990). A vision of the next-generation MRP II. Scenario S 300–339, Gartner Group, April 12, 1990.

Xu, L. D., Xu, E. L., & Li, L. (2018). Industry 4.0: State of the art and future trends. *International Journal of Production Research*, 56(8), 2941–2962.

Yen, H. R., Hu, P. J. H., Hsu, S. H. Y., & Li, E. Y. (2015). A multilevel approach to examine employees loyal use of ERP systems in organizations. *Journal of Management Information Systems*, 32(4), 144–178.

Youssef, M. A. E. A., & Mahama, H. (2021). Does business intelligence mediate the relationship between ERP and management accounting practices? *Journal of Accounting and Organizational Change*, 17(5), 686–703.

Zdravković, M., Panetto, H., & Weichhart, G. (2022). AI-enabled enterprise information systems for manufacturing. *Enterprise Information Systems*, 16(4), 668–720.

4. Enterprise resource planning systems as a tool for standardisation, centralisation, and control: insights from the qualitative accounting literature

Matt Kaufman and Erica Wagner

4.1 INTRODUCTION

This chapter examines 30 years of qualitative research into the effects of Enterprise Resource Planning (ERP) on financial and managerial accounting systems. Fieldwork by accounting scholars begins with initial installations in the early 1990s (Scapens & Jayazeri, 2003), and continues through the shift to cloud-based platforms in the late 2010s (Carlsson-Wall et al., 2021). Over that approximately 25-year period these studies describe remarkable technological and organisational change.

The median study within our sample performed approximately two years of fieldwork. Our goal is to knit fieldwork together from the initial (1993) to the most recent (2018). We hope this approach, and the results presented, are of broad interest to all members of the accounting community who study technological progress from a qualitative perspective. The resulting approach differs from a traditional literature analysis as we focus on only the methods and case analysis sections from each paper. Numerous papers within our sample have varying periods of delay between initial fieldwork and published manuscript. Such delays blur the relationship between evidence observed and conclusions reached. While author conclusions act as a lens through which case evidence is sifted for presentation, we hope the combined analysis of all available studies provides insight into the historical evolution of ERP in organisational life.

This chapter highlights the transition of ERP within the qualitative accounting literature from an organisational problem to a data platform with influence beyond corporate reporting. A review of qualitative accounting ERP studies highlights persistent tension between central and peripheral organisational actors as a central theme. It also suggests this conflict plays out through three subthemes: standardisation, centralisation, and sources of resistance/ drivers of change. These themes have continued relevance for a number of emerging Accounting Information System (AIS) topics. We synthesise findings from ERP studies and discuss implications for several accounting topics built upon and around the existing ERP infrastructure. Emerging examples include analytics, blockchain, and cybersecurity.

4.2 LITERATURE REVIEW METHODS

We utilise the Web of Science (WoS) database to compile a comprehensive list of all ERP studies published within academic accounting journals. ERP studies were identified through use of the search term 'Enterprise Resource Planning' and limited to accounting journals through the use of a 'Business Finance' category filter. On 21 November, 2021 this query returned an initial list of 101 total papers. We review methods from each paper to identify a subset of 31 qualitative studies. Further review identified varying levels of observation quality within each case. As such, we further filtered our initial list to include studies published in journals rated A or A* by the Australian Business Deans Council. The result was a final list of 15 studies.

To assess the completeness of the resulting list of papers we performed a detailed review of literature reviews and sources cited within each study. The WoS database excludes studies published before 2005. Additional review identified three studies that meet established study criteria but were published before WoS began aggregating papers. As such, our completeness check results in the manual addition of papers published before this date.

The final sample includes the 18 papers discussed in Section 3. For context, publishing journals include: *Accounting, Auditing and Accountability Journal* (1); *Accounting, Organizations and Society* (2); *European Accounting Review* (3); *Financial Accountability and Management* (1); *International Journal of Accounting Information Systems* (1); *Management Accounting Research* (3); *Managerial Auditing Journal* (1); *Qualitative Research in Management and Accounting* (6).

4.2.1   Case-Codex Compilation and Temporal Analysis

The typical qualitative accounting study is organised around six sections: introduction, literature review, case methods, case analysis, discussion, and conclusion. Our final case codex consists of information taken from the methods and case analysis sections from each of the 18 studies identified. A preliminary review of qualitative data collected across these studies notes conclusions reached are more accurately grouped by fieldwork date rather than publication date. As such, studies are arranged within the case codex by the period in which authors collect data. This shift clarifies a set of demarcations between qualitative accounting studies that roughly correspond to societal shifts around ERP specifically and information technology generally.

An initial group of studies perform fieldwork from 1993–2000. Primary drivers of ERP adoption in the 'ERP as Electronic Revolution' period include the need to consolidate disparate systems, adopt the euro currency, and address the Y2K problem. A noteworthy theme is the need to successfully implement the technologic aspects of a shared system, and difficulty changing related organisational process. Section 4.3.1 summarises six studies that conduct the majority of their fieldwork in this period, all of which were published in A* journals (100 per cent).

A second group conduct fieldwork from 2001–2007. Primary drivers of ERP adoption in the 'ERP as Control and Compliance' period include the need to improve financial and operational performance through standardised business process and reporting. Within this period, technological challenges are less pronounced and studies focus on the increasing ability of centralised actors to shape action firm-wide. Section 4.3.2 summarises seven studies that conduct the majority of their fieldwork in this period, three of which were published in A* journals (43 per cent).

The final group of studies gather field data after 2007. Studies within the 'ERP as Financial Platform' period primarily describe the adoption of systems designed to stack upon fully functioning ERP and provide additional functionality. The primary drivers of system implementation in this period are competitive pressure and financial distress, likely related to the global financial crisis from 2007–2008. Within this period the objections of local actors to centralised process are less pronounced and studies focus on the increasing sophistication of centralised reporting. Section 4.3.3 summarises five studies that conduct the majority of their fieldwork in this period, none of which were published in A* journals (0 per cent).

The bracketed analysis of these qualitative accounting studies allows for temporal and holistic analysis of ERP technology, related organisational adaptation/resistance, and complementary tools. The ability of qualitative research to observe differences in description across a 25-year period is distinct. It provides an archived description of technology-in-use and allows for a sort of qualitative meta-analysis to observe its evolution through time.

4.2.2   Case-Codex Compilation and Thematic Analysis

While significant insight is obtained through the temporal bracketing of qualitative ERP studies within the accounting literature, significant themes also emerge from a review of the case codex as a whole. These themes are present across each of the three time periods analysed, but with shifting relative impact. Case codex themes are discussed in detail within Section 4.4 below, alongside implications for future research.

Theme one is the impact of ERP on the relationship between accounting at the centre and periphery. The primary contrast is between attempts by headquarters to impose centralised, standardised reporting on disparate systems of divisional reporting that are customised to the needs of local actors. This theme is present in the vast majority of studies examined, and the dominant theme of every study published in an A* journal. A holistic review suggests the qualitative accounting literature is primarily interested in ERP because of its ability to centralise and standardise organisational activity.

ERP differentially impacts work performed by professionals at varying levels in a business hierarchy. Each qualitative ERP study pays special attention to the role of management accountants in facilitating information flow between, and within, distinct organisational units. The primary role for management accountants in these organisations is the creation of reports that meet internal information needs. This leads to tension between standardised systems used to aggregate divisional data for corporate use and localised systems that conform to work and analysis performed by local actors.

A final theme includes sources of resistance to standardisation and centralisation, as well as strategies used to enact change. A combination of temporal and thematic analysis not only highlights conflict between central and local actors around ERP, but also shifts in the nature of this conflict through time. Ties between conflict, continued technological development, and financial constraint are also considered with potential application for emerging technology.

4.3   CASE CODEX ANALYSIS

4.3.1   ERP as Electronic Revolution (1993–2000)

Granlund and Malmi (2002) use the phrase 'electronic revolution' to describe the overall impact of ERP from initial adoptions of the 1990s. Their study asks whether the minimal impact of ERP on management accounting practice is a temporal lag or a permanent outcome.

This question is consistent with the overall approach and findings from the six qualitative studies that conduct fieldwork during this period. Each of these studies note differential experience of ERP implementation by central and peripheral actors alongside significant, persistent barriers to the standardisation of work performed at local levels. When viewed alongside results from future studies, the electronic revolution period conclusively describes a temporal lag before significant future change.

Scapens and Jazayeri (2003) perform fieldwork at the European division of a multinational firm from pre-implementation in 1993 through post-implementation in 1999. Cited drivers of system implementation are the cost of maintaining a diverse set of legacy financial and manufacturing information systems, difficulties in managing currency translation, and the growing need for a coordinated information technology strategy. The authors note many employees required remedial training on unfamiliar topics in basic business and computer literacy. However, the primary problems preventing successful implementation stemmed from the diverse information systems ERP sought to replace.

> The European business is different from the American business. A global system doesn't fit because we don't work in a global market. There are differences in markets, customers, and so on. Scapens and Jazayeri (2003, p.207)

Even the earliest observation of ERP implementation highlights organisational, as opposed to technical, barriers to success. The quote above defines a general mindset that separates electronic revolution period studies from those that follow. The pre-ERP business environment was incredibly balkanised between different production centres, functional areas, and geographic units. Authors identify four specific problems a global system must overcome: 1) meeting the localised needs of individual plants with their own business and operating philosophies; 2) the need to transfer localised information to integrate local applications; 3) resistance from employees who fear resulting job loss; and 4) creating the formalised business processes necessary to meet the needs of a singular, rigid system.

The conclusion to the project is especially noteworthy. The authors note ERP resulted in an improved and standardised flow of global information, centralised authority for system design and control in the American headquarters, and the automation of routine information processing. However, the system was not used by the European division to manage the business because global reports did not meet the reporting needs of local managers. Authors conclude that management accounting information remains unchanged; but note fewer accounting staff who primarily meet the specialised information needs of specific managers.

Granlund and Malmi (2002) interview a set of 16 financial and information technology executives in ten different companies from 1999–2000. They observe divergent results in ERP implementation and use, and coin the term electronic revolution to ask if the limited impact of ERP on management accounting is a temporal lag or a permanent outcome.

Half of the interviewed companies perform key management accounting functions (for example, costing and profitability analysis) outside the ERP environment, typically within spreadsheets. The remaining half were able to incorporate management accounting functions into ERP by recreating a set of diverse, legacy systems within the new environment. Authors highlight reporting environment rigidity as a key limitation to ERP adoption, and question whether future systems could improve flexibility through database design and data warehousing.

On the one hand, due to ever-increasing automation there is less need for accountants to handle routine tasks. Some of them are needed in more analytical tasks, while others will be laid off...With advanced on-line analytical processing (OLAP) tools it is possible to process the data in many ways. However, our study showed that in most cases managers do not have the skills and/or time for this... The non-accountants we interviewed or spoke with never indicated that they would now perform management accounting tasks. Granlund and Malmi (2002, p.312)

In many ways this conclusion seems both prescient and short-sighted in two respects. First, it suggests the automation of routine transaction processing will result in a bifurcated outcome for accounting staff. Some accountants will pivot to increasingly complex reports with growing strategic relevance, while the majority will be downsized and eliminated. The centralising effect of these job losses is not remarked upon, but implied by a remaining few with increased authority. Second, authors suggest non-accountants would not take on management accounting tasks such as budgeting, costing, or other forms of analysis. ERP software would soon enable the diffusion of accounting work through the development of specialised reporting tools designed to stack upon a singular database.

Caglio (2003) conducts fieldwork from 1999–2000 with a variety of accounting, IT, management, and line employees within a medium-sized division of a multidivisional firm. Cited drivers of system implementation include euro adoption, Y2K risk, and the parent firm's acquisition by a German multinational in 1996. The study's primary research question involves shifts to accounting work brought on by ERP implementation and possible hybridisation of accounting with other management functions.

Case firm goals for the ERP project include the redesign of both business processes and information flows. Firm management explicitly states implementation should 'constrain people to a common platform' and avoid 'different approaches by different functions'. However, the study documents resistance by functional managers, including the head of the management accounting function, who feared a loss of control over data and general organisational influence. Corporate management pressed the initiative and called for accountants to help 'harmonise' interconnected parts of the organisation.

Despite what one would tend to argue, standardization has favored accountants, because even if the new ERP system has led accounting professionals to lose some control over their expertise and everyday activities, it has also legitimized a new role for them within [the case division] and has improved the overall perception of what value the accounting function creates for the whole firm. In fact, the standardization of practices has allowed the accounting department to guarantee a more consistent, quality service to all its internal clients. Caglio (2003, p.141)

The quote above highlights standardisation as a significant outcome from ERP adoption, a theme that would recur throughout the rest of the qualitative accounting literature. The authors note the automation of low-level accounting work and the loss of discretion for others. ERP implementation results in fewer, hybridised roles that require accounting, business process, and IT knowledge.

Authors describe initial shifts toward standardisation as a boon to accounting staff, allowing them to provide a higher quality work product and avoid time wasted cleaning and combining data. What is unanswered is whether the new role specified is temporary or permanent. Taken alongside other studies of the electronic revolution period this question takes on additional importance. Are accountants establishing a higher-value organisational role, or are they simply filling a gap between the standardised data established through ERP and later tools that could capitalise more fully? It will take time for this question to fully resolve.

Dechow and Mouritsen (2005) conduct fieldwork within business units of two multinational firms with reputations for successful ERP implementation. Interviews were conducted from 1999–2000. Cited drivers of system implementation include the need to expedite and improve the reliability of financial reporting, increase data visibility across firm boundaries, and decrease manual data processing. Their research question targets the integration of management and accounting control through ERP adoption, and findings suggest this synthesis is an unending process.

A case informant notes, 'Management decided that they wanted to get rid of all those spreadsheets, word documents, etc. that individuals used to integrate everything into one, centralised information system' (Dechow & Mouritsen, 2005, p.701). Similar to other studies in this period, employees pressed back against efforts to increase access to data under their control, or to standardise reporting away from the specific needs of local users. For example, because different business units were defined as production plants and not financial entities within SAP the firm was unable to compile unit-specific financial reports.

Significant repair work was required to ensure data reliability and ensure reliably comparable reports. System data was exported to other tools at the local level for analysis and reporting. Accounting must step in to repair damage to corporate reports caused by employees not understanding the integrated system and a general lack of firm-wide data discipline. Diverse local classifications conflict with global usage. Spreadsheets maintained by local actors contradict ERP-based reports. In the concluding section, IT personnel critique the need for integrative work as a failure to fully capitalise on ERP functionality and hope a future system would further integrate and automate organisational reporting.

> No one resisted integration as an idea, but informants had only vague ideas about what to do with it and attempted to use the ERP system as a tool to guarantee their own autonomy. Operations wanted to introduce a product-configurator in order to give them access to the entire supply chain and in particular to align sales with production. Yet they preferred to maintain physical Kanban card systems in order to secure themselves a place of informational darkness. In similar ways accountants chose not to do overhead calculations by the ERP system because data discipline was too low but in effect also because doing these calculations in spreadsheets also kept their activities in the dark. Dechow and Mouritsen (2005, p.724)

The quote above is perhaps the best description of sources of resistance to ERP implementation in the electronic revolution period. An asymmetry exists where employees enthusiastically accept standardisation for reports they might use, but resist the standardisation of their own work. Early studies document similar resistance to ERP by employees across locations, geographies, and functions.

Quattrone and Hopper (2005) perform fieldwork from 1997–1999 in business units and corporate headquarters of two multinational firms. Cited drivers of system implementation include regulatory changes around reporting for overseas subsidiaries, the need to replace a large number of legacy information systems, and Y2K compliance. The primary research question asks how the implementation of ERP will impact management control within multinational firms. Findings focus on the spatial and temporal shifts that accompany, or impede, ERP implementation.

We are getting two servers – one in Japan and one in Europe. So, our template becomes the European template and then we have to find a way of interfacing. Now, in five years we will all be wishing: 'Oh slow down, let's get a global template'…We will say, 'Wait a minute! It is now time for the two servers to join. AHA!! But wait a minute…you have got a different standard there, you have got a different material number…why didn't we think of this five years ago!' Quattrone and Hopper (2005, p.750)

This study examines incremental ERP implementation as a suboptimal, but ultimately achievable, goal. Phased approaches avoid the need to rapidly flatten hierarchies or reduce headcount, minimise resistance, and foster collaboration around successful implementation. The quote above provides insight into the incremental nature of ERP implementation in the electronic revolution period, where continued support at all levels of the organisation was a key driver of success. This strategy comes at a cost however, where the full benefits of ERP require successive rounds of iteration and re-implementation. The authors ask a manufacturing leader when three ERPs would be merged into a single, common platform and they jokingly reply, 'Not at least until 2017!' (Quattrone & Hopper, 2005, p.753). Given findings within subsequent qualitative studies this apparent joke proved a reasonable estimate.

Phased implementations include significant customisation to replace centralised best practices embedded in SAP with locally accepted legacy workflow. Data integrity issues result similar to those observed in other cases. Even when global standards are successfully put into place, such as a single chart of accounts across all subsidiaries, they are undermined by inconsistent use at the local level. The result in this case is not a singular system of centralised control, but a distributed access to data that empowered everyone to create their own report as control over data was lacking in implementation.

There is no single, unambiguous 'bottom line' in Think–Pink anymore. Anyone with access to ERPs database can create information to suit his or her purpose… [different] versions are not necessarily coherent with one another and, most importantly, change continuously and unpredictably. Quattrone and Hopper (2005, p.759)

The quote above comes from the case conclusion and highlights the extent to which ERP studies within the electronic revolution period provide a window on initial implementation and not a final result. ERP was an unsettling event often performed in phases to ensure success. The appearance of disorder within corporate reporting through ERP is very much an artifact of the technology and business culture of this period (1993–2000), not a description of ERP itself.

Wagner et al. (2011) conduct initial fieldwork between June 1999 and August 2000, with follow-up interviews through publication. Their study involves an Ivy League university seeking to replace legacy information systems through an integrated ERP. Central administrators sought to reduce unnecessary reconciliation, and improve overall financial performance and governance. Research questions ask how accounting logics are encoded within ERP systems and how new accounting practices emerge around a reconfigured system.

The crux of the conflict described in this study is a desire by central campus managers to impose budgeting and reporting practices used by the Central Budget Office onto faculty members throughout the university. The result was significant work by staff to download information from the centralised system and use Excel to create customised reports for local users. Over time consolidation at the higher level increased pressure for conformity and oversaw an iterative process of training and standardisation to build support.

Why not design [current practice] as the integrated, standardized technology? It worked for faculty for years...I hope you understand that it's not [the ERP] itself that's the issue. It's the lack of understanding and regard for the people bringing in the money and the people doing the work that's so frustrating. Wagner et al. (2011, p.189)

[Case firm] really missed an opportunity to understand the business... [we] focused way too much on giving [central managers] information and not worrying about giving [line employees] information needed to manage the business. We just focused on the wrong things first. Wagner et al. (2011, p.190)

The quotes above highlight two latent themes within the electronic revolution period that would emerge with more force in later studies. First, ERP is a standardising force that requires everyone within an organisation to perform assigned tasks according to a system template. Second, ERP is also a centralising force that focuses on aggregating newly standardised data in ways that meet the needs of central (or senior, corporate) management. The key takeaway from early qualitative accounting studies of ERP is the amount of time and effort required to implement a system that achieves these objectives. Early studies describe the compromise necessary to implement a standardised, centralised system with local buy-in around use. Resulting tensions would not fully resolve for a decade (see additional discussion of 2010 follow-up interviews below).

4.3.2   ERP as Control and Compliance (2001–2007)

Three interrelated influences mark the primary point of demarcation within early-ERP implementation studies. First, the Sarbanes–Oxley Act of 2001 requires ERP to meet newly stringent internal control documentation and testing requirements. Second, the tech bubble recession in 2000 gave central managers leverage to enact business process change. Finally, technological innovation continued to develop additional reporting functionality, both within ERP itself as well as through reporting tools meant to stack upon the ERP database. The combined result of these changes is an increase in successful implementation and a decline in documented resistance.

Hyvönen et al. (2006, 2008) observe the implementation of profitability management software (PMS) in an operating division of a multidivisional firm from 2002–2005. The primary driver of adoption is the corporate parent's need to standardise reporting across companies acquired from 1998 to 2002. This study marks a clear break from earlier cases, as the PMS system must operate on top of an established ERP. The resulting report manager allows for product/customer/market analysis across more than 30 different dimensions in a standardised format.

Authors note earlier attempts at an ERP-enabled reporting platform proved difficult to accomplish across different production facilities. Attempts led to disparate sets of locally customised spreadsheets. The new system went forward despite complaints from local actors that a single set of standardised, centralised reports would not meet local information needs.

In 2002, [business unit] accounting personnel who were interviewed saw the new PMS mainly as extra reporting (and additional work) that was going to be of some use to senior management. The division-level controllers interviewed saw the situation in another light. According to them, the new PMS system would eventually replace the former management reporting/responsibility accounting structure, thus the [unit's] internal reporting did not have a future. Hyvönen et al. (2008, p.56)

The new reporting tool was meant to replace many existing cost and profitability reports at the local level. Legacy systems persisted alongside the new reporting tool, as new reports were considered less accurate and less useful to local level actors. Central actors initially allowed legacy routines and reports to continue, so long as they did not conflict with PMS. Authors observe diminished resistance with each round of fieldwork performed.

> The main goal of these developments was standardisation, which would then enable the model to be rolled out in other locations. This standardisation has two aspects, namely: (1) the standardised activities and definitions in the model; and (2) standardised links to the ERP system that allow for integration with the information systems containing the cost data. Thus, [centralised reporting] enabled efficient dis-embedding of local knowledge into such a form that it could later be transformed to other contexts. However, the re-embedding would likely have been impossible without [PMS] being linked to the corporation-wide ERP system. Hyvönen et al. (2006, p.153)

Local accountants continued to supplement centralised reports with additional context, but gradually admitted the information provided by the centralised system was the primary driver of organisational decisions. The quote above highlights key themes of the control and compliance period. First, additional reporting tools are developed to subsume localised reporting into a standardised set of centralised templates. Second, this process can only take place upon the singular database enabled by ERP. The authors conclude their case noting the full strategic potential of the initial ERP project was only realised upon successful implementation of a global reporting tool.

Hyvönen et al. (2009) perform fieldwork around an ERP implementation by the Finnish Defence Forces from 2003 to 2006. The primary driver of implementation was the need to consolidate a large number of legacy systems into a singular database that covers the entire entity. ERP replaced 19 information systems covering materials management, procurement, and financial management. This paper primarily deals with implementation specifics for a large defence department with minimal generalisability beyond that setting.

Jayazeri et al. (2011) perform fieldwork within an operating division of a multinational defence contractor from 2002–2003. ERP implementation was primarily driven by increased market pressure and a desire by senior management and the board of directors to fundamentally restructure internal control through Kaizen, activity-based costing (ABC), and ERP. The combination of cost savings and organisational disruption led to significant turnover throughout the organisation. Authors document significant conflict between previously empowered local divisions and pressure to establish a single corporate authority.

> [Corporate reporting] was now well communicated to all levels within the company. An ERP system was used to do this effectively. As mentioned above, there were easy-to-read summarized reports available online … [Corporate reports] became a tool that senior managers used to communicate their key values to the business units, to help managers achieve their strategic intent. It linked to business unit strategic objectives and performance measures, and focused on achieving targets set out in the strategic plan. Jayazeri et al. (2011, p.305)

The quote above highlights the specific form of standardised, centralised reporting that became commonplace within the control and compliance period. A corporate reporting platform stacked upon the ERP database to provide a singular set of reports aligned with the strategic goals of corporate management. This marks a distinct change from the lack of common measures and reports described during earlier ERP studies.

Beaubien (2013) performs qualitative case study at a financial services firm deploying an ERP-enabled control system from 2004–2006. The primary driver of implementation was a desire to standardise management, operations, and controls across 15 regional units by centralising operations at headquarters. Goals for the implementation include improved operational performance and internal control.

Similar to prior studies, authors note dissonance between local actors who object to cumbersome new processes and central actors who found legacy processes to lack sufficient internal control. The focus on internal control shows the growing influence of Sarbanes–Oxley requirements on business culture throughout the control and compliance period. Firm management explicitly focuses on centralising operational decision-making at corporate headquarters.

> There was no uniform, complete acceptance of the [ERP enabled] audit/assurance function... Individuals sought to recreate the processes and end-results with which they had come to believe to be correct from past experience. The reliance on past perceptions and modes of work is an enactment of the inertia of the past. Beaubien (2013, p.61)

Local actors persisted in actions outside, and around, the system, eroding the perceived level of control offered by the ERP-enabled reporting system. However, the authors document growing acceptance of centralised solutions as employees face multiple cycles of economic contraction, technical investment, and process redesign. The persistence of legacy process within and around an ERP system is a theme of electronic revolution studies. The control and compliance era suggests this was a temporary lag before a standardised, centralised reporting system enabled by ERP.

4.3.3   ERP as Financial Platform (2008–2018)

The third era of qualitative ERP studies in accounting begins with continued technological development and another recessionary business environment. Technology in this period pivoted to the use of web-based platforms constructed upon large databases enabled by cloud computing technology. This period saw the widespread launch of Amazon Web Services in 2006, then Google Cloud and Microsoft Azure in 2008. Additionally, the recession that followed the 2008 financial crisis was severe and long-lasting. It led to a prolonged period of business process redesign centring on information technology, software as a service, and cloud-based IT infrastructure; a trend formally termed Digital Transformation in the late 2010s. Studies from this period document significant standardisation and centralisation of accounting work. Sources of resistance documented in earlier studies remain but with continually declining influence.

Wagner et al. (2011) includes an epilogue describing the continued evolution from conclusions reached during initial fieldwork from 1999–2000. As of 2008, a centralised reporting platform constructed around a single corporate standard remained a nonstarter at the local level. However, over the intervening period central campus had successfully prompted local actors to enter key information into the ERP system for centralised use alongside legacy reports. In 2010, following a period of financial instability during the housing crisis, the central campus system was fully implemented.

> Finally, after 10+ years, time-phased budgeting is now being done. We just started [reinstating the approach] when the US financial crisis began and we needed to cut expenses across the board

and more carefully monitor spending. The administration used this financial situation to leverage time-phased budgeting. They argued that more careful monitoring of cash flows month-by-month and budgeting monthly was necessary…It is not that faculty are more receptive, it is just that the climate is different. Wagner et al. (2011, p.192)

This illustration is chosen to emphasise the extent to which many conclusions reached in earlier ERP studies describe intermediary steps on a prolonged implementation curve. Significant cultural, organisational, and technological changes had to take place for ERP to fully standardise and centralise reporting. Many of these changes required periods of financial instability and staff turnover to overcome internal resistance.

Rautiainen and Scapens (2013) perform an initial series of interviews within the operational and financial divisions of a Finnish city from 2005 to 2007, with follow-up interviews in 2009, that sought to revise performance management and financial control through ERP adoption. Financial pressures associated with the recession in 2001–2002 led to increased focus on improving the efficiency of operational routines. Many legacy processes persisted despite the efforts of the city manager and city board. A consolidated ERP system was proposed as a solution to integrate operations and municipalities in the region.

> By the autumn of 2007, all SAP modules had been adopted, except for some parts of the materials management and human resource modules. Basically, everything worked despite some initial problems in billing and reporting, allowing myths of both success and failure in SAP use. Nevertheless, reporting did not improve significantly until a new reporting system (Cognos 8) was adopted in late 2009, almost two and a half years after the adoption of SAP. Rautiainen and Scapens (2013, p.117)

Similar to the Wagner et al. study, follow-up interviews describe the adoption of a specialised reporting tool (COGNOS) in 2009 to extend ERP reporting functionality. We describe this case as part of the financial platform period as anticipated benefits required a prolonged period of negotiation around legacy business process, another round of financial disruption, and continued technological innovation. The authors note, with some criticism, that the eventual success of the ERP platform was achieved by conforming organisational routines to standardised system interfaces causing organisations to become 'average' and isomorphic. The authors note some practices remain untouched due to legislative mandates resistant to change, but expect continued waves of standardisation and centralisation into the future.

Sánchez-Rodríguez and Sraakman (2012) interview controllers from major Canadian firms regarding the influence of ERP systems on management accounting practice. Interviews took place from December of 2008 through to March of 2009 and document the growing ubiquity of ERP platforms across all organisational types. The authors go as far as to say management accounting is no longer possible without an ERP backbone to enable financial and operational reporting. The study pays special attention to specific improvements that helped to ensure firms achieved anticipated benefits through ERP. A standardised chart of accounts maintained by central management is held out as an especially important innovation toward this end.

> Getting the full benefits from an ERP system implementation took even longer, and then there was often the need for complementary software such as Cognos and Hyperion to access the information from the ERP database. In this ERP environment, one important attribute of ERP systems identified by respondents was the extensive and standardized chart of accounts. This change in chart of accounts enabled performance measures to become more extensive, more detailed, and standardized. Sánchez-Rodríguez and Sraakman (2012, p.407)

The quote above highlights multiple themes from the financial platform period of qualitative ERP studies: the long time period required to fully achieve anticipated ERP benefits; the need for supplementary reporting software to stack upon the ERP database; an increasingly standardised business process. The authors hold up a single, standardised chart of accounts as both an outcome of these changes as well as a symbol of increasing effect. There are no longer multiple data sets, reports, and interpretations of corporate life. ERP not only crafts a single data set available to all organisational actors, but its use is also required to work in a contemporary firm.

Bradford et al. (2014) conduct a case study analysis of two higher education institutions' use of consolidated ERP to support the provisioning, scoping, and deprovisioning of employee IT access. Interviews with IT staff took place from late 2011 through to early 2012 and focused specifically on the use of a centralised end-to-end identity and access management system (change to: CIAM – customer identity access management). The authors note the organic growth of information systems within complex organisations will naturally lead to the development of non-standardised process and the devolution of decision-making authority. Case universities sought additional control through an ERP-enabled identity management platform, but use was voluntary due to the strong federated environment within the university.

> Only if a system interacts with the ERP system do we know about it because that group needs to work with OIT to create a feed or file share to or from ERP. Otherwise, the system is out there and university-wide IAM policies and procedures are not enforced...One of the key ways that ERP systems facilitate the implementation of a CIAM is through integration and standardization of identities as it serves as the authoritative data source for all other systems. A CIAM will manage identities separately, but must by synced to the ERP system since this is where the initial data resides. Bradford et al. (2014, p.156)

The quote above highlights multiple themes observed within financial platform era studies. A common database constructed within an ERP system not only provides a foundation for standardised transaction processing and reporting, but also a singular data set that can be used by other software applications. It is the common touchpoint for an increasingly large set of software adopted during this period. ERP systems standardise and centralise a single set of organisational identities that are then available for use elsewhere. The result is a deepening software stack constructed upon the foundational data provided through ERP.

Shin et al. (2013) perform fieldwork on the implementation of continuous auditing systems within the ERP environment of two large companies. Implementations of continuing audit software were largely driven with Korean-Sarbanes–Oxley (K-SOX) compliance. Time ranges for fieldwork are not provided and much of the case narrative is a technical description of automated risk analysis within an established ERP environment.

Technical discussion of continuous auditing has limited relevance to the aims of this study, but the case analysis provides further evidence of an increasingly deep stack of software applications and related business processes dependent upon ERP data. Throughout the financial platform period ERP becomes less a primary focus and instead begins to serve as the taken for granted infrastructure on which successive waves of automation and innovation take place.

Oliviera and Clegg (2015) study a large manufacturing firm from 2005–2008 to investigate the centralising influence of shared service centres enabled by ERP technology. The study notes ERP alone did not achieve desired levels of organisation-wide conformity due to persistent differences in business process and charts of account. To address persistent issues and promote cost efficiency, the firm created a centralised shared services centre (SSC) to manage financial accounting from corporate headquarters. Significant resistance was observed from local actors who objected to lost autonomy and feared downsizing. Resistance diminished over time through repeated cycles of standardisation, centralisation, and staff attrition. While the SSC was the primary driver of uniformity, it was constructed upon the visibility and restrictions on data access enabled through ERP.

> The definition of user profiles excluded local actors from creating accounts and posting transactions; by defining what each actor could and could not do in the system, human involvement and agency was shaped – and excluded...A second choice was embedding business rules within SAP during current operations, beyond the SAP FI module, to ensure certain sequences of actions were followed (e.g. no production could be planned without the prior definition of a product code and costing). Oliviera and Clegg (2015, p.438)

The quote above emphasises claims made by other studies on the reliability imposed on the organisation through a centralised ERP platform. Local resistance may prolong legacy platforms as evidenced by earlier qualitative ERP studies. However, financial platform era studies not only show such resistance to be short-lived, but also the growth of additional software used to impose further standardisation, centralisation, and control on other aspects of an organisation. This study shows significant work associated with noncompliance, and the eroding relevance of locally specific reporting over time.

Van Roekel and van der Steen (2019) investigate persistent difficulties encountered during ERP implementation within a healthcare subsidiary of a larger corporate parent. Fieldwork took place during 2013 and includes a series of interviews with company staff during a three-month implementation. The adoption decision was primarily driven by the reporting needs of the corporate parent. ERP was seen as a way to integrate reporting across a diverse set of subsidiaries and provide a 'true' result. The organisation was told an additional software package would customise the ERP platform for the healthcare industry and cover 90–95 per cent of their accounting and reporting needs. However, a heterogenous set of users and legacy user requirements prevented easy implementation. A familiar tension to prior studies is observed between reporting needs at local (division) and global (corporate parent) levels.

> These actors, including the parent company and the key-users thus continued to question the network and configuration choices that had been made. Consequentially, the complexity of the ERP system continued to be visible. As a manager remarks: 'various participants in the process are still questioning the system and the choices we all made. These questions pop up regularly and need to be addressed. As a result, we continue to deal with details that should have been settled by now'. Van Roekel and van der Steen (2019, p.25)

Case analysis concludes with the quote above, which highlights the extent to which many historical themes from prior cases persist within segments of an initial ERP implementation. The authors do not comment on the possibility that a three-month implementation is too brief a period to observe the standardisation and centralisation necessary for ERP to function effectively. Organisations are indeed complex and difficult to integrate during an initial implementation, but over a longer time horizon business process and related reports are much more malleable.

Carlsson-Wall et al. (2022) conduct fieldwork within a large Swedish municipality during 2018. They note the majority of accountants in the municipality work for divisions, with about 10 per cent working at a centralised headquarters. Throughout the case they refer to these groups as 'local' and 'central'. Central finance is responsible for budget preparation and reporting and Central IT with implementing a new cloud ERP system. Central administration pressed for the new system to expedite and simplify financial reporting, increase cost efficiency, and decrease unnecessary administrative reporting. Additional modules, such as customer relationship management, were designed to build upon the standardised data compiled by the ERP system.

Central administration sold the system implementation as a net benefit to local accountants, freeing them up from tedious 'bean counter' roles and allowing focus on 'strategic' activity. Local accountants, however, attributed most of the benefits to the centralised headquarters. There is no discussion of eventual repurposing or downsizing, which may be due to the relatively brief fieldwork period or the specifics of the municipal setting.

> Our case illustrates how a cloud-based system with restricted opportunities for customization can be welcomed by central management accountants but create frustrations on the part of their local counterparts. Prior to the implementation of the CERP, local management accountants were involved in developing their local AISs and could inscribe their local expertise in those systems. However, they are now confronted with an off-the-shelf solution that only grants limited influence. Influence on the system is only possible if they have a compelling case in that their request is beneficial for the whole organization, contributing to making processes easier, more efficient, and safer. Considering this, the new system setup triggered power dynamics that disciplined local management accountants in line with a centralized structure—even though the implementation of the CERP system was not part of a broader centralization strategy. Carlsson-Wall et al. (2022, p.194)

The quote above highlights that the relationship between control over ERP system configuration increasingly translates into control over work process. Pre-ERP and early-ERP environments featured pluralistic interfaces designed to meet the needs of local users and to gain acceptance for system use. Over time, centralised control over a singular system imposed a uniform standard. Central IT emerges throughout this case as a driver of standardisation and centralisation by imposing off-the-shelf configurations and refusing local adaptation. Central accounting exacerbates this trend with a company-wide chart of accounts and reporting template that is similarly binding. Many of the local accountants interviewed saw these impositions as intrusive and ill-suited to work performed. However, central accountants point to increased visibility, efficiency, and control as significant benefits of the change.

4.4   ANALYSIS AND OPPORTUNITIES FOR ADDITIONAL RESEARCH

The foundational promise of ERP is an ability to consolidate disparate systems across a complex organisation. Over 25 years of qualitative accounting studies show this promise fulfilled, but over a longer time horizon than originally anticipated. Each of the papers described above highlights the social, organisational, and technological barriers to success. The primary issue in each study is the need to standardise work across numerous divisions or business units. Business process in the pre-ERP environment was largely manual and conducted through offline spreadsheets and other locally hosted systems. ERP promised a singular database of firm-wide data, but for that data to exist it must be generated, entered, and reported in a uniform fashion. Qualitative studies continually highlight the differential experience of central (corporate) actors from peripheral (business unit) actors. The compiled case codex describes the systematic restructure of business process around new technology through years of sustained effort. Staff attrition and restructuring during recessionary business cycles may also be a requirement for firms facing significant resistance. This section reviews each of these themes in turn. We highlight the combined impact of standardisation, centralisation, and temporal resistance to those trends as a common set of impediments for any emerging technology.

4.4.1   Standardisation and Centralisation

ERP technology, alongside incremental innovations in internal control and corporate reporting, is more than the construction of a singular database. Employees must fill a database with uniformly structured data. Managers must base decisions on a common set of system generated reports. Much of the work that makes up a diverse firm must be standardised around a common process. The predominant theme in the qualitative accounting literature is how difficult organisations found such realignment to be in practice.

The qualitative accounting literature highlights the extent to which work process, not data structure, is the primary barrier to ERP implementation. Electronic revolution era studies describe manual processes based on the local requirements, constraints, or preferences of individual business units. The combined impact of Sarbanes–Oxley legislation, globalisation, and continued technological innovation in the control and compliance era prompted increasingly homogenous practice. Finally, the financial platform era describes construction of sophisticated reporting and monitoring tools upon the common database of fully functional ERP.

Centralisation is a natural result of the push toward a single, organisation-wide standard. A digital environment increases access to data, but also highlights areas of inconsistency and (from a corporate perspective) inefficiency. Automation places increasing pressure for uniform systems of entry, aggregation, and analysis. Central actors are a driving force behind automated reports and have the authority to press for firm-wide solutions. Peripheral accounting work remains to the extent that managers require translation between local information needs and centralised templates. However, increasingly granular (and user-friendly) data collection and system reporting shrink this gap through time. The importance of local accounting and analysis staff declines as standardised systems of reporting take root.

Contrary to questions raised in initial analysis by electronic revolution era studies, ERP-driven changes had a dramatic and observable impact on work performed by accountants working at all levels of an organisational hierarchy. System generated reports allow production staff to not only take on costing and analysis work, but to understand their work as a part of a firm-wide value chain. Automated systems perform many data entry, reporting, and audit tasks without the need for dedicated accounting staff. Increasingly reliable and available data empowers a smaller group of central financial accountants at the expense of local accountant authority.

Local accounting staff see their expertise gradually subsumed into a set of system generated data structures and reporting templates. Local accounting work persists, but is largely limited to manual data/reporting tasks beyond the functionality provided by an increasingly centralised system. A smaller number of central accountants benefit from these shifts through timely access to standardised data and reporting.

4.4.2 Strategies for Resistance and Change

The technological trend of the past decade toward automated, centralising data platforms raises the question of how these systems can be (at least partially) resisted at local levels. How do local actors preserve a diversity of practice/data/reporting around a homogenising system? The primary answer observed in the qualitative ERP literature is empowered experts within institutional settings. Examples include professors, medical professionals, and city employees. Other possibilities include legal barriers/requirements that are specific to a particular setting (industry, union, government) or geographic region.

Understanding sources of peripheral resistance also requires an understanding of how central actors effectively overcome local objections. The qualitative ERP literature features multiple accounts of protracted conflict surrounding implementation. Documented drivers of central authority in the face of resistance include budgetary constraint, acquisition, and the tech-assisted diffusion of specialised knowledge into the broader organisation. To resist these forces local actors must be able to articulate a case for the added value of a specific, localised reporting over a global corporate template. A comprehensive review of the qualitative accounting literature shows this form of argument is initially persuasive. However, it erodes over time from increasing system functionality, and homogenous business process, and automation.

Local reporting was able to add significant value during the electronic revolution period due to reporting limitations within ERP environments and the extent to which local workflow and decision-making failed to conform to ERP templates. Emphasis on firm-wide systems of internal control brought increasing conformity throughout control and compliance studies. The development of powerful and customisable reporting tools that stack upon the ERP database led to further erosion during the financial platform studies. Future literature should investigate the extent to which this phenomenon applies to other emerging technologies such as blockchain or cybersecurity.

REFERENCES

Beaubien, L. (2013). Technology, change, and management control: A temporal perspective. *Accounting, Auditing & Accountability Journal*, 26(1), 48–74.

Bradford, M., Earp, J. B., & Grabski, S. (2014). Centralized end-to-end identity and access management and ERP systems: A multi-case analysis using the Technology Organization Environment framework. *International Journal of Accounting Information Systems,* 15(2), 149–165.

Caglio, A. (2003). Enterprise resource planning systems and accountants: Towards hybridization? *European Accounting Review*, 12(1), 123–153.

Carlsson-Wall, M., Goretzki, L., Hofstedt, J., Kraus, K., & Nilsson, C. J. (2022). Exploring the implications of cloud-based enterprise resource planning systems for public sector management accountants. *Financial Accountability & Management*, 38(2), 177–201.

Dechow, N., & Mouritsen, J. (2005). Enterprise resource planning systems, management control and the quest for integration. *Accounting, Organizations and Society*, 30(7–8), 691–733.

Granlund, M., & Malmi, T. (2002). Moderate impact of ERPS on management accounting: A lag or permanent outcome? *Management Accounting Research*, 13(3), 299–321.

Hyvönen, T., Järvinen, J., & Pellinen, J. (2006). The role of standard software packages in mediating management accounting knowledge. *Qualitative Research in Accounting & Management*, 3(2), 145–160.

Hyvönen, T., Järvinen, J., & Pellinen, J. (2008). A virtual integration – the management control system in a multinational enterprise. *Management Accounting Research*, 19(1), 45–61.

Hyvönen, T., Järvinen, J., Pellinen, J., & Rahko, T. (2009). Institutional logics, ICT and stability of management accounting. *European Accounting Review*, 18(2), 241–275.

Jazayeri, M., Wickramsinghe, D., & Gooneratne, T. (2011). Convergence versus divergence of performance measurement systems: Lessons from spatial variations. *Qualitative Research in Accounting & Management*.

Oliveira, J., & Clegg, S. (2015). Paradoxical puzzles of control and circuits of power. *Qualitative Research in Accounting & Management*, 12(4), 425–451.

Quattrone, P., & Hopper, T. (2005). A 'time–space odyssey': Management control systems in two multinational organizations. *Accounting, Organizations and Society*, 30(7–8), 735–764.

Rautiainen, A., & Scapens, R. W. (2013). Path-dependencies, constrained transformations and dynamic agency: An accounting case study informed by both ANT and NIS. *Qualitative Research in Accounting & Management*, 10(2), 100–126.

Sánchez-Rodríguez, C., & Spraakman, G. (2012). ERP systems and management accounting: A multiple case study. *Qualitative Research in Accounting & Management*, 9(4), 398–414.

Scapens, R. W., & Jazayeri, M. (2003). ERP systems and management accounting change: Opportunities or impacts? A research note. *European Accounting Review*, 12(1), 201–233.

Shin, I. H., Lee, M. G., & Park, W. (2013). Implementation of the continuous auditing system in the ERP-based environment. *Managerial Auditing Journal*, 28(7), 592–627.

van Roekel, H. J., & van der Steen, M. (2019). Integration as unrealised ideal of ERP systems: An exploration of complexity resulting from multiple variations of integration. *Qualitative Research in Accounting & Management*, 16(1), 2–34.

Wagner, E. L., Moll, J., & Newell, S. (2011). Accounting logics, reconfiguration of ERP systems and the emergence of new accounting practices: A sociomaterial perspective. *Management Accounting Research*, 22(3), 181–197.

PART III

USING INFORMATION TO SUPPORT DECISIONS

5. Using accounting information to support venture capital decisions

Tibah Al Harbi, Renzo Cordina and David Power

5.1 INTRODUCTION

Financial information has traditionally played a crucial role in investment decisions (Arnold and Moizer, 1984). Despite the limitations associated with such information (Amir and Lev, 1996), the valuation of businesses on the basis of earnings, dividends, assets or cash flows has a long pedigree dating back to Graham and Dodd (1934). These pioneers suggested that investors could estimate the fundamental value or intrinsic worth of a business based on financial statement numbers. A comparison of this intrinsic value with the current price of a listed entity would then help investors to identify undervalued companies that were suitable for investment. Several academics have suggested trading strategies for investors based on such mispricing of securities that appear to yield abnormal returns (Alexakis et al., 2010; Lewellen, 2002; Oppenhiemer, 1984; Ou and Penman, 1989). Although there is significant literature about the use of accounting numbers in decision-making processes by investors (see, for example, Arnold and Moizer, 1984; Imam and Spence, 2016; Pike et al., 1993), its role in decision-making within the VC (venture capital) industry is not well understood.[1]

Venture capitalists (VCs), unlike shareholders who invest in public companies, have different information needs, and face different constraints in terms of the financial information available. The nature of the environment where VCs operate is different from that of typical investors who purchase a stake in a listed company. In particular, obtaining information about unquoted companies is more difficult (Hassan and Leece, 2007) since they have fewer disclosure requirements and do not need to comply with stock exchange listing rules.[2] Obtaining this information from the unquoted companies themselves is often problematic since issues such as information asymmetry and adverse selection arise (Amit et al., 1993). In addition, the legal protection afforded to investors in private companies may not be as robust since the safeguards associated with share ownership are conditions linked to stock exchange rules. The remainder of this chapter will discuss the role played by accounting information in aiding VC investors to decide on which enterprise should be funded. Specifically, this chapter will identify the extent to which VC investors in Saudi Arabia use financial statement information when arriving at their investment decision. Saudi Arabia was selected for the research site because a thriving VC market has developed in the country as a result of the Kingdom's attempt to reduce its dependence on oil; this desire to diversify the economy of the country was signalled in the government's Vision 2030 plan which was published in 2016 (Kingdom of Saudi Arabia, 2022). The plan has sought to encourage entrepreneurs who want to set up their own non-oil related businesses and aid those who seek to fund such ventures. As a result, the VC market in Saudi Arabia has become one of the largest in the Middle East and one of the fastest growing outside of Europe and the USA. The Saudi VC industry has grown tremendously during the years 2019–2021; most of this growth has been attributed to two main funds: the Saudi Venture Capital Company and JADA[3] which were established by the Saudi government in 2018 with initial grants in excess of $1bn each to stimulate VC investments in start-ups as well as to encourage angel investments in the Kingdom (JADA, 2021; Saudi Venture Capital, 2022). The total amount of subsequent funds raised by these and other Saudi VCs for investment in start-up businesses has increased from $59m in 2018 to $584m in 2021; as a result, Saudi Arabia has achieved the second highest rate of growth in this form of funding within the Middle East/North Africa (MENA) region after the United Arab Emirates (UAE).[4] Yet very little is known about the information which Saudi VCs require or the details which Saudi entrepreneurs are willing to supply in order to secure funding. Very little research has investigated the relative importance of financial or nonfinancial information in Saudi Arabian VC funds. Further, no research exists about the different sources of information available to VC investors or the emphasis placed on an investee-firm's information systems when Saudi VCs are deciding to take a stake in a potential investee company. Whilst such questions have been addressed in the USA and in Europe, the current chapter examines these issues in an emerging market setting where the legal framework governing VC investment is still developing.[5] Thus, the current chapter seeks to plug these gaps in the literature by addressing two research objectives: first, the chapter examines the importance of financial and nonfinancial accounting information in the VC decisions about investment in Saudi companies; the usefulness of financial data relative to nonfinancial information is considered. Second, the chapter gathers perceptions about the role played by an investee firm's accounting information system (AIS) in VC decisions. These objectives are examined in a context characterised by very few financial analysts and limited nonfinancial information where the VC investment community is relatively new.

5.2   INSIGHTS FROM THE MAINSTREAM LITERATURE

Studies about VC practices in developed countries suggest that before investing VC investors follow three steps when deciding on whether or not to invest in a firm. These are: collecting investee company information, using this information to estimate the risk and expected return from the possible investment, and applying an appropriate valuation method to calculate the percentage of equity they would require for the funding they are willing to provide (Hassan and Leece, 2007). A debate exists in the literature about these steps on whether or not financial statement information is relevant for VC investors. Studies have highlighted that the importance attached to accounting information contained in business plans such as income statements, balance sheets and unaudited management projections varies across countries and regions. For example, evidence indicates that more importance is given to financial information amongst European VC managers than among their counterparts in the USA (Manigart et al., 1997; Manigart et al., 2000). Manigart et al. (1997) attributed this difference to the fact that fewer VC investors in the USA concentrate on early-stage companies relative to their VC counterparts in Europe; early-stage companies suffer from a lack of available financial information. In addition, Hand (2005) argues that financial information is less significant for early-stage businesses seeking VC funding since the emphasis is on innovation and business growth. As firms mature, however, financial information becomes more important in the VC investment decision. With mature firms, greater importance is placed on assets and financial capital when arriving at company valuations. In contrast, early-stage firms tend to suffer from a shortage of physical and financial assets, relying mainly on human capital (Zimmerman, 2015). When Armstrong et al. (2006) examined the financial statements of early-stage companies, they found that certain costs were used by VC firms when looking at a broad range of industries. They found items such as the cost of sales, selling, marketing, and general administrative expenses as well as Research & Development (R&D) expenditure, were seen as crucial variables that influenced a VC's decision to invest since they provided information about the revenue-generating potential of an investee firm.

Cassar (2009) has examined the role of interim financial reports in securing VC funding for new ventures in the USA. In the absence of any disclosure requirements, Cassar (2009) found a positive relationship between (i) the frequency with which interim financial statements were produced by entrepreneurs seeking VC funding and (ii) the need for external financing, the level of competition among VCs to supply funding, and the stage of an investee firm's product development. The author concluded that 'non-stewardship factors, … that reduce competitive and fundamental uncertainty, [were] influential' (Cassar, 2009, p.28). This suggests that the provision of interim financial statements by entrepreneurs reduced information asymmetry and helped secure VC funding at more competitive rates. This was especially true for the income statement and cash flow information; very little emphasis was placed on balance sheet data.[6] Also, projections and forecasts were more frequently prepared in start-ups that involved patents and R&D (Cassar, 2009).

Zimmerman (2015) built on Cassar's (2009) work by exploring the role of accounting information in the valuation of investee firms by US VCs. He argued that the importance of accounting information is declining due to the growth of knowledge-based capital and other intangibles amongst start-ups seeking VC funding. He found that within companies with predominantly human-based capital, current earnings were a very poor predictor of future income and growth (Zimmerman, 2015). However, other accounting information appeared to be used by US VC investors such as revenues, cash flows, cost reduction targets, and working capital (Zimmerman, 2015).

Consistent with Zimmerman's (2015) findings, Smith and Cordina (2014) argue that accounting information only plays a limited role in investment decisions by VC investors within a European context. They interviewed a number of representatives from early-stage VC associations representing investors in the UK and mainland Europe between August and December 2011. They found that VC investors tended to use financial statements as a 'starting point' to conduct their due diligence on funding applications from entrepreneurs. VCs within the UK considered projected rather than historical financial statements arguing that 'historic financial statements are not a very major component of due diligence; … when you are investing, you are investing in future value, not past value' (Smith and Cordina, 2014, p.316). The respondents in Smith and Cordina's European study indicated that VCs never relied entirely on financial statements to produce a holistic view of the company's value; indeed, one of the investors interviewed by Smith and Cordina (2014, p.316) highlighted that 'financial statements are always not the whole truth and sometimes they're not even very close to the truth'. Although VC investors were sceptical about the figures provided by entrepreneurs within the annual report, they suggested that financial statements might still be useful except 'when talking about intangibles [where] there is always an issue about the degree of uncertainty around some of the assumptions [employed]' (Smith and Cordina, 2014, p.316).

Hassan and Leece (2007), Manigart et al. (1997) and Wright and Robbie (1996), have all explored the common sources of information used by VC investors in different national settings. They have highlighted that the VC firm's own due diligence reports are the most important source of information; the financial information provided by the entrepreneur in the business plan which accompanied the funding application was ranked second. Manigart et al. (1997) and Wright and Robbie (1996) found income statements, unaudited financial statements, and management projections for the coming year were influential among VCs in preparing to value an investee firm.

However, the literature suggests that the views of VC managers in Europe vary from country to country; for example, Wright and Robbie (1996) indicated that a VC's own due diligence reports were considered more important than the due diligence documents of a third party (i.e. an accounting firm) in the UK. By contrast, Manigart et al. (1997) and Manigart et al. (2000) found external due diligence reports to be more critical in mainland Europe. Further, some accounting information, such as a qualified audit report and long-term management projections, was used more in mainland Europe than in the UK (Manigart et al., 2000). This led the authors to conclude that VC managers in Europe were more financially oriented while their counterparts in Anglo-Saxon countries (such as the UK) were more business-focussed (Manigart et al., 1997; Manigart et al., 2000; Sapienza et al., 1996).

Lockett et al. (2002) compared the different approaches used by VCs in the US, Hong Kong, India, and Singapore when gathering information on which to base their investment decisions. They suggested that information sources that a VC can trust might be more culturally determined rather than easily transferred from one country to another. As a result, there are less trusted sources of information for a VC to use in developing countries compared to the US market. However, the rationale behind such differences was unclear. Joshi and Subrahmanya (2019) suggested that this lack of trust was greater (and risk higher) where the 'nationality' of the VC firm and the location of the investee company were different.

Other researchers have considered different influences on the sources of information used by VCs when arriving at their funding decision. For example, Wright et al. (2004) documented no relationship between the source of information used by VCs and the VC type when looking at different countries. However, Hassan and Leece (2007) found differences across three different types of VC (independent, captive, and semi-captive)[7] both in terms of their usage of accounting data and the source of that information. According to Hassan and Leece's analysis, semi-captive VCs tended to use accounting information to a greater extent than the other two because they worked within a parent company; they needed to manage risk and justify their funding decision to the main board of their parent entity and used accounting information for this purpose (Hassan and Leece, 2007). Hassan and Leece (2007) suggested that the three types of VC had different organisational structures and invested at different stages of the start-up's journey leading to different agency risks. As a result, a greater emphasis was placed on some information sources rather than others by the three types of VC. However, all of the VC firms consulted believed that publicly available sources of information such as articles in the financial press and trade journals were ranked as unimportant by VC investors (Wright and Robbie, 1996; Hassan and Leece, 2007).

Given the differences in information (and information sources) used by VCs when evaluating potential investments further research is needed, especially relating to VCs investing in a developing country such as Saudi Arabia. The current chapter attempts to address this need for research; specifically, it examines the usage of financial as opposed to nonfinancial information by VCs in the Kingdom of Saudi Arabia (a developing country) and investigates the common sources of information which VCs employ. Finally, the chapter looks at the role of an enterprise's AIS in the decision by a VC to invest in a business seeking funding.

5.3   RESEARCH METHOD

This research employed semi-structured interviews to tackle the issues being investigated.[8] Specifically, each interviewee was asked about the sources of information used by (or supplied to) a VC as part of a funding application. Their views were also ascertained on perceptions about the relative importance of different types of financial information in the VC funding application process. Finally, participants were asked about the relative importance attached to the AIS in the potential investee firm by a VC when making their investment decision. Each interview lasted for between 1 and 1.5 hours. The interviews took place between November 2020 and December 2021. All of the interviews were conducted online via Zoom/Microsoft Teams because of travel restrictions and responses to questions were transcribed in Arabic and translated into English for the few interviews that did not take place in English. Each transcript was read several times and the responses of the interviewees distilled into a brief comment which was entered into an Excel spreadsheet. These comments were then summarised in tables, following a thematic analysis (King, 2004), and quotes extracted from the transcripts in order to illustrate the views being expressed. Therefore, a deductive approach was employed drawing on the themes from the questionnaire and the concepts from the literature (Johnson, 2004).

Table 5.1 shows an overview of the research participants. Some 11 worked for VCs while 8 were owners of investee, or potential investee firms. All of these investees (5 interviewees) and potential investee firms (3 interviewees) had either secured VC funding in the recent past or were actively looking for a VC investor to take an equity stake in their business. Thus, perspectives from the two main 'sides' of the VC funding decision were consulted for this research. Obtaining the perspective of investees/potential investees and VC investors was crucial as the literature indicates that the two groups can often hold different and conflicting views about the issues being considered in this chapter (Zacharakis et al., 2010). Participants worked in a range of different size VCs or firms; thus, the views expressed should not be unique to any size-category of entity. Sixteen of the interviewees were male and three were female; such a mix is not unusual in Saudi Arabia where the presence of female VC investors and female entrepreneurs is relatively low (Danish and Lawton Smith, 2012). All of the participants were experienced having spent many years, on average, either working as a VC investor or operating as an entrepreneur; as such, the views expressed should be insightful since participants were knowledgeable about the issues being discussed.

5.4   RESULTS

This section is divided into two parts: (i) the first will present the views of participants from VCs; (ii) the second part will discuss the perceptions of entrepreneurs working in investee (or potential investee) firms.

Table 5.1   *An overview of the research participants*

Participant	Type	Firm size	Gender	Education level
P1	VC	Medium	Male	BSc
P2	VC	Small	Male	MSc
P3	VC	Large	Male	MSc
P4	VC	Small	Male	MSc
P5	VC	Large	Male	MSc
P6	VC	Small	Male	MSc
P7	VC	Large	Male	BSc
P8	VC	Medium	Male	BSc
P9	VC	Small	Male	MSc
P10	VC	Large	Male	BSc
P11	VC	Large	Male	BSc
P12	Investee firm	Medium	Female	MSc
P13	Investee firm	Medium	Male	MSc
P14	Potential Investee firm	Small	Female	GradD
P15	Potential Investee firm	Small	Female	BSc
P16	Investee firm	Medium	Male	BSc
P17	Potential Investee firm	Small	Male	MSc
P18	Investee firm	Medium	Male	MSc
P19	Investee firm	Medium	Male	BSc

Note: The second column shows classification of participants whether from the VC side or from investee side. The third column shows the firm size, measured by the number of start-ups that they have funded for those who are VCs and company assets for those which are Investee or Potential Investee firms. The final column shows the highest education level attained by the respondent where GradD refers to a graduate diploma, BSc refers to a Bachelor's degree and MSc refers to a Master's qualification.

5.4.1   The VC Investors' Perceptions

All of the VC participants agreed that their investment decisions were characterised by uncertainty and information asymmetries; the VCs and the entrepreneurs operating the investee firms/potential investee firms often had different goals – especially in the pre-investment phase of the funding process. Thus, the quantity and quality of information provided to VC investors was often described as problematic. VC participants highlighted that they were targeting privately owned, relatively small and often young businesses to make an equity investment. These businesses typically had limited data available compared to publicly listed companies. This was especially true of financial or accounting data which VCs needed in order to estimate the equity stake that they should demand for their investment, the likely rate of return which they might achieve, and the time needed before an exit strategy could be acted upon. The information systems of the potential investee firms were typically less sophisticated as these businesses concentrated on production or marketing strategies to achieve market share. Table 5.2 summarises the views of the VC research participants on the usefulness of different accounting information in the VC funding decision. In contrast to findings from the literature, a sizeable majority of the participants believed that accounting information was useful for Saudi VCs when deciding to invest in a business. Most of the VCs interviewed indicated that accounting information was always useful; only two VCs suggested that the information was sometimes useful. Subtle differences about the usefulness of accounting information emerged amongst the interviewees when the stage of the investment and other factors were considered.

Table 5.2   *The usefulness of accounting information in the VC industry: perceptions of VC participants*

Participants	Usefulness of Accounting Information for VCs	Type of Accounting Information consulted	
		Internal management accounts	Audited financial statements
P1	Always Useful	Yes	Yes
P2	Always Useful	Yes	Yes
P3	Always Useful	Yes	No
P4	Always Useful	Yes	No
P5	Always Useful	Yes	No
P6	Always Useful	Yes	Maybe
P7	Sometimes Useful	Yes	No
P8	Always Useful	Yes	No
P9	Always Useful	Yes	No
P10	Sometimes Useful	Yes	No
P11	Always Useful	Yes	No

According to the interviewees, the management AIS was still viewed as useful for making an informed decision about whether or not to invest in a business although such management accounting information might lack complete accuracy, or it might exhibit a high level of optimism (when it came to forecasts); the VC interviewees suggested that information produced by entrepreneurs who were seeking to securing funding tended to be positive and biased in an upward direction. For some VC investors, accounting information was seen as a crucial factor in deciding on whether or not to take an investment opportunity further. For example, participant P2 explained that '[within his VC fund, they] do not invest in a company that does not have financials; [his VC fund] has invested in a company that did not have an audit but they must have financials'. This participant stressed that his fund would pass up on an investment opportunity if they learnt that an applicant did not produce any management accounts. As with Smith and Cordina (2014), this management accounting information acted as a starting point for the investment analysis of this participant's VC. He argued that without this source of accounting information, understanding the current financial position of the applicant was problematic. He stated that 'making decisions in a vacuum or [where financial information was] non-existent is always dangerous'. He added that 'starting from somewhere and then building on it always [leads to] a better decision'. Participant P1 supported this view. He highlighted that his fund took the applicants' internally produced 'financials and [went] ... forward from there'. The management accounts were viewed as a building block upon which the VCs valuation could be constructed.

A key issue was whether the usefulness of management accounting information related to the current financial position of the company or whether it played a role in helping VC investors to differentiate possible high growth deals from other applicants with less potential. Such information was seen as essential from a very early stage. Participant P11 highlighted the predictive ability of management accounting information, stating that 'it helped [his VC] to verify the past and forecast [the future allowing his firm to check] those assumptions, relating to new customers and growth'. He stated that his VC firm was interested in how 'costs were going to play out so [accounting information] was seen as very important'. P9 added that this management accounting information needed to show whether or not the company was performing in a satisfactory matter. For example, he stated that:

> If you do not have financial information, how can you know if this company is actually selling some-thing? How do you know if the start-up is getting a lot of customers? Part of the financial information is not only the income statement, the balance sheet and the cash flow statement. [In addition], I want to know what [certain ratios such as] the mark-up [indicate].

Participant P8 highlighted that any sensitivity analysis or scenario planning involving this management accounting information was not focussed solely on making predictions about the future but evaluating the plausibility of the information being considered. For example, he highlighted that:

> We [don't] want to see [only] healthy financials; we want to see entrepreneurs who know what is going on [with their business] – not only presenting [the VC] with any kind of numbers which might make them appear in a more favourable light. There is a difference. Sometimes we see a company with a weak financial position, but [the information] is genuine, and there is no evidence of fraud. Others just give you information that shows you tremendous growth that will never happen. We don't like that.

The alignment between the management accounting information and the narrative supplied by the investee firm was seen as crucial for P6. It gave him reassurance about the veracity of the financials and likely success of the applicant's business plan. His VC based their investment 'on two things: narratives (the story about the business) and the numbers in the financial state-ments.' His VC wanted 'to see alignment between narratives and numbers.'

Participant P7 expressed a different opinion when commenting on the usefulness of finan-cial information for VCs. He argued that the importance of the financials depended on the maturity of the potential investee firm being considered. Indeed, for some early businesses, the role of nonfinancial information was crucial:

> We invested in some companies that did not have adequate financials as long they were in the early stage [of their lifecycle]. In such cases, the big problem was not the [lack of] financial [information] but the validation of the product, the adoption of the product, the happiness of the customers, scala-bility issues, and growth potential. All of these things were much bigger problems than the financial [situation].

Similar to Hand (2005), P7 suggested that 'the financials were not seen as a priority for some VC investors'. He admitted that a 'better financial position for a company was definitely desirable but VCs had much bigger issues to consider [such as sales, market penetration and production] before looking at the financials'.

A smaller number of participants suggested that the annual reports of investee or potential investee firms were used by VCs – confirming the view expressed by Wright and Robbie (1996). They argued that any financial information provided by a business needed to be externally verified in order to be credible for the VC. This view depended on the stage of the investment, with several participants attaching greater weight to audited financial statements if the business being considered for investment was relatively mature. For newer businesses, the availability of audited financial statements was less common, and VCs did not require such information due to the cost and time constraints that this requirement would impose. For example, participant P5 highlighted that 'if you are looking for audited financial statements in early-stage companies … by the time you have them, they might be out-of-date – they might be 6 to 10 months old'. However, other participants were more supportive of the usefulness of audited financial statements for VC investment decisions. These audited financial statements provided some VCs with further assurance about the financial information being analysed. For instance, participant P1 highlighted:

> I'll be honest the most important thing in my personal opinion [is that the financial statements need to be audited]; maybe, it's because I am finance guy. In addition, the financials really need to be audited by a decent auditor. So, if it is not [one of the] big four, at least it should be one of the top 10. That really helps to give me comfort, whatever the founder or the company is saying is great; we need validation.

Other participants (P2, P5, P6, and P10) used their own checks in the absence of audited financial statements. They suggested that VC investors could perform different tests to examine the reliability of the accounting information provided. For instance, participant P1 noted that conducting interviews with the employees of the entity itself usually gave a lot of insight about what exactly was going on in the organisation. Others sought additional details by asking the management team at the potential investee firm 'multiple questions from different angles about the accounting information supplied'. However, they admitted that this approach was 'not as easy as one might think' as the answers received were not always truthful since some of these entrepreneurs were keen to see the business' funding bid succeed even if the accounting information provided was less accurate. For example, P2 highlighted that his VC verified the financials by asking for 'a monthly breakdown [of what the business] claim[s] that they sold this past year' noting that 'sometimes the monthly breakdown doesn't add up [to the annual revenue figure in the business' annual report]'. In addition, P2 highlighted that his VC occasionally asked for the applicant's revenue which they multiplied by 'the percentage profit margin in order to compare with reported earnings'; in his view, 'there are multiple ways of testing any accounting information provided'. More recently, P2 noted how VCs were seeking access to an applicant's dashboard; they looked to 'find any misalignment between the [information from the] dashboard and the [numbers reported in the] financial statements'.

If questions arose about the accounting information after performing checks, recourse to an auditing firm was a possible option according to P10. This individual mentioned that 'If [an applicant has no] audited financial statements, [his VC met with the entrepreneur] and [went] through numbers with them; [his VC] ask[ed] the [business' owners] questions to verify the numbers but had hired external auditors to verify the financials [previously], before investing'. Another option highlighted by P9 involved the VC's accountant talking to the investee firm's accountant (if the investee firm had an accountant) about the financial statement numbers.

However, these 'VC-audit' procedures did not apply to established applicant companies that had been trading for two/three years or those which were raising a sizeable amount of funding. In these cases, VC investors required such applicants to have audited financial statements. Participant P3 stressed that if the company has been operational for a long time and does not have audited financial statements, this will raise a lot of 'red flags' and give rise to questions about the reliability of the management. Participant P6 clarified that although his VC fund required companies at the later stages of development to have audited financial statements, sometimes his fund made an exception because some of those applying for funding may have radically changed their business in recent months. He stressed that it was not uncommon for companies to 'pivot the business based on market inputs'; in these cases 'the historical data in terms of financials' would not reflect the new path that the company was taking. Only data for the most recent months might reflect a business' current strategy; however, such data was still unaudited. Therefore, his VC skipped the requirement of having audited annual reports for such potential investees.

Some participants explained that if the potential investee firm was incorporated as a company, they had to submit audited financial statements according to Saudi government requirements. Thus, the interviewees suggested that the use of audited annual reports by VCs was unrelated to whether the potential investee firm was raising a sizeable amount of funding. Instead, it was linked to the legal status of the applicant – whether it was incorporated or not. Participant P11 agreed and commented that most Saudi companies had to file their accounts on an annual basis for tax purposes certified by a public accountant if they had been in business for more than a year. As a result, audited financial statements were available for such entities and typically consulted by VCs.

Participants were invited to comment on the sources of information which they consulted when making an investment decision. Although VC investors mentioned a number of different external information sources, an inspection of the interview transcripts showed that the two most common sources of information were the investment file which the VC produced (including a checklist), and the financial information provided by the potential investee firm. If VCs needed further details, they went back to the applicant and asked them to provide additional information. This is consistent with the observations of Reid and Smith (2007). An analysis of the results showed that VCs adopted different approaches to the sourcing of information: a checklist was typically prepared by VCs and sent to the entrepreneur requiring the disclosure of specific items that the VC was interested in; the potential investee firm had to complete the checklist. Participant P3 described this process as follows:

> [Our VC] usually shares a list of questions or a checklist [with the applicant]; basically, this checklist helps us gather specific information which [is] really helpful [for] learning quickly about the company; it is an efficient method of conducting the due diligence on each opportunity and really helps improve our basic analysis and decision-making [about the applicant].

The second method was to ask for a set of financial reports about the business applying for funding including a balance sheet and an income statement. The investment team at the VC then reviewed these reports internally, checking every detail. As participant P4 explained:

> [We] take the details they provide us with, whether it was actual accounts or projections. Those are the two main things we ask them [to provide], and [from these] we see if [the financial information] makes sense; if the projections are too optimistic; if they have done sensitivity analysis [or considered] different scenarios. If not, we will have to do [it]. Then we check if [their] valuation [of the business ties in with] their projections. So, if they're asking for a certain [amount of funds linked to a specific equity stake based on their] valuation, does that make sense with their current financial information and the amount they are raising.

Subsequently, VC investors may check further external sources to validate the information supplied, as documented in the literature by Fried and Hisrich (1994). In doing so, it is not necessarily new information that VCs are trying to find from different sources. Rather participant P7 suggested that they 'dig deeper and deeper to verify more of the information that they got in general terms at the beginning'. Participant P7 declared that such validation did not take place at the beginning but rather with the due diligence as the VC decides on whether or not to proceed with an investment:

We usually don't do intense validation at the screening stage; [for that], we [rely on] what the founders say about the company. Then in the due diligence [phase of the process], we try to validate every aspect [of the information supplied] by asking for the raw data on all of their company's transactions to make sure that what they said is true. So, the full validation comes in the due diligence phase of the analysis.

Participant P2 agreed, explaining that his VC 'start[ed] with the information [that the business had provided] and then grill it to see if it is credible or not'. After this, his VC brought in their own 'information from [other] sources'. His VC either did this 'exercise internally or found research that support[ed]' what the applicant was claiming. Such an approach was not uncommon. Indeed, participant P1 indicated that his VC had 'recently signed up with a service which helped find technical advisors who were able to come in and [offer advice] on a certain technical matter if so needed'.

5.4.2   The Views of Investee Firms

Having reviewed the thoughts of VC investors, this section will discuss the views of those participants from the investee side of the process. These participants were invited firstly to comment on whether they believed that VC investors relied on accounting data when taking a decision to invest in a business. The vast majority of respondents in Table 5.3 believed that such information was useful to VCs. However, participant P13 argued that accounting data offered only a partial perspective on the possible risk associated with an investment in a business. He suggested that 'VCs don't [rely fully on accounting data] because there is a risk [that the owners] will close the business after a couple of months'. He thought that VCs 'ask[ed] for the financial [data] just to understand how the company is doing and [whether] there is an opportunity and potential for the company to scale up the business in a couple of months'. In his view, most VCs 'invested in the person'; they invested 'in the entrepreneur [once] they saw his passion, his energy and the time he put into the start-up'. In his opinion, therefore, 'the reports, the numbers [and] the financials, [were] just to make the VCs feel [more] secure'.

Participants working in investee firms were also asked about whether VCs focus on the AIS of the start-up company when deciding to invest. In addition, their views were sought on whether VCs' expectations about the AIS varied according to the investee firm's maturity. An analysis of the interviews revealed that newer, younger start-ups in Saudi Arabia typically did not employ a full-time accountant; the founders themselves usually recorded financial transactions and prepared financial reports. Participant P16 suggested that VC expectations regarding the availability of accounting information varied according to business size and age as well as industry norms. He agreed that 'start-ups do not hire an accountant at first'. As the company grows 'then this would be the time that you should hire an accountant'; but he noted that such an individual 'is only a bookkeeper [who is hired to process] the invoices and [keep] track receipts'. He indicated that the accounting function in such firms 'will not be very sophisticated' with most of the work being 'done by the founders'. P16 noted that after they had secured some initial funding, his firm 'hired a CFO' to produce the 'financial numbers… need[ed] by the lawyers and the VCs'.

A variety of AISs were used by these investee firms including Xero, Google Drive, QuickBooks, Dashboards, and the ARB system. Participant P16 described how his firm used Google Drive to store accounting data:

We built our data rooms on Google Drive; we structured it in a way that the VC investor [could] check each and every file in the easiest [possible] way. So [we designed] a very nice archiving system that [allows transactions to] be tracked; we put it in a secure file, and we call[ed] it 'the data room'. This data room includes every detail about the company; then once the VCs start their due diligence, we share a list of [our files in] the data room, and they can check each file one at a time.

Table 5.3   The usefulness of accounting information in the VC industry: perceptions of entrepreneurs

Participants	Usefulness of Accounting Information for VCs	Type of Accounting Information consulted	
		Internal management accounts	Audited financial statements
P12	Always Useful	Yes	Maybe
P13	Always Useful	Yes	Yes
P14	Always Useful	Yes	NA
P15	Always Useful	Yes	No
P16	Always Useful	Yes	Maybe
P17	Always Useful	Yes	No
P18	Always Useful	Yes	No
P19	Always Useful	Yes	No

The interviews revealed that investee firms often had to change their AIS after a VC invested in a firm. For example, P13 reported that his business

'used a [particular AIS] in one of [their] companies [and now that the AIS had changed, the company was] not going back to the old system … as the VC ask[ed] [them] to submit a legally-audited financial report [using the new AIS] to them … certified by an accounting firm in Saudi Arabia'.

Participant P14 attributed the change in the AIS in his business to a change in the governance of the firm following the involvement of a VC (consistent with Sahlman,1990). He highlighted that:

After the VC investment, it became different. We now have a strong governance body that controls our communication with them. We define exactly what kind of reporting they will receive, how frequent [it will be] and if they have a seat on the board [as a] member or not. [We agree at the start if the VC] is playing an advisory role or not. So, we literally define our communication with the VC … at that moment when they decide to invest.

The interviewees supported the model developed by Fried and Hisrich (1994). The results from the participants revealed that investee firms categorised the accounting information provided to VCs into two kinds: where investee firms tended to share a limited amount of information before the VC investors showed an interest in making a deal; then VCs were given access to an online data room when they were performing a due diligence investigation of the firm which usually happened after the investment became more likely. The difference between the two is that the initial data supplied includes information about the financial model, revenue streams, costs, and financial statements of the business; but the data room includes detailed records of the company's management accounts, documents, contracts, liabilities, and every single transaction relating to the company. Participant P12 provided an example of the information that her business provided to VCs at a very early stage of the discussion about the possibility of investment. She reported that:

a good presentation of the … the business [was needed]; what kind of problems [they were] solving as well as the vision [of the future]; what [the business was] trying to do or what was the next step. Information about the management team was important as well; what kind of team [had the business] built, market opportunities, market size, and the growth potential? [For our business] the numbers were good because we grew our revenue by [a factor of] three during COVID when everyone else's sales stalled.

Participant 13 explained that the type of information provided to the VC may depend on what they ask for. He noted that 'some of them ask[ed] for all the financials, even the budgets – everything from the day you start[ed]. But some VCs didn't ask [for]anything. They just [looked at] the sales and the operating cash in the business and evaluated the potential investment in this way'. However, P13 indicated that 'about 80 per cent of the VCs ask to see the financials. The largest VCs will ask for a financial report certified by an auditing firm' before they hand over their investment.

Several participants from investee firms highlighted concerns over the confidentiality of their business' records and financial information. They noted that it was difficult to differentiate between VCs who were interested in investing and those who only wanted to get access to the records/financial data and the project's progress in order to benchmark their current investee firms or help their investees to increase their market shares. A number of participants recalled situations where a VC passed their information on to competitors who were in their portfolio or being considered for investment. Non-disclosure agreements were uncommon in the MENA region and VCs mostly refuse to sign these agreements. Even where they were signed, P18 indicated that there was no law in Saudi Arabia to protect a business against any breach of these agreements.

5.5   CONCLUSION

This chapter has discussed the use of accounting information in Saudi VC investments with the views of both VC investors as well as investee/potential investee firms being represented. Looking at the views of those who worked in VCs, the analysis showed that accounting information played a crucial role in the investment decision; management accounting information was scrutinised for new, young start-up firms while audited financial statements were consulted for more mature businesses. The management accounting information was used cautiously since the VC investors were concerned about any optimistic bias present in the data. The accounting information helped VCs to predict the potential growth and profitability of the investee firms which fed into VC valuations and decisions about the equity stake which VCs would demand for the funds being sought; one might argue that even when using the accounting information as the 'starting point' of investment analysis it helped to mitigate the risk associated with making an investment decision in the absence of other data. The results also revealed that audit played a less important role in VC investments compared to investing in publicly listed companies. Looking at the views of investee/potential investee firms, the participants highlighted difficulties faced in preparing detailed accounting information at very early stages of their companies' life due to the dearth of resources available. They were also concerned about the cost of audit if the VC required the financial information to be assured. The relative financial information varied depending on the stage of the investee company's development. For younger, less-mature companies, greater reliance was placed on nonfinancial data. As companies grew, the role of audited financial information became more important. AISs played a role in facilitating the exchange of accounting information between the two parties (the VCs and the investee/potential investee firm) at different stages of the company's life. The relationship between the VC and the investee was therefore a multistage process; the accounting used and the AIS employed by the investee firm changed to take account of the nature of the relationship between the two parties. Indeed, as firms matured, the emphasis placed on audited financial statements increased at the expense of internally produced management accounting data.

NOTES

1. A notable exception to this generalisation is Wright and Robbie (1996).
2. Holmes and Nicholls (1988) investigated the use of accounting information in Australian small businesses. The authors identified many factors that might affect the nature and the amount of published accounting information, namely: business size, business age, industrial grouping, and the owner/manager's level of education.
3. JADA was launched following a resolution of the Council of Ministers in Saudi Arabia, with an investment capital of SAR 4 billion (approximately 861m GBP). It aims to provide funding to Saudi small and medium-sized entities through VC and private equity investments. JADA was a key component of Saudi Arabia's economic and social development plan – Vision 2030.
4. Indeed, Saudi Arabia was ranked second both in terms of the total amount of VC funding raised as well as the number of deals agreed between VCs and businesses (MAGNiTT, 2022). The largest deals by Saudi VCs were in the Food and Beverage industry, followed by the Fintech, Logistics and E-commerce industries. The industry which received the smallest amount of VC funding was the IT solutions sector (MAGNiTT, 2022)
5. It is worth noting that the government of Saudi Arabia has recently updated the legal system underpinning VC investment. These changes are expected to come into force by the end of 2024. For example, Antaki (2022) noted that a new type of company will be permitted to meet 'the needs of entrepreneurship and venture capital growth'.
6. Cassar (2009) attributed this emphasis on the income statement and cash flow data to the lack of assets amongst start-ups which could be used as collateral.
7. A captive VC firm is typically a subsidiary of a large financial institution. This type of VC firm receives financing from the parent company (Osnabrugge and Robinson, 2001; Hassan and Leece, 2007). Independent VC firms receive financing from different external sources such as individual investors and pension funds (Hassan and Leece, 2007). The semi-captive firm is established when a subsidiary of a large institution establishes its own fund and invites external investors to contribute funding (Hassan and Leece, 2007).
8. These semi-structured interviews were guided by a questionnaire document split into eight different sections. The first section sought background information about the respondents. The next two sections asked interviewees about the pre-investment stages of the VC cycle. Interviewees' views on the role of financial information, valuations and the importance of nonfinancial information were elicited in the following three sections. Post investment considerations were included in the final two sections of the questionnaire.

REFERENCES

Alexakis, C., Patra, T. and Poshakwale, S. (2010) Predictability of stock returns using financial statement information: Evidence on semi-strong efficiency of emerging Greek stock market, *Applied Financial Economics*, 20(16), pp.1321–1326.

Antaki, T. (2022) Saudi Arabia introduces new Companies Law. Available at: https://www.roedl.com/insights/saudi-arabia-new-companies-law-economic-system (Accessed: 21 April, 2023).

Amir, E. and Lev, B. (1996) Value-relevance of nonfinancial information: The wireless communications industry, *Journal of Accounting and Economics*, 22(1–3), pp. 3–30.

Amit, R., Glosten, L. and Muller, E. (1993) Challenges to theory development in entrepreneurship research, *Journal of Management Studies*, 30(5), pp. 815–834.

Armstrong, C., Davila, A. and Foster, G. (2006) Venture-backed private equity valuation and financial statement information, *Review of Accounting Studies*, 11(1), pp. 119–154.

Arnold, J. and Moizer, P. (1984) A survey of the methods used by UK investment analysts to appraise investments in ordinary shares, *Accounting and Business Research*, 14(55), pp. 195–207.

Cassar, G. (2009) Financial statement and projection preparation in start-up ventures, *The Accounting Review*, 84(1), pp. 27–51.

Danish, Y.A. and Lawton Smith H. (2012) Female entrepreneurship in Saudi Arabia: Opportunities and challenges, *International Journal of Gender and Entrepreneurship*, 4(3), pp. 216–235.

Fried, V.H. and Hisrich, R.D. (1994) Toward a model of venture capital investment decision making, *Financial Management*, 23(3), pp. 28–37.

Graham, B. and Dodd, D.L. (1934) *Security analysis*. New York: Whittlesey House. New York: McGraw-Hill Book Company.

Hand, J.R. (2005) The value relevance of financial statements in the venture capital market, *The Accounting Review*, 80(2), pp. 613–648.

Hassan, A.E. and Leece, D. (2007) Agency and information problems in venture capital markets: An empirical study of the information needs of UK investors and the demand for accounting information, *The Journal of Private Equity*, 10(2), pp. 93–112.

Holmes, S. and Nicholls, D. (1988) An analysis of the use of accounting information by Australian small business, *Journal of Small Business Management*, 26(2), pp. 57–68.

Imam, S. and Spence, C. (2016) Context, not predictions: A field study of financial analysts, *Accounting, Auditing and Accountability Journal*, 29(2) pp. 226–247.

JADA (2021) Future Proofing the Saudi Economy – Year In Review 2021. Available at: https://jada.com.sa/en/about-us (Accessed: 15 October, 2022).

Johnson, P. (2004) 'Analytic induction' in C. Cassell, & G. Symon (eds.), *Essential guide to qualitative methods in organizational research*. Thousand Oaks, CA: Sage Publications, pp. 164–179.

Joshi, K. and Bala Subrahmanya, M.H. (2019) 'Information asymmetry risks in venture capital (VC) investments: Strategies of transnational VC firms in India' in *Transnational Entrepreneurship*. Singapore: Springer, pp. 117–142.

King, N. (2004) 'Using templates in the thematic analysis of text' in C. Cassell, & G. Symon (eds.), *Essential guide to qualitative methods in organizational research*. Thousand Oaks, CA: Sage Publications, pp. 257–270.

Kingdom of Saudi Arabia (2022) Saudi Vision Document. Available at: https://www.vision2030.gov.sa/v2030/overview/ (Accessed: 15 October, 2022).

Lewellen, J. (2004) Predicting returns with financial ratios, *Journal of Financial Economics*, 74(2), pp. 209–235.

Lockett, A., Wright, M., Sapienza, H.J. and Pruthi, S. (2002) Venture capital investors, valuation and information: A comparative study of the US, Hong Kong, India and Singapore, *Venture Capital: An International Journal of Entrepreneurial Finance*, 4(3), pp. 237–252.

MAGNiIT (2022) H1 2022 Saudi Venture Capital Report. Available at: https://tinyurl.com/3u7b86vu (Accessed: 15 October, 2022).

Manigart, S., Wright, M., Robbie, K., Desbrières, P. and De Waele, K. (1997) Venture capitalists' appraisal of investment projects: An empirical European study, *Entrepreneurship Theory and Practice*, 21(4), pp. 29–43.

Manigart, S., De Waele, K., Wright, M., Robbie, K., Desbrières, P., Sapienza, H.J. and Beekman, A. (2000) Venture capitalists, investment appraisal and accounting information: A comparative study of the USA, UK, France, Belgium and Holland, *European Financial Management*, 6(3), pp. 389–403.

Oppenheimer, H.R. (1984) A test of Ben Graham's stock selection criteria, *Financial Analysts Journal*, 40(5), pp. 68–74.

Van Osnabrugge, M. and Robinson, R.J. (2001) The influence of a venture capitalist's source of funds, *Venture Capital: An International Journal of Entrepreneurial Finance*, 3(1), pp. 25–39.

Ou, J.A. and Penman, S.H. (1989) Financial statement analysis and the prediction of stock returns, *Journal of Accounting and Economics*, 11(4), pp. 295–329.

Pike, R., Meerjanssen, J. and Chadwick, L. (1993) The appraisal of ordinary shares by investment analysts in the UK and Germany, *Accounting and Business Research*, 23(92), pp. 489–499.

Reid, G.C. and Smith, J.A. (2007) *Risk appraisal and venture capital in high technology new ventures.* London: Routledge.

Sahlman, W.A. (1990) The structure and governance of venture-capital organizations, *Journal of Financial Economics,* 27(2), pp. 473–521.

Sapienza, H. J., Manigart, S. and Vermeir, W. (1996) Venture capitalist governance and value added in four countries, *Journal of Business Venturing*, 11(6), pp. 439–469.

Saudi Venture Capital Company (2022) Impact on venture capital ecosystem in the Kingdom of Saudi Arabia. Available at: http://svc.com.sa/wp-content/uploads/2022/02/SVC_Impact-Report_Jan_2022 .pdf (Accessed: 15 October, 2022).

Smith, J.A. and Cordina, R. (2014) The role of accounting in high-technology investments, *The British Accounting Review*, 46(3), pp. 309–322.

Wright, M. and Robbie, K. (1996) Venture capitalists, unquoted equity investment appraisal and the role of accounting information, *Accounting and Business Research*, 26(2), pp. 153–168.

Wright, M., Lockett, A., Pruthi, S., Manigart, S., Sapienza, H.J., Desbrières, P. and Hommel, U. (2004) Venture capital investors, capital markets, valuation and information: US, Europe and Asia, *Journal of International Entrepreneurship*, 2(4), pp. 305–326.

Zacharakis, A., Erikson, T. and George, B. 2010. Conflict between the VC and entrepreneur: The entrepreneur's perspective. *Venture Capital*, 12(2), pp.109–126.

Zimmerman, J.L. (2015) The role of accounting in the twenty-first century firm, *Accounting and Business Research*, 45(4), pp. 485–509.

6. Non-accounting patent data and venture capital investment in the United Kingdom
Julia A. Smith and Renzo Cordina

6.1 INTRODUCTION

Previous studies have debated the role of accounting and non-accounting information in the financing of new start-up ventures (Wright and Robbie, 1996; Smith and Cordina, 2014b). Some of the prior literature suggests that non-accounting data such as evidence of patenting plays a crucial role in obtaining external funding from investors (Caviggioli et al., 2020; Hoenig and Henkel, 2015; Hottenrott et al., 2016; Hsu and Ziedonis, 2007; Smith and Cordina, 2015). They have pointed to the dearth of accounting information in start-up businesses, where cash flows are typically negative, profits non-existent and assets usually intangible in nature (Zimmerman, 2015). In such a situation, non-accounting information can often be employed to signal firm potential to outside investors. This is especially true for the UK, where research on the role of non-accounting information in the valuation of unlisted start-up entities by venture capital firms is relatively scarce; prior studies have failed to look at this issue from the British venture capital perspective.

Academics continue to draw on the idea put forward in the US by Stinchombe (1965), who argued that new organisations are more likely to fail when compared to their more established counterparts. The higher risk of failure makes funding difficult to secure from conventional sources, since evidence of accounting performance is often lacking leaving firms to seek out venture capital investment based on non-accounting information. Given this lack of accounting information, past research suggests that non-accounting data such as patents may serve as a signal (cf. Spence, 1973, 2002) to the venture capitalists about the quality of the start-up firm which is seeking funding allowing them to focus their investment on higher quality companies with a greater chance of success (Conti et al., 2011; Hoenig and Henkel, 2015; Hottenrott et al., 2016; Hsu and Ziedonis, 2007; Long, 2002; Smith and Cordina, 2015). Since very little information may be publicly available about new start-ups (Gompers, 1995), it has been argued that non-accounting data such as patents or other patent related measures may serve as a way of reducing information asymmetry to venture capital investors (Hsu and Ziedonis, 2007; Long, 2002; Zhou et al., 2016). This is perhaps not surprising since past research shows that patenting in innovative intensive industries is linked with improved accounting performance in the future (Maresch et al., 2016).

Most of the prior studies carried out in this area have relied on North American transactional data when conducting their empirical analyses (Hoenig and Henkel, 2015). However, there are notable differences between the venture capital sector in North America and its counterpart in the UK. In North America, venture capital tends to be larger in terms of the size of investment made (Manigart et al., 2000; Reid, 1998) and the level of syndication involved. For example, Manigart et al. (2006) argues that syndication in the North American venture capital sector is typically associated with providing specialist expertise and networks of assistance to investee firms. It also tends to focus on larger companies and investments during later stages in the start-up cycle. By contrast, UK investment by venture capital firms tends to occur at an earlier stage of the start-up process, and syndication occurs for different reasons. It tends to be associated with diversification of risk such that any one venture capital outfit is not overly exposed rather than for resource-based motives (Manigart et al., 2006).

In this study, we seek to investigate whether non-accounting information, such as patents, is associated with UK venture capital investment in early-stage companies, particularly within the technology sector. To investigate this contention, non-accounting information has been hand-collected from various data sources to facilitate the creation of a database which includes details of venture capital investments in UK start-ups between 2000 and 2013. Information on patents, industry, and firm age has been gathered. Attempting to obtain accounting information is difficult since all the firms are privately owned and unquoted.

6.2   PRIOR LITERATURE AND HYPOTHESES

North American-based studies point to a link between non-accounting information such as the existence of a patent application and the level of external investment which a start-up can obtain. For example, in a study focusing on US patents, Zhou et al. (2016) found a positive association between the amount of venture capital funding that a start-up could secure and the existence of a patent application – although industry differences were noted. This finding is in line with results from a study by Mann and Sager (2007) which focused exclusively on the software industry in the US; in their article, the authors identified a positive relationship between the existence of a granted patent and the amount of investment received. A similar relationship was identified by Conti et al. (2011), with their restricted data set relating to firms located at 'an incubator facility' within the Georgia Institute of Technology. Extending this logic to the UK scenario, we propose that:

Hypothesis 1: There is a positive relationship between the existence of a patent application and investment by UK-based venture capital firms

In an earlier UK study by Smith and Cordina (2015), interviewees highlighted the importance of broader protection to investors available from using multiple patents in a start-up firm. According to Smith and Cordina (2015), interviewees argued that a stand-alone patent might not provide adequate protection for venture capital investors or supply a clear signal about firm quality that would allow high quality start-up firms to be distinguished from their lower quality counterparts. In particular industries, such as the pharmaceutical sector, they suggested that one patent alone may not be a credible signal about firm quality and the likely future success of a start-up firm. Patents can be filed across different jurisdictions (Hall, 2007) and during the different stage of an invention's lifetime. For example, in the case of a drug manufacturer, a patent fencing approach might be adopted (Granstrand, 1999), i.e. where different patents are obtained to protect a whole line of research. A separate patent would be filed to protect the substance and compounds used; further patents would be filed to protect the drug formulation, and the dosage (Sternitzke, 2013). In the case of the software industry in the US, Mann and Sager (2007) suggested that a similar approach tended to be followed; they identified a positive relationship between the existence of multiple patents and the level of investment that a start-up firm secured, although the study focused on patents which were granted rather than patent applications. Therefore, based on the above findings we would expect that:

Hypothesis 2: *There is a positive relationship between the existence of multiple patents and the level of investment obtained from UK-based venture capital firms by start-up entities.*

Prior studies also suggest there is a positive association between the actual number of patent applications and the amount of venture capital funding received (Baum and Silverman, 2004; Conti et al., 2011; Hsu and Ziedonis, 2007). In some investigations evidence indicates that a relationship exists between the number of patents granted and the amount of funding received (Baum and Silverman, 2004; Mann and Sager, 2007); although, in this case there is less agreement among the empirical findings uncovered (Hoenen et al., 2014), presumably because it is easier to file a patent than to secure the granting of such a recognition from the patenting authority. The patent application may be viewed as a weaker signal by the venture capitalist funding bodies. Once again, the focus of most these studies has tended to be transactional North American venture capital and patent data (Hoenig and Henkel, 2015). Assuming the findings identified in North American studies were also applicable to the UK we would expect that:

Hypothesis 3: *There is a positive relationship between the number of patent applications and the level of investment from UK-based venture capital firms by start-up companies.*

One problem with using the number of patents as a signal is that multiple patents may relate to the same invention. Thus, some 'double counting' of innovations might arise if the focus is on the number of patents granted or the number of patents applied for. To overcome this problem, the 'family' of patents relating to a single invention may be viewed as a signal by a venture capital funding body. Interview participants in the study by Smith and Cordina (2015) adopted such a perspective; they outlined the importance of patent families to venture capital investors with multiple patents associated with the one invention being grouped together when funding decisions were being evaluated. By looking at the number of patent families (instead of the number of patent applications or patents granted), a researcher would ensure that patents protecting the same invention are only counted once (Martínez, 2011). Further, such an approach would fit in with the practice identified by Smith and Cordina (2015) in their investigation of the UK venture capital sector. Based on this analysis we would expect that:

Hypothesis 4: *There is a positive relationship between the number of patent families and the level of investment.*

6.3   DATA SOURCES, VARIABLES AND MODELS

For the purposes of this research three types of data (investment data, company data and patent data) were manually collected from numerous complementary data sources. Some 668 funding transactions to venture capital firms from early-stage companies were initially included in the data set. However, data were missing for 89 of these start-ups.[1] Thus, for the purposes of the multivariate analysis conducted in this chapter, these firms were omitted. As a result, the regression analysis only includes data relating to 579 investment rounds; 119 of these were in companies which had only been incorporated for a year or less at the point of investment.

6.3.1 Data Sources

6.3.1.1 Investment data
The availability of disaggregated data on investments by UK venture capital firms is limited; such information is usually only published in aggregate by means of statistical reports issued by the British Venture Capital Association (BVCA). To overcome this difficulty, we made use of Crunchbase, an online database which summarises key information on technology companies. Crunchbase gathers data from various news outlets and company websites and is increasingly being used as a reliable source for investment data in early-stage companies (Block et al., 2013; Zhou et al., 2016). In some cases, the amount invested was not disclosed within Crunchbase's database; in these situations, an attempt was made to identify the amount invested by venture capital firms manually using shareholder documents filed at Companies House if the investment being made was in a UK company. Investments made by UK venture capital firms who were members of the BVCA investing in the technology sector were included.

6.3.1.2 Company data
Industry classification data for each company were obtained (i) using SIC codes (standard industrial classification codes) from Companies House submissions if the investee companies were located in the UK, or (ii) using NAICS (North American Industry Classification System) data if the investee firm was from the US or Canada. These North American classifications were then regrouped using the main headings of the UK SIC codes (Office for National Statistics, 2002). The year in which the company was incorporated and the country of incorporation were obtained from Crunchbase. Since the study focuses on early-stage companies, any companies older than 10 years were excluded from our analysis; a similar cut-off has been employed by other researchers in this area (for example, Davila and Foster, 2005).

6.3.1.3 Patent data
Patent data were collected by means of manual queries in the Global Patents Index, by using the Patents Information for Experts facility available through the website of the European Patent Office.[2] The data obtained relate to the number of patent applications, patents granted and the number of patent families for each company in which a venture capital investment was made.

6.3.2 Variables

Multivariate ordinary least squares regression was used to examine the extent to which venture capital funding is associated with patenting information. In carrying out the regression analysis, Stata 13.0[3] statistical software was employed to generate the output. White standard errors which are robust to within-cluster correlation based on the year of investment (Petersen, 2009) were used to evaluate the statistical significance of any coefficient estimated.

The specification of the models follows from valid inference techniques in the wake of potential misspecifications which can arise in the model. In particular, we test for the heteroscedasticity and non-normality of the errors. Nonrelevant variables which have a highly insignificant p-value (based on robust standard errors) are removed from the regression. Under each combination of regressors are conventional tests of misspecification (such as tests for nonlinearity and heteroscedasticity). It is worth mentioning that since there are many dummy variables in the model, high collinearity is an issue which is best dealt with by dropping the statistically insignificant variables. All tests were performed at the 5 per cent significance levels.

6.3.2.1   Dependent variable

The dependent variable used in our regressions is the natural logarithm of the amount of funding received by a sample company from a venture capital organisation in millions of British pounds (GBP). Investments made by UK venture capital companies in other currencies were converted into GBP based on the exchange rate as at the first day of the investment using historical exchange rate information.[4] This approach was adopted since the exact date of investment was not always known.

6.3.2.2   Independent variable

Different regressions were run using a number of different patent measures. These represent different ways of looking at the patent data. In line with Mann and Sager (2007) we use a number of dummy variables which measure whether a firm had (i) a patent application lodged, (ii) a single patent granted or (iii) multiple patents granted before the first day of the month in which the investment was made. We also estimate the regressions with the actual number of patent applications and patents granted, and the number of patent familes – instead of the dummy variables. Since the patent measures using the 'actual' numbers were highly skewed, the natural log of each measure was employed. In some cases this was equal to zero, and in order to apply the transformation a constant of one was added.

6.3.2.3   Control variables

A number of control variables relating to the characteristics of the investee companies were also included in the analysis. In particular, we considered the age of the investee company at the date of investments (in years), dummy variables indicating whether the company was a US or a non-UK European investee company, and a dummy variable which was set equal to one if the company was in the information technology subsector. Dummies were also included to control for the period in which the UK was in financial crises (Campos et al., 2011). We also controlled for the interaction between the patenting variables and some of the control variables.

6.3.3   Models

The following models are estimated using the variables identified in the previous section. First, the log of the venture capital funding (LVCF) is explained by a model based on whether a patent application was held (Model M0), (PatApp), investee related variables (age of firm (AGE), member of IT related industries (SECTOR), region of incorporation (US) or (EUROPE)) and two dummy variables for the financial crisis (2008 and 2009) (CRISIS2008 and CRISIS2009). Interactions between the patent application variable and other variables are also included.

$$LVCF = \beta_0 + \beta_1(\text{PatApp}) + \beta_2(\text{Age}) + \beta_3(\text{Sector}) + \beta_4(\text{US}) + \beta_5(\text{Europe}) + \beta_5(\text{Crisis1}) +$$
$$\beta_6(\text{Crisis2}) + \beta_7(\text{PatApp} * \text{Age}) + \beta_8(\text{PatApp} * \text{Sector}) + \beta_9(\text{PatApp} * \text{US})$$
$$+ \beta_{10}(\text{PatApp} * \text{Europe}) + \beta_{11}(\text{PatApp} * \text{Crisis1}) + \beta_{12}(\text{PatApp} * \text{Crisis2}) + \varepsilon \qquad (6.1)$$

LVCF is also explained by similar models but instead of looking at whether a patent application was held, we considered whether patents were granted (PatGrant) (Model M1) and whether the firm held multiple patents (MultiplePat) (Model M2).

Third, the dependant variable is explained by a model based on the log of the actual number of patent applications (LNumberPatApp) (Model M3):

$$LVCF = \beta_0 + \beta_1(\text{LNumberPatApp}) + \beta_2(\text{Age}) + \beta_3(\text{Sector}) + \beta_4(\text{US}) + \beta_5(\text{Europe}) +$$
$$\beta_5(\text{Crisis1}) + \beta_6(\text{Crisis2}) + \beta_7(\text{LNumberPatApp} * \text{Age}) + \beta_8(\text{LNumberPatApp} * \text{Sector}) +$$
$$\beta_9(\text{LNumberPatApp} * \text{US}) + \beta_{10}(\text{LNumberPatApp} * \text{Europe}) +$$
$$\beta_{11}(\text{LNumberPatApp} * \text{Crisis1}) + \beta_{12}(\text{LNumberPatApp} * \text{Crisis2}) + \varepsilon \qquad (6.2)$$

Similar models which included the actual number of patents granted (instead of patent applications) (LNumberPatGrant) (Model M4) and the number of patent families (in respect of patents applied for) (LNumberPatFamilies) (Model M5) were also estimated.

6.4   RESULTS

6.4.1   Descriptive Statistics

Tables 6.1 and 6.2 show the key descriptive statistics relating to the data under consideration. The tables show the descriptives for the whole sample as well as for investments in companies which are a year old or less. Thus, the case of very early-stage companies can be examined in more detail to see if the role of patents in venture capital funding decisions is different for such firms. Moreover, by considering very early-stage investments separately we attempt to mitigate the causality problem identified in earlier studies relating to whether the act of patenting increases investment or venture capital funding increases patenting (Bertoni et al., 2010; Munari and Toschi, 2015).

Table 6.1   Descriptive statistics

Variable	Full Sample				Investees younger than 1 yr			
Investment	Mean	SD	Min	Max	Mean	SD	Min	Max
VC funding (mln of £)	5.58	7.84	0.01	92.06	2.46	3.62	0.01	20
Patent data								
Patents Applications								
No of patent applications	8.18	26.1	0	233	0.97	4.80	0	37
No of patent families	3.25	9.54	0	86	0.47	2.22	0	18
Patents Granted								
No of patent granted	1.72	7.90	0	96	0.80	0.38	0	3

Variable	Full Sample				Investees younger than 1 yr			
No of patent families	0.84	3.61	0	63	0.80	0.43	0	3
Company Data								
Age	3.82	2.58	0	10	0.66	0.48	0	1
	Frequency				Frequency			
	N				N	%		
Country incorporated								
United Kingdom	433	64.82%			98	74.81%		
USA	106	15.97%			14	10.69%		
Other Europe	120	17.96%			18	13.74%		
Other	9	1.35%			1	0.76%		
Industry								
Industry (Non-IT related)	387	57.93%			61	46.56%		
Industry (IT related)	281	42.07%			70	53.44%		

Overall, Table 6.1 highlights that the average investment was £5.58 million, however when looking specifically at the amount obtained by younger firms it was significantly ($t(367) =$ 6.84; p=0) smaller; companies less than a year old only attracted an average investment of £2.46 million from venture capital firms. As expected, established firms also had more patent applications and patent families than their younger counterparts. The typical company in the whole sample had over eight patent applications and just under two patents granted. Very few firms which were incorporated for less than a year before the venture capital investment had patents granted. The majority of the sample firms were incorporated in the UK and did not operate in the IT sector; for younger companies, nearly three quarters were incorporated in the UK although a majority of these firms were drawn from IT related industries.

Table 6.2   *Background information relating to the dummy variable patent metrics*

	All Sample		Investees younger than 1 yr	
	Frequency		Frequency	
Patent Application	N	%	N	%
(Yes)	298	44.61%	38	70.99%
(No)	370	55.39%	93	29.01%
Patent Granted				
(Yes)	127	19.01%	6	95.42%
(No)	541	80.99%	125	4.58%
Multiple Patents				
(Yes)	269	40.27%	0	80.15%
(No)	399	59.73%	26	19.85%

6.4.2 Results and Discussion

Table 6.3 and 6.4 show the results of the multivariate regressions analysis conducted. As discussed above, investments in companies that are less than a year old are considered in a separate model. An inspection of these tables indicates that a positive relationship exists between venture capital investment and the existence of a patent application or a granted patent although at varying levels of signficance. *Ceteris paribus*, a firm having a patent received 74.9 per cent more investment than one without (as shown in the results of the model considering all firms irrespective of age ($p < 0.1$, model M0). If we consider Model M0a which shows the same relationship but only for investee companies which are less than a year old, we find that the increase is equal to approximately 119.5 per cent although once again this is only signficant at the 0.1 level. Therefore our results show some evidence in support of Hypothesis 1 (Model M0, Model M0a). Similarly we looked at the case of whether an investee had a patent granted, and once again we find evidence of higher investment amounts ($p < 0.05$). In view of the fact that within our data set there were only three instances where a firm which had only been incoporated for less than a year had a patent granted, this model was only estimated for the full data set (Model M1).

Our evidence also supports Hypothesis 2 with regards to the level of investments if multiple patent applications were held; the coefficient on the multiple patents dummy variable is 0.6212 (Model M2, $p < 0.1$). We find no evidence to support this hypothesis for investee firms which are less than a year old since although the coefficient is positive, it is not significantly different from zero. In view of the fact that very few of the youngest firms in the sample had filed multiple patent applications in the period, this result was not unexpected.

In all the models considered we find the age of the investee company to have a positive effect on the amount of financing received. This finding is not surprising, since the 'older' the firm, the less the information asymmetry problem; more information is available for scrutiny about investee companies which have been in existence for several years (Gompers, 1995). Some of these older firms may also have a number of patents granted, as evidenced in the descriptive statistics in Tables 6.1 and 6.2. Finally, the literature suggests that the risk of failure declines dramatically after a company has been in existence for a longer period (Hudson, 1987); such firms may represent relatively more attractive investment opportunities for venture capital funders.

In line with published statistics by the British Venture Capital Association (BVCA) (2013), we also find higher amounts of investment by UK venture capital firms in companies located outside the UK. Munari and Toschi (2015) explain that higher levels of investment would be expected for firms located in the US given that the market for venture capital investments in the US is more developed. We also note that investment amounts for firms in the IT industry tend to be lower than for other sectors. Once again, this result is consistent with the overall industry statistics published by the BVCA (2013) which show that the average investment in pharmaceuticals and biotechnology was over three times higher than that in the IT industry. This finding is also in line with conclusions from earlier studies carried out in the US (Gompers, 1995). Interestingly, the interaction dummy included to show the joint effect of having a patent and operating in the IT industry was not signifcant. This reflects the views identified in interview-based studies carried out by Smith and Cordina (2014a). According to their analysis, interviewees had stated that alternative forms of investor protection were more effective in the software industry and investors were therefore less concerned about the existance of patents or patent applications.

Surprisingly, the control variable for the financial crisis period in 2008 is positive and significant. Upon closer investigation this may be due to the nature of our data set which includes

Table 6.3   *The effect of patenting on the level of investment (using 'dummy' patent related variables)*

Dependent variable: Natural log of VC financing in a funding round in GBP (£)

	Model M0	Model M0a	Model M1	Model M2	Model M2a
	(Investee > 1 yr)	(Investee < 1 yr)	(Investee > 1 yr)	(Investee > 1 yr)	Investee (< 1 yr)
Patent related variables					
Patent application (dummy)	0.5593*	0.7862*			
	(0.2692)	(0.3631)			
Patent granted (dummy)			0.6427**		
			(0.2585)		
Multiple patents (dummy)				0.6212*	0.7273
				(0.3026)	(0.5374)
Investee related variables					
Age of investee firms	0.1417***		0.1502***	0.1425***	
	(0.0228)		(0.0160)	(0.0233)	
IT industry (dummy)	-0.5408***	-0.4689*	-0.5884***	-0.5272***	-0.4983*
	(0.1246)	(0.2340)	(0.1661)	(0.1142)	(0.2570)
US investee (dummy)	1.1713***	1.1887***	1.2047***	1.1926***	1.2275***
	(0.1725)	(0.2537)	(0.1682)	(0.1579)	(0.2678)
European investee (dummy)	1.1396***	1.2138***	0.9558***	1.0593***	0.9920***
	(0.2110)	(0.3538)	(0.1763)	(0.1939)	(0.2359)
Financial crisis dummies					
Financial crisis (2008) (dummy)	0.3480***	0.4213*	0.3493***	0.3367***	0.4468**
	(0.0855)	(0.1923)	(0.0825)	(0.0907)	(0.1895)
Financial crisis (2009) (dummy)	0.0190	0.2562	0.0246	0.0009	0.3050
	(0.0712)	(0.2490)	(0.0762)	(0.0768)	(0.2639)
Interaction variables					
Patent related variables x all other variables	Yes	Yes	Yes	Yes	Yes
Number of investment rounds (N)	579	119	579	579	119
R-squared	0.270	0.146	0.252	0.271	0.132

Note: Robust standard errors (clustered by year of investment) in parentheses.
*** $p<0.01$, ** $p<0.05$, * $p<0.1$

all venture investment rounds in the period, irrespective of the stage of investment. Although Pierrakis (2010) explains that during the recession period there was a decline in seed funding and very early-stage investments, BVCA (2009, 2010) statistics show a move by venture capitalists towards later-stage (safer) investments in 2008 which tended to be larger size. The move towards 'larger', safer investment is reflected in the size of the investments within the data set.

Similar results (although at a higher significance level: $p < 0.01$) were obtained when the actual number of patents was considered, rather than dummy variables (Table 6.4). Model M3 and M3a consider the actual number of patent applications made prior to the investment data. We find evidence to support Hypothesis 3. A larger number of patent applications lead

Table 6.4   *The effect of patenting on the level of investment*

Dependent variable: Natural log of VC financing in a funding round in GBP (£)					
	Model M3	Model M3a	Model M4	Model M5	Model M5a
Patent related variables	(Investee > 1 yr)	(Investee < 1 yr)	(Investee > 1 yr)	(Investee > 1 yr)	Investee (< 1 yr)
Number of patents applied for	0.2314***	0.5025***			
(natural log)	(0.0261)	(0.0916)			
Number of granted patents			0.3862*		
(natural log)			(0.1866)		
Number of patent families				0.3382***	0.5442***
(based on patents applied for)				(0.0633)	(0.1148)
(natural log)					
Investee related variables					
Age of investee firm	0.1093***		0.1439***	0.1391***	0.6544*
	(0.0257)		(0.0186)	(0.0166)	(0.3011)
IT industry (dummy)	-0.4857***	-0.4023	-0.5712***	-0.4747***	-0.3355
	(0.1242)	(0.2612)	(0.1520)	(0.1211)	(0.2421)
US investee (dummy)	1.2561***	1.2362***	1.1992***	1.2647***	1.3138***
	(0.1768)	(0.2370)	(0.1677)	(0.1744)	(0.2575)
European investee (dummy)	1.1271***	1.1518***	0.9815***	1.1293***	1.3113***
	(0.1962)	(0.2707)	(0.1877)	(0.1999)	(0.3187)
Financial crisis control variables					
Financial crisis (2008) (dummy)	0.2921***	0.5612**	0.3455***	0.3281***	0.4844**
	(0.0843)	(0.1781)	(0.0851)	(0.0799)	(0.1881)
Financial crisis (2009) (dummy)	0.0167	0.3946	0.0242	0.0224	0.4701*
	(0.0673)	(0.2265)	(0.0799)	(0.0635)	(0.2168)
Interaction variables					
Patent related variables x all other variables	Yes	Yes	Yes	Yes	Yes
Number of investment rounds (N)	579	119	579	579	119
R-squared	0.294	0.197	0.252	0.297	0.233

Notes: Model uses the actual number for the stock of patents.
Robust standard errors (clustered by year of investment) in parentheses.
*** $p<0.01$, ** $p<0.05$, * $p<0.1$

to a higher amount of investment in the venture round ($p < 0.01$), both in the case of the full data set (Model M3) and also in the case of the subsample relating to firms less than a year old. The findings appear to be in line with the prior studies carried out amongst North American firms (Baum and Silverman, 2004; Conti et al., 2011; Hsu and Ziedonis, 2007). In the case of the full sample (Model M4) we also find some evidence that a similar result occurs when the number of patents granted is considered ($p < 0.1$) although this finding was not present for the sample of younger firms. As explained earlier, very few firms of a year or under had been granted patents at such an early stage in their lives. It is also worth recognising that the

European Patent Office indicates that the data on the number of granted patents needs to be treated with caution, since a number of patent records may have the data relating to whether a patent was granted or not omitted (European Patent Office, 2012).

In a unique approach, not considered in previous transactional North American studies, we also consider the number of patent families as an explanatory factor for venture capital funding. Having a number of patent families was considered important in a prior study by Smith and Cordina (2015) and the current analysis investigates whether similar findings arise across a large sample. Our results support Hypothesis 4 (p < 0.01,M5; p < 0.01, M5a). Having a larger number of patent families attracts a greater amount of financing since the coefficient is positive at 0.3382 for the whole sample; in fact, the coefficient is even larger at 0.5442 when the younger firms' data were considered separately. Similar results were obtained with regard to the significance of the control variables identified in the models included within Table 6.3.

6.5   CONCLUSION

Despite the differences between the venture capital markets in the UK and the US, our UK data have yielded results that are similar to findings in the North American literature; early-stage companies which have patents are able to obtain more venture capital funding. Apart from the actual number of patents held (or applied for), we find that whether or not a company holds (or has applied for) patents seems to make a difference in the amount of venture capital funding received. The impact of patent families, a group of related patents, on venture capital funding is also explored in the current chapter, and we confirm that this also seems to make a difference for venture capital investors; this finding confirms what has emerged from earlier interview-based studies by Smith and Cordina (2015). In fact, it would appear that multiple patents are expected in certain industries (Sternizke, 2013). The results also highlight the importance of non-accounting information in the financing of start-up companies; whilst these start-up companies often have no profits and limited financial history (Zimmerman, 2015), the link between the amount of funding and the non-accounting aspects (in this case, patent data) would suggest that in these early stages non-accounting information would be more important to investors (Smith and Cordina, 2014b).

Our results are supportive of some governments' policies to promote patenting (Smith and Cordina, 2015) such as the 'patent box' scheme. However, it is important to note that patenting is not the only intellectual property protection available and may not be suitable for every industry (Kitching and Blackburn, 2003; Neuhäusler, 2012; Smith and Cordina, 2014b; Thomä and Bizer, 2013). The findings of the current chapter also suggest that alternative incentives are required to encourage the funding of early-stage companies in sectors where patenting is deemed to be less relevant. For example, our study has indicated that the effect of patenting on venture capital financing is not significant for companies in the IT sector.

We acknowledge that there are some limitations to the study we have carried out, however we believe that our work will serve as a starting point for future research in this area. In particular, we note that the nature of venture capital investment, which usually takes the form of private deals, has made data collection difficult, and we have had to rely upon data collected from various news sources in Crunchbase. There is also the issue of whether venture capital itself is increasing patenting (Bertoni et al., 2010), but we have mitigated this problem by considering a subset of investments in companies which had only been incorporated for less than a year. In future research, it would be useful to explore further some of the industry differences identified and perhaps carry out fieldwork research with early-stage companies to examine the importance they ascribe to patenting, and why increasingly some companies are opting not to patent.

NOTES

1. Due to the nature of the venture capital investment, the amount invested was not always disclosed and, as a result, a number of investments were removed from the data set. In our data set, we also verified the existence of severe outliers using the resistant outlier detection approach based on the 'interquartile range' (Frigge et al., 1989; Hamilton, 1992). After applying logarithmic transformation to the amount invested (as discussed later on in Section 6.3.2.1) , and dropping investments in companies older than 10 years (as discussed in Section 6.3.1.2) the data set only included a small number of 'mild' outliers which do not affect the analysis carried out.
2. This is accessible from http://www.epo.org/searching-for-patents/technical/espacenet/gpi.html.
3. StataCorp (2013) Stata Statistical Software (Version 13), College Station, TX: StataCorp, LP.
4. Currency conversions were carried out using the tool provided by Oanda Corporation at https://www.oanda.com/currency/converter/.

REFERENCES

Baum, J.A.C. and Silverman, B.S. (2004) 'Picking winners or building them? Alliance, intellectual, and human capital as selection criteria in venture financing and performance of biotechnology startups', *Journal of Business Venturing*, 19(3), pp. 411–436.

Bertoni, F., Croce, A. and D'Adda, D. (2010) 'Venture capital investments and patenting activity of high-tech start-ups: A micro-econometric firm-level analysis', *Venture Capital: An International Journal of Entrepreneurial Finance*, 12(4), pp. 307–326.

Block, J.H., De Vries, G., Schumann, J.H. and Sandner, P.G. (2013) 'Trademarks and venture capital valuation', *Journal of Business Venturing*, 29(4), pp. 525–542.

British Venture Capital Associaton (2009) BVCA Private Equity and Venture Capital Report on Investment Activity 2008. London: British Venture Capital Associaton.

British Venture Capital Associaton (2010) BVCA Private Equity and Venture Capital Report on Investment Activity 2009. London: British Venture Capital Associaton.

British Venture Capital Associaton (2013) BVCA Private Equity and Venture Capital Report on Investment Activity 2012. London: British Venture Capital Associaton.

Campos, C., Dent, A., Fry, R. and Reid, A. (2011) Impact of the Recession. London: Office for National Statistics.

Caviggioli, F., Colombelli, A., De Marco, A. and Paolucci, E. (2020) 'How venture capitalists evaluate young innovative company patent portfolios: Empirical evidence from Europe', *International Journal of Entrepreneurial Behavior & Research,* 26(4), pp. 695–721.

Conti, A., Thursby, M.C. and Rothaermel, F. (2011). Show me the right stuff: Signals for high tech startups. Cambridge: National Bureau of Economic Research.

Davila, A. and Foster, G. (2005). 'Management accounting systems adoption decisions: Evidence and performance implications from early-stage/startup companies', *The Accounting Review,* 80(4), pp. 1039–1068.

European Patent Office (2012). GPI User Manual. Brussels: European Patent Office.

Frigge, M., Hoaglin, D.C and Iglewicz, B. (1989) 'Some implementations of the boxplot', *The American Statistician,* 43(1), pp. 50–54.

Gompers, P. (1995) 'Optimal investment, monitoring, and the staging of venture capital', *The Journal of Finance,* 50(5), pp. 1461–1489.

Granstrand, O. (1999) *The economics and management of intellectual property: Towards intellectual capitalism.* Cheltenham, UK and Northampton, MA, USA: Edward Elgar Publishing.

Hall, B.H. (2007) 'Patents and patent policy', *Oxford Review of Economic Policy*, 23 (4), pp. 568–587.

Hamilton, L.C. (1992) 'Resistant normality check and outlier identification', *Stata Technical Bulletin,* 1, pp. 15–18.

Hoenen, S., Kolympiris, C., Schoenmakers, W. and Kalaitzandonakes, N. (2014) 'The diminishing signaling value of patents between early rounds of venture capital financing', *Research Policy*, 43(6), pp. 956–989.

Hoenig, D. and Henkel, J. (2015) 'Quality signals? The role of patents, alliances, and team experience in venture capital financing', *Research Policy*, 44(5), pp. 1049–1064.

Hottenrott, H., Hall, B.H. and Czarnitzki, D. (2016) 'Patents as quality signals? The implications for financing constraints on R&D', *Economics of Innovation and New Technology*, 25 (3), pp. 97–217.

Hsu, D.H. and Ziedonis, R.H. (2007) 'Patents as quality signals for entrepreneurial ventures', *DRUID Summer Conference*, Copenhagen: 18–20 June.

Hudson, J. (1987) 'The age, regional, and industrial structure of company liquidations', *Journal of Business Finance & Accounting*, 14(2), pp. 199–213.

Kitching, J. and Blackburn, R. (2003) 'Innovation, intellectual property and informality', in: R.A. Blackburn (ed.), *Intellectual property and innovation management in small firms*. London: Routledge, pp. 16–34.

Long, C. (2002) 'Patent signals', *The University of Chicago Law Review*, 69(2), pp. 625–679.

Manigart, S., De Waele, K., Wright, M., Robbie, K., Desbrières, P., Sapienza, H. and Beekman, A. (2000) 'Venture capitalists, investment appraisal and accounting information: A comparative study of the USA, UK, France, Belgium and Holland', *European Financial Management*, 6(3), pp. 389–403.

Manigart, S., Lockett, A., Meuleman, M., Wright, M., Landström, H., Bruining, H., Desbrières, P. and Hommel, U. (2006) 'Venture capitalists' decision to syndicate', *Entrepreneurship Theory and Practice*, 30(2), pp. 131–153.

Mann, R.J. and Sager, T.W. (2007) 'Patents, venture capital, and software start-ups', *Research Policy,* 36(2), pp. 193–208.

Maresch, D., Fink, M. and Harms, R. (2016) 'When patents matter: The impact of competition and patent age on the performance contribution of intellectual property rights protection', *Technovation*, 57, pp. 14–20.

Martínez, C. (2011) 'Patent families: When do different definitions really matter?', *Scientometrics*, 86(1), pp. 39–63.

Munari, F. and Toschi, L. (2015) 'Do patents affect VC financing? Empirical evidence from the nano-technology sector', *International Entrepreneurship and Management Journal*, 11(3), pp. 623–644.

Neuhäusler, P. (2012) 'The use of patents and informal appropriation mechanisms – differences between sectors and among companies', *Technovation*, 32(12), pp. 681–693.

Office for National Statistics (2002) UK Standard Industrial Classification of Economic Activities 2003. London: Her Majesty's Stationery Office.

Petersen, M.A. (2009) 'Estimating standard errors in finance panel data sets: Comparing approaches', *Review of Financial Studies*, 22(1), pp. 435–480.

Pierrakis, Y. (2010) *Venture capital – now and after the dotcom crash.* London: NESTA.

Reid, G.C. (1998) *Venture capital investment: An agency analysis of practice.* London: Routledge.

Smith, J.A. and Cordina, R. (2014a) Reporting of intangible assets: Views from venture capitalists, *European Accounting Association Congress*, Tallinn: 21–23 May.

Smith, J.A. and Cordina, R. (2014b) 'The role of accounting in high-technology investments', *The British Accounting Review*, 46(3), pp. 309–322.

Smith, J.A. and Cordina, R. (2015) 'Patenting and the early-stage high-technology investor: Evidence from the field', *R&D Management*, 45(5), pp. 589–605.

Spence, M. (1973) 'Job market signaling', *The Quarterly Journal of Economics*, 87(3), pp. 355–374.

Spence, M. (2002) 'Signaling in retrospect and the informational structure of markets', *American Economic Review*, 92(3), pp. 434–459.

Sternitzke, C. (2013) 'An exploratory analysis of patent fencing in pharmaceuticals: The case of PDE5 inhibitors', *Research Policy*, 42(2) , pp. 542–551.

Stinchombe, A.L. (1965) 'Social structure and organizations', in J.G. March (ed.), *Handbook of organizations*. Chicago: Rand Mcnally, pp. 142–155.

Thomä, J. and Bizer, K. (2013) 'To protect or not to protect? Modes of appropriability in the small enterprise sector', *Research Policy*, 42(1), pp. 35–49.

Wright, M. and Robbie, K. (1996) 'Venture capitalists, unquoted equity investment appraisal and the role of accounting information', *Accounting and Business Research*, 26(2), pp. 153–168.

Zimmerman, J.L. (2015) 'The role of accounting in the twenty-first century firm', *Accounting and Business Research*, 45(4), pp. 485–509.

Zhou, H., Sandner, P.G., Martinelli, S.L. and Block, J.H. (2016) 'Patents, trademarks, and their complementarity in venture capital funding', *Technovation*, 47, pp. 14–22.

7. Information flow and investment decision-making in equity crowdfunding

Catherine Deffains-Crapsky and Abdel Malik Ola

7.1 INTRODUCTION

High-potential new ventures are understood to contribute to job creation and economic welfare (Lerner, 2010). The landscape of financing nascent new ventures is expanding with digitalisation disrupting the traditional financial sector (Bertoni et al., 2022; Block et al., 2018). For start-up capital, Equity Crowdfunding (ECF) began to play an important role in complementing Business Angel (BA) and Venture Capitalist (VC) funding. Through a Delphi study focused on Europe, North America and Asia, Tiberius and Haupmeijer (2021) show that experts expect a rapid growth of this market for SMEs (small-to-medium-sized enterprises) and start-ups. Ahlers et al. (2015, p. 958) define ECF as 'a method of financing, whereby an entrepreneur sells a specified amount of equity or bond-like shares in a company to a group of (small) investors through an open call for funding on Internet-based platforms', while for Estrin et al. (2022, p. 1761), ECF is 'an open digital marketplace for entrepreneurial equity finance that operates within a social media environment'.

ECF can be a viable source of equity funding for entrepreneurial firms if it can fill the funding gap (Cressy, 2002) despite the many challenges that it faces mainly due to a very high asymmetry of information and agency costs (Carpenter and Petersen, 2002; Cassar, 2004) as well as the risk of adverse selection (Akerlof, 1970). Indeed, ECF activity takes place on a two-sided platform (Rochet and Tirole, 2003) that matches the supply of capital on one side of the platform with the demand for capital on the other. On the demand side, it is well recognised that all young and small firms face difficulties when accessing finance (Ang, 1992). On the supply side, investors are a diverse group (Goethner et al., 2021; Feola et al., 2021) as ECF is not limited to sophisticated investors such as BAs or VCs. It allows early-stage financing through the participation of unsophisticated investors, only some of whom may have a strong relationship with the venture entrepreneurs. Therefore, while ECF increases the number of potential investors, most of them may not have the expertise to accurately assess the value proposition of projects seeking equity capital (Freear et al., 1994). In addition, they may not have the incentive to devote resources to due diligence as the amount they invest can be small (Vismara, 2018a). In such a context, perception of the project's quality may be difficult to ascertain. Therefore, the disclosure of information by entrepreneurs is very important to help investors decide whether or not to invest. The nature of the information, the credibility of the sender and the ability of investors to process it, are only beginning to be addressed in the literature on ECF (Johan and Zhang, 2020; Estrin et al., 2022; Kleinert et al., 2022). The digital platforms themselves represent a challenging environment, even for sophisticated investors who need to adapt to this new financing tool.

Signalling theory, developed by Spence (1973), has largely been applied to early-stage ventures (Colombo, 2021) and, in particular, investments via ECF platforms (Ahlers et al.,

2015; Vismara, 2016; Kleinert et al., 2020). In traditional signalling theory, investors prefer to consider costly information that is supposed to be an effective signal allowing them to separate high from low quality projects (Connelly et al., 2011). But the details of investments on ECF platforms have led researchers to question the relevance of classical signalling theory. Thus, Estrin et al. (2022) speak of an information deluge. Ventures seeking financing are not the only providers of these signals, given the network effects that are at work on these platforms (Acs et al., 2021). Therefore, some of the information, even if it is not costly, is taken into consideration by investors (Anglin et al., 2018). This refers to the costless signalling theory that considers that low cost or costless signals can be influential for an unsophisticated audience (Lowenstein et al., 2014). In this framework, the distinction between hard and soft information in the context of risk capital is developing (Liberti and Petersen, 2018). Finally, network effects must be considered when analysing investment decisions in ECF (Estrin et al., 2022).

The aim of this chapter is to highlight the signalling literature in relation to ECF and discuss what work has already been done and what research questions should be investigated in the near future. More precisely we look at this general research question: do ECF platforms improve the flow of information during the fundraising campaign, facilitating decision-making by investors and, if so, how? To answer this question, the first part of the chapter presents the difficulties of assessing the early stages of entrepreneurial firms seeking external funding. The challenges related to the nature of the information and the potential investor's ability to process it are discussed with a focus on traditional actors. The second part of this chapter focuses on the particularities of project assessment on ECF platforms and discusses how such platforms mitigate the information asymmetry which may be present when entrepreneurs seek funding. The conclusion highlights the advances in the ECF literature and the future research to be carried out in order to better understand the decision-making process of investors on these platforms.

7.2 EARLY-STAGE FINANCING, ASYMMETRY OF INFORMATION AND SIGNALS

7.2.1 Entrepreneurial Firms' Characteristics

ECF platforms target new businesses seeking external equity capital (Kleinert et al., 2022; Butticè and Vismara, 2022). The nature of new ventures is diverse and challenging to support, particularly for investors targeting potential high growth impact ventures (Smallbone et al., 2002). In an explanatory study, Morris et al. (2018, p. 454) propose a typology of the different 'emerging firms that may or may not grow, do or do not innovate, can fail or succeed, and vary considerably in their economic impact'. This broad delineation leads the authors to propose four types of emergent ventures: based on their entrepreneurial orientation, their growth orientation, their innovativeness, their risk-taking and the time dimension. The first two types represent the majority of emergent ventures. The authors call them 'survival ventures' and 'lifestyle ventures'. Both are characterised by weaker entrepreneurial identities in contrast to the other two types called 'managed growth' and 'aggressive growth' ventures. These latter two types are more established entrepreneurial firms. Innovation is a key characteristic of entrepreneurial firms and is linked to their growth potential.

The current definition of innovation, which seems to be the broadest, is that supplied by the Organisation for Economic Co-operation and Development (OECD, 2015, p. 16): 'the implementation of a new or a significantly improved product (good or service) or process, a new marketing method, or a new organisational method in business practices, workplace organization or external relations'. In an entrepreneurial context, innovation is called technological innovation, meaning development of new products and/or services. The commercial success aspect is crucial. Technological innovation is therefore linked to the acceptance of a change by the market. Entrepreneurial firms may involve a high degree of innovation; there may be a higher risk for radical innovation over an incremental change (Deffains-Crapsky and Sudolska, 2014). This is because any project involving radical or disruptive innovation is uncertain since it can be characterised as unique and new. The challenge for the external funder is to identify an investment opportunity while dealing with an idea which may disrupt the market. It can be a long-term, uncertain and idiosyncratic investment in intangible assets that requires exploration of an unknown future (Huang and Pearce, 2015: Ola et al., 2019). Due to their newness, these new ventures cannot provide public and audited financial data which is typically needed for financial assessment (Cosh et al., 2009; Jeffrey et al., 2016; Wallnöfer and Hacklin, 2013). A high degree of innovation represents a technological and commercial uncertainty (Ola et al., 2019; Packard et al., 2017) and suffers from a reputation deficit: an inability to guarantee the repayment of any funds borrowed (Ueda, 2004).

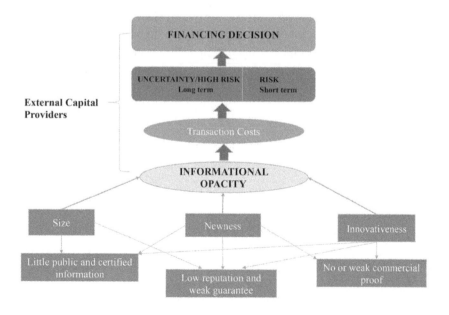

Figure 7.1   *Entrepreneurial firms and funding decision challenges*

Figure 7.1 above represents the challenges faced by different types of entrepreneurial firms. The uncertainty or the risk emerges from a dearth of information and/or information asymmetry between entrepreneurs and outside equity capital providers. The latter have to manage the risk of adverse selection, which increases the transaction costs of the assessment underlying the decision to invest in the business. While information is necessary to reduce the effects of adverse selection risk, there are many questions about the nature and the quality of the information, and the trust which can be placed in it by the various stakeholders.

According to signalling theory, in order to mitigate information asymmetries and attract external capital providers, new ventures use signals to convey their quality; potential investors respond to these signals and engage in screening. The two main issues regarding signals are: first the availability of information and its nature, and second the ability of the receiver to process this information. These issues are interdependent.

7.2.1.1   The challenge of information

The first issue relating to how information may convey news concerns the cost of the signal. Spence (1973) considers that those who receive signals pay much more attention to the signals that cost time, effort, or money. This cost is seen as evidence of credibility since such signals cannot be mimicked by low quality projects. Nevertheless, as Svetek (2022) points out, the environment of new ventures facilitates low-quality projects that can easily manipulate signals because the information supplied can be ambiguous, relatively cheap to produce, and easily copied. Any information sent to an external actor by the entrepreneur or a third party can be considered as a signal that may reflect a characteristic of the project. The early-stage context leads to information of several types, not all of which can be considered as relevant signals (Estrin et al., 2022).

A second issue relating to how information may convey news relates to the broad range of signals which can be sent. Three categories of information which have been analysed in the literature are, respectively, the intrinsic characteristics (technical and marketing) of the project, the financial parameters of the investment, and the characteristics of the entrepreneur (Alexy et al., 2012; Brush et al., 2012; Colombo, 2021; Maxwell et al., 2011; Sudek et al., 2008; Shafi, 2021). More recently, the social and environmental impact of the project has been used as a signal of quality (Harrer and Owen, 2022). Huang and Knight (2017) and Shafi (2021) note that research on entrepreneurial signalling behaviour distinguishes between interpersonal signals (an entrepreneur's behaviour and their interactions at work with others) and informational signals (an entrepreneur's or venture's ability to progress). In each category, there is objective and subjective information which can be qualitative or quantitative.

A final distinction that comes from the banking literature separates soft from hard information but with no clear dichotomy (Liberti and Petersen, 2018). The distinction between hard and soft information is more complex than that between qualitative and quantitative information (Estrin et al., 2022). To distinguish hard from soft information, Liberti and Petersen (2018) analyse three main characteristics. First, it appears that hard information is most often associated with numbers while soft information is typically conveyed more through text. However, soft information can also be expressed using numbers.

The importance of the context under which the information is collected also helps distinguish hard from soft information; hard information is usually public and easy to verify. Alharbey and Van Hemmen (2021) limit hard information to financial statements while soft information relates to future plans. For Estrin et al. (2022), hard information involves facts on which there is general agreement, which are verifiable and cannot be easily changed in the investment process; by contrast, soft information is open to debate, or alternative interpretations about its implications are available and more difficult to verify. Soft cues are tightly linked to sensemaking which conditions the knowledge that outsiders derive from them, whereas the meanings of hard cues are commonly understood by all. Soft cues represent opinions, projection and commentaries and are grounded in experience. Hard data are validated objective cues without equivocal meaning (Huang, 2017; Sudek, 2006). In contrast, soft information (also called subjective cues), are non-codifiable cues, collected and produced during the interaction between investors and the project team, and used to assess the skills required in entrepreneurship (Cardon et al., 2017; Murnieks et al., 2016). Finally, the collection of soft information cannot be separated from the decision-making process, unlike hard information, which can be collected without anyone other than the decision-maker being present.

There is a great deal of consensus in the literature on the view that soft information is crucial for the financing of entrepreneurial firms (Croce et al., 2021; Huang and Knight, 2017; Mason et al., 2019; Parhankangas and Ehrlich, 2014; Wood et al., 2020), but for investors it is costly to process. Estrin et al. (2022) argue that soft information may be the main component of information asymmetries that limit the entrepreneur's ability to raise equity. The importance of looking at hard data or soft information may depend on stage of assessment. For instance, there is some evidence that soft signals are mostly used in the screening stage while hard data are preferred during the final stage of evaluation (Cardon et al., 2017; Sudek, 2006).

7.2.1.2   The receiver's ability to accurately process the signalled information

As the nature and the quality of the information is partly dependent on the entrepreneur, the way it is collected or made available to external funders is another challenge associated with early-stage investment. BAs and VCs represent the main source of finance for entrepreneurial firms and, therefore, receivers of the information (Li et al., 2014; Mason, 2009; Maxwell et al., 2011; Morrissette, 2007; Shepherd et al., 2003; Shepherd and DeTienne, 2005). They have two characteristics in common: their experience and their network; both of which influence their ability to expose themselves to the information flow.

According to the literature, a very important advantage of VCs and BAs is in their entrepreneurial experience, which helps them to evaluate the value of the information provided by entrepreneurs. Morrissette (2007) finds that US BAs have entrepreneurship experience in common that helps them to perceive less risk in start-ups than other investors. This experience helps in validating the information provided by the entrepreneur and in securing access to key third-party information. Investment experience influences the effectiveness of techniques used at each subsequent stage of the investment process (Maxwell et al., 2011). In Japan, Tashiro (1999) notes that the main occupation of active BAs is either as founder or cofounder of a successful entrepreneurial firm. Some of them have been involved in providing financial services to small ventures, which exposes them to key data about the environment in which entrepreneurial firms operate. It appears that they draw on the network (friends and associates) that they have built through their past experiences (rather than business plans), which helps them obtain information about their investment opportunities.

In China, Li et al. (2014) also observe that the majority of BAs have entrepreneurial experience and/or a business background. This experience helps build large personal networks which become the most preferred source of information, although this kind of data may not fully satisfy investor demands for news. It is important to note that experience, in some cases, may inhibit the search for additional information and prevent the funders from fully considering all relevant information, thus reducing the quality of their decision-making (Zacharakis and Shepherd, 2001).

More than experience, access to reliable information also relies on exposure to ideas and opinions of other individuals (Mason et al., 2019). Indeed, the recent trend in the BA market shows that group interactions, both formal and informal, allow for the dissemination and integration of the information necessary for their decision (Wood et al., 2020; Ola et al., 2022). In the case of VCs, the reaction to and interpretation of information depends largely on the expertise and the social status of the firm (Shepherd et al., 2003; Shepherd and DeTienne, 2005). The study by Alexy et al. (2012) finds that the structural and relational aspects of VC's social networks give them superior access to information about current investment opportunities, which increases their willingness to invest in these ventures.

The above discussion highlights that the financing of the entrepreneurial firms involves a diversity of information that does not pass through conventional channels, nor does it take the usual forms: personal opinions, investor experience, formal and informal personal networks. A decision to finance an entrepreneurial firm involves taking and processing several pieces of information to reach a conclusion (McMullen and Shepherd, 2006; Wiltbank et al., 2009). This is particularly important as uncertainty calls into question the relevance of even widely available information. There is very little literature on the decision-making processes that underpin the interpretation of the potential of entrepreneurial firms. Most of them are focused on BA investment decision-making, individually or as part of a group.

Initial studies find that the assessment of uncertainty within entrepreneurial firms' funding requires the implementation of a multistep process (Duxbury et al., 1996; Macmillan et al., 1985; Maxwell et al., 2011; Osnabrugge, 2000; Paul et al., 2007; Riding, 2008) with a very low final selection rate. The main stages can be distinguished as follows: identification and screening, due diligence and closing negotiations. In the identification phase, the early-stage investor will interpret the recommendation of a project by a member of his network as a good quality signal (Amatucci and Sohl, 2004; Fried and Hisrich, 1994). Screening is done through pitches, where the investor will interpret the entrepreneur's ability to defend the potential of their idea and their propensity to collaborate (Clark, 2008; Elsbach and Kramer, 2003).

Focusing on the cognitive process at play at the individual level, early-stage investors have been described as intuitive investors. Indeed, at the early stage their decisions are supposed to be based on quick, non-conscious impulses and do not draw on all available information, some of which may be relevant. For example, Shepherd and Zacharakis (1999) and Zacharakis and Meyer (1998) found that VCs rely on recollections which make them subject to confirmation bias. Early-stage investors tend to interpret information in a way that confirms their preconceptions from previous decision-making. In this sense, they voluntarily limit the search for additional information. Thus, Maxwell et al. (2011) describe the selection stage by BAs as a cognitive operation that minimises the required effort to rapidly screen opportunities, while limiting the chance of discarding investments of high potential. The process involves a non-compensatory approach where a 'fatal flaw' (a predetermined minimum standard on a factor that is absent) may end the interaction between an investor and an entrepreneur, even though there may be a lot of other positive factors present in the funding bid. Shafi (2021) describes the heuristic where the investor reduces the information processing effort by focusing heavily on criteria that are easy to assess while paying less attention to criteria that appear difficult to evaluate.

Recent literature has focused on intuition as a characteristic of sophisticated investors. Based on their solid experience, they are able to see beyond the information by making an intuitive or new interpretation of the data at hand. According to Huang (2017), BAs follow an elaborated intuitive process that helps them see opportunities where others see projects that are too risky to support and likely to fail. This process involves interweaving many decision factors, whatever their nature, to form a narrative that sustains investment opportunities. Huang (2017) shows that some BAs first calculate risk using hard data and then compare the result with non-codifiable information, while others start by screening soft information about the entrepreneur and after prioritise data that confirm their initial feeling. In a similar vein, Ola et al. (2019) link the BA's intuition to the process of structural alignment. The latter implies that investors subjectively relate existing information in the context of the entrepreneurial firm to infer characteristics that are not available *in situ*. Svetek (2022) follows the same idea by arguing that informational signals are used to derive subjective values such as preparedness, confidence, and commitment while the interpersonal signals are transformed to derived subjective values like trustworthiness and coachability.

A final point about those who receive signals is that processing a venture's information often involves working in groups. Brush et al. (2012) describe groups of BAs who most often work together on due diligence, assessing business plans, based on regular meetings and interactions when listening to pitches. Wood et al. (2020) highlight the judgement about trust between peers. Ola et al. (2022) emphasise the importance and added value of intersubjective exchanges in assessing investment opportunities. These studies demonstrate that the actual cognitive process must be embedded in the collective in order to facilitate the interpretation of information about entrepreneurial firms.

The literature on the nature of information and its processing during early-stage investments allows us to outline the challenges faced by ECF platforms in bridging the equity gap. In order to answer the research question, the following section analyses the ECF literature on information flows and processing during the crowdfunding campaign.

7.3   EQUITY CROWDFUNDING PLATFORMS' BUSINESS MODELS TO HELP INVESTORS' DECISION-MAKING

7.3.1   ECF Platforms' Business Models

Within the financial growth-cycle paradigm (Berger and Udell, 1998), the funding of entrepreneurial firms follows a linear relationship between sources of funding and stages of development. Given the small amounts invested by each contributor and the average amount of capital raised by the venture through platforms, ECF often appear after the 'love-money' and before or at the same time as the BA and seed funds. Depending on its business model, the ECF platform offers a variety of services, ranging from identifying ventures to be funded to the management of the shareholding after a successful fundraising campaign, through different phases and using different marketing tools and partnerships with traditional players (Cumming et al., 2022; Girard and Deffains-Crapsky, 2016; Deffains-Crapsky and Daniel, 2016; Kleinert et al., 2022). To create value, ECF platforms must attract enough investors to satisfy entrepreneurs and vice versa (Belleflamme et al., 2015). It is expected that the development of ECF will enable entrepreneurial firms to access a larger number of small equity investors (Drover et al., 2017), thereby broadening the base of investors allowed to invest in ventures and diversifying the funding sources used (Cumming et al., 2018). This broadening of access to investment is one of the most important expectations of ECF (Cumming et al., 2018). This more diverse range of investors comes with the potential to harness the 'wisdom of the crowd' and create more efficiency in the market (Butticè and Vismara, 2022).

Therefore, although the business model may vary from one platform to another, its revenues rely on its ability to generate good investment opportunities and to expand the quantity and the quality of its community of investors. To this end, ECF platforms select projects that are presented online to their investor community. This selection can take different forms but is very strict (Kleinert et al., 2022). The aim is to take into account the presence of unsophisticated investors among the investor community. Some platforms offer registered investors the opportunity to participate in this selection via a phase known as 'e-voting' (Cumming et al., 2022). Only projects that have received a sufficient percentage of investment promises are likely to be financed on the platform. During the crowdfunding campaign, platforms help entrepreneurs to dynamically present themselves, their project, their value proposition and to answer a variety of questions asked by investors. The platform also helps the investors to access and process the information. Although the selection of projects by the platform is very important, the focus here is on the flow of information as soon as the crowdfunding campaign begins. Indeed, the specific context of entrepreneurial firms can lead to a mis-selection (Blaseg et al., 2021) and each investor must be able to form his or her own opinion.

Beyond a simple new financing process, the platform can be viewed as a social catalyst (Lehner and Harrer, 2019, p. 90) from a system perspective that 'highlights the systemic interplay that arises from the interaction between individual actor and the surrounding structure (institutions), and hence provides a holistic, societal perspective on entrepreneurial finance'. The financial brokerage offered by ECF platforms follows country-specific regulations. For European platforms, a new European regulation has been implemented and should be applied by all equity-based and lending-based platforms by the end of 2023. This European regulation will replace national regulations, standardising the regulatory framework in this area throughout the EU; it will allow platforms to apply for an EU Passport and makes it easier to offer services to both investors and businesses. Another objective of this regulation is to better protect small, unsophisticated investors, i.e. the crowd.

This raises the question of the platform's ability, through its economic model, to provide access to information throughout the investment process and to enable optimal processing of the information provided. In the previous section, we highlighted the characteristics of early-stage information and its processing by traditional early-stage actors, namely BAs and VCs. To answer the research question, we adopt the same approach through the ECF literature. First, we characterise and discuss the information that flows through these platforms during a campaign. Secondly, we question the capacity of each participant who receives information to process it efficiently.

7.3.1.1   The flow of information during an equity crowdfunding campaign

According to Estrin et al. (2022, p. 1762), a digital platform is a means 'to produce, disseminate and store an unprecedented deluge of information'. It increases the amount of hard information available but more importantly the supply of soft information by providing direct access and knowledge of the new venture and the entrepreneur before the funding round. An advantage of the digital platform is that it helps to reduce the cost of information disclosure by entrepreneurs (Attuel Mendes et al., 2019; Tomczak and Brem, 2013). Entrepreneurs can easily provide soft information helping to reduce any limit on their ability to raise funds. They can easily and cheaply spread the word about their project. Indeed, a platform manager gives advice and screens the format of the video pitch provided by entrepreneurs before making it available to the members (Estrin et al., 2018). Therefore, entrepreneurs can be more confident in sharing subjective cues and dynamically influencing the perceptions of investors.

Traditionally, the pitch is the main channel through which projects are brought to the attention of the BA and VC. According to Moritz et al. (2015, p. 320), ECF has made pseudo personal forms of communication such as video possible: 'A high-quality video posted on the platform can address common question asked by investors...becoming a substitute of the private conversation between investees and investors, and a written business plan'. Such videos disseminate information about the technological and commercial value of the project. They can also convey personal impression signals such as empathy, trustworthiness, open mindedness, reliability, authenticity, and a willingness to share information (Moritz et al., 2015). This is soft information as defined by Liberti and Petersen (2018). Indeed, during an ECF campaign, a huge amount of soft information is produced and shared. Investors pay attention to the way the entrepreneur answered questions, and to the extent that they provided fast and credible answers (Estrin et al., 2022). Johan and Zhang (2020) analyse the power of qualitative information revealed by entrepreneurs during ECF campaigns to mitigate information asymmetry. Their empirical results confirm that qualitative information reveals quality helping investors to evaluate projects. Nevertheless, they highlight a difference between sophisticated and unsophisticated investors. The latter are less resistant to promotional language used by some entrepreneurs, meaning that they have more difficulty in assessing the quality of soft information.

The most recent literature emphasises the dynamics of the information flow on ECF platforms, mainly soft information (for example, Estrin et al., 2018, 2022; Johan and Zhang 2020; Kleinert et al., 2020; Stevenson et al., 2019). First, the platform is structured to facilitate the publication of investors' comments and entrepreneurs' responses in an accessible and easy-to-use format (Estrin et al., 2018). Online exchanges with the entrepreneur help to see his or her enthusiasm. Crowdfunding investors pay more attention to person-to-person information (direct exchanges with the team through the online platform chat) rather than formal sources such as project websites and media publications (Polzin et al., 2018). They consider this information to be more accurate and proprietary with low cost.

Second, during the campaign, the opinion and behaviour of the other investors represent another category of soft information (Estrin et al., 2018). Indeed, the interaction frequency, the synchronous and the asynchronous nature of discussions, the number of times a pitch is viewed, are key items of information that are available around the project. Stevenson et al. (2019) introduce the term 'crowd cues' that includes the crowdfunder's endorsement and collective opinions displayed during a campaign. According to these authors, there are 'qualified' crowd cues where the collective opinion is representative of the true objective value of the project, while other cues may be inaccurate ('unqualified'). This is the case when the opinion of an individual potential investor is not aligned with the true value of the project. The big challenge remains to be able to distinguish between qualified and unqualified crowd cues.

Third, to ensure the success of fundraising campaigns, platforms may also choose to make leaders' opinions visible in order to induce herding behaviours. Leaders are the most active members of the platform's community of investors regarding a venture proposal. They have experience, expert knowledge about the company and/or its products, networks, and professional investment skills. They represent a very small group and are interested in being involved in the business; they want to have direct contact with entrepreneurs – to meet them in person. They tend not to use pseudo communication tools (video, chat on Internet). Instead, they ask more questions and influence peer behaviours sometimes triggering social contagion. Their decisions are well-informed based on their experience. Opinion leaders often pledge large amounts of funding.

Sometimes, platforms reward these investors when they achieve a certain investment frequency or reach a cumulative amount invested. In this situation, the behaviour of highly active investors in the crowd is an important social cue (Shafi, 2021) to other investors. A project that received funding from a BA and/or a VC increases its chances to raise all of the funds that it seeks (Kleinert et al., 2020). According to Moritz et al. (2015), retail investors contact the lead investor as he is considered to have more complete information. Their profile gives them the opportunity to get in direct contact with the entrepreneur and recommend the investment to others. Therefore, the flow of information inside the community increases due to the interactions between different types of investors. Block et al. (2018) confirm that the presence of investors with public profiles makes a project more appealing to early investors often inducing information cascades.

In addition, Estrin et al. (2018) argue that the platform's members observe lead investors to see what they were thinking and to discern their response to different perspectives and investment rationales. Shen et al. (2020) focus on the role of a lead investor in ECF in China. More specifically, they provide evidence that the percentage of money invested by the lead investors in the project and their investment experience positively affect the behaviour of followers. Furthermore, platforms have a 'memory', which means that information is stored, coded and available for a long time on the platform. The cost of accessing this information is low or non-existent since each member of the platform can see the characteristics of previous campaigns and the comments left by actors in relation to a project. According to Svetek (2022), this aspect is very important for reducing information asymmetry. Indeed, information related to previous investments can influence an investor's attitude through feedback mechanisms. Nevertheless, some previous valuable signals may, over time, become uninformative as their relationship with future performance dissipates.

Figure 7.2 (adapted from Lehner and Harrer, 2019) is a simplified representation of the dynamics of information flows between distinct categories of players on an ECF platform during a fundraising campaign.

This figure clearly shows the key role played by the platform as the focal actor and the mechanisms used to facilitate the flow of information between stakeholders. Compared to traditional approaches to early-stage financing, it is clear that information, whatever its nature, is more abundant with more diverse sources on ECF platforms. Moreover, the ECF model better operationalises the information dynamics, particularly for soft information.

Whatever the platform's business model, information cascades are favoured because the platform helps network participants to observe each other's willingness to invest, the amount invested and the timing of each other's investment (Estrin et al., 2018). A large number of initial early investors is a valuable signal which increases the number of subsequent investors, the total funding amount, and the success probability (Vismara, 2018a). Moritz et al. (2015) confirm the existence of the social effect of peer investors in ECF platforms. Participants are used to following the first investors that pledge money. They do this because they do not

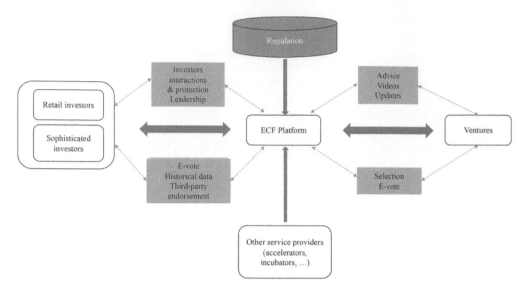

Figure 7.2   ECF platform, stakeholders and information flows mechanisms

have the time and the necessary expertise to assess the project's potential. Investors following the opinions of informed peers seem to ignore or re-evaluate their own private information. However, this effect is positive only if some peer investors do the job of scrutinising the investment's potential. If only friends and family are amongst the early investors, the information cascade will not be effective. Therefore, the behaviours of lead investors are important. It is believed that they carry out due diligence on projects and take the initiative to fund a project that they feel has potential. Lead investors provide third-party endorsement that reduces information asymmetry and lowers the importance of the pseudo personal communication (Moritz et al., 2015). Indeed, some investors may ignore their own private information or any video produced by the entrepreneur only because they have identified leading opinions to follow. Investors on ECF platforms consider the funding momentum at the beginning of the campaign and the reaction over time of other investors as key signals. This has become a social norm. Endorsement can also come from customers' comments, the reputation of business partners and other external credentials.

It is also important to note that beyond making information, in its various forms, accessible to members, platforms can also play a role in processing information. As Cumming et al. (2022) point out, the platform model can reduce the degree of subjectivity associated with some soft information. Indeed, platforms may provide the possibility to rate the subjective quality of the team or other characteristics of the project. Thus, 'soft' information can become 'hard', making it easier for the crowd to use and reducing the cost of collecting it.

Nevertheless, Kleinert and Volkmann (2019) provide a nuanced picture of the added value of online discussions by showing that information on topics like market risk and shareholder rights harm funding success. Moritz et al. (2015), Cumming et al. (2022) and Estrin et al. (2018) provide a differentiated view of the ability of digital platforms to increase the flow of reliable information. Some information fails to predict the actual investment. Cumming et al. (2022) observe that investment intentions during the e-voting phase are significantly larger than the final contribution if the participant ultimately contributes to the campaign. Indeed, they observed a very high non-transformation rate of funding intentions between the e-voting and the funding phases. Moreover, they found that there is no correlation between the average assessment and its dispersion (on the project interest scale) and the success of a funding campaign. It suggests that social cues can have limited value. Estrin et al. (2018) highlight another drawback associated with the high level of transparency and the public nature of information on ECF platforms: failure is always public, and entrepreneurs are not willing to share all sensitive financial and/or strategic data in the public domain.

7.3.1.2 Ability of unsophisticated investors as signal recipients to assess the information received

To the extent that platforms increased the flow of soft information between all actors in a fundraising campaign, the question here is whether, with the digitisation enabled by the ECF, investors are better able to assess signals in order to distinguish between projects of different quality (Blaseg et al., 2021). This issue is linked to the composition of the platform's investor community. Indeed, ECF platforms attract professional and nonprofessional investors who are described as unsophisticated and form the so-called 'crowd'. However, this crowd itself is heterogeneous (Goethner et al., 2021; Feola et al., 2021).

Cumming et al. (2022) observe different investor behaviours according to income, location, the level of education and gender. For example, women respect more their investment intentions communicated during the e-voting phase. Feola et al. (2021) segment ECF investors into four clusters. In the first one, they identify 'venture trustful investors' who are more confident in the digital technology offered by the platform and very motivated to deal with it. They are younger and less driven by social and ethical values. A second cluster refers to 'crowdfunder technicians' who are more than 50 years old, use the platform with ease, and are more motivated by intrinsic values when dealing with ECF. A third cluster concerns 'financial investor talent scouters', aged between 30 to 50, who experience difficulties when participating in campaigns but are loyal to this mode of financing. They need to collect more soft information about factors such as founder motivation, skills, capabilities, and other personal values.

Finally, in the fourth cluster there are 'social dreamers' who experience more difficulties in participating in the ECF campaign, display less confidence in the technology, have lower intrinsic motivation, and are more driven by financial pledges, project characteristics, and social as well as ethical values. Polzin et al. (2018) divided the crowd into two families: the in-crowd which includes investors with strong or weak ties with the project teams; the out-crowd which includes investors with no personal ties to the project owner. Their study shows that in-crowd investors place more importance on the team and their previous project outcomes, than the out-crowd. Out-crowd investors rely more on information about financial planning and risk (hard data) than soft data (planning about technology and the market).

The fact that all these studies have identified different kinds of investors with diverse behaviour confirms an advantage of ECF; such platforms pool together investors with different information needs and expertise. It allows for the development of personal networks between investors enabling them to source information. According to Estrin et al. (2018), platforms make possible a learning process between experienced and novice investors. It is apparent that novice investors focus on a single dimension (the product or the entrepreneur) when investing in early-stage ventures while experienced investors consider many aspects such as the business model, the concept, the entrepreneurial team and the technology. The fact that they can learn from each other facilitates a useful complementarity. Moreover, Estrin et al.

(2022) describe a network effect that leads to economies of scale in the provision of information. Indeed, a large community of investors may reduce considerably the cost of information gathering, which counterbalances the fact that early-stage retail investors will not be motivated to perform due diligence.

Platforms are able to generate the direct exchange of information between investors and facilitate the flow of signals. Less experienced and less expert investors can easily assess the skills of their more sophisticated counterparts. Platforms can make and keep visible for a long time the projects that have raised funds, and provide the public with continuous updates about them. This publicity can attract more investors, and perhaps additional professional funders. This is an indirect effect of the network that may contribute to increasing the wisdom of the crowd. The larger the proportion of knowledgeable investors, the more the crowd members can read signals to distinguish between entrepreneurs of different quality.

Nevertheless, Cumming et al. (2022) raise concerns related to this plurality of communities within the members of a platform. Some investors follow a community logic, which distances them from any idea of in-depth due diligence. Thus, such investors as leaders can cause a cascade of misinformation. According to Stevenson et al. (2019), investors on ECF platforms are not able to uniformly observe and understand information. ECF gives an example of crowd bias which describes the tendency to follow the opinions of the crowd despite the presence of contrary objective information. Amateur investors (who are not professional decision-makers) are more likely to be part of the crowd. They are less likely to react to negative video pitch cues when positive crowd cues are present, leading them to invest more in poor quality projects (Johan and Zhang, 2020).

As highlighted in the first part of this chapter, an important challenge regarding the processing of information in the context of entrepreneurial firms is the required interpretation of soft information (Estrin et al., 2022). Sensemaking is at the heart of early-stage assessment. Apart from considering the three usual families of criteria in the early-stage valuation process, easier access to more information and the network dimension, the literature on ECF provides relatively little information on the underlying decision process used to integrate and process information. Shafi (2021) is one of the few who deal with such an issue. According to him, equity crowdfunders follow a heuristic of evaluability which supposes that financial information is difficult to process, so then little attention is devoted to it. Their focus is on the quality of the team and the quality of the business – soft information according to the study.

The quality of the business refers to the innovativeness of the product, the lead time advantage, the size of the market and the growth potential. For Blaseg et al. (2021), informed due diligence is difficult in ECF for three reasons. First, the absence of face-to-face interaction limits the assessment of the quality of the management team. Second, due to the small amount and small expected return of their investment, investors are not motivated to spend time and effort in assessing the project potential. Third, crowd investors are mostly amateurs with uncoordinated money pledges. Then, they will adopt a herding behaviour instead of active and consistent information processing. Ultimately, we still lack knowledge about what is or can be done by the ECF platform to improve the efficiency of information processing in the uncertain/risky context of entrepreneurial firms.

7.4   CONCLUSION

The context of entrepreneurial firm financing is undeniably characterised by information asymmetry. Based on a review of the literature, this chapter focused on the contribution of a rather new actor, the ECF platform, in managing this asymmetry. This actor responds to an important challenge as it facilitates access to external equity for projects but also aims to 'democratise' VC investment. The notable contribution of the ECF platform refers to the availability of usable information in the early-stage investment decision. The model is widely recognised as facilitating the production and dissemination of more information. It outperforms the BA network model by expanding the influence of leaders' opinions. Platforms provide proxies to allow others to quantify and qualify the opinions of so-called 'professional' investors or those with solid investment experience. They also make it legitimate for the public to base an investment decision on subjective parameters such as personal opinion or intuition. Equity investment, even in entrepreneurial firms, is increasingly seen as accessible to unsophisticated investors, and this is not only related to the small amounts that the ECF allows such investors to invest. The ECF model helps to emphasise the importance of 'intuition' in early-stage investments. However, not enough research has been done so far on the decision-making process during fundraising campaigns. Indeed, if information is more accessible, several challenges to the development of ECF arise.

First of all, the credibility of the sources of various opinions appears fundamental, without necessarily linking it to cost as advocated by traditional signalling theory. The work of Cumming et al. (2022) offers an interesting avenue where the platform could work to increase the transformation rate of investment intentions disclosed during the e-voting period. Second, the platform must take account of the effects of the community logic that can sometimes prevail among the first movers (Cumming et al., 2022; Josefy et al., 2017). If the latter are to send a signal, the most visible should already be the most capable of making a serious assessment.

To this end, different solutions have been implemented or suggested. Thus, the French platform Sowefund has chosen to base its model on a strong partnership with traditional investors who select, together with the platform, the projects to be the subject of campaigns and in which they coinvest with the platform's community of investors. In such a model, the investor community can effectively distinguish between the initial contributions made by the close circle of the entrepreneur (friends and family), and the contributions made by more professional and expert investors (Hornuf and Schwienbacher, 2018; Zhang and Liu, 2012). The choice could be to make the experience of investors more visible, which is essential in BA networks, both in terms of the amount invested in projects and the exits achieved. For example, investor profiles could include speeches on the life of an investment, which would be widely visible to the entire crowd. Indeed, for Le Bon (2009), the 'wisdom of the crowd' and the associated information cascade exist when a sense of responsibility to the community is present only in a non-anonymous crowd. Otherwise, a large number of people gathered for a task would not always be more capable than a small number of people of making a relevant decision on a given subject. According to the study by Attuel et al. (2020), the tools made available by ECF platforms therefore do not sufficiently optimise the production and dissemination of information required by the crowd and for the crowd. Future research can help platforms evolve their model by insisting on the perfect mix between different categories of contributors, with a focus on credibility and accountability of the opinion source.

Third, there is a need to better understand how platforms can respond to Stevenson et al.'s (2019) finding that the ECF gives an example of crowd bias which describes the tendency to follow the inaccurate opinions of the crowd despite the presence of contrary objective information. While peer judgement is a significant advantage, it should not undermine alternative sources of information. Rather, platforms should insist that each capital provider exercise his or her personal intuition to confront the opinions of peer leaders in their decision-making. The form that interactions need to take to enable this approach to information processing needs to be studied further. Moreover, community members considered as experts/leaders themselves need to interact with the less expert, since such interactions allow them to question their own opinions and any underlying arguments (Surowiecki, 2008). Research could be inspired by the study of Ola et al. (2022) which highlights the form that collective events take in the construction of individual thought in BA groups. Platforms may also pay attention to how the sophisticated investors can increase proximity with a project as they represent an important source of information.

Finally, in Europe, the new regulation that is due to come into force and which should allow nonprofessional investors to withdraw for a period of a few days may result in the benefits of ECF platforms being undermined to the detriment of the financing of entrepreneurial firms. This is another aspect that will also require further investigation into the contribution of the investor collective to the decision-making process of individual investors, professional or otherwise.

REFERENCES

Acs, Z., Song, A., Szerb, L., Audretsch, D., & Komlosi, E. (2021). The evolution of the global digital platform economy: 1971–2021, *Small Business Economics, 57*(4), pp. 1629–1659.

Akerlof, G. A. (1970). The market for 'lemons': Quality uncertainty and the market mechanism, *Quarterly Journal of Economics, 84*(3), pp. 488–500.

Alexy, O. T., Block, J. H., Sandner, P., & Ter Wal, A. L. (2012). Social capital of venture capitalists and start-up funding, *Small Business Economics, 39*(4), pp. 835–851.

Alharbey, M. & Van Hemmen, S. (2021). Investor intention in equity crowdfunding. Does trust matter? *Journal of Risk and Financial Management, 14*(2), pp. 53–73.

Ahlers, G. K., Cumming, D., Günther, C., & Schweizer, D. (2015). Signaling in equity crowdfunding, *Entrepreneurship Theory and Practice, 39*(4), pp. 955–980.

Amatucci, F. M. & Sohl, J. E. (2004). Women entrepreneurs securing business angel financing: Tales from the field, *Venture Capital, 6*(2/3), pp. 181–196.

Ang, J. (1992). On the theory of finance for privately held firms, *Journal of Small Business Finance, 1*(3), pp. 195–203.

Anglin, A. H., Short, J. C., Drover, W., Stevenson, R. M., McKenny, A. F., & Allison, T. H. (2018). The power of positivity? The influence of positive psychological capital language on crowdfunding performance, *Journal of Business Venturing, 33*(4), pp. 470–492.

Attuel-Mendes, L., Soulas, C., & Ola, A. M. (2020). Le paradoxe du crowdfunding: La sous-utilisation de la foule dans la fabrique de la décision individuelle d'investissement, *Systemes d'information management, 25*(1), pp. 89–121.

Belleflamme, P., Omrani, N., & Peitz, M. (2015). The economics of crowdfunding platforms, *Information Economics and Policy, 33*(3), pp. 11–28.

Berger, A. & Udell, G. (1998). The economics of small business finance: The roles of private equity and debt markets in the financial growth cycle, *Journal of Banking & Finance, 22*(6–8), pp. 613–673.

Bertoni, F., Bonini, S., Capizzi, V., Colombo, M. G., & Manigart, S. (2022). Digitization in the market for entrepreneurial finance: Innovative business models and new financing channels, *Entrepreneurship Theory and Practice, 46*(5), pp. 1120–1135.

Blaseg, D., Cumming, D., & Koetter, M. (2021). Equity crowdfunding: High-quality or low-quality entrepreneurs? *Entrepreneurship Theory and Practice*, *45*(3), pp. 505–530.

Block, J. H., Colombo, M. G., Cumming, D. J., & Vismara, S. (2018). New players in entrepreneurial finance and why they are there, *Small Business Economics*, *50*(2), pp. 239–250.

Brush, C. G., Edelman, L. F., & Manolova, T. S. (2012). Ready for funding? Entrepreneurial ventures and the pursuit of angel financing, *Venture Capital*, *14*(2–3), pp. 111–129.

Butticè, V. & Vismara, S. (2022). Inclusive digital finance: The industry of equity crowdfunding, *The Journal of Technology Transfer*, *47*(4), pp. 1224–1241.

Cardon, M. S., Mitteness, C., & Sudek, R. (2017). Motivational cues and angel investing: Interactions among enthusiasm, preparedness, and commitment, *Entrepreneurship Theory and Practice*, *41*(6), pp. 1057–1085.

Carpenter, R. E. & Petersen, B. C. (2002). Capital market imperfections, high-tech investment, and new equity financing, *The Economic Journal*, *112*(477), pp. F54–F72.

Cassar, G. (2004). The financing of business start-ups, *Journal of Business Venturing*, 19(2), pp. 261–283.

Clark, C. (2008). The impact of entrepreneurs' oral 'pitch' presentation skills on business angels' initial screening investment decision, *Venture Capital*, *10*(3), pp. 257–279.

Colombo, O. (2021). The use of signals in new-venture financing: A review and research agenda, *Journal of Management*, *47*(1), pp. 237–259.

Connelly, B., Certo, S. T., Ireland, R. D., & Reutzel, C. R. (2011). Signaling theory: A review and assessment, *Journal of Management*, *37*(1), pp. 39–67.

Cosh, A., Cumming, D., & Hughes, A. (2009). Outside entrepreneurial capital, *The Economic Journal*, *119*(540), pp. 1494–1533.

Croce, A., Ughetto, E., Bonini, S., & Capizzi, V. (2021). Gazelles, ponies, and the impact of business angels' characteristics on firm growth, *Journal of Small Business Management*, *59*(2), pp. 223–248.

Cumming, D., Hervé, F., Manthé, E., & Schwienbacher, A. (2022). Testing-the-waters policy with hypothetical investment: Evidence from equity crowdfunding, *Entrepreneurship Theory and Practice*, *46*(4), pp. 1019–1053.

Cumming, D., Johan, S., & Zhang, Y. (2018). Public policy towards entrepreneurial finance: Spillovers and the scale-up gap, *Oxford Review of Economic Policy*, *34*(4), pp. 652–675.

Cressy, R. (2002) Introduction: Funding gaps: A symposium, *Economic Journal*, *112*(477), pp.1–16.

Deffains-Crapsky, C. and Sudolska, A. (2014). Radical innovation and early-stage financing gaps: Equity based crowdfunding challenges, *Journal of Positive Management*, *5*(2), pp. 3–19.

Deffains-Crapsky C. & Daniel C. (2016). Quels modèles de gouvernance de la foule en Equity Crowdfunding? Le cas français, *Revue française de gouvernance d'entreprise*, 18, pp. 194-222.

Drover, W., Wood, M. S., & Zacharakis, A. (2017). Attributes of angel and crowdfunded investments as determinants of VC screening decisions, *Entrepreneurship: Theory and Practice*, *41*(3), pp. 323–347.

Duxbury, L., Haines J. R., G. H., & Riding, A. L. (1996). A personality profile of Canadian informal investors, *Journal of Small Business Management*, *34*(2), pp. 44–55.

Elsbach, K. D. & Kramer, R. M. (2003). Assessing creativity in Hollywood pitch meetings: Evidence for a dual-process model of creativity judgments, *Academy of Management Journal*, *46*(3), pp. 283–301.

Estrin, S., Gozman, D., & Khavul, S. (2018). The evolution and adoption of equity crowdfunding: Entrepreneur and investor entry into a new market, *Small Business Economics*, *51*(2), pp. 425–439.

Estrin, S., Khavul, S., & Wright, M. (2022). Soft and hard information in equity crowdfunding: Network effects in the digitalization of entrepreneurial finance, *Small Business Economics, 58*(4), pp. 1761–1781.

Feola, R., Vesci, M., Marinato, E., & Parente, R. (2021). Segmenting 'digital investors': Evidence from the Italian equity crowdfunding market, *Small Business Economics*, *56*(3), pp. 1235–1250.

Freear, J., Sohl, J. E., & Wetzel Jr,W. E. (1994). Angels and nonangels: Are there differences? *Journal of Business Venturing*, *9*(2), pp. 109–123.

Fried, V. H. & Hisrich, R. D. (1994). Toward a model of venture capital investment decision making, *Financial Management*, *23*(3), pp. 28–37.

Girard C., & Deffains-Crapsky C. (2016). Les mécanismes de gouvernance disciplinaires et cognitifs en Equity Crowdfunding: Le cas de la France, Finance Contrôle Stratégie, 19-3, pp. 1-17.

Goethner, M., Sebastian, L., & Regner, T. (2021). Crowdinvesting in entrepreneurial projects: Disentangling patterns of investor behavior, *Small Business Economics*, *57*(2), pp. 905–926.

Hornuf, L. & Schwienbacher, A. (2018). Market mechanisms and funding dynamics in equity crowd-funding, *Journal of Corporate Finance*, 50, pp. 556–574.

Harrer, T. & Owen, R. (2022). Reducing early-stage Cleantech funding gaps: An exploration of the role of Environmental Performance Indicators, *International Journal of Entrepreneurial Behavior & Research*, 28(9), pp. 268–288.

Huang, L. (2017). The role of investor gut feel in managing complexity and extreme risk, *Academy of Management Journal*, 61(5), pp. 1821–1847.

Huang, L. & Pearce, J. L. (2015), Managing the unknowable: The effectiveness of early-stage investor gut feel in entrepreneurial investment decisions, *Administrative Science Quarterly*, 60(4), pp. 634–670.

Huang, L. & Knight, A. P. (2017). Resources and relationships in entrepreneurship: An exchange theory of the development and effects of the entrepreneur-investor relationship, *The Academy of Management Review*, 42(1), pp. 80–102.

Jeffrey, S. A., Lévesque, M., & Maxwell, A. L. (2016). The non-compensatory relationship between risk and return in business angel investment decision making, *Venture Capital*, 18(3), pp. 189–209.

Johan, S. & Zhang, Y. (2020). Quality revealing versus overstating in equity crowdfunding, *Journal of Corporate Finance*, 65(C), pp. 101741.

Josefy M., Dean T. J., Albert L. S. & Fitza M. A. (2017). The role of community in crowdfunding success: Evidence on cultural attributes in funding campaigns to 'Save the Local Theater', *Entrepreneurship Theory and Practice*, 41(2), pp. 161–182.

Kleinert, S. & Volkmann, C. (2019). "Equity crowdfunding and the role of investor discussion boards", *Venture Capital*, 21(4), pp. 327–352.

Kleinert, S., Bafera, J., Urbig, D., & Volkmann, C. K. (2022). Access denied: How equity crowdfunding platforms use quality signals to select new ventures, *Entrepreneurship Theory and Practice*, 46(6), pp. 1626–1657.

Kleinert, S., Volkmann, C., & Grunhagen, M. (2020). Third-party signals in equity crowdfunding: The role of prior financing, *Small Business Economics*, 54(1), pp. 341–365.

Le Bon, G. (2009), *Psychologie des foules*, Le Monde Flammarion, Paris, (édition originale 1895).

Lehner, O. M. & Harrer, T. (2019). Crowdfunding revisited: A neo-institutional field-perspective, *Venture Capital*, 21(1), pp. 75–96.

Lerner, J. (2010). The future of public efforts to boost entrepreneurship and venture capital, *Small Business Economics*, 35, pp. 255–264.

Li, Y., Jiang, S., Long, D., Tang, H., & Wu, J. (2014). An exploratory study of business angels in China: A research note, *Venture Capital*, 16(1), pp. 69–83.

Liberti, J. M. & Petersen, M. A. (2018). Information: Hard and soft, *The Review of Corporate Finance Studies*, 8(1), pp. 1–41.

Loewenstein, G., Sunstein, C. R., & Golman, R. (2014). Disclosure: Psychology changes everything, *Annual Review of Economics*, 6(1), pp. 391–419.

Macmillan, I. C., Siegel, R., & Narasimha, P. N. S. (1985). Criteria used by venture capitalists to evaluate new venture proposals, *Journal of Business Venturing*, 1(1), pp. 119–128.

Mason, C. (2009). Business angels. In: *Encyclopaedia of entrepreneurship. Edward Elgar. (In Press)*. http://strathprints.strath.ac.uk/15915/

Mason, C., Botelho, T., & Harrison, R. (2019). The changing nature of angel investing: Some research implications, *Venture Capital*, 21(2–3), pp. 177–194.

Maxwell, A. L., Jeffrey, S. A., & Lévesque, M. (2011). Business angel early stage decision making, *Journal of Business Venturing*, 26(2), pp. 212–225.

McMullen, J. S.
& Shepherd, D. A. (2006). Entrepreneurial action and the role of uncertainty in the theory of the entrepreneur, *The Academy of Management Review*, 31(1), pp. 132–152.

Moritz, A., Block, J., & Lutz, E. (2015). Investor communication in equity-based crowdfunding: A qualitative-empirical study, *Qualitative Research in Financial Markets*, 7(3), pp. 309–342

Morris, M., Neumeyer, X., Jong, Y., & Kuratko, D. (2018). Distinguishing types of entrepreneurial Ventures: An identity-based perspective, *Journal of Small Business Management*, 56(3), pp. 453–474.

Morrissette, S. G. (2007). A profile of angel investors, *Journal of Private Equity*, 10(3), pp. 52–66.

Murnieks, C. Y., Cardon, M. S., Sudek, R., White, T. D., & Brooks, W. T. (2016). Drawn to the fire: The role of passion, tenacity and inspirational leadership in angel investing, *Journal of Business Venturing*, *31*(4), pp. 468–484.

OECD (2015), The Innovation Imperative. *Organisation for Economic Co-operation and Development*.

Ola, A. M., Deffains-Crapsky, C., & Dumoulin, R. (2019). Vers une nouvelle approche de l'investissement en amorçage: Un raisonnement à travers la théorie de l'alignement structurel, *Finance Contrôle Stratégie,* NS-5. https://doi.org/10.4000/fcs.3091

Ola, A. M., Deffains-Crapsky, C., & Dumoulin, R. (2022). Cognition collective et investissement en Early-stage: Le cas des groupes de business angels, *La Revue de l'Entreprneuriat, 21*(4), pp. 129–166.

Osnabrugge, M. (2000). A comparison of business angel and venture capitalist investment procedures: An agency theory-based analysis, *Venture Capital, 2*(2), pp. 91–109.

Paul, S., Whittam, G., & Wyper, J. (2007). Towards a model of the business angel investment process, *Venture Capital, 9*(2), pp. 107–125.

Packard, M. D., Clark, B. B., & Klein, P. G. (2017). Uncertainty types and transitions in the entrepreneurial process, *Organization Science, 28*(5), pp. 840–856.

Parhankangas, A. & Ehrlich, M. (2014). How entrepreneurs seduce business angels: An impression management approach, *Journal of Business Venturing, 29*(4), pp. 543–564.

Polzin, F., Toxopeus, H., & Stam, E. (2018). The wisdom of the crowd in funding: Information heterogeneity and social networks of crowdfunders, *Small Business Economics, 50*(2), pp. 251–273.

Rochet, J-C. & Tirole, J. (2003). Platform competition in two-sided markets, *Journal of the European Economic Association, 1*(4), pp. 990–1029.

Riding, A. L. (2008). Business angels and love money investors: Segments of the informal market for risk capital, *Venture Capital, 10*(4), pp. 355–369.

Shafi, K. (2021). Investors' evaluation criteria in equity crowdfunding, *Small Business Economics, 56*(1), pp. 3–37.

Shen, T., Ma, J., Zhang, B., Huang, W. & Fan, F. (2020). "I Invest by Following Lead Investors!" *The Role of Lead Investors in Fundraising Performance of Equity Crowdfunding, Frontiers in Psychology*, 11:632, pp. 1.9.

Shepherd, D. A. & DeTienne, D. R. (2005). Prior knowledge, potential financial reward, and opportunity identification, *Entrepreneurship Theory and Practice, 29*(1), pp. 91–112.

Shepherd, D. A. & Zacharakis, A. (1999). Conjoint analysis: A new methodological approach for researching the decision policies of venture capitalists, *Venture Capital, 1*(3), pp. 197–217.

Shepherd, D. A. Zacharakis, A., & Baron, R. A. (2003). VCs' decision processes: Evidence suggesting more experience may not always be better, *Journal of Business Venturing, 18*(3), pp. 381–401.

Smallbone, D., Baldock, R., and Burgess, S. (2002). Targeted support for high-growth start-ups: Some policy issues, *Environment and Planning C, 20*(2), pp. 195–209.

Spence, M. (1973). Job market signaling, *Quarterly Journal of Economics, 87*(3), pp. 355–374.

Stevenson, R. M., Ciuchta, M. P., Letwin, C. & Dinger, J. M. & Vancouver, J. B. (2019). "Out of control or right on the money? Funder self-efficacy and crowd bias in equity crowdfunding," Journal of Business Venturing, *34*(2), pp. 348-367

Sudek, R. (2006). Angel investment criteria, *Journal of Small Business Strategy, 17*(2 Fall/Winter), pp. 89–103.

Sudek, R., Mitteness, C. R., & Baucus, M. S. (2008). Betting on the horse or the jockey: The impact of expertise on angel investing. In *Academy of Management Proceedings*, No. 1, pp. 1–6.

Surowiecki J. (2008), *La sagesse des foules*, Jean-Claude Lattès, Paris.

Svetek, M. (2022). Signaling in the context of early-stage equity financing: Review and directions, *Venture Capital, 24*(1), pp. 71–104.

Tashiro, Y. (1999). Business angels in Japan, *Venture Capital, 1*(3), pp. 259–273.

Tiberius, V. & Hauptmeijer, R. (2021). Equity crowdfunding: Forecasting market development, platform evolution, and regulation, *Journal of Small Business Management, 59*(2), pp. 337–369.

Tomczak, A. & Brem, A. (2013). A conceptualized investment model of crowdfunding, *Venture Capital, 15*(4), pp. 335–359.

Ueda, M. (2004). Banks versus venture capital: Project evaluation, screening, and expropriation, *Journal of Finance, 59*(2), pp. 601–621.

Vismara, S. (2016). Equity retention and social network theory in equity crowdfunding, *Small Business Economics*, *46*(4), pp. 579–590.

Vismara, S. (2018a). *Signalling to overcome inefficiencies in crowdfunding markets.* In *The Economics of Crowdfunding,* edited by Cumming, D. & Hornuf, L., pp. 29–56, Palgrave Macmillan, Switzerland.

Vismara, S. (2018b). Information cascades among investors in equity crowdfunding, *Entrepreneurship Theory and Practice*, *42*(3), pp. 467–497.

Wallnöfer, M. & Hacklin, F. (2013). The business model in entrepreneurial marketing: A communication perspective on business angels' opportunity interpretation, *Industrial Marketing Management*, *42*(5), pp. 755–764.

Wiltbank, R., Read, S., Dew, N., & Sarasvathy, S. D. (2009). Prediction and control under uncertainty: Outcomes in angel investing, *Journal of Business Venturing*, *24*(2), pp. 116–133.

Wood, M. S., Long, A., & Artz, K. (2020). Angel investor network pitch meetings: The pull and push of peer opinion, *Business Horizons*, *63*(4), pp. 507–518.

Zacharakis, A. L. & Meyer, D. G. (1998). A lack of insight: Do venture capitalists really understand their own decision process? *Journal of Business Venturing*, *13*(1), pp. 57–76.

Zacharakis, A. L. & Shepherd, D. A. (2001). The nature of information and overconfidence on venture capitalists' decision making, *Journal of Business Venturing*, *16*(4), pp. 311–332.

Zhang, J. & Liu, P. (2012). Rational herding in microloan markets, *Management Science*, *58*(5), pp. 892–912.

PART IV

USING INFORMATION TO CONTROL AND MANAGE BEHAVIOUR

8. Development of costing systems as a process not outcome: a field study of Patient Level Information and Costing Systems (PLICS) in UK health care[1]

Christopher S. Chapman and Anja Kern

8.1 INTRODUCTION

The challenge of developing and implementing information systems is subject to a vast literature. In this chapter we approach it in relation to the further challenges presented in the area of developing costing systems since this is a task which brings distinctive technical and organisational challenges of its own. Development of information technology has led to increased practicality of adopting a more real-time approach to costing, for example, but conceptual concerns about when this might or might not be a good idea remain (for example, Cooper and Kaplan, 1998), and the issue has still received relatively little attention in the costing literature (cf. Wouters and Stecher, 2017, for a notable exception).

In considering why this might be, we begin by noting that there is still debate over conceptual concerns about how to treat costs (for example, Noreen and Soderstrom 1994, 1997; Foster and Gupta, 1990). This chapter proposes that a part of the explanation for this is that not only do costing systems face technical challenges such as errors (Christensen, 2010; Labro and Vanhoucke, 2007), but also they present organisational challenges since costing systems feed into many other control and performance evaluation systems and thus are centrally bound up with the politics of organisational priorities (for example, Laguecir et al., 2019).

This situation is further complicated by the growing literature that has emphasised the importance of involving non-accountants in cost system design (Eldenburg et al., 2010; Hoozeé and Bruggeman, 2010; Wouters and Wilderom, 2008; Wouters and Roijmans, 2010). This need arises because other organisational members have information that can be relevant for the costing system (as illustrated in the case study of Wouters and Stecher, 2017) requiring a 'data discovery process'; but also presents challenges, since it can be the case that cost system designers have insufficient knowledge about operational processes. It can also be the case that it is the decisions made by these non-accountants that are required in order to achieve benefits from costing data. Thus the ambition of articles such as Kaplan and Porter (2011) is not just to see a change in the form of calculation but also in patterns of thinking and collaboration through which organisational information is marshalled towards flexible but shared ends.

In this chapter we seek to contribute to our understanding of this challenge based on a field study undertaken in a high-performing and high-participation UK hospital. In doing so, we build on research about the participation of non-accountants in cost system design (Eldenburg et al., 2010; Wouters and Wilderom, 2008; Wouters and Roijmans, 2010; Wouters and Stecher, 2017).We find that there is a recursive process of making cost systems more accurate that transcends the data discovery problem of finding and drawing upon diverse sources of information scattered across organisational information systems. For whilst there are many such sources that can potentially be mobilised in costing activity, these often reside in systems designed and managed with very different purposes in mind, and so discussion between accountants and non-accountants can usefully bridge such conceptual gaps and highlight previously unseen patterns. This challenge therefore goes beyond the sourcing of correct cost data, such as estimates for activities in time-driven ABC (activity-based costing) approaches (for example, Hoozeé and Bruggeman, 2012; Scott et al., 2018).

Thus, non-accountants participating in cost system design increase accuracy and usability of costs for decision-making. But in achieving this, patterns presented prompt reflection on operational process which, in turn, can lead to reshaping services with the aim of improving efficiency and effectiveness. Undertaking such changes might well mean that assumptions or costing choices built into the system become obsolete, and so this requires further refinement of the cost system jointly between accountants and non-accountants. The implication is that cost systems may not be converging on some optimal level of error; rather, they might be in a continuous process of becoming accurate. This depends however on a constructive engagement in which the emphasis is on mutual learning, rather than fear of enforced compliance (for example, Hoozeé and Bruggeman, 2010).

This understanding has significant implications for designers and users of costing systems alike, since it suggests that traditional framing of cost system design and implementation may set up an unhelpful set of expectations around the participation of non-accountants in this ongoing process and the nature of support that might be required from those managing an organisation's information and information system support. This insight can be of particular importance in health care settings given concerns in many countries to engage clinicians in the cost effectiveness of health care (Chapman et al., 2022), coupled with the potentially antagonistic relationship that has been documented between clinicians and costing (for example, Fischer and Ferlie 2013; Kurunmäki 1999; Abernethy and Vagnoni 2004).

The remainder of the chapter is organised as follows. In the next section, we develop a model of the ongoing development of costing systems. We then explain our research design before presenting findings from the field and analysis before drawing some general conclusions.

8.2   DEVELOPING A MODEL OF THE DEVELOPMENT OF COSTING SYSTEMS

The role of the costing system as an information system is to produce costing information for specific purposes, such as accurate costs at the product or service level, to inform pricing or costs at the process level, in order to manage the efficiency of processes. The difficulty for cost system design is to model complex organisational arrangements within costing information and then, ultimately, to assign costs to specific products and specific processes. The cost system design choices have also been seen to depend upon the different purposes and contexts faced by firms (Labro and Vanhoucke, 2007; Callahan and Gabriel, 1998; Christensen and Demski, 1997; Labro and Stice-Lawrence, 2020).

This understanding emphasises the point that cost system design goes beyond producing a representation of the structure of the firm, but also requires consideration of specific managerial objectives (Thibodeau et al., 2007; Ittner and Larcker, 2001; Christensen, 2010). Far from being a neutral and objective representation, cost systems are tools to influence behaviour and decision-making (Brüggen et al., 2011; Hopwood, 1983; Ahrens and Chapman, 2007). Understanding the accuracy of a cost system therefore relies upon two main elements. First, a consideration of the material properties of the organisational processes, i.e. the relations between resources, organisational processes and outputs; and second, the managerial objectives of the firm. These two elements are interdependent, as the question of how to represent material properties of organisational processes depends also on the objectives of the firm. In other words, in order to produce accurate costs, cost system design must be aligned with material properties of organisational processes and their managerial objectives.

Accordingly, we define the accuracy of costs here as aligning cost system design with organisational processes, including the material properties of the processes and their managerial objectives. In practice this will be a dynamic recursive process. In order to help to structure our understanding of this, in the next section we build a simple theoretical model to help delineate two reciprocal dynamics of ongoing management activity which create a recursive process of cost system design: seeking to correct representations in the system which in turn leads to rethinking service delivery which in turn creates new misrepresentations.

Figure 8.1 presents the model of the process of producing accurate costs. The model consists of two reciprocal dynamics. The first dynamic describes one aspect of the process of making cost systems accurate: participation of clinicians in cost system design aligns cost systems and organisational processes, leading to an increased usability of cost data for decision-making. The second dynamic describes the simultaneous effect that increased usability of cost data for decision-making leads to misalignment of costs systems and organisational processes, triggering the participation of clinicians in cost system design. The remainder of this section provides theoretical analysis to support the model.

In complex operational contexts, cost system designers may not have sufficient knowledge about operations and must rely on the participation of non-accountants in cost system design. This is particularly the case for professional and service organisations such as hospitals. In many real-world situations, front-line clinical staff face change, risk and high uncertainty. Given this, service design and innovation cannot be neatly separated from actual production: a clinician may frequently change method or explore new methods if a patient does not respond well to a certain treatment. This leads to an unpredictable relationship between outputs (patient outcomes) and inputs (patient treatments) for many patient conditions (for example, Ahern, 1993). This technical challenge for cost system design is amplified by the wide range of services generally provided in public hospitals.

Participation allows integrating expert knowledge about organisational processes into the cost system (Wouters and Wilderom, 2008; Wouters and Roijmans, 2010; Eldenburg et al., 2010). This allows relevant tacit knowledge to be considered in the cost system design (Wouters and Roijmans, 2010). Such knowledge concerns both the material properties of the organisational processes and the managerial objectives linked with them. Participation of non-accountants in cost system design thus enhances alignment of cost system design and organisational processes.

An important characteristic of alignment is that it is a collaborative and ongoing process. The knowledge of non-accountants is translated by the cost system designers, i.e. the management accountant, in cost vocabulary such as cost pools or cost drivers. Wouters and Roijmans (2010) show that this process can benefit from the experiment with prototypes. Through prototypes users can experiment to use the data and refine alignment during the experimentation stage.

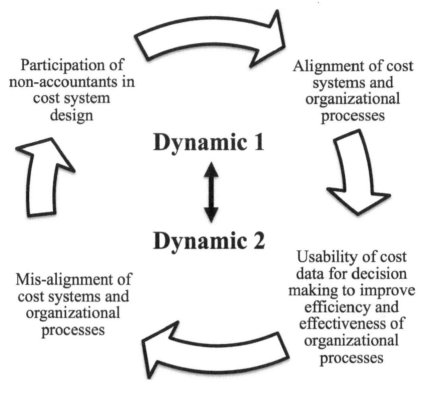

Figure 8.1   The ongoing cost system development process

Pizzini (2006) observes in her study that cost-system functionality had not been successfully introduced into clinical management in some hospitals. A central limitation undermining perceived usefulness was the failure of the cost system to present a detailed understanding of the nature of the entities in the cost system. Instead, it is thought that the classification of costs in strictly accounting terms such as direct and indirect or the hope that the discipline of frequent reporting and or standard costing and variance analysis would be sufficient. These latter attributes of cost system design were found not to influence outcomes (Pizzini, 2006).

On the other hand, accounting systems are perceived as being useful when they address the needs of operational managers (Wouters and Roijmans, 2010). For example, Eldenburg et al. (2010) describe how non-accountants in a hospital were involved in designing the information collection method to identify activities and track resources. The information provided by non-accounting staff leads to a new cost system design with new cost pools and drivers. This also leads to a redesign of monthly reports. An additional report is edited to enable physicians to evaluate the impact of clinical decision-making on costs detailing financial performance, teaching, and research activities, and the amount of revenues from patient treatment. These new reports allowed physicians to better understand how their clinical activities were linked with financial outcomes. Most importantly this study finds evidence that such participation and increased usability of accounting information leads to increased financial performance. Alignment of cost systems and organisational processes then does not only increase usability, but also financial performance.

This confirms empirical studies on the effect of costing systems. Ittner et al. (2002) find evidence that 'the relation between ABC and financial performance varies with the extent to which the decision to use ABC "matches" the plant's operational characteristics'. This is consistent with evidence in the health care sector that, if the process of embedding cost systems is coordinated with organisational context, it has a positive impact on financial performance (Thibodeau et al., 2007). Cost systems increase financial performance when they are embedded in organisational processes and used for operational decision-making (Banker et al., 2008; Maiga and Jacobs, 2008l; Da Silva and Gago, 2020). The impact of cost systems on financial performance is therefore not direct, but indirect via operational performance.

Consequently, we formulate dynamic 1:

Dynamic 1: *Participation of clinicians in cost system design aligns cost systems and organisational processes, leading to an increased usability of cost data for decision-making to increase the efficiency and effectiveness of organisational processes.*

During their use, accounting systems are regularly redesigned (Henri, 2010; Hopwood, 1987). An important reason behind such redesign stems from misalignment of cost systems and organisational processes. As managerial decisions concerning organisational processes are taken, this can lead to a redesign of organisational processes resulting in a misalignment of cost systems and organisational processes. Reducing such misalignment requires the participation of non-accountants.

Wouters and Roijmans (2010) describe how non-accountants and accountants participate in designing a performance measurement system (PMS) in a logistics department of a manufacturing company. In the design process organisational members experiment with a prototype of the PMS. In this experimentation organisational members use data to analyse operational processes of transportation services. Using the data, they become aware of discrepancies between transportation times and driver time which should theoretically be the same. They find that this difference is due to legal resting times of the drivers. Further experimentation with the data leads to exploring which times are invoiced and if resting times are invoiced. The discovery of this misalignment requires close collaboration between the organisational members of the contract, invoicing, and operational processes. This creates new knowledge about the organisational processes, which informs the construction of the new accounting information.

If the cost system is seen to offer usable data, then while seeking to use the data, further misalignments are discovered and opportunities for refinement of both cost system design and organisational processes will likely present themselves, leading to dynamic 2:

Dynamic 2: *Increased usability of cost data for decision-making leads to misalignment of costs systems and organisational processes, thus triggering the participation of clinicians in cost system design initiating dynamic 1 processes.*

The relation between user participation in cost system design, alignment of costs and organisational processes, usability for decision-making and misalignment is therefore circular. Most importantly this circular relation points out that specification and management of costs are linked. For example, the question of what a relevant error is, how to define accurateness and economically relevant costs must be seen in relation to the context in which these terms operate, for example, the managerial objectives.

8.3   RESEARCH DESIGN

Given our interest in the dynamics of cost system design we undertook a field study in a UK hospital[2] between December 2010 and July 2011. Based on exploratory fieldwork undertaken in several other UK hospitals (Chapman and Kern, 2010) together with existing theory, we presented in the last section a model of the process of developing accurate cost systems. The role of the theoretical model developed in the previous section is to help structure our understanding of the process of cost system design in the field setting. The model is then confronted in the next section with data collected in the field study to help provide a plausible and theory consistent account of the field (Ahrens and Chapman, 2006).

The field study was carried out in a purposefully selected hospital, which had implemented a patient level costing more than 18 months prior to our study, in which there was a commitment of clinicians, managers and accountants to use cost systems for operational management and which had relatively good organisational performance.[3] This theoretical approach to sampling was essential given our objective of studying and elaborating the process of how accurate cost systems are developed.

Process theories aim at providing 'explanations in terms of the sequence of events leading to an outcome' (Langley 1999, p. 692). Process data brings with it challenges in terms of complexity and volume of data. Specific strategies support the task of identifying empirical regularities and understanding the 'generative mechanisms' that are driving them (Langley, 1999; Tsoukas, 1989). Using the model as a visual map of the process allows us to analyse the sequence of events and their circular relation. As we confront the model with data collected in the field study, each element of the process map is enriched with field data. The 'contextual detail in the narrative will allow the reader to judge the transferability of the ideas to other situations' (Langley 1999, p. 695). The discipline of the theoretical model is an essential support to the articulation of knowledge arising from our fieldwork that achieves a level of generality (Ahrens and Chapman, 2006).

Following the granting of ethical approval for this case study,[4] we relied on three data collection methods: observations of meetings, documents and presentations used in the case organisation and interviews with organisational members. Observations and internal documents from archives constitute evidence from real-life context of the phenomenon under study and provide a direct understanding of how the members of the organisation sought to define and carry out their tasks. This contrasts, but also complements, interviews, in which the researcher guides and questions and therefore may focus the orientation of the interview. Interviews were undertaken by one of the authors using a semi-structured interview protocol (see Appendix for interview guide) relating to cost system design and use of costing information. All interviews were recorded and subsequently transcribed. Meetings were recorded and transcribed where possible. For all observations and interviews detailed field notes were also taken. Details on the specifics of the field research in the case company may be found in Tables 8.1, 8.2 and 8.3 below.

In seeking to put together the field material and analysis in the section that follows, we undertook an iterative analysis and review of both meeting and interview transcripts alongside gathered archival material. The intention was to select excerpts that effectively convey the dynamics and motivations of organisational members' interactions in ways that illuminate the interest and limitations of the theoretical model derived in the previous section of the chapter (Ahrens and Chapman, 2006). Whilst the field excerpts have been chosen in relation to our

Table 8.1   *Interviews*

Date	Recording time	Interviewee
2.12	29 M 53 S	Physician 1
2.12	55 M 42 S	Physician 2
31.1	39 M 25 S	Physician 3
31.1	42 M 12 S	Physician 4
31.1	32 M 29 S	Physician 5
2.12	35 M 58 S	Accountant 1
2.12	54 M 22 S	Accountant 2
2.12	28 M 36 S	Manager 1
2.12	60 M 35 S	Manager 2
2.12	17 M 22 S	Manager 3
2.12	22 M 40 S	Manager 4
31.1	109 M 19 S	Accountant 2
31.1	17 M 47 S	Accountant 3
1.3	19 M 51 S	Accountant 4
16.3	25 M 15 S	Manager 5

Table 8.2   *Observations*

Date	Observation time	Title of meeting	Description
31.1	51 M 45 S	Performance meeting at service line level	Meeting 1: Meeting at service line level to discuss latest service-line reporting (SLR) report. Participants: Physician 6, Senior technician, Accountant 2, Manager 1, Physician 7
31.1	82 M 47 S	Performance meeting at hospital level	Meeting 2: Meeting at hospital level to discuss the development of service-line management (SLM). In particular how to design performance reports to engage clinicians. Participants: Physician 8, Manager 3, Accountant 2, Manager 1
1.3	60 M (not recorded)	Internal costing training	Meeting 3: Internal training session of PLICS/SLR
1.3	60 M (not recorded)	Executive board meeting	Meeting 4: Monthly board meeting at executive level. Head of PLICS/SLR team presents performance report which is subsequently discussed by board members
27.6	45 M (not recorded)	Executive board meeting	Meeting 5: Monthly board meeting at executive level. Head of PLICS/SLR team presents performance report which is subsequently discussed by board members
4.7	30 M	Performance meeting at service line level	Meeting 6: Meeting at service line level to discuss latest SLR report
			Participants: Accountant 2, Physician 2, Head nurse and manager 1

theoretical model, care and attention has been given to guarding against the suppression of potentially inconvenient evidence gathered. This analytical interplay and tension between elements of field evidence gathered is frequently called triangulation.

The final stage in the engagement with the field was a presentation of the theoretical model and field material excerpts and analysis to both the executive board of the hospital and to a group of participants in the interviews and observations. This took place in June 2011.

Table 8.3   *Documents*

Date received	Document title	Description	Source
1.12	SLM Project Overview	Document on the introduction of SLM in the hospital. It consists of a summary of objectives and different steps on how to transform SLR to SLM within the hospital. This document was drafted by the PLICS/SLR team and presented to the hospital board	
1.12	SLM Progress Report 1	Report on the progress of SLM introduction. This document summarises the progress towards the objectives outlined initially. It was drafted by the PLICS/SLR team and was presented to the hospital board, 2 months after initiating SLM project	Accountant 2
1.12	SLR Issues	Issues which arose during the SLM introduction and solutions on how to solve them. Presentation of the PLICS/SLR manager to other members of the hospital	Accountant 2
1.12	SLM Progress Report 2	Report on the progress of SLM introduction. It summarises the progress towards the objectives outlined initially. This document was drafted by the SLR/PLICS team and presented to the hospital board, 6 months after first report	Accountant 2
1.12	SLM Monthly Report	Monthly SLR report at hospital level with main performance key figures and action points. This document was drafted by the PLICS/SLR team and presented by the head of PLICS/SLR to the board	Accountant 2
28.1	Clinician Presentation SLR	SLR presentation of a senior clinician to colleagues from his respective Royal College. The presentation has the objective to explain to other clinicians how to transform SLR into a useful tool for management of clinical practice (how to turn it into SLM)	Physician 3
28.1	Capacity Work Plan	This document is a capacity assessment for a specific service line based on PLICS data. It calculates the current excess capacity for a certain procedure. It was made by the PLICS/SLR team for use at the hospital and service line level	Accountant 2
28.1	Activity Planner 1	This document is an excel table. It contains a planner for the activity of certain procedures. Its objective is to analyse the impact of activity variation on costs and revenue. The planner is based on historic data. It was made by the PLICS/SLR team for use at the hospital and service line level	Accountant 2
28.1	SLR Presentation Hospital Board	Presentation of the SLR/PLICS team to the hospital board on how SLR can be used for strategic decision-making	Accountant 2
28.1	Activity Planner 2	This document is an excel table. It contains a planner for the activity of certain procedures. Its objective is to analyse the impact of activity variation on costs and revenue. The planner is based on historic data. It was made by the PLICS/SLR team for use at the hospital and service line level	Accountant 2
28.1	Business Case	This document contains a detailed business case to support the introduction of a new technology	Manager 4
		The business case is based on PLICS data. It was presented to the hospital board. This document was drafted by the performance manager of the service line	

Date received	Document title	Description	Source
4.7	Performance Review	Performance review	Accountant 2
15.7	Performance Report	Report on the performance of a service line 2: costs and revenue for diagnostic catheter procedure	Accountant 2
15.7	Performance Report	Report on the performance of a service line 2: analysis of patient level data for three selected patients	Accountant 2

8.4   FIELD STUDY EVIDENCE AND ANALYSIS

8.4.1   Episode 1

Speaking participants in meeting 1:
A2: Accountant 2
ST: Senior technician (clinical staff)
P6: Physician 6

A2:   … for ICD [one type of clinical procedure] we have had 89 patients. For pacing [a related clinical procedure] we had 169 patients, okay. And I tried to match between [the inventory management] and your register [Clinician maintained records], okay, and I did that exercise. What I found was, these patients were not found in [consumption report of our inventory management software], they were found in the register, they were not found in [our inventory management software]. The total is about 8 patients of ICD and 8 patients of pacing.

ST: I think I know what is happening there. We've got two pacing theatres but only one has cabinets [run by inventory management software]. So if you work in theatre B, the doctor could say to you, I don't know whether I would want to put a [a brand name for a device] in or a [a brand name of another device] in…so the technician goes to the theatre cabinet takes both [devices] under the patient's name and I think they are not returning the unused to the cabinet. I think they take out multiple devices to cover every eventuality but not returning devices to the cabinet under the proper patient name…

P6:   So we assign double device costs on some patients, is that what you're saying?

A2:   Yeah. Device costs were wrong… So that is what I'm coming to…

P6:   Okay. So, we've just got to make sure they go back on this…

     […]

A2:   Right, okay, he's the Technical Director of… […]the inventory management system, you know, […]What he says is, he has written a sort of software, which checks the anomalies within the system, […]and he's going to send weekly that list to key people and then they can go and correct the data.

     […]

P6:   So that is what is going to happen, that should reduce this kind… [of problems]

ST: But what I've ordered as well, to make it easier, I've ordered a scanner so they can scan…

A2:   But until… Until… Until… Can I request you one thing? Until that is being done, can you ask somebody to check within the register on this?

ST: No, it's too time consuming for the technicians at the moment. I can't do that. I haven't got the time to sit and do that sort of check, what's been taken out of the cupboards, because have you seen the […] lists [of the inventory management]? They're just ridiculous…

P6:   What we'll do is speak to everyone and say, you must put them back. […]

The central point of discussion here arises from the fact that a cabinet for devices was placed in one theatre, but not the other. This mundane fact leads to distortions in reported costs at the patient level. The nature of activity in the theatre without a cabinet means that patients are assigned an average rather than the actual device consumption. Further, more devices than actually consumed are assigned. As device costs per patient represent several thousand pounds and vary considerable among different sorts of devices, this leads to distortions in what should in principle be direct costs.

Accountant 2, responsible for the cost system design, discovers this distortion which is caused by a misalignment between actual costs and costs in the cost system. He discovers it when comparing numbers and patients from the record produced by clinicians and from the inventory management software, which feeds into the cost system. There is a difference between the costs in the system and the actual costs. Cost system and organisational processes are not aligned.

While Accountant 2 discovers this misalignment, he has no explanation for it. It is only with the combined knowledge of the clinical staff that an explanation for this misalignment can be found. The participation of clinical staff is essential for identifying the origin of the misalignment between actual costs and costs reported in the cost system.

Organisational members subsequently consider ways to decrease this misalignment. Again, the participation of clinical staff is important to align cost systems and organisational processes. Which solution is chosen depends on the feasibility in terms of time and resources in the operating theatre, as well as in the accounts team and data recording infrastructure. It also becomes clear that identifying a misalignment, and even identifying possible solutions to reduce it, does not resolve the problem immediately. It takes time to implement solutions to align cost systems and operational processes. Also, this example shows how cost data depends on other sources of operational data, here the inventory management system. This episode emphasises the processual, collaborative and interconnected dimension of aligning cost systems and operational processes.

The process of aligning cost systems and operational processes increases not only the usability of cost data, but it also leads to identifying inefficiencies linked with the misalignment. The fact that the inventory management system was not up to date led to problems in the management of orders: if items are placed in the cupboards without updating the inventory system, staff order items too early. This in turn leads to too many items on the inventory and creates problems for the management.

Other inefficiencies linked with this misalignment were the resources used to perform the inventory count. Accountant 2 compared the actual inventory with the inventory in the inventory management system and had to rectify differences. If inventory count is a necessary feature of all inventory management, using the resources of an accountant to perform it is not efficient. Also, if there is an ongoing misalignment between the inventory management system and the actual inventory this raises the question about the return on investment of the system.

To summarise, alignment in this episode goes beyond correcting a misreported figure and thereby making cost data more usable. Indeed, as cost systems and organisational processes are misaligned, inefficiencies are revealed. The process of alignment does then not only correct a misreported figure, but it makes processes more efficient. Further the episode shows that the process of alignment is an organisational challenge. Indeed, it requires not only considering the knowledge of non-accountants who are directly involved in operations, but also managing organisational processes, to change them to improve their efficiency. Hence alignment between cost systems and organisational processes is an ongoing process striving to improve efficiency.

8.4.2   Episode 2

Speaking participants in meeting 2:
P8: Physician 8
A2: Accountant 2

P8:   Can you provide an update on one of the comments I made previously when I saw an iteration of this work on the Consultant Allocated Costs [report of the costing system], there was a real gap in that if a Consultant did one case in a day and went on till three in the afternoon, and a second case wasn't done, then they showed the costs for the one case and not the opportunity lost costs because they didn't do two cases in a day, and that is an unfair reflection on the productivity of a consultant if you don't include the lost opportunity in that, and that was something we've asked...

A2:   It'll be, this has been approached in a different way, slightly different, it may not satisfy your question in full but I'll tell you what I am doing, I have divided the theatre costs, total cost of the content of the theatre as in the case of a surgeon to reflect with their job plan; like we have so many theatres and so many surgeons to operate, to utilise the theatre. The sessions are allocated to each in turn, they have got to find patients if not the patient that the authority found has to share the costs, so if you consider in the whole year or in a period of time, consultants having equal theatre sessions allocated to them through their job plan and the theatre schedule, the total costs allocated for these patients will be distinctive [...]

The physician in this meeting excerpt had demanded a modification of the cost system design. He wants the cost system to better reflect how he judges and evaluates physicians. His demand is a proposition to improve the alignment between cost system design and organisational processes. The initial design of the costing system followed closely the guidance of the costing standards (DH, 2011). In this guidance there is a strong emphasis on the use of cause-and-effect cost drivers, in the case of operating theatres this equates to 'cut' time.

The physician demands a modification to take into account capacity. This is a sophisticated intervention, not an initial one, since it requires the physician to have taken on board enough of the meaning of the nature of the accounting system to begin to propose the new interactions between system design, operational process and motivational effect. The alignment concerns the integration of his managerial objectives in cost system design.

Subsequently the physician had another request linked to a misalignment. His objective was to use the cost data for physician appraisals in his service. But to make the data more usable for the appraisals he wanted to add a measure to integrate the complexity of patients in the cost data. Not considering the complexity of patients in the cost figures represented for him a misalignment of cost system and organisational processes. To achieve alignment, the physician, the manager responsible for cost system design and the quality manager decide to integrate specific clinical measures such as the EuroSCORE[5] in the cost figures.

To sum up, when cost systems are used for operational management, aligning cost systems with operational processes requires considering specific managerial objectives such as the management of capacity and clinical quality. As cost data is used for decision-making, objectives evolve, and cost systems need to be realigned. As the managerial objectives include quality standards as well as efficiency gains, the costs system must reflect these objectives. It is ongoing designing of the system in this way which increases alignment and thus the accuracy of costs and enables to manage effectiveness and efficiency of the processes.

8.4.3   Episode 3

Speaking participants in meeting 6:
A2: Accountant 2
P2: Physician 2

A2:   Right, […], here is my answer, first I learned that in this particular service line, […] we do something like 158 cases every month so we may have to look at one month and then I'll have more confidence and then we can look at it. So, out of this 158 cases for this particular procedure which is coming in as simple catheter, they made a loss of £108,000 and what I see is when I am alerted, they all seem to be in the same ballpark so we can go to the next thing, there's no difference between [physicians] there. If you go by elective, non-elective and non-elective and emergency what I find is again it is spread equally, the losses, … I found 20 episodes there, we seem to have used some of the items that is used for [treatments], the items like I recognise as pressure wire, guide wire and radial sheath and…

P2:   Just a point, the six-inch radial sheath [can also be used for diagnosis not only for treatment].

A2:   Maybe, […] maybe I'm wrong. What I am trying to say here is: are these really simply catheter cases? […]

P2:   Well it could be the coding, but the coding will probably be for pressure wire …[…]

A2:   We need to look at it…

In this meeting (meeting 6) organisational members use cost data to understand why certain services are lossmaking. The hospital expects service line 2 to be making profit, but it turns out to be a lossmaker. The discussion in the meeting revealed that there are two types of interventions: simple diagnostic catheter interventions and treatment interventions. The latter are more costly as expensive devices are implanted. In some cases, patients who were scheduled for a diagnostic procedure receive also a treatment, even if such treatment was initially not foreseen. While expensive devices were implanted in the heart, the procedure stayed coded as a simple diagnostic procedure in the system and therefore less revenue is received. When

Table 8.4   Comparative analysis of profit(loss) – archival document 14

	Patient 1	Patient 2	Patient 3
Performed in separate sessions	£ 704.62	£ 1,079.32	£ (389.00)
Performed in the same session	£ 808.61	£ 1,145.32	£ (241.49)
Benefit of same session approach	£ 103.99	£ 66.00	£ 147.51

becoming aware of this misalignment between costs in the cost system and actual costs, the physicians improved their description of the intervention. Subsequently this led to improved coding and thus more revenue.

In subsequent meetings this led to a discussion about the organisation of clinical practice. Physicians became aware that if they treated the patient in two separate procedures this would generate additional revenue: revenue for diagnostics and revenue for treatment. If done as one procedure they only receive revenue for treatment. Basing their economic reasoning on income logic, physicians adopted an unofficial rule: it is preferable to perform diagnostics and treatment separately as this generates additional income for the hospital. Clinical practice was aligned to the income logic.

The adoption of this unofficial rule was, however, challenged by Accountant 2. When analysing cases of patients, who came separately for diagnostics and treatment, he pointed out that the hospital would in fact end up with a higher profit when performing the procedures (diagnostics and treatment) at once. Table 8.4 compares the profit/loss for three patients of the reporting month when procedures were performed separately and at once.

Performing procedures separately did not generate a higher total profit. Instead, it was more advantageous for the hospital to carry out procedures at once if possible. There was thus a misalignment between actual costs and the economic reasoning of the physicians based on income logic. Physicians analysing Table 8.4 then aligned their economic reasoning with the evidence and explored new ways of carrying out clinical practice. If it was more advantageous to carry out both procedures at the same time, the schedules for the interventions should have spare capacity (in terms of time) so that physicians can perform both diagnostic and treatment if it is possible.

To sum up, this episode provides evidence that aligning cost systems and organisational processes is going beyond data quality issues. What started with an issue of data quality, i.e. miscoded clinical procedures, turned into an issue of improving the efficiency and effectiveness of clinical processes. Further this episode supports that the process of alignment is ongoing when using cost systems to improve efficiency and effectiveness.

8.5   CONCLUSION

Producing accurate costing systems is both a technical and organisational challenge. Based on our analysis of the literature and fieldwork undertaken in the UK health care sector, we develop a model on the process of developing accurate cost systems. Consistent with our theoretical model, participation of non-accountants in cost system design is necessary to identify and correct misalignments and make costs more accurate. Cost data is not only made more accurate and therefore more usable for non-accountant decision-making however, but also new perspectives on efficiency and effectiveness gains are made visible. This is consistent with dynamic 1. Increased usability leads to new perspectives on organisational processes and on costs system accuracy, underlining thus the limitations of current approaches to capturing and analysing operational and cost data. The result may be understood as the discovery of further misalignments, which in turn require the participation of clinicians in cost system design. This confirms dynamic 2.

Firstly, we seek to contribute to the literature on the process of cost system design. While previous literature finds that the participation of both accounting and non-accounting knowledge is needed to increase the usability of cost data (Wouters and Roijmans, 2010; Eldenburg et al., 2010), we add to the literature by providing evidence that this process of making cost data more accurate through the participation of non-accountants can be ongoing during the use of the system with no necessary end point at which further refinement offers insufficient value. The implication is that a neat separation between design and implementation of costing systems is not appropriate in certain sectors. Cost system design in complex settings where operational processes frequently require redesign as they are performed, as seen in our field study, requires the continuous evolution of the design of the cost system. Therefore, we contribute to a reconceptualisation of cost system design both on a theoretical and practical level.

Secondly, this study seeks to contribute to the literature on cost system errors, confirming that errors due to misalignments between organisational processes and the cost system have an important role in the cost system design process (Christensen, 2010). Organisational members are key actors to reduce misalignments between cost systems and organisational processes. Their knowledge contributes to identifying misalignments and their origin and finding solutions for alignment. Our study suggests that identifying and correcting errors is, itself, an ongoing process, which has the potential not only of reducing misalignments and thus increasing the accuracy of cost systems, but also of achieving efficiency and effectiveness gains.

NOTES

1. We gratefully acknowledge the constructive comments of the following individuals on earlier versions of this chapter: David Dugdale, Joan Luft, Wim van de Stede, Sally Widener, Marc Wouters.
2. The UK offers an institutional context that reinforces the use of management accounting tools at the clinical level. In the UK context public hospitals underwent a major change in terms of funding and governance involving the implementation of new costing systems to produce more accurate data at the clinical level.
3. The hospital selected has more than 200 beds, more than ten service lines. It is known for high clinical quality and care quality and has experienced a significant increase in profit recently. In contrast to many US hospitals, clinicians are all employed by the hospital and are paid based on a fixed monthly salary.
4. REC Reference Number 09/H0718/67 under the UK National Research Ethics Service.
5. EuroSCORE (European System for Cardiac Operative Risk Evaluation) is a risk model which allows the calculation of the risk of death after a heart operation.

REFERENCES

Abernethy, M. A., and E. Vagnoni. (2004). Power, organization design, and managerial behaviour. *Accounting, Organizations and Society* 29 (3–4):207–225.
Ahern, M. (1993). The softness of medical production and implications for specifying hospital outputs. *Journal of Economic Behavior & Organization* 20 (3):281–294.

Ahrens, T., and C. S. Chapman. (2006). Doing qualitative accounting research: Positioning data to contribute to theory. *Accounting, Organizations and Society* 31 (8):819–841.

Ahrens, T., and C. S. Chapman. (2007). Management accounting as practice. *Accounting, Organizations and Society* 32 (1–2):1–27.

Brüggen, A., R. Krishnan, and K. L. Sedatole. (2011). Drivers and consequences of short-term production decisions: Evidence from the auto industry. *Contemporary Accounting Research* 28 (1):83–123.

Callahan, C. M., and E. A. Gabriel. (1998). The differential impact of accurate product cost information in imperfectly competitive markets: A theoretical and empirical investigation. *Contemporary Accounting Research* 15 (4):419–455.

Chapman, C. S., and A. Kern. (2010). Costing in the National Health Service: From reporting to managing: Chartered Institute of Management Accountants.

Chapman, C. S., A. Kern, A. Laguecir, N. Algele-Halgand, G. Doyle, A. Hansen, F. Hartman, C. Mateus, P. Perego, V. Winter, and W. Quentin. (2022). Managing quality of cost information in clinical costing: Evidence across seven countries. *Journal of Public Budgeting, Accounting and Financial Management* 34 (2):310–329.

Christensen, J. (2010). Accounting errors and errors of accounting. *The Accounting Review* 85 (6):1827–1838.

Christensen, J., and J. Demski. (1997). Product costing in the presence of endogenous subcost functions. *Review of Accounting Studies* 2 (1):65–87.

Cooper, R., and R. S. Kaplan. (1998). The promise – and peril – of integrated cost systems. *Harvard Business Review* (July/August):109–119.

DH, D. o. H. (2011). Acute Health-Clinical Costing Standards 2011/2012, edited by D. o. Health. Bristol: HFMA.

Eldenburg, L., N. Soderstrom, V. Willis, and A. Wu. (2010). Behavioral changes following the collaborative development of an accounting information system. *Accounting, Organizations and Society* 35 (2):222–237.

Ferreira Da Silva, A., B. Fernandez-Feijoo, and S. Gago. (2020). Accounting information tools in managerial clinical service decision-making processes: Evidence from Portuguese public hospitals. *International Public Management Journals* 23 (4):535–563.

Fischer, M. D., and E. Ferlie. (2013). Resisting hybridisation between modes of clinical risk management: Contradiction, contest and the production of intractable conflict. *Accounting, Organizations and Society* 38 (1):30–49.

Foster, G., and M. Gupta. (1990). Manufacturing overhead cost driver analysis. *Journal of Accounting and Economics* 12 (1–3):309–337.

Henri, J.-F. (2010). The periodic review of performance indicators: An empirical investigation of the dynamism of performance measurement systems. *European Accounting Review* 19 (1):73–96.

Hoozeé, S., and W. Bruggeman. (2010). Identifying operational improvements during the design process of a time-driven ABC system: The role of collective worker participation and leadership style. *Management Accounting Research* 21 (3):185–198.

Hoozeé, S., and W. Bruggeman. (2012). The impact of refinement on the accuracy of time-driven ABC. *Abacus* 48 (4):439–472.

Hopwood, A. G. (1983). On trying to study accounting in the contexts in which it operates. *Accounting, Organizations and Society* 8 (2–3):287–305.

Hopwood, A. G. (1987). The archeology of accounting systems. *Accounting, Organizations and Society* 12 (3):207–234.

Ittner, C. D., and D. F. Larcker. (2001). Assessing empirical research in managerial accounting: A value-based management perspective. *Journal of Accounting and Economics* 32 (1–3):349–410.

Ittner, C. D., W. Lanen, and D. F. Larcker. (2002). The association between activity-based costing and manufacturing performance. *Journal of Accounting Research* 40 (3):711–726.

Kaplan, R. S., and M. Porter. (2011). How to solve the cost crisis in healthcare. *Harvard Business Review* (September):47–64.

Kurunmäki, L. (1999). Professional vs financial capital in the field of health care – struggles for the redistribution of power and control. *Accounting, Organizations and Society* 24 (2):95–124.

Labro, E., and L. Stice-Lawrence. (2020). Updating accounting systems: Longitudinal evidence from the healthcare sector. *Management Science* 66 (12):6042–6061.

Labro, E., and M. Vanhoucke. (2007). A simulation analysis of interactions among errors in costing systems. *The Accounting Review* 82 (4):939–962.

Laguecir, A., C. S. Chapman, and A. Kern. (2019). Profitability calculations under trial of strength: Insights into intra-accounting variation in a social housing organization. *Accounting, Auditing and Accountability Journal* 33 (4):727–751.

Langley, A. (1999). Strategies for theorizing from process data. *The Academy of Management Review* 24 (4):691–710.

Noreen, E., and N. Soderstrom. (1994). Are overhead costs strictly proportional to activity? Evidence from hospital departments. *Journal of Accounting and Economics* 17 (1–2):255–278.

Noreen, E., and N. Soderstrom. (1997). The accuracy of proportional cost models: Evidence from hospital service departments. *Review of Accounting Studies* 2 (1):89–114.

Pizzini, M. J. (2006). The relation between cost-system design, manager's evaluations of the relevance and usefulness of cost data, and financial performance: An empirical study of US hospitals. *Accounting, Organizations and Society* 31 (2):179–210.

Scott, D. J., E. Labro, C. T. Penrose, M. P. Bolognesi, S. S. Wellman, & R. C. Mather III. (2018). The impact of electronic medical record implementation on labor cost and productivity at an outpatient orthopaedic clinic. *Journal of Bone & Joint Surgery* 100 (18), 1549–1556.

Thibodeau, N., J. H. Evans III, N. J. Nagarajan, and J. Whittle. (2007). Value creation in public enterprises: An empirical analysis of coordinated organizational changes in the veterans health administration. *Accounting Review* 82 (2):483–520.

Tsoukas, H. (1989). The validity of idiographic research explanations. *The Academy of Management Review* 14 (4):551–561.

Wouters, M., and D. Roijmans. (2010). Using prototypes to induce experimentation and knowledge integration in the development of enabling accounting information. *Contemporary Accounting Research* 28 (2):708–736

Wouters, M., and C. Wilderom. (2008). Developing performance-measurement systems as enabling formalization: A longitudinal field study of a logistics department. *Accounting, Organizations and Society* 33 (4–5):488–516.

Wouters, M., and J. Stecher. (2017). Development of real-time product cost measurement: A case study in a medium-sized manufacturing company. *International Journal of Production Economics* 183 (A):235–244.

APPENDIX: SEMI-STRUCTURED INTERVIEW GUIDE

1. Presentation of the research project

Question: How is PLICS/SLR implemented and used at the service line level?
Objective: Getting more insights on the factors which enhance and hinder the use of PLICS/SLR for clinical decision-making.

2. Introducing question: How did you first get in contact with PLICS/SLR?

- Embedding PLICS/SLR in clinical practice
  Is there a standard PLICS report which you consult regularly
  In which meetings is PLICS data discussed?
  How has PLICS informed discussion and analysis of patient care?
  What is demonstrable experience of how PLICS informs management of healthcare processes?
  Which service lines use PLICS? Which ones use it most effectively?
  Which are the factors linked with an effective use of PLICS?

- Linking PLICS/SLR with wider organisational structure
  Are there incentives/sanctions linked with PLICS/SLR-use?
  Which kind of incentives/sanctions?
  What was the observed effect of introducing incentives/sanctions?
  Does PLICS inform appraisals?
  How does PLICS inform career development?

- Organisational issues of PLICS/SLR design/implementation
  Were/are you involved in PLICS/SLR design? How?
  Who is leading the design/implementation process?
  How would you describe the involvement/role of managers, clinicians, IT, executive and operational levels, and consulting firms?
  What resources do you commit to designing PLICS/SLR (including time, cost, staff)?
  What were the key steps of the design/implementation process?

- Technical issues of PLICS/SLR design/implementation
  Does your system meet standards defined by the Clinical Costing Standard Association of England?
  Does your system allow you to drill down to patient level processes systematically?
  How did you carry out the analysis of clinical processes?
  How can the system be accessed? Who has access?
  Which dimensions can be compared?
  Which technical problems did you face? How did you solve them?

9. Mobilising accounting information systems in mergers and acquisitions

Marjo Väisänen and Janne Järvinen

9.1 INTRODUCTION

Mergers and acquisitions (M&A) and other corporate restructurings are an essential part of the business world today, offering organisations ways to grow, enter new markets, and gain new technologies (Graebner et al., 2017). Typically, M&A relate to organisations striving to create value, with the integration process between the parties being a critical factor that can either facilitate or impede value creation (Haspeslagh and Jemison, 1991). Previous studies on M&A have indicated that a shift of power from the acquired firm's senior executives to the acquiring firm is common in these situations (Jones, 1985a; Roberts, 1990; Granlund, 2003). To date, research has tended to highlight that managers and employees often respond negatively to M&A and the subsequent integration, and have detailed the challenges faced by employees dealing with the changes (Burke, 1988; Vaara, 2003; Sinkovics, Zagelmeyer and Kusstatscher, 2011). These challenges have been associated with a range of dysfunctional emotional and behavioural outcomes, including power games, job dissatisfaction, increased stress, unproductive behaviour, mistrust, increased staff turnover and absenteeism (for example, Appelbaum et al., 2000; Risberg, 2001; Krug, 2003; Vaara, 2003). Therefore, in order for organisations to succeed after M&A, it is crucial that they integrate and formalise their accounting information systems (AIS) within their new subsidiaries in a way that overcomes the challenges (Chenhall, 2003; Granlund, 2003; Väisänen, 2022).

A major task in post-acquisition integration is the implementation of information systems that integrate the subsidiary with the parent company (see, for example, Bondarouk and Friebe, 2014). Such integration may appear forced due to the inflexible nature of enterprise resource planning (ERP) systems often used in these situations, as well as tight schedules which prevent any customisation. In such situations, successful and fast ERP integration can make it easier to facilitate compliance (Hough, Haines and Giacomo, 2007). Because systems such as ERP, supply chain management (SCM), and customer relationship management (CRM) are complex and their implementation is tied to a particular set of circumstances, their integration is a focal issue during M&A. As IT integration is such a resource-consuming task in post-acquisition integration, the risk exists that it can compromise other important areas, resulting in employees having negative views of the integration process and related controls.

However, information system integration may have design features that allow for flexibility and self-empowerment and result in enabling views (Chapman and Kihn, 2009). To play an enabling role in M&A integration, an information system should optimally be part of the company's acquisition strategy. For instance, Sliwa (2000) reports how the company Monsanto, when implementing an ERP system, made sure that it designed a global system that would be flexible enough to handle any potential mergers.

Approaching the issue from a managerial angle, the literature suggests that firms should move quickly and firmly to avoid prolonging the uncertainty and distress experienced by the employees of the acquired firm (for example, Haspeslagh and Jemison, 1991; Sinkovics, Zagelmeyer and Kusstatscher, 2011). While some studies suggest that the gradual integration and co-existence of two separate systems represent an option in some cases (Boateng and Bampton, 2010), financial reporting legislation such as the Sarbanes–Oxley Act (SOX) stipulates that at least financial accounting information must be available shortly after the acquisition, putting pressure on AIS integration. As a result, systems are often implemented in a quick top-down manner (Jones, 1985b; Granlund, 2003), which could potentially lead to organisational members feeling coerced by the new controls. Accordingly, implementing internal controls, especially those related to the SOX, becomes intertwined in this process, which may cause additional coercive perceptions in the newly acquired firm (Väisänen, 2022). However, M&A can also be a credible explanation to help the management rationalise why controls are being implemented, and this could also reduce negative attitudes towards the imposed AIS (Christ, 2013). It is more likely that subordinates will be willing to accept imposed changes if the reasons are external to the superior and changes are effectively explained to them (Korsgaard, Sapienza and Schweiger, 2002; Christ, 2013; Väisänen, Tessier and Järvinen, 2021).

The aim of this chapter is to provide an overview of the scarce literature on the role of AIS in M&A situations. While previous research has discussed the role of management control in M&A, we find the role of information technology in such situations an important topic in need of synthesis. Perhaps this is due to the fact that the studies discussed in this chapter lie at the intersection of two disciplines that lack interest in in each another (Dechow, Granlund and Mouritsen, 2006). The following sections discuss the role of AIS in establishing vertical and horizontal control in acquired subsidiaries. Tensions created by the AIS integration process are illustrated using two examples reported in the literature.

9.1.1   Accounting Information Systems in Controlling Subsidiaries

Previous studies such as those by Busco et al. (2008) and Carlsson-Wall et al. (2019) have discussed decentralisation in integrating acquired subsidiaries, and the tensions that co-exist with the centralisation/decentralisation dilemma in such settings. The authors note that, in addition to vertical accountability relations, changing business environments may create a need for more flexibility and individual responsibility, which requires strengthening horizontal relations, either within the same function (for example, sales) inside the corporation, or with other subsidiaries (Busco, Giovannoni and Scapens, 2008). Importantly, Hempel et al. (2012) discuss how formalisation reduces uncertainty inherent in many organisational processes, thus facilitating an enabling view of control, whereas the formalisation of jobs and roles reduces flexibility and mitigates the benefits of decentralisation. Frow et al. (2005) discuss this in the context of budgeting systems, where strong vertical controls and budgetary accountability structures exist in conflict with horizontal cooperation. Organisations must find a way to manage such tensions to reconcile and accommodate the management's needs for predictability and centralised control with more informal horizontal relationships that encourage cooperation and creativity.

Regarding information system implementation, Schermann et al. (2012) argue that there are three main effects on control: increased transparency of vertical relationships, increased information about horizontal processes and the possibility to achieve integration by discarding silos and formalising control routines across the organisation (Volonino, Gessner and Kermis, 2004). Thus, in a decentralised organisation there exists tension between decentralised accountability relations and formalising horizontal processes. In addition, the vertical and horizontal relations are affected by other developments in the organisation, such as the adoption of internal (for example, SOX) controls and the potential centralisation of various administrative functions into shared service centres (SSC).

9.1.2 The Role of Accounting Information Systems in Formalising Vertical Accountability Relations

Organisational design, and, in particular, the decentralisation and delegation of responsibilities, lies at the heart of management control (Emmanuel, Otley and Merchant, 1990; see for example, Cooper and Ezzamel, 2013; Otley, Merchant and Emmanuel, 2013). The degree to which the head office is willing to delegate its power to subsidiaries is largely determined by its perception of how decision-making benefits from flexibility and the use of local information to adjust to varying circumstances and thus gain business opportunities. The head office will govern acquired companies by establishing vertical accountability relations (Roberts, 1990), but how these are received will depend largely on the local culture (Cruz, Major and Scapens, 2009). On the one hand, ERP will provide increased visibility to allow for self-empowerment (Chapman and Kihn, 2009). On the other hand, fast integration and formalisation of AIS without consulting the opinions of the new subsidiary's employees could be perceived as coercive by the new organisational members, who may experience it as alienating and demotivating (Adler and Borys, 1996).

Coercive perceptions could be remedied if firms are able to let employees participate in the design of the AIS to increase their commitment (Wouters and Wilderom, 2008; Wouters and Roijmans, 2011). However, such participation requires time and is often impossible at the fast pace at which the integration of ERP systems, especially, in a post-acquisition setting, should take place for the global organisation to manage its daily business. Achieving efficiency in M&A requires standardisation across sites, and in modern business conglomerates ERP systems are the key to achieving this. For instance, Teittinen et al. (2013) record the challenges in companies adapting their processes to those modelled in a standard version of a software system, and not the other way around. Similarly, Hyvönen et al. (2006) note that standardised software packages in an 'expert system' codify best practice in a way that allows for its implementation across firms in differing circumstances.

Regarding the use of AIS, previous research indicates that information system integration can play a role in the enabling and interactive use of vertical controls. ERP systems enable interactive controls by providing an organisation with a view that may otherwise be broken into separate data sources, such as operations, marketing and accounting (Chapman, 1997), thus avoiding organisational silos. This makes it possible to direct employees and empower them at the same time, allowing for the control system to stimulate learning and innovation (Bisbe and Otley, 2004; Mundy, 2010). However, ERP systems can be implemented in a particular order that assumes a certain pre determined control design (Dechow and Mouritsen, 2005; Hyvönen et al., 2009). Thus, an ERP system that is built on a logistics module may have different control implications to a system that implements financial control first and expands from there on. This inflexibility can be addressed by various business analytics tools (Libby,

Schwebke and Goldwater, 2022), as well as governance, risk management, and compliance information systems (GRCIS) (Schermann, Wiesche and Krcmar, 2012), allowing managers to identify weak signals outside of the formalised control system (Speklé, 2001). Importantly, integrated systems can empower employees with improved internal and global transparency (Chapman and Kihn, 2009), increasing their understanding of local processes and how these fit into the organisation as a whole (Ahrens and Chapman, 2004; Jordan and Messner, 2012).

Increased transparency between the head office and the subsidiaries can also establish panoptic control (Quattrone and Hopper, 2001, 2005; Dechow and Mouritsen, 2005) by decreasing both the physical distance as well as the time between them. In essence, panoptic visibility is provided by the shared database of the ERP system, where the transactions of subsidiaries are visible to the head office in real time. This can facilitate enabling views, but at the same time enable increased control-at-a-distance (Dechow and Mouritsen, 2005; Quattrone and Hopper, 2005). The possibility of drilling down into reports as well as accessing information in real time and from multiple physical locations makes the issue all the more relevant. However, centralising management controls and standardising work practices are not always achieved, as local conditions, views and institutionalised patterns often deviate from the prescriptions of the designers and users at the head office (Cruz, Scapens and Major, 2011). Thus, it may not be possible to create a unique centre of calculation (Quattrone and Hopper, 2005). Rather, being able to access the system from many points creates multiple and previously unanticipated uses for information, which may not be in line with the control design the head office originally had in mind.

Indeed, Yazdifar et al. (2008) illustrate how the internal information requirements of a subsidiary can be in conflict with the reports required by the head office, and how subsidiary employees rely on the information provided by other sources for decision-making. In such cases, the acquired firm may develop vernacular accounting systems that go beyond the scope of official information systems (Kilfoyle, Richardson and MacDonald, 2013; Goretzki, Strauss and Wiegmann, 2018), and that would optimally, from a global, organisation-wide perspective, be replaced by an integrated system or abandoned (Dechow and Mouritsen, 2005; Hyvönen et al., 2009). This, combined with the inherent inflexibility of the information system itself, can also lead to working around controls (Pernsteiner, Drum and Revak, 2018). The studies reviewed above would suggest that ERP implementation reflects, but also partially drives, the management control of an organisation, but as ERP is implemented, the organisation will face new problems of coordination and control.

9.1.3   Internal Controls

Internal controls represent a special case of vertical controls, as they are forced upon the organisation by the SOX or corporate governance regulation in general. Since it was implemented in 2002, SOX has had a definite impact on the development of new AIS, which have since become prominent in practice (Volonino, Gessner and Kermis, 2004; Hagerty and Kraus, 2009). SOX provides a comprehensive set of legal and ethical standards applicable to all public companies listed in the US concerning their boards and management, as well as to public accounting firms. The provisions of the Act that relate most directly to AIS are sections 302 and 404, which deal with the disclosure of internal controls, procedures and fraud assurance and the responsibility related to maintaining adequate internal controls. Section 404 relates especially to authorisation and control, for example, the person with the authority to create vendors within an ERP system is not supposed to have the ability to authorise payments to vendors. These rules can only be applied if there are sufficient internal control systems.

According to Schermann et al. (2012), different practitioner groups emphasise different reasoning for the controls that have varying effects for management control. For instance, some internal auditors may focus on control deficiencies and their effects on financial outcomes, while those focusing on compliance may weigh the effectiveness of controls and cost efficiency, and the integrity of IT (Ramakrishnan, 2008). Likewise, software vendors are likely to emphasise the segregation of duties (Hagerty and Kraus, 2009). The strict rules of segregation of duties can cause serious problems in small subsidiaries with just a few people working in the accounting department, and therefore compliance with SOX can be costly and cause inefficiency.

Regarding the relationship between management control and internal controls, Schermann et al. (2012) argue that management also implements internal control systems to provide transparency about their activities to stakeholders. Such data can be used to produce reports to assess whether an organisation has been compliant with standards, rules and guidelines (Fisher, 2007). Ultimately, firms must balance and integrate such an external compliance perspective with its internal controls. It has become clear that it is no longer possible to implement effective internal controls without information systems such as ERP to support the processing of massive amounts of real-time data (Schermann, Wiesche and Krcmar, 2012).

9.1.4   Accounting Information Systems in Formalising and Standardising Horizontal Processes

In addition to vertical processes, horizontal relationships within organisations have become increasingly important for coordination (Simons, 2005; Chenhall, 2008; van der Meer-Kooistra and Scapens, 2008; Brivot and Gendron, 2011). According to Simons (2005, p. 11), 'successful organisation designs must take into account not only the vertical hierarchy – the ladders – but also the horizontal networks – the rings – needed to coordinate information, decisions, and workflows'. Traditional vertical organisational structures need to be complemented by horizontal forms of control to coordinate task interdependence and to utilise economies of scale (Dent, 1987), increasingly so during dynamic changes such as M&A. Indeed, corporate acquisitions typically entail changes in management controls, particularly in acquired organisations (for example, Jones, 1985b, 1985a; Busco, Giovannoni and Scapens, 2008; Yazdifar et al., 2008), which can therefore create tensions between different members of the organisation.

Through AIS, organisations can be decomposed into profit centres, which sometimes leads to profit centres working against each other and creating horizontal tensions. This 'silo thinking' could be avoided by managers emphasising joint responsibility and shared interests and learning processes (Goretzki and Messner, 2016). Horizontal relationships are best facilitated through informal and spontaneous communication (Dent, 1987; Berry et al., 2009), supported by familiarity among managers from different departments (Goretzki and Messner, 2016).

The integration of information systems is the key element in supporting process standardisation and achieving the benefits of scale and scope. Problems may arise if the acquired local business culture comes into conflict with the culture of the acquirer, causing difficulties in coordination and identifying local business opportunities (Cruz, Scapens and Major, 2011). Thus, the centralisation–decentralisation dilemma is influenced by the need to balance corporation-wide integration and listening to local needs (Busco, Giovannoni and Scapens,

2008; Carlsson-Wall et al., 2019), which materialises in the decision to implement AIS to standardise practices and implement horizontal control processes.

9.1.5   Accounting Information Systems and Centralising Corporate Services

In addition to centralising accountability relationships between the head office and the business areas, AIS enables centralising corporate services. In discussing centralisation, Scapens and Jazayeri (2003) argue that it is important to consider both the centralisation of control and the centralisation of other support activities, such as transaction processing and financial accounting. Centralisation of support activities is made possible by AIS and has given rise to SSCs, which have emerged as an alternative solution to the problem of how far decentralisation should go.

According to Schulman et al. (1999), an SSC centralises certain functions from the decentralised business units to a single semi-autonomous organisational unit, with the aim of lower costs and standardised processes. Increased flexibility facilitates the ability to react to the needs of different business areas across a corporation (Anthony et al., 2014). To achieve such benefits, SSCs redefine their services as service packages or 'products'; in other words, controlling sales invoices is now something that has well-defined content and a price to be paid internally. Information technology and process automation are used extensively to achieve economies of scale (Tuomela and Partanen, 2001). The SSC can be physically located away from both the head office and the decentralised business units. In some cases, SSCs are independent to the extent that they can negotiate with business areas about their services and how these are financed. In other cases, SSCs represent a step towards outsourcing, as the centre could potentially be sold to an external vendor who operates many such centres.

An SSC can be created between business areas in one part of an organisation (typically a legal entity or geographical area), or it can be created at the group level. In addition, services can be shared between several organisations, that is, an inter-organisational SSC can be created, which borders on outsourcing (see, for example, Hyvönen et al., 2012). Normally, SSCs are 'intra-organisational', and created by centralising certain administrative functions from various business areas into one single department. Often, the main idea is to avoid replication of certain tasks in several business units to achieve efficiency (for example, Quinn, Cooke and Kris, 2000). Usually the SSC serves all business areas within the group (Janssen and Joha, 2008). The unique aspects of centralisation (in relation to the accountability relations detailed above) relate to management control systems that partially overlap with the reporting and accountability structures between a business unit and the head office. From a control perspective, an SSC can be a business area, as it has a budget (complete with anticipated internal sales) and its own administrative functions, and therefore enjoys a certain degree of autonomy with respect to the upper levels of the corporation. Naturally, the degree of this autonomy in relation to the corporate head office is dependent upon many case-specific features of the business (Bergeron, 2003).

In the past, SSCs have aimed primarily at decreasing the cost per transaction, but later they have developed a business orientation to provide additional value for internal customers. Thus, while most SSCs budget their activities to break even, some may adopt a market price for their services and aim for profit (see Anthony et al., 2014). In any case, the increased autonomy most likely also entails pressure to standardise processes to improve efficiency (Bondarouk and Friebe, 2014), a development which in turn will also support horizontal process standard-isation (see above).

The next section illustrates the use of AIS to establish controls during M&A integrations. Specifically, the tension between vertical and horizontal controls is discussed in relation to two empirical case studies. The first example describes the top-down implementation of controls using ERP. The second example illustrates how ERP can be configured to enable future acquisitions.

9.2 TWO EXAMPLES OF ERP-ENABLED MERGERS

9.2.1 Vertical and Horizontal Controls in Acquisitions: Case Study of Gretzky and Finski

This section focuses on the tension between vertical and horizontal controls, and how IT systems both create and help manage this tension in corporate acquisitions. To illustrate this, the example of the case study presented by Väisänen, Tessier and Järvinen (2021) and Väisänen (2022) is discussed. The case study describes the post-acquisition integration of Finski which was acquired by Gretzky in 2010. At the time of the acquisition, Finski was a privately owned company with its head office in Finland, whereas Gretzky was a much bigger operator in the same global telecom industry. Gretzky's shares were listed on the Nasdaq and the Toronto Stock Exchange, and its head office was located in North America. The reasons behind M&A are often strategy related, with different value-adding objectives. Gretzky had made several acquisitions before acquiring Finski, and the takeover was a good fit for its long-term strategy to acquire complementary technologies in high-growth markets and to increase penetration within the customer sector in which Finski had gained a strong foothold.

The first months after the merger were turbulent times for Finski, as the integration of the two very different companies was not easily accomplished. After struggling for several months with separate systems, Gretzky's top management decided to integrate the AIS systems step by step. Due to its long history of previous acquisitions, Gretzky has developed a system for managing the tasks of integrating new subsidiaries. Using an ERP system would be an effective tool for merging and harmonising Finski's systems and processes to match those of Gretzky.

The ERP integration project was launched in December 2011, and the go-live date was set for 1st September, 2012 because this was the beginning of the 2013 fiscal year for the Gretzky Group. This would allow the firms to start the new fiscal year together, and it would be easier to consolidate the financial information at group level. Gretzky had a large team experienced in ERP, specifically SAP, and this team of experts ran the developmental process, keeping customisation to a minimum.

Having learned from previous experiences in integrating acquired companies, Gretzky decided to form a team of dedicated persons from both firms to deal with issues arising during all phases of the ERP integration. On Finski's side, the ERP team typically consisted of one manager and one employee for each function. These members were responsible for dealing with all the practical issues arising during the integration related to their respective functions. On Gretzky's side, there were managers from different functions but also several ERP and other experts (for example, accounting technicians and logistics analysts) to deliver specific information about the processes to be integrated. This team broke up into smaller teams, focusing on finance, logistics, production, purchasing, etc. This was a very efficient way of solving the issues that arose during the integration.

For implementation, Gretzky used a methodology created by SAP, called 'ASAP Methodology for Implementation'. ASAP is the SAP road map for implementing SAP solutions in a cost-effective, speedy manner. It consists of six 'gates' which were fully executed in Finski's ERP project. The schedule for the ERP project is presented in Figure 9.1.

Figure 9.1   Finski's ERP project schedule

The ERP modules implemented by Finski consisted of the following core functions: financial accounting, controlling, production planning, materials management, and sales and distribution. The ERP project was successful in terms of timing since it was completed within one year. The project also stayed within the budget that was set at the beginning. The AIS integration was important for top management to ensure the availability of financial data, as well as offering visibility of the global management to the subsidiaries in terms of sales, purchases, inventories, etc. In this sense, ERP effectively served the purpose of vertical control.

During the AIS integration process, Gretzky decided to change the organisation structure of Finski, which meant that the accountability relations were completely changed. Finski's old organisational structure was replaced by the Gretzky Group's organisation model. Finski's former vice presidents (VPs) became directors or managers who reported directly to Gretzky's global VPs and directors, located mainly in North America. The local R&D function was merged with the global R&D team, led by the VP of R&D in Canada. Similarly, the local sales team was incorporated into the global sales organisation, led by the VP of Sales in the US. As no superiors, such as a site manager, were present at the local level, the situation helped form strong and formal vertical relationships between Finski and Gretzky, fostered by organising regular meetings between the two firms. Typically, Gretzky's managers arranged weekly online meetings with their subordinates in Finski, where they did not necessarily have a formal agenda, but simply listened to what was on their subordinates' minds. For Gretzky managers, these frequent meetings were a way of having an open-door policy, even if they were not physically in the same location. This helped the Finski managers and employees accept and rationalise the changes in the AIS systems (see also Väisänen, Tessier and Järvinen, 2021).

The rationale behind these actions was to ensure vertical control. First, the integration of financial and managerial accounting systems was crucial in order to fulfil the reporting obligations to external and internal stakeholders, Gretzky's investors, as well as their top managers.

Second, compliance with SOX had to be ensured. According to section 404, listed companies can exclude newly acquired units from the internal control assessment only for the first fiscal year. Implementing the SOX controls was not easy; for example, the segregation of duties was a big issue at Finski. Before the acquisition, it used to be a normal day-to-day routine for Finski's accountants to enter invoices into the ERP system and pay them via a banking program without anyone else checking, approving, or controlling the procedure. There were many other changes like this, also in the distribution and logistics department; for example, previously the logistics coordinators were used to creating vendors, issuing orders, approving orders and shipping goods with no segregation of duties. Gretzky effectively used the implementation of ERP to ensure SOX compliance by setting the user rights in the ERP accordingly, so that risky work combinations could be avoided.

The segregation of duties meant that employees were no longer allowed to go beyond their own tasks, although there were no physical barriers preventing local managers from discussing issues. However, since vertical controls prevented them from making decisions at the local level, managers felt that there was no point discussing issues locally, resulting in feelings of working in organisational silos. Rather than solving problems at the local level, Finski's managers turned to their superiors at the head office. This meant that, in addition to vertical control, also horizontal controls needed attention.

To help coordinate horizontal processes, a new CRM system, SalesForce, was implemented at Finski and, at the same time, within the whole Gretzky Group. The new system brought together all customer information into a single platform. The salespeople saw the systems as helping them in their work tasks and especially valued the usability of the system (Väisänen, Tessier and Järvinen, 2021). These changes also produced positive effects for everyone involved with the sales process by providing transparency in terms of the respective horizontal functions, for example, improving the visibility of production for future sales estimates. The CRM introduced two effects that employees appreciated and that were needed at the time. According to them, the new system provided 'a common terminology' and a 'united way of working', which facilitated multilateral understanding. This was considered important, also by the global managers, because then 'people can communicate and help each other'. After the formalisation and standardisation of sales processes with the new CRM system, the processes and their interdependence were visible to employees. The CRM system helped break up organisational silos with improved visibility and standardised processes.

In post-acquisition integration, firms tend to concentrate on the integration of AIS supporting vertical control, which is obviously very important for managing the global organisation. However, attention should also be paid to forming horizontal networks, which can also be facilitated by IT systems, providing visibility and real-time information between functions. Furthermore, the study by Väisänen et al. (2021) demonstrates that taking the time to rationalise changes and give support to local subsidiaries helps in gaining the new organisational members' commitment to the new head office. Organisational members' perceptions and commitment matter in order for the whole firm to aim for shared goals. Therefore, the role of AIS is crucial in helping organisations to integrate after M&A and be united and successful in the future.

9.2.2   Vertical and Horizontal Controls in Acquisitions: Case Study of PaperCo

This section reviews a case study from the literature, the PaperCo case presented by Hyvönen et al. (2006, 2008), which focuses on the tension between vertical and horizontal controls and how IT systems can resolve this tension in corporate acquisitions. While PaperCo's core business had for a long time been centred on the highly efficient production of paper and pulp, more customer-oriented strategies began to emerge in the early 2000s. The previous industry logic was to sell paper to customers in bundles, which had been cut and taken to printing before delivery. The paper industry rapidly changed to a business model where an increasing variety of products was produced. The product was no longer understood as simply 'paper', but there were brands of different quality, with varying paper sizes and constantly evolving packaging solutions. These trends, increasing customer orientation and the increasing number of new products, created both the opportunity for industry consolidation through M&A, as well as the need for new management control mechanisms aligned with such opportunities.

Traditionally, the paper industry's responsibility structures are characterised by rather autonomous profit centres that are created around physical factory sites. Such developments have been documented in budgeting research by, for example, Ihantola (2006, 2010) and Henttu-Aho and Järvinen (2013). At the time, budgetary accountability could be characterised as a vertical process, where the managers of a highly decentralised and geographically dispersed organisation negotiated with the head office. It can be said that in most cases the head office did not have much visibility in terms of the financial circumstances of the profit centres, aside from responsibility accounting reports that focused on returns on assets or investments. As the industry globalised through M&A, divisional structures were created, which entailed IT and support services in each division, and the corporate head office drilling down to obtain factory-level information. The new ERP systems allowed for integrated and consolidated financials from all PaperCo's locations around the globe.

As PaperCo's strategy was to grow through acquisitions, the company created an ICT strategy that would enable such actions. Also, the growth strategy included explicitly establishing new, IT-enabled management controls for the acquired companies that could be implemented quickly. The main idea was to configure ERP in a way that allowed for quick implementation. However, the core of the management control to be established in the acquired company – the profitability management system (PMS) – was deemed too complex to program in ERP. A separate software solution transferred best practices to the acquired factories while allowing for quick and flexible implementation (Hyvönen, Järvinen and Pellinen, 2006). Bridging software would then link the PMS to ERP for data acquisition and to the data warehouse for reporting. In essence, this was an activity-based costing system that allowed for transparency of the cost structure and created visibility for the divisional controllers of various activities that took place at the levels of the factory and the profit centre level.

At the divisional level, the ERP as well as the PMS interacted with various legacy systems and factory-level applications. In some acquisitions, if the acquired company had a different version of the ERP, it was not necessarily replaced (mainly due to the links and interfaces with the underlying factory systems), and the company ended up with several ERP versions. To counter this, PaperCo decided to implement most of the controls in separate software solutions that were linked to SAP. The activity-based costing solution allowed for a new 'centre of calculation' with respect to profitability management. Relating to this, PaperCo introduced the concept of 'virtual integration' to illustrate how, instead of individual factories and production sites, profitability was now sought by configuring the wood–pulp–paper–packaging supply chain to seek solutions that optimised efficiency and profitability. At this stage, the traditional responsibility structure based on production sites as physical locations was complemented by establishing a new AIS-enabled PMS, which played a central role in the divisional management (Hyvönen et al., 2008). While maintaining the traditional responsibility structure, where acquired companies' physical production sites remained local profit centres in the division, the new concept of a virtually integrated production chain became the strategic arm of acquisition management.

While standardising corporate control as a top-down process, most accounting functions were at the same time centralised to an SSC, which was later outsourced for the most part. This partially reflects a rationale introduced by, for example, Quinn et al. (2000), of avoiding overlapping work in a divisionalised organisation. The physical location of transaction-processing accountants became irrelevant, and only a few minor functions remained in Finland. As new companies were acquired, one of the first steps after the initial ERP rollout was to centralise the transaction-processing activities to the SSC. This also had the effect of unbundling control-related accounting activities from the rest, as previously the accounting personnel would perform both financial and management accounting tasks. Thus, as the ERP and the related cost accounting controls were implemented at the new production sites, the tasks of the remaining accountants (SSC almost inevitably meant a decrease in headcount) shifted towards controlling related activities.

At PaperCo, acquisitions changed the hierarchical structure of the company but led to disparate horizontal work processes and systems. While the main goal of the process standardisation was mostly related to increasing productivity in paper production, establishing horizontal controls interacted with vertical accountability controls. As the factory infrastructure was a source of high fixed costs, minimising excess capacity was prioritised as the aim of supply-chain-oriented controls. PaperCo attempted to resolve the tension between horizontal and vertical controls by retaining its old sales management software that had interfaces with factory-level systems instead of trying to integrate such controls as a module of the ERP system. As production diversified – mainly because of acquisitions – establishing horizontal controls became a source of much debate; especially the fact that PaperCo, having acquired new factories, now offered a diverse product portfolio with a wide variety of paper sizes was seen as problematic because of difficulties with sales forecasting, paper machine set-up costs, as well as overheads related to complexity. The dilemma related to the extent to which IT solutions could be implemented to efficiently provide operative solutions for such problems, and the extent to which PaperCo should adopt a strategy of improving profitability by focusing on fewer products. At the time, discussion around activity-based costing provided input to such portfolio-optimising considerations. A related concept, which was widely debated in the firm, was to abandon transfer pricing in the context of the virtual organisation's profitability calculations, although they naturally existed in financial and tax accounts, as mandated by legislation. This way, the formal accountability relations, together with profit centres and accounting reports based on the organisational structure, differed from the more horizontal profitability calculation of the AIS-enabled 'virtual organisation'.

In the end, the company implemented AIS tools for both the horizontal and vertical axes of control, with the concept of virtual integration acting as an instrument of reconciling the tension between the two. As for the horizontal control, sales forecasting and predictive analytics were developed alongside CRM implementation to improve capacity allocation decisions and estimate the costs of logistical processes for different market areas (see for example, Huikku, Hyvönen and Järvinen, 2017). The aim was to develop better intercompany planning and supply chain capabilities. Eventually, this IT-driven change in horizontal controls was also reflected in how the management accounting function was organised. A group of sales and logistics controllers (as opposed to divisional controllers responsible for top-down vertical control) were given responsibility for the product and supply chain information (Hyvönen, Järvinen and Pellinen, 2015; Henttu-Aho, 2016). Over time, the IT landscape developed into a single-instance ERP that would reconcile both aspects of control.

9.3   CONCLUSION

To summarise, while part of many multinationals' growth strategies, are high-risk operations in the sense that the benefits are hard to realise. Part of this risk is the need to integrate AIS and other controls in a quick and effective manner. The enforced way in which AIS are implemented results in controls that are often vertical in nature, dealing with, for example, how the accounting systems of the acquired business units are integrated with those of the acquirer. A primary example of this is establishing SOX controls, which are required for US-listed companies in a tight schedule after M&A. Indeed, the first step is to integrate the financial accounting systems, which is usually done quickly due to external and legal reporting requirements.

However, integrating management accounting goes hand in hand with integrating operations. Therefore, while prioritised for legislative reasons, establishing vertical controls is not the only required task after acquisition, nor is it related to the original motivations for the acquisition, which lie in business processes. Naturally, companies make acquisitions for business reasons, such as acquiring R&D knowledge, new customers, or entry into new market areas. This means that horizontal controls must also be established to integrate the acquired company with the processes and supply chain management of the acquirer. Thus M&A often create a situation where the inflexible nature and disregard of local circumstances of top-down vertical controls interact with horizontal controls, which require simultaneously efficient standardisation and the flexible accommodation of local practices. This poses a major challenge for AIS.

This chapter presented two examples based on the literature of how AIS can be mobilised in corporate acquisitions. First, the case study of Finski (Väisänen, 2022) illustrated forced and top-down ERP adoption to implement SOX controls and to integrate the product structure of the acquired company with the larger organisation. The tension between vertical and horizontal controls was mostly resolved by a new organisational structure. In practice, this meant that the staff in Finland were directly incorporated into a larger function, and they had to report to its head. While there was a legal entity in Finland, there was no site manager or local superior. Thus, the R&D and procurement people were part of the respective global teams, which managed their processes in ERP and reported to a superior abroad. Likewise, the local sales team was incorporated into the global sales division, which operated using a CRM system as its primary tool. This allowed for configuring the horizontal controls so that they did not get in the way of the vertical profit centre organisation. This means that, although it is clear that AIS can be configured to enable decentralised as well as network structures in multinational companies (for example, Bartlett and Ghoshal, 2002), this case study illustrates how geographical decentralisation is no longer a necessity. Operational managers and administrative functions need not be physically present at the profit centre.

The other example from the literature presented here, PaperCo (Hyvönen, Järvinen and Pellinen, 2006, 2008), created a management model labelled 'virtual integration', which, instead of focusing on business unit profitability and the trade of semifinished products between factories, created calculations that allowed for the comparison of different combinations of factories, paper mills and logistical options. While ERP was used to integrate the vertical controls, the virtual organisation concept was necessary to allow for flexibility in configuring and introducing new items originating from the acquired production sites to the supply chain. This was done by utilising separate, ERP-linked, activity-based costing software, with the numbers transferred to a reporting cube. In the end, the rollout of the ERP was quick, which was necessary to establish financial and internal controls, but left the decision-maker considerable flexibility in designing horizontal processes.

From a management control perspective, AIS play various roles in M&A. First, they allow for effectively establishing vertical decentralised controls. In this way, the legal requirements of acquisition are fulfilled and the internal controls are efficiently implemented. As the control in the acquired company is centralised, part of its administrative functions can also be eliminated or moved to an SSC (Quinn, Cooke and Kris, 2000). Second, the acquired company's product portfolio, R&D and procurement processes, as well as the sales function, can be integrated with the larger whole. Effective, integrated AIS ensure control-at-distance in a way that enables managing subsidiaries, even without local supervisors. For example, the R&D projects can be managed by virtual teams situated in different countries with the supervisor in yet another country, reporting to the global head office. Third, and importantly, AIS can be invoked to resolve the conflict between the two mentioned axes controls by establishing virtual organisations facilitated by information systems.

Our examples from the literature demonstrate that resolving tensions between the horizontal and vertical axes in acquisition can take place by, for example, establishing a virtual supply chain where the profitability of various production and logistical options is constantly calculated, or by practically abolishing the acquired company as a decentralised organisational structure by establishing virtual teams across global functions (for example, R&D). Interestingly, while both the case study companies ran SAP, their sales management software was independent from it, and run as a separate module. We speculate that customer orientation may be an area where a top-down approach may be seen as risky or ineffective and which, instead of solving the tension between controls, retains its relative independence. This might prove an interesting avenue for future research.

REFERENCES

Adler, P.S. and Borys, B. (1996) Two types of bureaucracy: Enabling and coercive, *Administrative Science Quarterly*, 41(1), pp. 61–89. doi:https://doi.org/10.2307/2393986.

Ahrens, T. and Chapman, C.S. (2004) Accounting for flexibility and efficiency: A field study of management control systems in a restaurant chain, *Contemporary Accounting Research*, 21(2), pp. 271–301. doi:https://doi.org/10.1506/VJR6-RP75-7GUX-XH0X.

Anthony, R.N. et al. (2014) *Management control systems*. 1. European edition. Maidenhead, Berkshire: McGraw-Hill Education.

Appelbaum, S.H. et al. (2000) Anatomy of a merger: Behavior of organizational factors and processes throughout the pre-, during-, post- stages (part 2), *Management Decision*, 38(10), pp. 674–684. doi:10.1108/00251740010360579.

Bartlett, C.A. and Ghoshal, S. (2002) *Managing across borders: The transnational solution.* 2nd ed. Boston, MA: Harvard Business School Press. Available at: https://oula.linneanet.fi/vwebv/holdingsInfo?bibId=867314.

Bergeron, B. (2003) *Essentials of knowledge management.* Hoboken, New Jersey: John Wiley & Sons, Inc.

Berry, A.J. et al. (2009) Emerging themes in management control: A review of recent literature, *The British Accounting Review*, 41(1), pp. 2–20. doi:10.1016/j.bar.2008.09.001.

Bisbe, J. and Otley, D. (2004) The effects of the interactive use of management control systems on product innovation, *Accounting, Organizations and Society*, 29(8), pp. 709–737. doi:http://dx.doi.org/10.1016/j.aos.2003.10.010.

Boateng, A. and Bampton, R. (2010) Integrating management accounting systems in mergers and acquisitions: The role of management accountants, *Research Executive Summaries Chartered Institute of Management Accountants*, 6(5), pp. 1–8.

Bondarouk, T. and Friebe, C.-M. (2014) 'Shared services – standardization, formalization, and control: A structured literature review', in *Shared services as a new organizational form.* Emerald Group Publishing Limited, Bingley (Advanced Series in Management), pp. 39–65. doi:10.1108/S1877-636120140000013003.

Brivot, M. and Gendron, Y. (2011) Beyond panopticism: On the ramifications of surveillance in a contemporary professional setting, *Accounting, Organizations and Society*, 36(3), pp. 135–155. doi:http://dx.doi.org/10.1016/j.aos.2011.03.003.

Burke, R.J. (1988) Managing the human side of mergers and acquisitions, *Business Quarterly (1986-1998)*, 52(3), p. 18. Available at: https://search.proquest.com/docview/222576681?accountid=13031.

Busco, C., Giovannoni, E. and Scapens, R.W. (2008) Managing the tensions in integrating global organisations: The role of performance management systems, *Management Accounting Research*, 19(2), pp. 103–125. doi:https://doi.org/10.1016/j.mar.2008.02.001.

Carlsson-Wall, M. et al. (2019) The role of technocratic and socio-ideological controls in managing tensions when integrating international subsidiaries, *Qualitative Research in Accounting & Management*, 16(3), pp. 434–455. doi:https://doi.org/10.1108/QRAM-05-2018-0032.

Chapman, C.S. (1997) Reflections on a contingent view of accounting, *Accounting, Organizations and Society*, 22(2), pp. 189–205. doi:10.1016/S0361-3682(97)00001-9.

Chapman, C.S. and Kihn, L.-A. (2009) Information system integration, enabling control and performance, *Accounting, Organizations and Society*, 34(2), pp. 151–169. doi:https://doi.org/10.1016/j.aos.2008.07.003.

Chenhall, R.H. (2003) Management control systems design within its organizational context: Findings from contingency-based research and directions for the future, *Accounting, Organizations and Society*, 28(2–3), pp. 127–168. doi:https://doi.org/10.1016/S0361-3682(01)00027-7.

Chenhall, R.H. (2008) Accounting for the horizontal organization: A review essay, *Accounting, Organizations and Society*, 33(4–5), pp. 517–550. doi:https://doi.org/10.1016/j.aos.2007.07.004.

Christ, M.H. (2013) An experimental investigation of the interactions among intentions, reciprocity, and control, *Journal of Management Accounting Research*, 25(1), pp. 169–197. doi:10.2308/jmar-50443.

Cooper, D.J. and Ezzamel, M. (2013) Globalization discourses and performance measurement systems in a multinational firm, *Accounting, Organizations and Society*, 38(4), pp. 288–313. doi:https://doi.org/10.1016/j.aos.2013.04.002.

Cruz, I., Major, M. and Scapens, R.W. (2009) Institutionalization and practice variation in the management control of a global/local setting, *Accounting, Auditing & Accountability Journal*, 22(1), pp. 91–117. doi:10.1108/09513570910923024.

Cruz, I., Scapens, R.W. and Major, M. (2011) The localisation of a global management control system, *Accounting, Organizations and Society*, 36(7), pp. 412–427. doi:10.1016/j.aos.2011.08.001.

Dechow, N., Granlund, M. and Mouritsen, J. (2006) Management control of the complex organization: Relationships between management accounting and information technology, *Handbooks of Management Accounting Research*, 2, pp. 625–640. doi:10.1016/S1751-3243(06)02007-4.

Dechow, N. and Mouritsen, J. (2005) Enterprise resource planning systems, management control and the quest for integration, *Accounting, Organizations and Society*, 30(7–8), pp. 691–733. doi:https://doi.org/10.1016/j.aos.2004.11.004.

Dent, J.F. (1987) 'Tensions in the design of formal control systems: A field study in a computer company', in Bruns, W.J. and Kaplan, R.S. (eds). Harvard Business School Press Boston, MA (*Accounting and management: Field study perspectives*), pp. 119–145.

Emmanuel, C.R., Otley, D. and Merchant, K. (1990) *Accounting for management control*. 2nd ed. London: Chapman and Hall.

Fisher, J. (2007) Compliance in the performance management context, *Bank Accounting and Finance*, 20(6), p. 41.

Frow, N., Marginson, D. and Ogden, S. (2005) Encouraging strategic behaviour while maintaining management control: Multi-functional project teams, budgets, and the negotiation of shared accountabilities in contemporary enterprises, *Management Accounting Research*, 16(3), pp. 269–292. doi:http://dx.doi.org/10.1016/j.mar.2005.06.004.

Goretzki, L. and Messner, M. (2016) Coordination under uncertainty: A sensemaking perspective on cross-functional planning meetings, *Qualitative Research in Accounting & Management*, 13(1), pp. 92–126. doi:https://doi.org/10.1108/QRAM-09-2015-0070.

Goretzki, L., Strauss, E. and Wiegmann, L. (2018) Exploring the roles of vernacular accounting systems in the development of "enabling" global accounting and control systems, *Contemporary Accounting Research*, 35(4), pp. 1888–1916. doi:10.1111/1911-3846.12357.

Graebner, M.E. et al. (2017) The process of postmerger integration: A review and agenda for future research, *Academy of Management Annals*, 11(1), pp. 1–32. doi:https://doi.org/10.5465/annals.2014.0078.

Granlund, M. (2003) Management accounting system integration in corporate mergers: A case study, *Accounting, Auditing & Accountability Journal*, 16(2), pp. 208–243. doi:https://doi.org/10.1108/09513570310472822.

Hagerty, J. and Kraus, B. (2009) GRC in 2010: $29.8 b in spending sparked by risk, visibility, and efficiency, *AMR Research*.

Haspeslagh, P.C. and Jemison, D.B. (1991) *Managing acquisitions: Creating value through corporate renewal*. New York: The Free Press. Available at: https://oula.finna.fi/Record/oula.1521530.

Hempel, P.S., Zhang, Z.-X. and Han, Y. (2012) Team empowerment and the organizational context: Decentralization and the contrasting effects of formalization, *Journal of Management*, 38(2), pp. 475–501. doi:10.1177/0149206309342891.

Henttu-Aho, T. (2016) Enabling characteristics of new budgeting practice and the role of controller, *Qualitative Research in Accounting & Management*, 13(1), pp. 31–56. doi:10.1108/QRAM-09-2014-0058.

Henttu-Aho, T. and Järvinen, J. (2013) A field study of the emerging practice of beyond budgeting in industrial companies: An institutional perspective, *European Accounting Review*, 22(4), pp. 765–785. doi:10.1080/09638180.2012.758596.

Hough, J.R., Haines, R. and Giacomo, S. (2007) Contextual factors affecting the integration of enterprise systems in post-merger oil and gas companies, *Enterprise Information Systems*, 1(4), pp. 421–441. doi:10.1080/17517570701630404.

Huikku, J., Hyvönen, T. and Järvinen, J. (2017) The role of a predictive analytics project initiator in the integration of financial and operational forecasts, *Baltic Journal of Management*, 12(4), pp. 427–446. doi:10.1108/BJM-05-2017-0164.

Hyvönen, T. et al. (2009) Institutional logics, ICT and stability of management accounting, *European Accounting Review*, 18(2), pp. 241–275. doi:https://doi.org/10.1080/09638180802681511.

Hyvönen, T. et al. (2012) Contracting out municipal accounting: The role of institutional entrepreneurship, *Accounting, Auditing & Accountability Journal*, 25(6), pp. 944–963. doi:10.1108/09513571211250198.

Hyvönen, T., Järvinen, J. and Pellinen, J. (2006) The role of standard software packages in mediating management accounting knowledge, *Qualitative Research in Accounting & Management*, 3(2), p. 145.

Hyvönen, T., Järvinen, J. and Pellinen, J. (2008) A virtual integration – The management control system in a multinational enterprise, *Management Accounting Research*, 19(1), pp. 45–61. doi:10.1016/j.mar.2007.08.001.

Hyvönen, T., Järvinen, J. and Pellinen, J. (2015) Dynamics of creating a new role for business controllers, *Nordic Journal of Business*, 64(1), pp. 21–39.
Ihantola, E.-M. (2006) The budgeting climate concept and its application to case organizations' budgeting – an explorative study, *Scandinavian Journal of Management*, 22(2), pp. 138–168. doi:https://doi
   .org/10.1016/j.scaman.2006.03.004.
Ihantola, E.-M. (2010) An historical analysis of budgetary thought in Finnish specialist business journals
   from c.1950 to c.2000, *Accounting, Business & Financial History*, 20(2), pp. 135–161. doi:10.1080/
   09585206.2010.485745.
Janssen, M. and Joha, A. (2008) Emerging shared service organizations and the service-oriented enterprise,
   Strategic Outsourcing: An International Journal, 1(1), pp. 35–49. doi:10.1108/17538290810857466.
Jones, C.S. (1985a) An empirical study of the evidence for contingency theories of management
   accounting systems in conditions of rapid change, *Accounting, Organizations and Society*, 10(3),
   pp. 303–328. doi:https://doi.org/10.1016/0361-3682(85)90022-4.
Jones, C.S. (1985b) An empirical study of the role of management accounting systems following takeover or merger, *Accounting, Organizations and Society*, 10(2), pp. 177–200. doi:https://doi.org/10
   .1016/0361-3682(85)90015-7.
Jordan, S. and Messner, M. (2012) Enabling control and the problem of incomplete performance indicators, *Accounting, Organizations and Society*, 37(8), pp. 544–564. doi:https://doi.org/10.1016/j.aos
   .2012.08.002.
Kilfoyle, E., Richardson, A.J. and MacDonald, L.D. (2013) Vernacular accountings: Bridging the
   cognitive and the social in the analysis of employee-generated accounting systems, *Accounting,
   Organizations and Society*, 38(5), pp. 382–396. doi:http://dx.doi.org/10.1016/j.aos.2013.08.001.
Korsgaard, M.A., Sapienza, H.J. and Schweiger, D.M. (2002) Beaten before begun: The role
   of procedural justice in planning change, *Journal of Management*, 28(4), pp. 497–516.
   doi:10.1177/014920630202800402.
Krug, J.A. (2003) Executive turnover in acquired firms: An analysis of resource-based theory and the
   upper echelons perspective, *Journal of Management & Governance*, 7(2), pp. 117–143. doi:https://doi
   .org/10.1023/A:1023607012229.
Libby, T., Schwebke, J.M. and Goldwater, P.M. (2022) Using data analytics to evaluate the drivers of
   revenue: An introductory case study using microsoft power pivot and power BI, *Issues in Accounting
   Education*, 37(4), pp. 97–105. doi:10.2308/ISSUES-2021-057.
van der Meer-Kooistra, J. and Scapens, R.W. (2008) The governance of lateral relations between and
   within organisations, *Management Accounting Research*, 19(4), pp. 365–384. doi:https://doi.org/10
   .1016/j.mar.2008.08.001.
Mundy, J. (2010) Creating dynamic tensions through a balanced use of management control systems,
   Accounting, Organizations and Society, 35(5), pp. 499–523. doi:https://doi.org/10.1016/j.aos.2009
   .10.005.
Otley, D., Merchant, K. and Emmanuel, C.R. (2013) *Readings in accounting for management control*.
   Springer, New York, NY.
Pernsteiner, A., Drum, D. and Revak, A. (2018) Control or chaos: Impact of workarounds on internal
   controls, *International Journal of Accounting and Information Management*, 26(2), pp. 230–244.
   doi:10.1108/IJAIM-12-2016-0116.
Quattrone, P. and Hopper, T. (2001) What does organizational change mean? Speculations on a taken
   for granted category, *Management Accounting Research*, 12(4), pp. 403–435. doi:http://dx.doi.org/10
   .1006/mare.2001.0176.
Quattrone, P. and Hopper, T. (2005) A "time–space odyssey": Management control systems in two multinational organisations, *Accounting, Organizations and Society*, 30(7–8), pp. 735–764. doi:https://doi
   .org/10.1016/j.aos.2003.10.006.
Quinn, B., Cooke, R. and Kris, A. (2000) *Shared services: Mining for corporate gold*. London: Financial
   Times Prentice Hall.
Ramakrishnan, S. (2008) Eliminate the weak links in your GRC process, *Operational Risk and
   Regulation (6)* [Preprint].
Risberg, A. (2001) Employee experiences of acquisition processes, *Journal of World Business*, 36(1),
   p. 58. Available at: http://search.ebscohost.com/login.aspx?direct=true&db=bth&AN=4166638&site
   =ehost-live.

Roberts, J. (1990) Strategy and accounting in a U.K. conglomerate, *Accounting, Organizations and Society*, 15(1–2), pp. 107–126. doi:https://doi.org/10.1016/0361-3682(90)90017-O.

Scapens, R.W. and Jazayeri, M. (2003) ERP systems and management accounting change: Opportunities or impacts? A research note, *European Accounting Review*, 12(1), pp. 201–233.

Schermann, M., Wiesche, M. and Krcmar, H. (2012) The role of information systems in supporting exploitative and exploratory management control activities, *Journal of Management Accounting Research*, 24(1), pp. 31–59. Available at: http://search.proquest.com/docview/1247632077?accountid =13031.

Schulman, D.S. et al. (1999) *Shared services: Adding value to the business units.* New York, Wiley.

Simons, R. (2005) *Levers of organization design: How managers use accountability systems for greater performance and commitment.* Boston, MA: Harvard Business School Press.

Sinkovics, R.R., Zagelmeyer, S. and Kusstatscher, V. (2011) Between merger and syndrome: The intermediary role of emotions in four cross-border M&As, *International Business Review*, 20(1), pp. 27–47. doi:https://doi.org/10.1016/j.ibusrev.2010.05.002.

Sliwa, C. (2000) Drug Giants' Merger to Bring Systems Integration Hurdles, *Computerworld*.

Speklé, R.F. (2001) Explaining management control structure variety: A transaction cost economics perspective, *Accounting, Organizations and Society*, 26(4–5), pp. 419–441. doi:http://dx.doi.org/10 .1016/S0361-3682(00)00041-6.

Teittinen, H., Pellinen, J. and Jarvenpaa, M. (2013) ERP in Action – Challenges and Benefits for Management Control in SME Context, *International Journal of Accounting Information Systems*, 14, PP. 278–296. https://doi.org/10.1016/j.accinf.2012.03.004

Tuomela, T.-S. and Partanen, V. (2001) In search of strategic contribution and operative effectiveness: Developing competencies within the finance function, *Finnish Journal of Business Economics*, 50(1), pp. 502–538.

Vaara, E. (2003) Post-acquisition integration as sensemaking: Glimpses of ambiguity, confusion, hypocrisy, and politicization, *Journal of Management Studies*, 40(4), pp. 859–894. doi:10.1111/1467-6486.00363.

Väisänen, M. (2022) *Enabling control in post-acquisition integration.* Oulu: University of Oulu (Acta Universitatis Ouluensis). Available at: http://urn.fi/urn:isbn:9789526233222.

Väisänen, M., Tessier, S. and Järvinen, J. (2021) Fostering enabling perceptions of management controls during post-acquisition integration, *Contemporary Accounting Research*, 38(2), pp. 1341–1367. doi:https://doi.org/10.1111/1911-3846.12639.

Volonino, L., Gessner, G.H. and Kermis, G.F. (2004) Holistic compliance with Sarbanes–Oxley, *Communications of the Association for Information Systems*, 14(1), p. 11.

Wouters, M. and Roijmans, D. (2011) Using prototypes to induce experimentation and knowledge integration in the development of enabling accounting information, *Contemporary Accounting Research*, 28(2), pp. 708–736. doi:http://dx.doi.org/10.1111/j.1911-3846.2010.01055.x.

Wouters, M. and Wilderom, C. (2008) Developing performance-measurement systems as enabling formalization: A longitudinal field study of a logistics department, *Accounting, Organizations and Society*, 33(4–5), pp. 488–516. doi:https://doi.org/10.1016/j.aos.2007.05.002.

Yazdifar, H. et al. (2008) Management accounting change in a subsidiary organisation, *Critical Perspectives on Accounting*, 19(3), pp. 404–430. doi:https://doi-org.pc124152.oulu.fi:9443/10.1016/ j.cpa.2006.08.004.

10. Measuring the effectiveness of the accounting information system in the Malaysian Federal Government

Sharinah Binti Puasa and Julia A. Smith

10.1 INTRODUCTION

Effective decisions require high-quality data. Generally, the quality of information is determined by the way the data is processed. Nowadays, many large organisations have to adapt and upgrade their technology to optimise their performance (Shagari et al., 2017) or the service offered (cf. Hung et al., 2009; Loo et al., 2009). In accounting, such improvements are embodied in an Accounting Information System (AIS). Technically, the AIS is described as the use of computers and technology to process accounting data (Puasa, 2017; Pierre et al., 2013; Nicolaou, 2000). Given the necessity for high-quality information to support decision-making, the AIS must effectively process accounting data (Ali & Abu-AlSondos, 2020; Chalu, 2012; Sajady et al., 2008). Most importantly, an organisation needs an effective AIS to achieve the organisation's strategic and operational objectives (Al-Okaily et al., 2020). AIS also plays a significant role in mediating the relationship between internal control and employee performance (Alawaqleh, 2021). Thus, the full potential of AIS must be used to get better information and better results (Alim and Siswantoro, 2019).

To realise the benefits of an improved AIS, most large organisations have decided to invest considerable amounts of money in developing and upgrading their systems. However, there are considerations surrounding whether or not this will be worthwhile, and whether such expenditure will guarantee an effective system (Al-Okaily et al., 2020). Without observed improvements, the investment might prove to be a burden on the organisation. It is challenging to create and implement a system that meets organisational requirements (Chalu, 2012). It is often argued that the investment in AIS is not worth the results from its implementation (Iskandar, 2015). In other cases, the system implemented is believed not to result in its expected benefit (Al-Okaily et al., 2020; Cohen et al., 2007).

Therefore, a practical evaluation is needed to assess the system's condition. It shows that a tool for measuring system effectiveness is vital. As such, the objectives of this study are: (i) to investigate the criteria of AIS effectiveness; and (ii) to develop a parsimonious model to assess AIS effectiveness. To achieve that, this study is seeking to answer the following questions:

(i) What are the criteria of effective AIS?
(ii) Which of the identified criteria are reliable and valid for the measurement of AIS effectiveness?

This study is an empirical exploration of AIS effectiveness of the Malaysian Federal Government. The Government's efforts to continuously support the advancement of technology and improvement of financial management in the public sector were brought to light in the Tenth Malaysia Plan (2011–2015), in which approximately 650 million in Malaysian ringgit (approximately \$157m) was budgeted for the advancement of technology (Jabatan Perdana Menteri, 2010). This advancement, which incorporated the AIS, was aimed at improving operational effectiveness and efficiency, as well as minimising task redundancy through an integrated and centralised system. In addition, in 2011, the Malaysian Government announced the plan to transition from a modified cash basis to accruals-based accounting. The Government upgraded its accounting system to support the accruals accounting modules so that this change could be made.

The existing accounting system was customised for cash-based accounting, and used at the Accountant General's Department (AGD) and the accounting office of each ministry for retrieving and processing accounting transactions and producing information for reporting purposes. The input of accounting data was carried out at the relevant responsibility centre, using the Electronic Budget Control and Planning System (eSPKB) to record expense transactions and the Standard Collection and Receipting System (eTerimaan) to record revenue collection transactions. The changes were made to facilitate the transition from decentralisation, with different servers, to centralisation with one server for the AGD, the accounting offices and the responsibility centres.

10.2   LITERATURE REVIEW

Previous studies have mentioned the difficulties in evaluating the return on investment from AIS (Al-Okaily et al., 2020), as it is inclusive of both tangible and intangible benefits (Puasa et al., 2019). Furthermore, it is difficult to assess from a single dimension (Al-Okaily et al., 2020). The measurement of AIS effectiveness is found to be inconsistent from one study to another (Chalu, 2012; Sabherwal et al., 2006; Choe, 1996). One of the reasons that give rise to such inconsistencies is the definition of effectiveness itself (Thong and Yap, 1996).

Effectiveness is multidimensional in nature (DeLone and McLean, 1992; Hamilton and Chervany, 1981). Thus, it is difficult to measure effectiveness directly, though some have tried, from the top management perspective (Al-Okaily et al., 2020) or a citizenship perspective assessing the eGovernment systems in Taiwan (Wang & Liao, 2008) which is, however, limited in its scope. Measurement of AIS efficacy typically relies on proxies, but the researchers rarely provide a convincing justification for their selection (Puasa, 2017). This has led to inconsistency of measurement and continuous debate; and no consensus has yet been achieved. A wider context of research is therefore required to investigate the measurement of AIS effectiveness.

Specifically, this study focuses on the perspective of the user of the system. For the purposes of this study, we define the system's users as those involved in applying the AIS to processing or transforming accounting data into accounting information. The success of AIS is largely determined by the people who use the system (Al-Okaily et al., 2020). Their perceptions and acceptance of the system is crucial in representing the system's performance. Previous work has considered the needs of external or end users of Government information systems (for example, Chu et al., 2004; Detlor et al., 2013; Loo et al., 2009; Verdegem & Verleye, 2009).

A system is considered a poor system if its users perceived it to be a poor system (Ives et al., 1983). Given the potential costs of failure of an information system, particularly in public sector settings (cf. Gauld, 2007), there are strong incentives for ensuring that the system is effective and efficient prior to its implementation. In addition, previous studies have viewed system effectiveness as a system that is meeting its users' requirements (for example, Puasa et al., 2019; Shagari et al., 2017; Ilias and Razak, 2011; Salehi et al., 2010; Mohamed et al., 2009). The latter can be measured by the extent of user satisfaction towards given or accepted criteria of an effective system (cf. Hung et al., 2009; Loo et al., 2009; Puasa, 2017).

In a Saudi Arabian e-Government effectiveness study, Santa et al. (2019) found that operational effectiveness and information quality are the primary drivers of user satisfaction. Consistent with literature in the information system field of study, user satisfaction is mentioned as an appropriate measure for effectiveness (DeLone and McLean, 1992). And Gatian (1994) confirmed the validity of user satisfaction in measuring information system effectiveness.

Nevertheless, previous studies use satisfaction to evaluate effectiveness differently. Some studies measure satisfaction on a five-point Likert scale ranging from 'Highly Disagree' to 'Highly Agree', in order to assess respondents' agreement with a given set of statements about the effectiveness of the system. Alternatively, others simply use satisfaction as the scale of measurement itself, for example from 'Very Dissatisfied' to 'Very Satisfied'. Furthermore, the use of satisfaction as an item or scale in previous studies has not always been adequately explained. Therefore, the application of user satisfaction in measuring effectiveness requires improvement, in order to strengthen existing instruments and research models (Puasa, 2017).

AIS effectiveness has been studied and discussed in various contexts due to the multidimensional nature of its effectiveness (Al-Okaily et al., 2020; Puasa et al., 2019). As evidence, prior studies (cf. Table 10.1) have measured AIS effectiveness from the perspective of decision-makers (Al-Okaily et al., 2020; Kouser et al., 2011; Nicolaou, 2000), operational efficiency (Ali & Abu-AlSondos, 2020), coordination and control (Kouser et al., 2011), organisational performance (Chalu, 2012), employee performance (Alawaqleh, 2021) and features of information (Pornpandejwittaya, 2012). However, different users at different levels may have different intentions towards and requirements from the system (Puasa, 2017). Internally, systems users can range from lower management to upper management. Thus, a specific investigation is needed to improve the understanding of AIS effectiveness and to further refine the measure of system effectiveness.

In the broader context of information systems, effectiveness has been shown to contribute to success in DeLone and McLean's Information System Success Model (D&M IS Success Model) 1992. This model has been subsequently debated, respecified, extended and modified by other researchers (for example, Ifinedo and Nahar, 2006; de Guinea et al., 2005; Seddon, 1997; Pitt et al., 1995). Nevertheless, effectiveness is not just about successfully implementing an information system. Effectiveness is beyond success. An effective system is 'a successfully implemented system that is capable of meeting a user's requirements (Salehi et al., 2010) and satisfying them' (Puasa, 2017, p. 24). In other words, effectiveness refers to ongoing and sustainable success.

Specifically relating to the AIS, AIS effectiveness is defined as the perceived ability of the system to provide information that meets the requirements of users of the system for coordination and control (Kouser et al., 2011; Nicolaou, 2000). In particular, AIS implementation is aimed at improving business operations and reporting (Sajady et al., 2008), as well as

Table 10.1   *Summary of the review on AIS effectiveness*

Criteria	Source
Ease of use	Cohen et al. (2016); Ilias and Zainudin (2013); Ifinedo (2006); Ifinedo and Nahar (2006); Davis (1989)
Benefit/Usefulness	Seddon (1997); Davis (1989)
Satisfaction (i.e. either overall or in a specific context)	Chalu (2012); Kouser et al. (2011); Ilias and Razak (2011); Al-Maskari and Sanderson (2010); Ilias et al. (2009); Ismail (2009); Mohamed et al. (2009); Ilias et al. (2007); de Guinea et al. (2005); DeLone and McLean (2003); Hung et al. (2009); Loo et al. (2009); Rai et al. (2002); Myers et al. (1997); Seddon (1997); Kettinger and Lee (1994); Thong and Yap (1996); Thong et al. (1994); Pitt et al. (1995); Gatian (1994); DeLone and McClean (1992); Torkzadeh and Doll (1991); Santa et al. (2019); Verdegem & Verleye (2009)
Information quality (e.g. accurate, complete, reliable, relevance, timely etc.)	Cohen et al. (2016); Fitriati and Mulyani (2015); Rapina (2014); Chalu (2012); Detlor et al. (2013); Komala (2012); Rahayu (2012); Dehghanzade et al. (2011); Ismail (2009); Ifinedo (2006); Ifinedo and Nahar (2006); DeLone and McLean (2003); Myers et al. (1997); Pitt et al. (1995); DeLone and McLean (1992); Santa et al. (2019)
Quality of the system	Cohen et al. (2016); Chalu (2012); Ismail (2009); Ifinedo (2006); Ifinedo and Nahar (2006); DeLone and McLean (2003); Myers et al. (1997); Pitt et al. (1995); DeLone and McLean (1992)
Impact	Ismail (2009); Ifinedo (2006); Ifinedo and Nahar (2006); Myers et al. (1997); Thong et al. (1994)
Smooth procedure and operation	Rahayu (2012)
Enhance productivity	Myers et al. (1997)
Reduce cost (e.g. paperless)	Myers et al. (1997)
Support decision-making	Kharuddin et al. (2010)
Perform accounting function	Belfo and Trigo (2013); Pierre et al. (2013); Salehi et al. (2010)
Improve accounting operation and report	Ilias and Zainudin (2013); Sacer and Oluic (2013)
Manage business activities	Dalci and Tanis (2002)

Source: Compiled for this study.

making better decisions (Kouser et al., 2011; Sajady et al., 2008). AIS effectiveness has also been measured according to the system's capacity for providing expected information, in terms of legal obligations, financial report preparation and adequacy of the control structure (Dehghanzade et al., 2011). Further, AIS effectiveness has been viewed in a broader context of four dimensions: viz. accounting information quality; system quality; user satisfaction; and organisational performance (Chalu, 2012). A recent study viewed AIS effectiveness as reflecting system quality, information quality, service quality, training quality and organisational benefits (Al-Okaily et al., 2020). Focusing specifically on information criteria, AIS effectiveness has been examined according to the features of information quality (i.e. reliability, relevance and timeliness) (Pornpandejwittaya, 2012). These definitions are more likely to focus on the role of the AIS in providing information for its users. Theoretically, a good decision requires a substantial amount of high-quality information. For example, Detlor et al. (2013) suggest that the quality of information provided may strongly affect a citizen's decision to utilise, or to continue to use, a government website. However, not all AIS users are using the system to retrieve information for decision-making (Chalu, 2012).

Therefore, this study aims to fill the research gap on the inconsistency of AIS effectiveness measurement by proposing an instrument that comprehensively measures AIS effectiveness.

Additionally, it applies in-depth investigation to provide empirical support for the development of a parsimonious AIS effectiveness model, within the novel context of the central government of an emerging economy.

10.3   METHODOLOGY

We have examined the internal users of the AIS in the Malaysian Federal Government at 26 ministries and a prime minister's department. The sample for this study focuses on accounting personnel, encompassing top and middle management at the ministry-level accounting office, using a purposive sampling technique (cf. Etikan et al., 2016). The accounting office processes data entered by responsibility centres throughout the country before forwarding it to the AGD for consolidation and use in top-level Malaysian Federal Government decision-making. This study used purposive sampling to ensure the respondents are relevant to the scope of study and had some diversity in relevant criteria or characteristics to better represent the phenomenon (Ritchie et al., 2003). A manager often has a better vision of the implemented information system compared to his or her subordinates (Wiechetek, 2012). Therefore, the top and middle management at the accounting office were chosen for the qualitative study. Conversely, the survey questionnaire for the quantitative study was distributed to all levels of management at the accounting office of the Malaysian Federal Government.

We employ multiple methods, using both qualitative and quantitative techniques. The qualitative method applies a semi-structured interview and framework refinement. This study used primary-source fieldwork. First, unstructured preliminary fieldwork collected data from group discussions and participant observation. This fieldwork sought to understand government AIS practices. It took place at the AGD and in the accounting offices, under the Ministry of Finance, Malaysia in April and May 2015. This phase provided an initial understanding of government AIS practices, accounting operations, and information flows, AIS factors, and system users' perceptions on system effectiveness. The understanding and findings from this phase, as well as insights from the literature, were comprehensively used in the development of semi-structured interview questions.

As recommended by Gillham (2000), the interview agenda was sent in advance to the interviewees to ensure they were prepared. The semi-structured interview questions were developed based on previous literature (for example, Appiah et al., 2014) and refined using the seven guidelines suggested by Cameron and Whetton (1983). See Appendix Table A10.1 for the application of the seven guidelines used in this study and Table A10.2 for the complete set of interview questions. In addition, a pilot study was conducted with academics and practitioners from the accounting field to improve the qualitative findings on identified measures of AIS effectiveness. This pilot study sought specific views of the terms used, including the words and categories of dimensions in the framework.

Next, the quantitative method used evidence gathered through a survey questionnaire that was developed following the findings from the earlier, qualitative, part of the study. Semi-structured interviews were used to explore AIS effectiveness, based on the interviewees' responses to predetermined factors for effective systems operation. In addition, their perceptions of the definition and criteria for an effective system were discussed. See Table A10.4 for the instrument of AIS effectiveness measurement. Specifically, their expectations towards the ability of the system to satisfy their requirements were explored to understand the criteria of an effective AIS. The interviews were conducted in August and September 2015 at the accounting office (i.e. ministry level). The findings from semi-structured interviews were used to refine the draft list of the critical factors of AIS effectiveness. We then use SPSS to apply factor analysis, using Principal Components Analysis (PCA), to examine the suitability of our proposed criteria for AIS effectiveness.

10.4   FIELDWORK EVIDENCE

The accounting system of the Malaysian Federal Government is known as the Government Financial Management Accounting System (GFMAS). Prior to this, the Malaysian Federal Government used a Branch Accounting System (BAS), a semi-manual accounting system in which some accounting tasks (for example, reconciliation, review, analysis, etc) were done manually before the accounting data was entered into the system. As the volume of accounting transactions increased, the need grew for a more sophisticated and automated system to cater for the high volume of transactions and improve the accounting processes.

The Government also uses a Budget Planning and Control System to process payment and expenses-related transactions (eSPKB), which was put in place in 2000 to control and manage the Federal Government's budget. This system was integrated with BAS prior to the implementation of GFMAS, and has additional links to the Human Resources Management Information System, the Project Monitoring System and others. Data entered into eSPKB is processed and forwarded to GFMAS for further action.

Finally, eTerimaan is a Standard Collection and Receipting System that processes the Government's collection and accounting records related to revenue. This was implemented in 2008 to smooth the accounting process, replacing the Government's manual collection system. eTerimaan is integrated with GFMAS through eSPKB. Both eSPKB and eTerimaan use the same server and platform. The integration between systems allows reconciliation to be done between the accounting records at responsibility centres and reporting in the accounting office, as well as at the headquarters.

The GFMAS, eSPKB and eTerimaan are intranet-based networks that can be accessed through any computer within the organisation that has the application installed. The main functions of the accounting system are to manage the accounting data and to produce financial statements. The accuracy of data and classification of accounts entered into eSPKB and eTerimaan are ensured through digital checks and approval in GFMAS at the accounting's office.

10.5   QUALITATIVE DATA ANALYSIS

In response to a formal invitation to all chief accountants at the Malaysian Federal Government, 22 interviewees from ten ministries agreed to be interviewed. This resulted in 12 interview sessions of approximately one-and-a-half hours per session. Almost all the interviewees are members of the Malaysian Institute of Accountants (MIA), of which the majority are female. The highest educational level of the interviewees is a Master's degree, and the lowest, a bachelor's degree. Some of them had mixed qualifications and educational backgrounds. For example, one interviewee might have a bachelor's degree in accounting and a Master's in another field (for example, business, human resource, marketing, etc.).

10.5.1   Qualitative Findings

Semi-structured interviews were transcribed using MS Word and analysed using NVivo 11 software (cf. Bazeley & Jackson, 2013). Coding analysis was applied to the qualitative data in this study. Saldaña (2013) perceives coding to be a cyclical, rather than a linear, process. The process commonly starts with a move from wider to narrower contexts. In this study, five coding types were used through two cycles. The 1st cycle implemented open coding (attaching concepts or codes to the observed data and phenomena), in-vivo coding (assigning labels to sections of data using words or short phrases) and simultaneous coding (where two or more codes are applied to the same parts). Next, the 2nd cycle applied focused coding (identifying recurrent patterns and multiple layers of meaning) and axial coding (constructing linkages between data.). See Table A10.3(i) and (ii) for an example of the extracted coding analysis performed in this study. The codes extracted were cross-referenced iteratively and compared to prior literature to refine and improve the overall findings. For the purposes of this study, we accept interviewees' views that their needs from and expectations towards the AIS are significant indicators of the criteria for the system's effectiveness.

To illustrate, the qualitative evidence from this study found that most interviewees perceived a good system to be one which was both easy to use and user-friendly. Both refer to the features of the system (i.e. 'simple commands', and 'easy to understand'). Usually, a highly complicated system will discourage users from learning and exploring, and is time-consuming to use and understand, both of which may limit the actual potential performance of the system. For example:

> The system should be simple and easy to understand. It will be difficult if the system is not user friendly.

> We have to bear in mind that the system is not only used by the accounting personnel. The system is also used by an Administration and Diplomatic Officer [PTD], engineer, lawyer, doctor and so on. Thus, it is important that the system is user friendly. In other words, the system is easy to understand … and uses layman language for accounting that everybody can understand.

> The system should be user friendly. So, it is not difficult to understand each component in the system.

The interviewees also emphasised system quality, including system operation and the quality of the information produced. System quality is crucial in ensuring the quality of produced information. The interviewees viewed system quality from the perspective of operational and system performance; for example, whether it offered real-time updates; processing speed; and the automation of accounting tasks, such as calculation and single entry. Furthermore, automatic functions of the AIS, including auto-matching details and the auto-checking of balances, all help to minimise human error.

> The system should be able to provide the current balance. Let's say the information is requested at nine o'clock, the system should be able to show the information as at nine o'clock.

> In my view, if the system is good, it would be able to [create] auto entry to the relevant journal when we key in the data; meaning that, we only have to put one entry.

> As for the system's performance, is it slow? Is it quick enough?

> In designing the system … we want to make sure the system can minimise all errors. To minimise all errors. That is the system I expect there to be.

Additionally, the interviewees want a system with the capacity to produce various types of reports, with a summary that meets the requirements of relevant management. In practice, top management generally wants a summary of information to get an overview, whereas lower and middle management usually need more detailed and specific information (Hall, 2010). Some of the interviewees believe that a variety of reports produced by the system may add value in the decision-making process.

> The system should be able to produce many types of report. As I said just now, can the system separate between the collection of cash and credit cards?

Furthermore, high-quality information is needed to support decision-making. A system that is incapable of producing high-quality information is a useless system. The common features of information quality are accuracy, completeness, timeliness, relevance and summarisation (Hall, 2010). Suggestions from our respondents were as follows:

> The information given must, firstly, be complete; second, accurate.

> Good information is accurate information, that has integrity and is genuine. So, we do not doubt the information. It is correct.

Over and above the benefits from having more accurate information, applying technology to the accounting process simplifies the process, especially for producing documents and submitting reports. The use of technology reduces the consumption of paper and speeds up the accounting process, as most of the data can be processed online. Further, automating the process of particular accounting tasks has helped to make the production of financial statements faster than before (Sori, 2009). In addition, the integrated function of an AIS offers a platform for sharing information within management, whilst having broader access through an online system. This feature adds value to the organisation as a whole and motivates staff to be more competitive, in line with the tremendous changes in technology around the world.

> We can retrieve whatever information [from the system] is requested by the top management.

> I remember the last time that we had to print three copies [of payment voucher]. But now we only have to print one copy.

> Previously, when you submitted a claim, … it would take you one month [to get processed]. But now, … if you submit your claim today, you can get your payment by tomorrow.

> Through GFMAS, the Government has introduced Electronic Fund Transfer [EFT] payment, which will benefit the stakeholders as well. Before this, we need to issue a cheque, but now it is directly transferred to their account.

User requirements may vary from one person to another, depending on their level and use of the system. Nevertheless, the main criteria for system effectiveness remain similar across the board. Consequently, the qualitative part of this study found three preliminary dimensions of AIS effectiveness: system quality; information quality; and benefit or usefulness of the system, encompassing all 13 criteria. These criteria are now refined and explained further in the next section of this chapter. In addition, we use 'satisfaction level' below to represent the level of effectiveness of a given criterion, whereby satisfaction is applied as a scale for measuring each of the criteria, rather than as an item or variable in its own right.

10.6   REFINEMENT OF AIS EFFECTIVENESS DIMENSIONS AND CRITERIA

The AIS effectiveness criteria identified from the literature review and semi-structured interview preliminary findings were next refined through a pilot study with academics and practitioners from the accounting field. The feedback from this exercise mainly recommended combining the redundant items. The qualitative findings and amendments from this stage of the study are shown in Table 10.2. As a result, AIS effectiveness is represented by the three dimensions of System Quality, Information Quality and Benefit/Usefulness of the System.

Table 10.2   Criteria refinement after pre-testing within the accounting field

Qualitative Preliminary Findings		Qualitative Final Result	
Dimension	Item	Amendment	Item
System Quality	– User friendly – Easy to understand – Easy to use – Processing time (speed) – Ability to produce reports in a required format	– The criteria of user friendly and easy to understand were removed and represented by easy to use	– Ease of use (user friendly) – Processing time (i.e. speed) – Ability to produce a report in a required format
Information Quality	– No doubt – Accurate – Completeness (all transaction are captured accordingly) – Relevant for use in decision-making	– The criterion of no doubt was removed as it was represented by accurate	– Accurate (no doubt) – Completeness (all transactions are captured accordingly) – Relevant for use in decision-making
Benefit/ Usefulness of the System	– Improve individual productivity – Improve decision-making – Minimise unintentional human error – Reduce hard copy submissions (paperless)	– No change	– Improve individual productivity – Improve decision-making process – Minimise unintentional human error – Reduce hard copy submission (paperless)

10.7   QUANTITATIVE EVIDENCE

A survey questionnaire was designed and applied to explore the AIS users' opinions of the effectiveness of the system. The questionnaire instrument for AIS effectiveness measurement represents three dimensions comprising ten items, measured using a five-point Likert scale of satisfaction from 'Very Dissatisfied' to 'Very Satisfied'. This study collected 177 questionnaires from AIS users in the Accounting Office of the Malaysian Federal Government. A number of incomplete (n=17) questionnaires were removed, and five questionnaires were noticed to have suspicious response patterns (i.e. half of the variables were answered 'neither satisfied nor satisfied', suggestive of ignorance towards the questions). Thus, the final number of questionnaires is 155, and considered to be acceptable, from a statistical standpoint.

The majority of respondents were female. Those aged between 31 and 40 years represented more than half of all respondents, and the majority held a bachelor's degree. Approximately 80 per cent of respondents had work experience of more than six years, and 66 per cent had work experience in the private sector before they joined the Government sector. About 41 per cent of respondents were members of the MIA. Overall, all respondents had experience in using the AIS of the Federal Government of Malaysia (including GFMAS, eSPKB, eTerimaan, etc).

10.7.1   Descriptive Statistics of AIS Effectiveness

AIS effectiveness in this study is measured according to our three dimensions, incorporating ten items. The three dimensions are System Quality (three items), Information Quality (three items) and Benefit/Usefulness of AIS (four items), as developed according to the qualitative findings of this study. The items measuring AIS effectiveness are scaled according to satisfaction level (i.e. five-point Likert scale, 'Very Dissatisfied' to 'Very Satisfied').

Table 10.3   Descriptive statistics of AIS effectiveness measures

Measurement Item	Mean	Min.	Max.	Std Deviation
System Quality				
Ease of use	4.04	2	5	0.602
System processing time (i.e. speed)	3.94	1	5	0.667
Ability to produce report in a required format	3.90	2	5	0.672
Information Quality				
Accurate	4.05	1	5	0.628
Completeness (all transactions are captured accordingly)	3.99	2	5	0.669
Relevant for the use in decision-making	3.99	1	5	0.688
Benefit/Usefulness of AIS				
Improves individual productivity	4.03	2	5	0.597
Improves decision-making process	4.01	2	5	0.619
Minimise unintentional human erro	3.92	2	5	0.702
Reduces hard copy submissions (paperless)	3.71	1	5	0.933

The frequency statistics given in Table 10.3 show that the modal outcome for all components of the measures of Systems Quality, Information Quality and Benefit/Usefulness of AIS, used to measure AIS effectiveness, was 4 ('Satisfied'). In other words, the majority of respondents were satisfied with the AIS, indicating perceived system effectiveness. In the context of this study, point 4 on the scale ('Satisfied') demonstrates moderate effectiveness of the system. A highly effective system should reach a high level of satisfaction among its users. Table 10.3 contains the descriptive statistics for all measures of AIS effectiveness used in this study.

10.7.2   Factor Analysis

The ten items proposed in this study were examined using Principal Components Analysis (PCA) using IBM SPSS Statistics (cf. IBM, 2015). Suitability of the data for factor analysis was assessed prior to performing PCA. A correlation matrix reported all coefficients to be above 0.3 with a minimum value of 0.350. The Kaiser–Meyer–Olkin (KMO) value is 0.856

(significance at p = .000), exceeding the threshold of 0.6, as suggested by Kaiser (1974). This result suggested factorability of the correlation matrix.

Furthermore, eigenvalues for all items are well above 1 with a minimum value of 1.280. 'Ease of Use' reported the highest eigenvalue, explaining approximately 56 per cent of the variance. This is expected, as the item of 'Ease of Use' has been widely accepted and applied in the literature for defining 'system success', 'acceptance' and 'intention to use', as well as effectiveness. The remaining items ranged from 1.280 to 9.362.

On the other hand, the Component Matrix reported an extraction of one component for the ten items. This finding indicates support for all items to be applied as AIS effectiveness measurements. In addition, all items load strongly above 0.7 except for one item under System Quality (i.e. 'The information is complete', with a loading = 0.697) and another one item under Benefit/Usefulness of AIS (i.e. 'The system reduces hardcopy submission', loading = 0.662). Both are retained in the AIS effectiveness model because the loadings are just slightly below 0.7 and both support the findings from the qualitative part of this study. The other items reported in the range of loading from 0.712 to 8.61. Overall, the results support all ten items representing our three dimensions of AIS, to be applied as AIS effectiveness measurements.

10.8   PROPOSED ACCOUNTING INFORMATION SYSTEM (AIS) EFFECTIVENESS MODEL

Prior studies have measured system effectiveness using proxies for the criteria that represent the utility of the system (for example, quality, output, cost, benefit and performance). Most of these studies adopted or adapted dimensions and criteria from the DeLone and McLean (1992) D&M IS Success Model, Technology of Acceptance Model (TAM) and End-User Computing Satisfaction (EUCS) model to measure system effectiveness. Nevertheless, the existing criteria need improvement to reflect the reality of system effectiveness in our current setting.

Therefore, the existing dimensions and criteria listed in previous studies are referenced accordingly, for the development of AIS effectiveness in this study. Also, the qualitative findings of this study were added and modified to develop a more parsimonious AIS effectiveness model. Specifically, it was found that AIS users perceived the system to be effective if it were able to meet their requirements and satisfy their needs. Thus, this finding suggested that the level of user satisfaction represents well the level of system effectiveness. In other words, a high satisfaction level (i.e. scale point 5, 'Very Satisfied') indicates a highly effective system, a moderate satisfaction level (i.e. scale 4, 'Satisfied') demonstrates a moderate effectiveness of the system, and so on. Hence, we propose that user satisfaction is suitable, and should be applied as a scale in which we measure each individual component of the AIS effectiveness criteria, rather than simply measuring effectiveness as a single measure.

Moreover, most of the criteria found during the fieldwork have been discussed by prior researchers. Note that some criteria are sub-criteria of other items. Further, and more crucially, this study has revealed some measures in the specific context of the Malaysian Federal Government, with additional criteria, as follows:

i.   Ability to produce reports in a required format.
ii.   Improved individual productivity.
iii. Minimisation of unintentional human error.

iv. Reduced hard copy submission (paperless).

Significantly, this study refined the long list of AIS effectiveness criteria from the literature review into ten criteria. The use of a satisfaction scale to measure the system's effectiveness is consistent with the definition of system effectiveness by Kouser et al. (2011), Salehi et al. (2010) and Nicolaou (2000), in which an effective system is a system that is capable of meeting its users' requirements. The definition is also consistent with Ives et al. (1983) about the concept of a good system (i.e. being capable of convincing its users). The proposed measurement reflects the perspective of AIS users for a stable and ongoing system that is currently

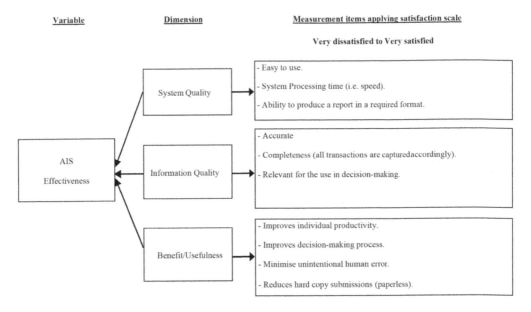

Figure 10.1   AIS effectiveness model

used by the Malaysian Federal Government. Figure 10.1 illustrates the research model developed in this study.

10.9   CONCLUSION AND FUTURE RESEARCH OPPORTUNITIES

This study contributes to the literature by refining the existing criteria of AIS effectiveness. The refined criteria were used to develop an AIS effectiveness model, in order to produce a comprehensive measure that takes into account the three essential dimensions of the system effectiveness (system quality, information quality and benefit/usefulness of the system). This study provides qualitative evidence from the perspective of system users in strengthening the research model and producing an instrument of AIS effectiveness. Moreover, the implementation of user satisfaction level to measure the criteria of AIS effectiveness is considered as a contribution to the existing literature. A high level of satisfaction translated as a highly effective system. This improvement provides a more accurate measurement of each criterion of system effectiveness, which shed light on the ambiguity and arguments on the AIS measurement in the literature.

Further, this study has enlightened the previous definition of AIS effectiveness as a successfully applied system that can convince its users about its capability to meet the users' requirements and provide the expected outcomes. The outcomes include high-quality information, a high-quality system and benefits/usefulness of the system. The research model of this study is not just limited to the AIS field, but is also appropriate for application in the information system, Enterprise Resource Planning (ERP) and IT management areas.

Despite the thorough analysis performed, some limitations should be noted. First, this study applied a qualitative method for collecting system user perspectives of the AIS. As such, bias in opinion might exist because opinion can easily be influenced by other factors, such as experience, background and environment. However, neglecting their opinion might not reflect the real phenomenon. Second, this study applies a factor analysis using PCA. Other techniques (for example, Hierarchical Components Model in SmartPLS) should be considered in future studies to statistically examine the three dimensions of AIS effectiveness. And third, the sample for this study is limited to ministry level only. Other contexts (for example, private sector, state government) are suggested for future research. In the meantime, we propose that our parsimonious means of assessing AIS effectiveness within a government setting presents a new way of analysis that future researchers will find useful and can easily utilise in their own settings.

REFERENCES

Al-Maskari, A., and Sanderson, M. (2010) A review of factors influencing user satisfaction in information retrieval. *Journal of the American Society for Information Science and Technology*, 61 (5), pp. 859–868.

Al-Okailya, A., Al-Okailyb, M., Shiyyab, F., and Masadah, W. (2020) Accounting information system effectiveness from an organizational perspective. *Management Science Letters*, 10, pp. 3991–4000.

Alawaqleh, Q. A. (2021) The effect of internal control on employee performance of small and medium-sized enterprises in Jordan: The role of accounting information system. *Journal of Asian Finance, Economics and Business*, 8 (3), pp. 855–863.

Ali, B. J. A., and Abu-AlSondos, I. A. (2020) Operational efficiency and the adoption of accounting information system (AIS): A comprehensive review of the banking sectors. *International Journal of Management (IJM)*, 11 (6), pp. 221–234.

Alim, D. L., and Siswantoro, D. (2019) The effect of the accounting information system (AIS) on accounting and financial task efficiency at the Depok City local government finance office. *Advances in Economics, Business and Management Research*, 89, pp. 408–413.

Appiah, K. O., Agyemang, F., Agyei, Y. F. R., Nketiah, S., and Mensah, B. J. (2014) Computerised accounting information systems: Lessons in state-owned enterprise in developing economies. *Journal of Finance and Management in Public Services*, 12 (1), pp. 69–91.

Bazeley, P., and Jackson, K. (Eds.) (2013) *Qualitative data analysis with NVivo*. London: SAGE Publications Ltd.

Belfo, F., and Trigo, A. (2013) Accounting information system: Tradition and future directions. *Procedia Technology*, 9, pp. 536–546.

Cameron, K. S. (1986) A study of organizational effectiveness and its predictors. *Management Science*, 32 (1), pp. 87–112.

Cameron, K. S., and Whetton, D. A. (1983) Some conclusions about organizational effectiveness. In B. L. Myers, L. A. Kappelman & V. R. Prybutok (Eds.), *A comprehensive model for assessing the quality and productivity of the information systems function: Toward a theory for information systems assessment* (pp. 261–277): New York: Academic Press.

Chalu, H. (2012) Analysis of stakeholder factors influencing the effectiveness of accounting information systems in Tanzania's local authorities. *Business Management Review*, 16 (1), pp. 1–32.

Choe, J.-M. (1996) The relationships among performance of accounting information systems, influence factors and evolution level of information systems. *Journal of Management Information Systems*, 12 (4), pp. 215–239.

Chu, P. Y., Hsiao, N., Lee, F. W., and Chen, C. W. (2004) Exploring success factors for Taiwan's government electronic tendering system: Behavioral perspectives from end users. *Government Information Quarterly*, 21 (2), pp. 219–234.

Cohen, J. F., Coleman, E., and Kangethe, M. J. (2016) An importance-performance analysis of hospital information system attributes: A nurses' perspective. *International Journal of Medical Informatics*, 86, pp. 82–90.

Cohen, S., Kaimenaki, E., and Zorgios, Y. (2007) Assessing IT as a key success factor for accrual accounting implementation in Greek municipalities. *Financial Accountability & Management*, 23 (1), pp. 91–111.

Dalci, I., and Tanis, V. N. (2002) Benefits of computerized accounting information systems on the JIT production systems. *Review of Social, Economic and Business Studies*, 2, pp. 45–62.

Davis, F. D. (1989) Perceived usefulness, perceived ease of use, and user acceptance of information technology. *MIS Quarterly*, 13 (3), pp. 319–340.

de Guinea, A. O., Kelley, H., and Hunter, M. G. (2005) Information system effectiveness in small business: Extending a Singaporean model in Canada. *Journal of Global Information Management*, 13 (3), pp. 55–70.

Dehghanzade, H., Moradi, M. A., and Raghibi, M. (2011) A survey of human factors' impacts on the effectiveness of accounting information systems. *International Journal of Business Administration*, 2 (4), pp. 166–174.

DeLone, W. H., and McLean, E. R. (1992) Information systems success: The quest for the dependent variable. *Information Systems Research*, 3 (1), pp. 60–95.

DeLone, W. H., and McLean, E. R. (2003) The DeLone and McLean Model of information systems success: A ten-year update. *Journal of Management Information Systems*, 19 (4), pp. 9–30.

Detlor, B., Hupfer, M. E., Ruhi, U., and Zhao, L. (2013) Information quality and community municipal portal use. *Government Information Quarterly*, 30 (1), pp. 23–32.

Etikan, I., Musa, S. A., and Alkassim, R. S. (2016) Comparison of convenience sampling and purposive sampling. *American Journal of Theoretical and Applied Statistics*, 5 (1), pp. 1–4.

Fitriati, A., and Mulyani, S. (2015) Factors that effect accounting information systems success and its implication on accounting information quality. *Asian Journal of Information Technology*, 14 (5), pp. 154–161.

Gatian, A. W. (1994) Is user satisfaction a valid measure of system effectiveness. *Information and Management*, 26 (3), pp. 119–131.

Gauld, R. (2007) Public sector information system project failures: Lessons from a New Zealand hospital organization. *Government Information Quarterly*, 24 (1), pp. 102–114.

Gillham, B. (2000) *The research interview*. New York, USA: Continuum.

Hall, J. A. (Ed.) (2010) *Introduction to Accounting Information Systems*. Boston, Ma, United States: South-Western Cengage Learning.

Hamilton, S., and Chervany, N. L. (1981) Evaluating information system effectiveness – part I: Comparing evaluation approaches. *MIS Quarterly*, 5 (3), pp. 55–69.

Hung, S. Y., Tang, K. Z., Chang, C. M., and Ke, C. D. (2009) User acceptance of intergovernmental services: An example of electronic document management system. *Government Information Quarterly*, 26 (2), 387–397.

IBM (2015) IBM SPSS Statistics for Windows, Version 23.0. Armonk, NY: IBM Corp.

Ifinedo, P. (2006) Extending the Gable et al. Enterprise Systems Success Measurement Model. *Journal of Information Technology Management*, 17 (1), pp. 15–34.

Ifinedo, P., and Nahar, N. (2006) Quality, impact and success of ERP systems: A study involving some firms in the Nordic–Baltic Region. *Journal of Information Technology Impact*, 6 (1), pp. 19–46.

Ilias, A., and Razak, M. Z. A. (2011) End-User Computing Satisfaction (EUCS) towards Computerised Accounting System (CAS) in the public sector: A validation of instrument. *Journal of Internet Banking and Commerce*, 16 (2), pp. 1–17.

Ilias, A., Razak, M. Z. A., Rahman, R. A., and Yasoa', M. R. (2009) End-User Computing Satisfaction (EUCS) in Computerised Accounting System (CAS): Which the critical factors? A case in Malaysia. *Computer and Information Science*, 2 (1), pp. 18–24.

Ilias, A., Yasoa', M. R., Razak, M. Z. A., and Rahman, R. A. (2007) The Study of End-User Computing Satisfaction (EUCS) on Computerised Accounting System (CAS) among government sectors: A case study in the responsibility centres. *Labuan e-Journal of Muamalat and Society*, 1, pp. 1–13.

Ilias, A., and Zainudin, N. N. B. (2013) Factors affecting the Computerised Accounting System (CAS) usage in public sector. *Journal of Internet Banking and Commerce*, 18 (1), pp. 1–29.

Iskandar, D. (2015) Analysis of factors affecting the success of the application of accounting information system. *International Journal of Scientific and Technology Research*, 4 (2), pp. 155–162.

Ismail, N. A. (2009) Factors influencing AIS effectiveness among manufacturing SMEs: Evidence from Malaysia. *The Electronic Journal on Information Systems in Developing Countries*, 38 (10), pp. 1–19.

Ives, B., Olson, M. H., and Baroudi, J. J. (1983) The measurement of user information satisfaction. *Communications of the ACM*, 26 (10), pp. 785–793.

Jabatan Perdana Menteri (2010) *Rancangan Malaysia Kesepuluh* 2011–2015, Putrajaya, Malaysia.

Kaiser, H. F. (1974) An index of factorial simplicity. *Psychometrika*, 39 (1), pp. 31–36.

Kettinger, W. J., and Lee, C. C. (1994) Perceived service quality and user satisfaction with the information services function. *Decision Sciences*, 25 (5/6), pp. 737–766.

Kharuddin, S., Ashhari, Z. M., and Nassir, A. M. (2010) Information system and firms' performance: The case of Malaysian small medium enterprises. *International Business Research*, 3 (4), pp. 28–35.

Komala, A. R. (2012) The influence of the accounting managers' knowledge and the top management support on the accounting information system and its impact on the quality of accounting information: A case of zakat institutions in Bandung. *Journal of Global Management*, 4 (1), pp. 53–73.

Kouser, R., Rana, G. e., and Shahzad, F. A. (2011) Determinants of AIS effectiveness: Assessment thereof in Pakistan. *International Journal of Contemporary Business Studies*, 2 (12), pp. 6–21.

Loo, W. H., Yeow, P. H., and Chong, S. C. (2009) User acceptance of Malaysian government multipurpose smartcard applications. *Government Information Quarterly*, 26 (2), pp. 358–367.

Mohamed, N., Hussin, H., and Hussein, R. (2009) Measuring users' satisfaction with Malaysia's electronic government systems. *Electronic Journal of e-Government*, 7 (3), pp. 283–294.

Myers, B. L., Kappelman, L. A., and Prybutok, V. R. (1997) A comprehensive model for assessing the quality and productivity of the information system function: Toward a theory for information systems assessment. *Information Resources Management Journal*, 10 (1), pp. 6–25.

Nicolaou, A. I. (2000) A contingency model of perceived effectiveness in accounting information systems: Organizational coordination and control effects. *International Journal of Accounting Information Systems*, 1 (2), pp. 91–105.

Pierre, A.-K., Khalil, G., Marwan, K., Nivine, G., and Tarek, A. (2013) The tendency for using accounting information systems in Lebanese firms. *International Journal of Computer Theory and Engineering*, 5 (6), pp. 895–899.

Pitt, L. F., Watson, R. T., and Kavan, C. B. (1995) Service quality: A measure of information systems effectiveness. *MIS Quarterly*, 19 (2), pp. 173–187.

Pornpandejwittaya, P. (2012) Effectiveness of accounting information system: Effect on performance of Thai-listed firms in Thailand. *International Journal of Business Research*, 12 (3), pp. 84–94.

Puasa, S. (2017) *A phenomenon of the critical factors of Accounting Information System (AIS) effectiveness*. PhD thesis. University of Strathclyde, Glasgow.

Puasa, S., Smith, J. A., and Amirul, S. M. (2019) Perceptions of accounting information system effectiveness: Preliminary findings from The Malaysian Federal Government. *Labuan e-Journal of Muamalat and Society*, 1, pp. 48–59.

Rahayu, S. K. (2012) The factors that support the implementation of accounting information system: A survey in Bandung and Jakarta's taxpayer offices. *Journal of Global Management*, 4 (1), pp. 25–52.

Rai, A., Lang, S. S., and Welker, R. B. (2002) Assessing the validity of IS success models: An empirical test and theoretical analysis. *Information Systems Research*, 13 (1), pp. 50–69.

Rapina. (2014) Factors influencing the quality of accounting information system and its implications on the quality of accounting information. *Research Journal of Finance and Accounting*, 5 (2), pp. 148–154.

Ritchie, J., Lewis, J., and Elam, G. E. (2003) Designing and selecting samples. In J. Ritchie & J. Lewis (Eds.), *Qualitative research practice: A guide for social science students and researchers* (pp. 77–108). London: SAGE Publications Ltd.

Sabherwal, R., Jeyaraj, A., and Chowa, C. (2006) Information system success: Individual and organizational determinants. *Management Science*, 52 (12), pp. 1849–1864.

Sacer, I. M., and Oluic, A. (2013) Information technology and accounting information systems' quality on Croatian middle and large companies. *Journal of Information and Organizational Sciences*, 37 (2), pp. 117–126.

Sajady, H., Dastgir, M., and Nejad, H. H. (2008) Evaluation of the effectiveness of accounting information systems. *International Journal of Information Science and Technology*, 6 (2), pp. 49–59.

Saldaña, J. (2013) *The coding manual for qualitative researchers*. London: SAGE Publications Ltd.

Salehi, M., Rostami, V., and Mogadam, A. (2010) Usefulness of accounting information system in emerging economy: Empirical evidence of Iran. *International Journal of Economics and Finance*, 2 (2), pp. 186–195.

Santa, R., MacDonald, J. B., & Ferrer, M. (2019) The role of trust in e-Government effectiveness, operational effectiveness and user satisfaction: Lessons from Saudi Arabia in e-G2B. *Government Information Quarterly*, 36 (1), pp. 39–50.

Seddon, P. B. (1997) A respecification and extension of the DeLone and McLean Model of IS Success. *Information Systems Research*, 8 (2), pp. 240–253.

Shagari, S. L., Abdullah, A., and Saat, R. M. (2017) Accounting information system effectiveness: Evidence from the Nigerian banking sector. *Interdisciplinary Journal of Information, Knowledge and Management*, 12, pp. 309–335.

Sori, Z. M. (2009) Accounting Information Systems (AIS) and knowledge management: A case study. *American Journal of Scientific Research*, 4, pp. 36–44.

Thong, J. Y. L., Yap, C.-S., and Raman, K. S. (1994) Engagement of external expertise in information systems implementation. *Journal of Management Information Systems*, 11 (2), pp. 209–231.

Thong, J. Y. L., and Yap, C.-S. (1996) Information systems effectiveness: A user satisfaction approach. *Information Processing and Management*, 32 (5), pp. 601–610.

Torkzadeh, G., and Doll, W. J. (1991) Test-retest reliability of the end-user computing satisfaction. *Decision Sciences*, 22 (1), pp. 26–37.

Verdegem, P., and Verleye, G. (2009) User-centered e-government in practice: A comprehensive model for measuring user satisfaction. *Government Information Quarterly*, 26 (3), pp. 487–497.

Wang, Y. S., and Liao, Y. W. (2008) Assessing e-government systems success: A validation of the DeLone and McLean model of information systems success. *Government Information Quarterly*, 25 (4), pp. 717–733.

Wiechetek, Ł. (2012) Effectiveness of information systems implementation: The case of the Polish small and medium enterprises. *Management, Knowledge and Learning International Conference* 2012, Celje, Slovenia. 20th–22nd June, 2012. pp. 193–202.

APPENDIX

Table A10.1   *The application of seven guidelines by Cameron and Whetton (1983) in assessing AIS effectiveness*

Effectiveness Guideline	Applied in This Study	Interview Question
i. From whose perspective is effectiveness being judged?	AIS users that used the system to manage and process accounting data and information.	What is your (interviewee) role in the organisation?
ii. On what domains of activity is the judgment focused?	AIS process from input, to output.	What are the objectives of the AIS in your organisation?
iii. What level of analysis is used?	Individual perception/opinion.	–
iv. What is the purpose of the assessment?	To evaluate AIS effectiveness based on user satisfaction towards the system.	How will you define the effectiveness of the AIS in your organisation? What are the criteria of an effective AIS?
v. What time frame is employed?	Periodically depending on the activity performed. Input and processing activity requires users perception based on their experience using the system in daily basis. On the other hand, output and impact gained on daily, monthly, quarterly or yearly basis.	–
vi. What types of data are sought?	Subjective, in which user perception and opinion are used.	–
vii. What is the referent against which effectiveness is judged?	User expectation towards an effective AIS.	What do you expect from the system in order to satisfy your requirements? What do you want from the system?

Source: Adapted from Cameron and Whetton (1983) in Cameron (1986, pp. 93 & 94) for this study.

Table A10.2   Semi-structured interview questions

Question
A. General Information: Respondent's Background
1. Please tell me about your education background and working experience relative to accounting and information system.
2. What is your role in your organisation?
B. Overview of Accounting Information System (AIS)
1. How do you define the AIS from the perspective of your organisation? Or what is AIS?
2. What are the objectives of the AIS in your organisation (e.g. budgeting, expenses, planning, decision-making and etc.)?
C. Accounting Information System (AIS) Effectiveness
1. How will you define the effectiveness of AIS in your organisation? Or what are the criteria of effective AIS?
2. What do you expect from the system in order to satisfy your requirements?
3. How important is the effectiveness of the AIS in contributing to your organisation?
D. Others
Do you have other opinions too? Or any key area that is not mentioned in the outlined questions, but highly relevant to the effectiveness of the system?

Source: Developed for this study.

Table A10.3   Extracted coding analysis

(i) First Cycle of Coding

Direct Quotation from the Transcript	Translated Quotation	Initial (Open) and In Vivo Coding	Simultaneous Coding
"Masa dulu I ingat lagi, dulu kita kena print tiga salinan [payment voucher]. tapi sekarang satu salinan instead."	"I remember the last time that we had to print three copies [of payment voucher]. But now we only have to print one copy."	– Only have to print one copy	– Paperless – Speed up process – Save time
"Dulu you buat claim, … sebulan [untuk diproses]. Tapi sekarang, … kalau you boleh hantar hari ni, you can get your payment tomorrow."	"Last time when you submitted a claim, … it would take you one month [to get processed]. But now, … if you submit your claim by today, you can get your payment by tomorrow."	– If you can submit your claim by today, you can get your payment by tomorrow	– Speed up process – Save time

(ii) Second Cycle of Coding

Direct Quotation from the Transcript	Translated Quotation	Focused Coding	Axial
"Masa dulu I ingat lagi, dulu kita kena print tiga salinan [payment voucher]. tapi sekarang satu salinan instead."	"I remember the last time that we had to print three copies [of payment voucher]. But now we only have to print one copy."	– Save cost – Speed up accounting process – Save time in processing	– Benefit from the system
[untuk diproses]. Tapi sekarang, … kalau you boleh hantar hari ni, you can get your payment tomorrow."	"Last time when you submitted a claim, … it would take you one month [to get processed]. But now, … if you submit your claim by today, you can get your payment by tomorrow."	– Speed up accounting process – Save time in processing	– Benefit from the system

Table A10.4   AIS effectiveness measurement

	Your Level of Satisfaction with the Current System				
	Very Dissatisfied	Dissatisfied	Neither Satisfied nor Dissatisfied	Satisfied	Very Satisfied
System Quality					
i. The system is easy to use (user friendly)	1	2	3	4	5
ii. The processing time (i.e. speed) of the system	1	2	3	4	5
iii. The system is able to produce report in a required format	1	2	3	4	5
Information Quality					
i. The information is accurate (no doubt)	1	2	3	4	5
ii. The information is complete (all transactions are captured accordingly)	1	2	3	4	5
iii. The information is relevant for use in decision-making	1	2	3	4	5
Benefit and Usefulness of AIS					
i. The system improves individual productivity	1	2	3	4	5
ii. The system improves the decision-making process	1	2	3	4	5
iii. The system minimises unintentional human error	1	2	3	4	5
iv. The system reduces hard copy submissions (paperless)	1	2	3	4	5

PART V

PRACTICAL APPLICATIONS OF ACCOUNTING INFORMATION SYSTEM RESEARCH

11. Going concern audit opinion: reducing information asymmetry

Dusica Stevcevska Srbinoska

11.1 INTRODUCTION

The financial scandals of the past few decades have called for greater scrutiny of the assurance process given the role of auditing as a social control mechanism in reducing information asymmetry between insiders and external stakeholders. The audit opinion is the main information vehicle used by auditors to provide public disclosure about the reliability of the entity's financial reporting and on the financial difficulties that may impede the auditee's ability to endure as a going concern. Given the importance of the aforementioned, the primary goal of this research is to examine the predictors and accuracy of going concern audit opinions (GCAOs). Scholars have embarked on examining the determining factors that shape audit opinions (Mareque, López-Corrales and Pedrosa, 2017; Czerney, Schmidt and Thompson, 2014; Christensen, Glover and Wolfe, 2014; Carson et al., 2013; Vermeer, Raghunandan and Forgione, 2013; Ettredge, Li and Emeigh, 2011; Reichelt and Wang, 2010; Boone, Khurana and Raman, 2010; Francis and Yu, 2009; Gaeremynck, Van Der Meulen and Willekens, 2008; Arnedo, Lizarraga and Sánchez, 2008; Geiger and Rama, 2006; Carey and Simnett, 2006; Choi, Doogar and Ganguly, 2004; Spathis, 2003; DeFond, Raghunandan and Subramanyam, 2002; Reynolds and Francis, 2001; Mutchler, Hopwood and McKeown, 1997; Dopuch, Holthausen and Leftwich, 1987; Mutchler, 1985 and many others). These scholars study different sets of variables that describe the auditor and the audited firm in order to establish associations with the opinion expressed by the auditor.

Some authors focus on examining the influence of company and auditor factors on going concern modifications in the report of the auditor (Mareque, López-Corrales and Pedrosa, 2017; Czerney, Schmidt and Thompson, 2014; Christensen, Glover and Wolfe, 2014; Vermeer, Raghunandan and Forgione, 2013; Carson et al., 2013; Arnedo, Lizarraga and Sánchez, 2008; DeFond, Raghunandan and Subramanyam, 2002; Mutchler, 1985), while others study the occurrence of earnings management in financially stressed entities (Lara, Osma and Neophytou, 2009; Rosner, 2003; Smith, Kestel and Robinson, 2001). In spite of this large body of literature, there is insufficient evidence concerning accounting behaviour in emerging economies and the relationship between earnings management and GCAO, which explains the need for the current research (for literature gaps see Dutzi and Rausch, 2016; Charitou, Lambertides and Trigeorgis, 2007).

Variations in national accounting legislation pose a viable hurdle when it comes to comparing the financial performance and position of domestic firms with firms operating in other national economies or even globally (Weygandt, Kimmel and Kieso, 2011). As capital markets and creditors become hungry for comparable performance data, the pressure for quality accounting in emerging economies has surfaced. Ergo, this chapter will look into the determinants of GCAOs as well as the going concern information asymmetry across audit firms in North Macedonia.

When the long-term financial well-being of the audited entity is uncertain, ISA 570, *Going Concern*, provides that the auditor is liable to elaborate and document this material uncertainty (International Standard on Auditing 570, 2015). Studying multiple auditee operating, financial and regulatory or market-specific parameters, the auditor needs to convey a message of material uncertainty in a separate paragraph indicating the auditee's disability to proceed as a going concern. Yet, even though ISA 570 foresees that the Emphasis of Matter paragraph will attract the reader's attention to a going concern uncertainty, auditors sometimes fail to gather sufficient audit evidence in making this decision. In consequence, the decision may trigger two kinds of information asymmetry: type I where a GCAO is issued to a subsequently viable entity, and type II where a GCAO is lacking although the entity subsequently files for bankruptcy.

Francis (2004) argues that erroneous audit opinions stand for audit reporting negligence. However, this discrepancy may also occur when the auditee voluntarily ceases operations or following a subsequent event. Many regulators have criticised auditors for failing to issue a timely warning on imminent auditee bankruptcy (Geiger, Raghunandan and Rama, 2005; Raghunandan and Rama, 1995). The inability to observe a material uncertainty (type II error) or erroneously detecting a considerable uncertainty when there is none (type I error) has been thoroughly studied by many researchers, especially knowing that national legislators are mainly concerned with type II errors (Geiger and Rama, 2006; Breeden, 2002; Dietz, 2002; Elias, 2001; Weil, 2001).

With this empirical research, we seek to enhance the existing accounting and auditing literature by assessing going concern audit reports in North Macedonia as a developing economy, thus contributing to future legislation amendments as well as to practitioners and certified accountants to better assess and disclose situations of financial distress. We also seek to investigate GCAO information asymmetry across audit firms. The data base is hand-collected from the SEI net site of the MSE (https://www.seinet.com.mk/default.aspx) and encompasses 93 public nonfinancial companies for the years 2015–2018, with 2014 as a lagged period. Out of 61 going concern opinions in total, 22 are first time. We place a particular emphasis on assessing the accuracy of GCAO in stressed versus healthy entities whereby we use Zmijewski's index (1984) as our financial distress indicator. Zmijewski's index has been used as a bankruptcy predictor in prior literature exploring audit report content (Carcello, Hermanson and Huss, 1995; Wheeler, Pany and Chewning, 1993). Our tests detected a positive albeit insignificant relationship between earnings management and GCAOs, as well as lower information asymmetry in non-Big4 auditors given the lower type II error rate in local brands.

This chapter is organised in the following manner: the first section introduces the research problem significance. Section 11.2 proceeds with a literature overview, enabling for specific hypotheses development. The design of the empirical study and the data collection process are presented in Section 11.3, whereas Section 11.4 presents the test results and summarises the key findings. Section 11.5 concludes the chapter while pinpointing our research limitations and future study opportunities.

11.2   HYPOTHESES DEVELOPMENT

11.2.1   Earnings Management and Going Concern Audit Opinion

Most accounting scandals from the past several decades revolved around management-orchestrated corporate fraud that has been largely linked to earnings management. As per Healy and Whalen (1999) and Schipper (1989), earnings management has been associated with the use of executive judgement to report results and structure transactions with the intention to mislead stakeholder opinion about corporate performance or to impact contracts that are based on reported corporate performance. Therefore, multiple studies have been concerned with exploring earnings management in various settings. Authors like Lara, Osma and Neophytou (2009), Rosner (2003) and Smith, Kestel and Robinson (2001) inspected the occurrence of earnings management in financially stressed entities. Univariate measurements indicate that stressed entities profess downward earnings manipulation before filing for bankruptcy after having previously inflated their financial performance. That is, upward earnings management pervades the entities that are not imminently financially strained. For that matter, Charitou, Lambertides and Trigeorgis (2007), Rosner (2003) and Kallunki and Martikainen (1999) detect more professed earnings manipulations in auditees with unqualified audit reports several years before filing for bankruptcy.

Auditees that were issued a qualified opinion professed elevated fraud occurrence as opposed to entities with a clean audit opinion, thus relating audit qualifications to fraud suspicion which goes beyond financial discomfort detection. Arnedo, Lizarraga, and Sánchez, (2008), Bradshaw, Richardson and Sloan (2001) and Bartov, Gul and Tsui (2000) perceive a significant relationship between audit modifications and substandard corporate reporting quality proxied by accounting accruals. Butler, Leone and Willenborg (2004) dispute this stance stating that the audit standards do not prompt for a GCAO in entities with deficient corporate reporting quality. Consistently, these researchers detect an association between outsized negative accruals, representing financial distress rather than earnings manipulation, and GCAOs. To the contrary, the work of Campa and Camacho-Miñano (2014) examining non-public Spanish entities three years before declaring bankruptcy provides evidence about upward earnings manipulation.

Given the lack of empirical consensus regarding accrual-based earnings management in relation to GCAOs, we can formulate our first hypothesis:

Hypothesis 1: *Ceteris paribus, earnings management will increase the likelihood of a going concern audit opinion.*

11.2.2   Going Concern Information Asymmetry

Agency theory defines the entity as agreements between self-regarding parties whereby the owners (principals) give power to managers (agents) to act on their behalf. Before diving into the going concern factor relationship, we need to discuss the concept of materiality as it is the pillar of the audit work and opinion statement. Stakeholder theory goes several steps further and defines the entity as a collection of agreements between multiple parties with differing interests, thereby adding creditors, vendors, customers, employees and others to the complex equation (Freeman, 1984). Conflicts of interest can harm the delicate relationship balance igniting agency problems or interest corrosion when some of the other parties are involved (DeAngelo, 1981). Stakeholder theory is of utmost importance for the current research as it seeks to establish the link between going concern opinions on one hand and audit quality as measured by the audit firm size on the other, thus inspecting the behaviour and material information asymmetry confines of a vital stakeholder, the auditor.

The International Standard on Auditing 320 defines materiality in the assurance context as 'misstatements, including omissions ... if they, individually or in the aggregate, could reasonably be expected to influence the economic decisions of users taken on the basis of the financial statements' (International Standard on Auditing 320, 2009). Materiality impacts the audit scope, risk assessment, and audit tests and is a determinant to planning, timing, and conducting the assurance steps and procedures. Setting and computing the materiality benchmark figure resides in the hands of the professional in charge of the audit especially given the lack of well-founded stands on materiality levels for various industries and entity sizes. Therefore, multiple researchers have studied the materiality decisions of auditors, focusing on variances in materiality thresholds between international and local audit firms (Ryu and Roh, 2007; Chewning, Pany and Wheeler, 1989; Messier, 1983; Holstrum and Messier, 1982). These studies detected major discrepancies in the materiality limits between audit firms of varying sizes. Namely, larger materiality thresholds exist in the big international audit firms leading to less going concern modifications for financially stressed auditees. Other authors tested the share of entities with GCAOs that do not enter bankruptcy (type I errors), or the share of entities going bankrupt without having received a going concern modification (type II errors). These authors rely on type I and type II reporting errors as a measure of audit quality and assert that the Big4 profess significantly lower error rates in both instances (Geiger and Rama, 2006; Lennox, 1999). Yet, Mutchler, Hopwood and McKeown (1997) failed to detect a significant difference in type II errors between the renowned global brands and local audit firms in issuing GCAOs to entities filing for bankruptcy within one year of the annual financial report.

GCAOs may be consequential for the auditor and the auditee. Specifically, if the auditor fails to detect a material going concern uncertainty and the auditee declares bankruptcy in the aftermath, the auditor may face litigation proceedings and be charged severe court fees (Geiger, Raghunandan and Rama, 2005; Geiger and Raghunandan, 2002; Krishnan and Krishnan, 1996; Carcello and Palmrose, 1994). To the contrary, literature also puts forth the idea of a self-fulfilling prophecy whereby an auditor may not go for a going concern modification in financially stressed firms fearing that the report itself may prompt failure (Kida, 1980). Type II error studies have generally established that less than 50 per cent of audit reports contain a GCAO.

Prospects for future benefits (or loss prevention) can inspire current decisions (Frederick, Loewenstein and O'Donoghue, 2002; George and Jones, 2000; Tversky and Kahneman, 1991). The auditor may face client and therefore revenue losses should they issue a GCAO and the auditee remains financially viable subsequently (Geiger, Raghunandan and Rama, 1998). Type I errors studies detect that 80 to 90 per cent of auditees with a GCAO remain financially viable (Geiger, Raghunandan and Rama, 1998; Nogler, 1995; Garsombke and Choi, 1992; Mutchler and Williams, 1990). Auditors are hired on behalf of company owners, but stakeholder theory has it that they may be inclined to act in their best self-interest should client loss be impending, thus damaging external audit report users (Bolten and Crockett, 1979). To this end, Numan and Willekens (2011) link GCAOs with audit market competitiveness and find a decrease in opinion modifications when market shares get close, which places market structure in the interest of regulators.

We therefore detect the need to assess audit information asymmetry by studying the GCAO accuracy through type I and type II errors in Big4 and non-Big4 audit brands. Hence, the ensuing hypothesis:

Hypothesis 2: There is less information asymmetry in Big4 auditors as reflected through lower type I and type II error rates.

11.3   SAMPLING PROCEDURE AND RESEARCH DESIGN

11.3.1   Sample Selection

The current research was conducted using a sample of all publicly traded nonfinancial firms listed on the Macedonian Stock Exchange (MSE). We hand-collected auditor and auditee information from the audited consolidated annual reports published on the MSE reporting system (https:// www .seinet .com .mk). Financial entities are not part of the research base given their regulation peculiarities. The sample contains information on 93 public firms over a four-year observation frame, from 2015–2018. 2014 was also retrieved for use in lagged variables. As per the Macedonian regulatory framework, MSE-listed companies comply with International Financial Reporting Standards (IFRS) for corporate reporting purposes, while the external auditing is compliant with the International Standard on Auditing (ISA) of the International Federation of Accountants (IFAC).

To arrive at the final sample, industry classifications containing less than eight observations were removed and so were missing data on financials and audit opinions. Outliers were also removed. Tables 11.1 and 11.2 explain the data set industry classification, the sampling process and data selection.

Table 11.1   Industry segmentation of the sample

	Observation count
Hospitality and transportation	106
Merchandising	36
Food and beverages	88
Chemicals and pharmaceuticals	12
Textile industry	27
Construction industry	27
Mining and metal industry	56
Preliminary observations	352

11.3.2   Research Models

We will hereby explain the two research models used to assess the influence of accrual-based earnings management on the issuance of going concern audit modification and the incidence of type I and type II error rates in audit reports. Given the importance of studying going

Table 11.2   Data sampling

Nonfinancial firms	93
Timeframe in years	4
No. of observations	372
Missing data and delisted firms	-20
Preliminary observations	352
Outliers	-11
Complete observations	341

concern modifications with the goal of reducing information asymmetry, there is a necessity to set an algorithm-driven threshold that will require auditors to issue a GCAO upon examining the client's annual accounts. This is even more vital in the context of emerging markets where a lack of literature is evident. The algorithm outcome may further be calibrated once reflecting upon industry and market specifics, but such an alteration will require the auditor to provide additional elaboration on the reasons not to proceed with a GCAO.

11.3.2.1 Empirical model: earnings management and going concern audit opinion

We define an empirical model to gauge the impact of earnings management on the issuance of GCAO. The first hypotheses will be tested by means of the following logistic regression model:

$$GCAO = \alpha + \beta 1 Lag + \beta 2 QAR + \beta 3 Big4 + \beta 4 CYLoss + \beta 5 LnAssets +$$
$$\beta 6 LnInt + \beta 7 Financing + \beta 8 CR + \beta 9 Lever + \beta 10 ROE + \beta 11 AssetTurnover +$$
$$\beta 12 Manuf + \beta 13 Inv + \beta 14 Rec + \beta 15 \Delta Sales + \beta 16 LagCFO + \beta 17 DA + \varepsilon \qquad (11.1)$$

where:

GCAO = 1 if the firm was issued a going concern audit opinion and 0 otherwise,

Lag = audit report delay computed as the number of days between the fiscal year-end and the audit report publication date,

QAR = 1 for a qualified, adverse or opinion disclaimer and 0 otherwise,

Big4 = 1 if the audit firm is PricewaterhouseCoopers, Deloitte, KPMG, Ernst and Young, 0 otherwise,

CYLoss = current-year loss, performance indicator, 1 when the firm incurs a current-year loss and 0 otherwise,

LnAssets = natural logarithm of total assets, company size measure,

LnInt = natural logarithm of intangibles,

Financing = 1 if external financing (debt and equity issued in Cash Flow Statement) exceeds 2 per cent of assets, 0 otherwise,

CR = current ratio, liquidity measure computed as the ratio of current assets to current liabilities,

Lever = leverage indicator computed as total liabilities to total equity,

ROE = profitability indicator computed as net profit to total equity,

AssetTurnover = activity measure, the ratio of sales to assets,

Manuf = 1 for listed manufacturing firms and 0 otherwise,

Inv = efficiency gauge calculated as inventory to assets,

Rec = efficiency gauge calculated as trade receivables to sales revenues,

ΔSales = the difference between current- and previous-year revenues,
LagCFO = operating cash flows to lagged assets,
DA = earnings management gauge (Model 1: DA, Model 2: DAroa, Model 3: DAcfo).

We are primarily interested in DA, a continuous variable that measures the extent of earnings management through discretionary accruals (DAs). Given Hypothesis 1 and prior research, we expect DA to profess a significant and negative association with the issuance of a going concern audit modification. Three DA models are applied to test the robustness of equation (11.1).

11.3.2.1.1 Model 1 for measuring earnings management – the modified Jones model
Our study of opportunistic managerial behaviour employs the modified Jones model to measure earnings manipulation. This approach goes one step beyond the original Jones model (Jones, 1991) as it controls for the effect of changes in the firm's financial position on non-DA items and relates noncash sales to earnings management (Dechow, Sloan, and Sweeney, 1995).

DA are our earnings management proxy employed to deter from ongoing weaknesses in financial results or to safeguard for future use (Reynolds, Deis and Francis, 2004; Gul, Sun and Tsui, 2003; Francis, Maydew and Sparks, 1999).

We first compute the total accruals of firm i in year t:

$$Acc_{it} = NI_{it} - CFO_{it} \qquad (11.2)$$

where Acc_{it} represents entity i's total accruals in year t, NI_{it} stands for firm i's posttax profit in year t whereas CFO_{it} denotes firm i's operating cash flows in year t.

We proceed with industry classifications following the Macedonian national classification of economic activities and generate the modified Jones model:

$$\frac{Acc_{it}}{A_{it-1}} = \alpha1\left(\frac{1}{A_{it-1}}\right) + \alpha2\left(\Delta Sales_{it} - \frac{\Delta REC_{it}}{A_{it-1}}\right) + \alpha3\left(\frac{PPE_{it}}{A_{it-1}}\right) + \varepsilon_{it} \qquad (11.3)$$

where Acc_{it} represents entity i's total accruals in year t, A_{it-1} firm i's total assets in year t – 1, $\Delta Sales_{it}$ the annual sales difference of firm i in year t computed as follows: $\Delta Sales_{it} = Sales_{it} - Sales_{it-1}$, ΔREC_{it} is firm i's year-over-year difference in receivables in year t computed as follows: $\Delta REC_{it} = REC_{it} - REC_{it-1}$, and PPE_{it} is firm i's property, plant and equipment in year t. The coefficients from equation (11.3) are then used in equation (11.4) for the computation of non-discretionary accruals (ND):

$$ND_{it-i} = \alpha1\left(1/A_{it-1}\right) + \alpha_2\left(\frac{(\Delta Sales_{it} - \Delta REC_{it})}{A_{it-1}}\right) + \alpha_3\left(PPE_{it}/A_{it-1}\right) \qquad (11.4)$$

where the elements are as discussed above.

Lastly, the discretionary accruals (DA) are the difference between total accruals and non-discretionary accruals:

$$DA = Acc_{it} - ND_{it} \qquad (11.5)$$

11.3.2.1.2 Model 2 for measuring earnings management – modified Jones model including previous-year ROA

Following Kothari, Leone and Wasley (2005), firms with unusual performance are expected to employ accruals to manage earnings. We therefore include ROA in the modified Jones model in an effort to exercise an improved control on performance:

$$\text{Acc}_{it}/A_{it-1} = \alpha_1 (1/A_{it-1}) + \alpha_2 (\Delta\text{Sales}_{it} - \Delta\text{REC}_{it}/A_{i,t-1}) +$$
$$\alpha_3 (\text{PPE}_{it}/A_{it-1}) + \alpha_4 (\text{ROA}_{it-1}) + \varepsilon_{it} \qquad (11.6)$$

where ROA $_{it-1}$ represents the ratio of net profit to total assets for the preceding year. The remaining variables follow the definitions set in equation (11.3).

We then employ these fitted values to arrive at the DA figure (DAroa).

11.3.2.1.3 Model 3 for measuring earnings management – modified Jones model including cash flow from operations

Following Larcker and Richardson (2004), we add CFO to Dechow, Sloan and Sweeney's modified Jones model (1995), thus aiming for an enhanced DA computation accuracy:

$$\text{Acc}_{it}/A_{it-1} = \alpha_1 (1/A_{it-1}) + \alpha_2 (\Delta\text{Sales}_{it} - \Delta\text{REC}_{it}/A_{it-1}) +$$
$$\alpha_3 (\text{PPE}_{it}/A_{it-1}) + \alpha_4 (\text{CFO}_{it}/A_{it-1}) + \varepsilon_{it} \qquad (11.7)$$

where CFO $_{it}$ represents the firm's operating cash flows, and remaining variables are as in equation (11.3).

We then employ these fitted values to arrive at the DAs figure (DAcfo).

11.3.2.1.4 Control variables

Considering existing research, we control for multiple auditee and auditor features to test Hypothesis 1 where the going concern modification is the dependent variable. These features are encompassed but not limited to the requirements of ISA 570 that prompt the auditor to assess going concern uncertainty by studying multiple auditee operating, financial and market-specific parameters. Following Behn, Kaplan, and Krumwiede (2001), Carcello, Hermanson and Iluss (1995), and McKeown, Mutchler and Hopwood (1991), we employ auditee size (LnAssets), audit opinion delay (Lag), and solvency risk (Lever) as control variables. To begin with, even though big entities are in a better negotiation position, auditors may take a more conservative stance given the accentuated lawsuit perils (Reynolds and Francis, 2001; McKeown, Mutchler and Hopwood, 1991). Yet, Mutchler, Hopwood and McKeown (1997), McKeown, Mutchler and Hopwood (1991) and Dopuch, Holthausen and Leftwich (1987) link smaller firms to GCAOs. Audit report delay is another factor in financially stressed firms since modified reports are more intricate to prepare given the auditee complexities, internal control lacks, and audit procedures required (Ettredge, Li and Sun, 2006; DeFond, Raghunandan and Subramanyam, 2002; Mutchler, Hopwood and McKeown, 1997; Carcello, Hermanson, and Huss, 1995).

We gauge industry risk by adding an industry indicator variable (Manuf), whereby manufacturing firms denote risky operating sectors prone to elevated material internal control weaknesses (Kasznik and Lev, 1995). As previous research emphasises significant drawbacks in internal controls, we seek to control for complex, fast-growing and less profitable company features given that they may modify the audit report for going concern (Jiang, Rupley and

Wu, 2010; Jiao, Mertens and Roosenboom, 2007; Doyle, Ge and McVay, 2007; Lee, Jiang and Anandarajan, 2005; Ge and McVay, 2005; Mutchler, 1985). Companies lacking sufficient profitability or expressing a bottom-line loss have elevated failure prospects. Thus, we further enhance the industry risk specifics by adding relevant proxies in our logistic regression model: the levels of assets tied up in inventory (Inv) and receivables (Rec), profitability (ROE), current-year loss (CYLoss), level of activity (AssetTurnover), and growth pace (ΔSales). As technology can promote the quality of audited accounting data and support stakeholder economic decisions, we introduce investments in intangibles (LnInt) as a control variable (Almasria et al., 2021; Handoko, Sabrina and Ayuanda, 2019). Finally, given that under-performing cash flows from operations impede the financial viability and increase financial failure prospects, we add operating cash flow to lagged assets (LagCFO) as our financial performance indicator.

Should material errors or lacking evidence prevail, auditors proceed to form a qualified opinion, adverse opinion or a disclaimer of opinion as regulated by the ISA 705, *Modifications to the opinion in the independent auditor's report* (International Standard on Auditing 705, 2015). Given the premise that unsatisfactory corporate reporting quality ignites the issue of modified opinions in auditors (Arnedo, Lizarraga and Sánchez, 2008; Bradshaw, Richardson and Sloan, 2001; Bartov, Gul and Tsui, 2000), we proceed by adding a predictor variable (QAR) for qualified, adverse or opinion disclaimer.

Financing is a predictor that expresses the company's aptitude to swiftly raise cash. Entities with elevated financing aptitude have more resources in hand to fight off financial failure and are less prone to GCAOs (DeFond, Raghunandan and Subramanyam, 2002; Behn, Kaplan and Krumwiede, 2001). In addition, going concern opinions are directly correlated with debt covenant violations and elevated leverage (Menon and Williams, 2010; Mutchler, Hopwood and McKeown, 1997; Mutchler, 1985; Kida, 1980), which calls for the use of our default indicator, (Lever), computed as total liabilities to total equity. Lower liquidity is often linked to GCAOs (Raghunandan and Rama, 1995; Koh, 1991; Mutchler, 1985; Kida 1980), triggering the use of current ratio (CR) as our liquidity gauge. As noted in Weber and Willenborg (2003) and DeFond, Raghunandan and Subramanyam (2002), going concern modifications are more frequent in the Big4 global auditors as opposed to other brands. This stance contrasts DeFond, Francis and Hu (2011), Reichelt and Wang (2010), and Geiger and Rama (2003), which necessitates the use of the audit firm type determinant (Big4) as our control variable.

11.3.2.2 Empirical model: information asymmetry
Considering existing literature (Carcello, Vanstraelen and Willenborg, 2009; Knechel and Vanstraelen, 2007; Geiger and Rama, 2006), we define the following empirical model to gauge the probability of type I and type II errors upon issuance of GCAO and test the second hypotheses:

$$GCAO_i = \alpha_0 + \beta1Big4_i + + \beta2Lag_i + \beta3LnAssets_i + \beta4CR_i + \beta4CYLoss_i \qquad (11.8)$$

where:

GCAO= 1 if the firm was issued a going concern audit opinion and 0 otherwise,
Big4 = 1 if the audit firm is PricewaterhouseCoopers, Deloitte, KPMG, Ernst and Young,
0 otherwise,
Lag = audit report delay computed as the number of days between the fiscal year-end and
the audit report publication date,
LnAssets = natural logarithm of total assets, company size measure,
CR = current ratio, liquidity measure computed as the ratio of current assets to current
liabilities.
CYLoss = current-year loss, performance indicator, 1 when the firm incurs a current-year
loss and 0 otherwise.

Nonetheless, our model differs somewhat from the approach of the above-mentioned researchers. This is due to several factors. We first needed to incorporate the market specifics using profitability and liquidity parameters. In addition, the sole way to distinguish between auditors was by applying the Big4/non-Big4 classification given the lack of legal obligation to report on audit/non-audit fee per client. There is also no public information on age, sex, education, specialisation and experience of auditors in the Macedonian market.

The model is applied separately to financially stressed and financially viable firms. Following Reynolds and Francis (2001) and Carcello, Hermanson and Huss (1995), we used Zmijewski's bankruptcy probability to gauge the financial distress level. Given the strain in assessing the subsequent financial stability of GCAO firms as a result of delayed filings or company status changes (Rama, Raghunandan and Geiger, 1997; Nogler, 1995), we will classify the firms in our sample as financially stressed if the Zmijewski index exceeds 0. The Zmijewski index is calculated using the coefficients and determinants set by Zmijewski (1984):

$$Zmijewski = -4.336 - 4.513 \left(\text{Profit After} \frac{\text{Tax}}{\text{Total}} \text{Assets} \right) +$$
$$5.679 \left(\text{Total} \frac{\text{Liabilities}}{\text{Total}} \text{Assets} \right) + 0.004 \text{ (Current ratio)} \qquad (11.9)$$

Within the financially viable group of firms, those who were issued a GCAO represent type I reporting errors. Likewise, the firms that were not presented with a GCAO within the financially stressed company lot are considered type II errors.

We encompass variables to control for determinants that influence the auditor decision to issue a going concern modification, which helps us avoid correlated omitted factor issues. Following Reynolds and Francis (2001), McKeown, Mutchler and Hopwood (1991), Mutchler, Hopwood and McKeown (1997) and Dopuch, Holthausen and Leftwich (1987), we add auditee size variable (LnAssets) given their contrasted size-related test results. Considering the lower likelihood of issuing a GCAO to big firms, we expect size to have a negative coefficient for the non-stressed group of firms and positive for the stressed groups of firms. Audit report timeliness (Lag) is also found to be intricate in bankrupt entities (Ettredge, Li and Sun, 2006; DeFond, Raghunandan and Subramanyam, 2002; Mutchler, Hopwood and McKeown, 1997; Carcello, Hermanson, and Huss, 1995), followed by drops in liquidity (Raghunandan and Rama, 1995; Koh 1991; Mutchler 1985; Kida 1980), eliciting the use of current ratio (CR) as our liquidity control variable. Lastly, we control for profitability or rather the lack of it (CYLoss) given that GCAOs are more frequent in entities with poor financial results (Lee, Jiang and Anandarajan, 2005; Reynolds and Francis, 2001; Mutchler, 1985; Kida, 1980).

11.4   RESULTS

11.4.1   Earnings Management and Going Concern Audit Opinion

As inferred from Table 11.3, there is a limited incidence of going concern modifications in North Macedonia (18 per cent of the total opinions observed), and a raised prevalence of report qualifications (47 per cent). Given the low rating of the country's legislative system and deficient anticorruption implementation (Evaluation report: North Macedonia, 2019), it can be discerned that potential legal proceedings costs are not of particular concern to Macedonian audit firms. Nonetheless, auditors do perceive a risk in growing and preserving the existing client base, a status further endangered by the high concentration of the Macedonian audit market where 44 audit firms tap the same revenue base (Sovet za unapreduvanje i nadzor na revizijata na Republika Makedonija [SUNRRM], 2018); hence, the relationship to type II error in audit reports that link revenue incentives to the avoidance of GCAOs (Carcello, Vanstraelen and Willenborg, 2009; Branson and Breesch, 2004).

Furthermore, the entities in our sample have an elevated liquidity score (mean CR = 4.54). However, receivables have a large presence in the current ratio calculation, and they are considered the least liquid current asset given that receivables collection in North Macedonia has averaged over three months as opposed to two months in the developed European countries (Janev, 2021). The audit opinion timeliness averages around four months which is aligned with the five-month cut-off date as per the Macedonian Law on securities (2018). Fifty-one firms denote a publication lag, 17 of which have a going concern modification, elucidating the delay deviance. Operating in a developing economy, the entities from our sample have low and negative profitability indicators, a momentum which preconditions the elevated levels of earnings manipulation demonstrated by the average DA.

The logistic regression test results for Hypothesis 1 are laid out in Table 11.5.

The models depicted in Table 11.5 are significant ($p < .001$). The regression results show that the three DA gauges for measuring earnings management models have a positive but statistically insignificant association with the issuance of going concern modifications. We can thus reject Hypothesis 1. Considering the above-stated, earnings management and discretionary accounting will rather be reflected in an opinion qualification than a going concern paragraph. That is, going concern opinions are impacted by material uncertainties, not material errors or lack of evidence that entail opinion qualifications.

As for the remaining contributing factors, and in conformity with authors like Jiang, Rupley and Wu (2010); Jiao, Mertens and Roosenboom (2007); Ettredge, Li and Sun (2006); Reynolds and Francis (2001); DeFond, Raghunandan and Subramanyam (2002); Mutchler, Hopwood and McKeown (1997); Carcello, Hermanson and Huss (1995); and Kida, (1980), going concern modifications are directly and significantly associated with negative bottom line results (CYLoss), delay in publishing the audit opinion (Lag), and operating complexity (Inv).

We also denote that lower liquidity (CR) is linked to GCAOs (Kida, 1980; Mutchler, 1985; Koh, 1991; Raghunandan and Rama, 1995). However, unlike prior research, the sample shows an inverse relationship between GCAOs and manufacturing entities (Manuf). This may be

Table 11.3   *Descriptive statistics, equation (11.1) variables*

		Mean	SD	Minimum	Maximum		No.
Predictor variables							
Lag	Days lag	116.45	37.08	36.00	345.00		341
Audite size	LnAssets	13.25	1.57	7.00	17.00		341
Intangibles	Lnint	4.42	4.23	0.00	14.81		341
Current ratio	CR	4.54	10.00	0.00	124.41		341
Debt to equity	Lever	0.51	3.61	-3.97	15.25		341
Return on equity	ROE	-0.02	0.59	-10.17	0.55		341
AssetTurnover	AssetTurnover	0.58	0.59	0.00	5.36		334
Inventory to assets	Inv	0.13	0.14	0.00	0.71		341
Receivables to sales	Rec	0.74	5.13	0.00	68.49		341
Change in sales	ΔSales	49710	507448	-1986277	4413267		341
CFO to lagged assets	LagCFO	0.05	0.12	-0.34	1.01		341
Discretionary accrual, Model 1	DA	0.14	0.19	-0.26	0.97		341
Discretionary accrual, Model 2	DAroa	0.11	0.41	-5.86	0.99		341
Discretionary accrual, Model 3	DAcfo	0.10	0.27	-2.23	1.06		341
Dependent variable		*n*	*%*		*n*	*%*	*No.*
Going concern audit opinion	GCAO	61	17.9	No-GC	280	82.1	341
Predictor variables		*n*	*%*		*n*	*%*	*No.*
Qualified audit opinion	QAR	161	47.2	Clean opinion	180	52.8	341
Audit firm size	Big4	44	12.9	Non-Big4	297	87.1	341
Current-year loss	CYLoss	87	25.5	Profit	254	74.5	341
Debt and equity issued	Financing	31	9.1	Non-financing	310	90.9	341
Manufacturing	Manuf	203	59.5	Non-manufacturing	138	40.5	341

Note: The multicollinearity test using the Pearson correlation matrix depicted in Table 11.4 designates weak correlations between the predictors given that the scores are below the 0.7 threshold (Landau and Everitt, 2004). These results are further supported by the VIF scores as the highest value does not exceed 2.0.

explained by the greater vigilance auditors dedicate to assessing complex industries, thus seeking to reduce audit risk.

11.4.2   Going Concern Information Asymmetry

Table 11.6 presents the descriptive statistics and univariate tests for information asymmetry in our financially viable and stressed samples. Conforming to the results of Francis (2011) and Louwers (1998), type I reporting errors constitute 8 per cent of the viable firms' sample: 24 healthy entities received a GCAO. Type I errors were less prevalent among Big4 auditors (Big4: 4 versus 9 per cent). Furthermore, type I errors are more widespread in entities with current-year loss than in profitable firms (CYLoss: 27 versus 4 per cent), entities with larger audit report publication lag (Lag: 137.33 versus 110.71) and higher liquidity (CR: 8.79 versus 4.87).

As for type II errors (distressed entities lacking a GCAO), 21 per cent (10 entities) were not issued a going concern modification. This outcome is in line with Myers, Schmidt and Wilkins (2014) and Koh (1991). Type II errors were less frequent among local audit brands (Big4: 10 versus 39 per cent). Moreover, distressed entities lacking a GCAO were bigger (LnAssets: 13.60 versus 12.00), and more profitable (CYLoss: 36 versus 17 per cent).

Table 11.4   Correlations

	Lag	QAR	Big4	CY-Loss	LnAssets	LnInt	Financ-ing	CR	Lever	Asset-Turnover	Manuf	Inv	Rec	ΔSales	LagCFO	DA	DAroa	DAcfo	ROE
Lag	1																		
QAR	.277**	1																	
Big4	.004	-.066	1																
CYLoss	.252**	.147**	.096	1															
LnAssets	-.156**	-.134*	.329**	-.348**	1														
LnInt	-.229**	-.167**	.306**	-.221**	.548**	1													
Financing	.119*	.048	.243**	.072	.177**	.122*	1												
CR	-.139*	-.064	-.114*	-.038	-.056	-.106	-.064	1											
Lever	.024	-.015	-.086	.161*	-.088	-.046	.079	-.051	1										
Asset-Turnover	-.110*	-.099	.399**	-.106	.375**	.386**	.138*	-.080	-.028	1									
Manuf	.080	-.106	.175**	-.120*	.209**	.203**	.115*	-.144**	-.085	.199**	1								
Inv	.077	-.126*	.064	-.004	.241**	.233**	.200**	-.071	.046	.276**	.548**	1							
Rec	.016	.021	.070	.148**	-.148**	-.091	-.028	.047	-.007	-.100	-.024	-.075	1						
ΔSales	-.038	.015	.176**	-.005	.133*	.074	.093	-.009	-.016	.432**	.019	.053	-.018	1					
LagCFO	-.175**	-.185**	.162**	-.136*	.080	.157**	-.237**	.045	-.081	.138*	.054	-.089	-.012	.073	1				
DA	.171**	-.058	.202**	.124*	.080	.090	.217**	-.062	-.008	.040	.229**	.094	.040	.041	.128*	1			
DAroa	.007	.038	-.121*	-.096	.179**	.124*	.113*	.011	-.008	.048	.041	.098	-.120*	.023	-.298**	.320**	1		
DAcfo	.182**	.070	.028	.074	.074	-.014	.174**	-.066	.000	-.009	.079	.122*	.065	-.036	-.574**	.444**	.598**	1	
ROE	-.096	-.018	.048	-.227**	.017	.051	-.175**	.032	-.608**	.026	-.010	-.135*	-.010	.031	.241**	-.037	-.012	-.091	1

** Correlation is significant at the 0.01 level (two-tailed)

* Correlation is significant at the 0.05 level (two-tailed)

Table 11.5   *Logistic regression results for Hypothesis 1: earnings management and going concern audit opinion (dependent variable = GCAO, n = 341)*

	Model 1: DA				Model 2: DAroa				Model 3: DAcfo		
	B	S.E.	Sig.		B	S.E.	Sig.		B	S.E.	Sig.
Lag	.047	.020	.020		.047	.020	.021		.048	.021	.020
QAR	1.465	.986	.137		1.426	.979	.145		1.439	.980	.142
Big4	.274	2.104	.896		.352	2.079	.866		.667	2.056	.746
CYLoss	3.088	1.500	.040		3.168	1.530	.038		3.035	1.495	.042
LnAssets	.031	.434	.944		.018	.436	.966		.022	.435	.950
LnInt	.078	.149	.602		.083	.150	.578		.081	.150	.588
Financing	2.182	2.056	.289		2.056	2.064	.319		2.101	2.021	.299
CR	-8.572	2.453	.000		-8.601	2.492	.001		-8.687	2.515	.001
Lever	.716	.433	.098		.693	.435	.111		.701	.435	.107
ROE	-11.399	6.259	.069		-10.919	6.426	.089		-11.226	6.191	.070
AssetTurnover	-6.401	3.514	.068		-6.481	3.524	.066		-6.750	3.574	.059
Manuf	-2.777	1.346	.039		-2.752	1.335	.039		-2.833	1.364	.038
Inv	11.969	5.698	.036		12.072	5.710	.034		12.517	5.854	.033
Rec	.711	.595	.233		.725	.596	.224		.704	.587	.230
ΔSales	.000	.000	.449		.000	.000	.432		.000	.000	.415
LagCFO	12.208	8.875	.169		12.035	8.845	.174		13.021	8.945	.145
DA/DAroa/DAcfo	2.364	2.090	.258		2.512	2.048	.220		2.372	2.149	.270
Constant	-3.106	6.039	.607		-2.915	6.061	.631		-2.973	6.057	.624
Model 1 tests					Model 2 tests				Model 3 tests		
Model Chi-sq. = 157.98 (p < .001)					Model Chi-sq. = 158.20 (p < .001)				Model Chi-sq. = 157.90 (p < .001)		
Pseudo R2 = .847					Pseudo R2 = .848				Pseudo R2 = .847		
*PAC = 97.2%					*PAC = 97.2%				*PAC = 97.2%		
All p-values are two-tailed											
The variables are defined in equation (11.1)											

Note: *PAC = percentage accuracy in classification

Table 11.6   *Descriptive statistics for information asymmetry: type I and type II errors*

	Financially viable sample (n = 294)					Financially stressed sample (n = 47)				
	GCAO (N = 24)		Non-GCAO (N = 270)		Differences	GCAO (N = 37)		Non-GCAO (N = 10)		Differences
Variable	Mean	SD	Mean	SD	t-statistic	Mean	SD	Mean	SD	t-statistic
Continuous										
Lag	137.33	19.93	110.71	35.82	-5.768*	141.16	40.60	129.70	33.41	-0.819
LnAssets	12.96	1.49	13.44	1.31	1.702	12.00	2.66	13.60	0.52	3.432*
CR	8.79	25.59	4.87	9.15	-0.746*	0.35	0.37	0.86	0.41	3.746
Dichotomous	n	%	n	%		n	%	n	%	
Big4	1	4	25	96	0.840	11	61	7	39	2.418
Non-Big4	23	9	245	91		26	90	3	10	
CYLoss	14	27	37	73	-4.254*	30	83	6	17	-1.199*
no-CYLoss	10	4	233	96		7	64	4	36	
* Correlation is significant at the 0.05 level										

Table 11.7   Logistic regression for Hypothesis 2: information asymmetry, type I and type II errors

Type I errors: Financially viable data set (n = 294)				Type II errors: Financially stressed data set (n = 47)		
	B	S.E.	Sig.	B	S.E.	Sig.
Big4	-.766	1.141	.502	-9.005	4.139	.030
Lag	.017	.006	.003	.022	.033	.510
LnAssets	.113	.201	.573	1.263	.581	.030
CR	0.024	0.014	.080	-12.058	4.580	.008
CYLoss	2.186	0.505	.000	2.756	1.707	.106
Constant	-6.805	2.933	.020	-6.955	5.877	.237
Model tests				Model tests		
Model Chi-sq. = 33.54 ($p < .001$)				Model Chi-sq. = 31.73 ($p < .001$)		
Pseudo R2 = .250				Pseudo R2 = .761		
*PAC = 91.2%				*PAC = 95.7%		
All p-values are two-tailed						
Variables are defined underneath equation (11.1)						
*PAC = percentage accuracy in classification						

The regression outcomes for information asymmetry in our two samples are depicted in Table 11.7. Given the statistical significance of our model in the type I error sample ($p < .001$), we can conclude that there is greater accuracy in issuing going concern modifications in entities that publish their annual reports on time (Lag) and entities that incur positive financial results (CYLoss).

In addition, the logistic regression model is also statistically significant for our financially stressed company sample ($p < .001$). We can infer from Table 11.7 that type II errors are less frequent in local auditors (Big4), larger firms (LnAssets), and entities with lower liquidity (CR).

11.5   CONCLUDING REMARKS

Who checks the work of accountants? And why does the accounting profession require great commitment and responsibility? Aside from the role of state institutions in assuring accounting data quality, the auditor acts as an indispensable external control mechanism, so this chapter looked into the interplay between two seemingly opposing professions, accountants and auditors. Given that stakeholder decisions are shaped using data obtained from accounting, the audit opinion communicates essential information on the quality of financial reporting and the company's ability to proceed as a going concern. Therefore, this chapter examined two different aspects in relation to GCAOs: the impact of earnings management on the issuance of GCAO, and the extent of information asymmetry in GCAOs measured by the occurrence of type I and type II reporting errors.

Given the insufficient body of literature that assesses the impact of earnings manipulation on GCAOs, the first model encompassed multiple auditor, auditee and industry sector determinants that have historically been linked with going concern reporting. Using a data set of 93 MSE-listed nonfinancial firms, we tested whether earnings management increases the likelihood of a GCAO. The results point out a positive but statistically insignificant association between earnings management measured via DAs and going concern modifications. However, our model indicates that traditional material uncertainty parameters such as auditee profitability and liquidity, annual report timeliness, and sector complexity do play a significant role in the modification process.

Moreover, given the mixed literature evidence, our research also sought to assess the GCAO reporting accuracy and information asymmetry in Big4 versus other auditors. Categorising the same observation sample into financially viable and financially stressed entities using Zmijewski's index, we tested if Big4 audit firms exhibit lower information asymmetry and better assurance quality measured by less frequent type I and type II reporting errors. The results point to lower information asymmetry among local audit brands when it comes to type II errors. That is, non-Big4 auditors depict a greater reporting accuracy in issuing GCAOs to financially stressed companies. Furthermore, type II error information asymmetry is lower in larger and less liquid entities. The audit firm affiliation proves to have no impact on the incidence of type I reporting errors where lack of profitability and timeliness are significantly associated with opinion modifications.

The Hypothesis 1 test results indicate that, although largely present, DAs and earnings manipulation do not trigger a GCAO. As in Butler, Leone and Willenborg (2004), going concern modifications are primarily focused on material uncertainties rather than material financial statement misrepresentations and errors. As for Hypothesis 2, we can seek plausible explanations for the information asymmetry in the Macedonian legislation and institutional gaps (Evaluation report: North Macedonia, 2019). Lawsuit and reputation risks are not of particular concern to the Big4 audit firms considering the loose institutional and legal environment. But, the Big4 are aware of the market share preservation risk given the concentrated Macedonian assurance market; hence, the relationship to type II error in audit reports that link revenue incentives to the avoidance of GCAOs (Carcello, Vanstraelen and Willenborg, 2009; Branson and Breesch, 2004).

Lastly, our findings are subject to a few limitations. To begin with, although we applied three different models for measuring managerial discretion in earnings management, they have all been subject to multiple critiques concerning their accuracy (Dechow, Sloan and Sweeney, 1995). However, they are handy gauges, Model 2 and 3 in particular, as they account for entity profitability and cash flows, parameters which are important considering the hampered liquidity and profitability of the Macedonian nonfinancial sector. Secondly, information asymmetry measured by type I and II errors in audit reports is not a unique indicator of audit quality in going concern decisions. Finally, our financially stressed data set is comprised of 47 observations which may hamper the applicability of the conclusions reached. These aspects can be embraced by future research to further calibrate the empirical models and research results.

REFERENCES

Almasria, A. N., Airout, R. M., Samara, A. I., Saadat, M. and Jrairah, T. S. (2021). The role of accounting information systems in enhancing the quality of external audit procedures. *Journal of Management Information and Decision Sciences*, 24 (S2), 1–23.

Arnedo, L., Lizarraga, F. and Sánchez, S. (2008). Going-concern uncertainties in pre-bankrupt audit reports: New evidence regarding discretionary accruals and wording ambiguity. *International Journal of Auditing*, 12 (1), 25–44.

Bartov, E., Gul, F. A. and Tsui, J. S. L. (2000) Discretionary-accruals models and audit qualifications. *Journal of Accounting and Economics*, 30 (3), 421–452.

Behn, B. K., Kaplan, S. E. and Krumwiede, K. R. (2001) Further evidence on the auditor's going concern report: The influence of management plans. *Auditing: A Journal of Practice and Theory*, 20 (1), 13–28.

Bolten, S. E. and Crockett, Jr. J. H. (1979) How independent are the independent auditors? *Financial Analysts Journal*, 35 (6), 76–78.

Boone, J., Khurana, I. and Raman, K. (2010) Do the Big 4 and the second-tier firms provide audits of similar quality? *Journal of Accounting and Public Policy*, 29 (4), 330–352.

Bradshaw, M., Richardson, S. A. and Sloan, R. (2001) Do analysts and auditors use information in accruals? *Journal of Accounting Research*, 39 (1), 45–74.

Branson, J. and Breesch, D. (2004) Referral as a determining factor for changing auditors in the belgian auditing market: An empirical study. *International Journal of Accounting*, 39 (3), 307–328.

Breeden, R. (2002) *Testimony: Oversight hearing on accounting and investor protection issues raised by Enron and other public companies*. U.S. Senate Committee on Banking, Housing and Urban Affairs, U.S. Senate, 12 February.

Butler, M., Leone, A. J. and Willenborg, M. (2004) An empirical analysis of auditor reporting and its association with abnormal accruals. *Journal of Accounting and Economics*, 37 (2), 139–166.

Campa, D. and Camacho-Miñano, M. (2014) Earnings management among bankrupt non-listed firms: Evidence from Spain. *Spanish Journal of Finance and Accounting*, 43 (1), 3–20.

Carcello, J. V. and Palmrose, Z.-V. (1994) Auditor litigation and modified reporting on bankrupt clients. *Journal of Accounting Research*, 32 (Supplement), 1–30.

Carcello, J.V., Vanstraelen, A. and Willenborg, M. (2009) Rules rather than discretion in audit standards: Going concern opinions in Belgium. *Accounting Review*, 84, 1395–1428.

Carcello, J. V., Hermanson, D. and Huss, F. (1995) Temporal changes in bankruptcy-related reporting. *Auditing: A Journal of Practice and Theory*, 14 (Fall), 133–143.

Carey, P. and Simnett, R. (2006) Audit partner tenure and audit quality. *Accounting Review*, 81 (3), 653–676.

Carson, E., Fargher, N., Geiger, M. A., Lennox, C., Raghunandan, K. and Willekens, M. (2013) Auditor reporting on going-concern uncertainty: A research synthesis. *Auditing: A Journal of Practice and Theory*, 32 (1), 353–384.

Charitou, A., Lambertides, N. and Trigeorgis, L. (2007) Managerial discretion in distressed firms. *British Accounting Review*, 39 (4), 323–346.

Chewning, G., Pany, K. and Wheeler, S. (1989) Auditor reporting decisions involving accounting principle changes: Some evidence on materiality thresholds. *Journal of Accounting Research*, 27 (1), 78–96.

Choi, J. H., Doogar, R. K. and Ganguly, A. R. (2004) The riskiness of large audit firm client portfolios and changes in audit liability regimes: Evidence from the U.S. audit market. *Contemporary Accounting Research*, 21 (4), 747–785.

Christensen, B. E., Glover, S. M. and Wolfe, C. J. (2014) Do critical audit matter paragraphs in the audit report change nonprofessional investors' decision to invest? *Auditing: A Journal of Practice and Theory*, 33 (4), 71–93.

Czerney, K., Schmidt, J. J. and Thompson, A. M. (2014) Does auditor explanatory language in unqualified audit reports indicate increased financial misstatement risk? *Accounting Review*, 89 (6), 2115–2149.

DeAngelo, L. E., (1981) Auditor size and audit quality. *Journal of Accounting and Economics*, 3 (3), 183–199.

Dechow, P., Sloan, R. and Sweeney, A. (1995) Detecting earnings management. *Accounting Review*, 70 (2), 193–225.

DeFond, M. L., Francis, J. R. and Hu, X. (2011) *The geography of SEC enforcement and auditor reporting for financially distressed clients*. Working paper, University of Southern California, University of Missouri at Columbia, and University of Oregon.

DeFond, M. L., Raghunandan, K. and Subramanyam, K. R. (2002) Do non-audit service fees impair auditor independence? Evidence from going concern audit opinions. *Journal of Accounting Research*, 40 (4), 1247–1274.

Dietz, D. (2002) *Auditors are timid. They failed to warn in most big firm bankruptcies since 1996*. *Pittsburgh Post-Gazette*, 26 April .

Dopuch, N., Holthausen, R. and Leftwich, R. (1987) Predicting audit qualifications with financial and market variables. *Accounting Review*, 62 (3), 431–454.

Doyle, J., Ge, W. and McVay, S. (2007) Determinants of weaknesses in internal control over financial reporting. *Journal of Accounting and Economics*, 44 (September), 193–223.

Dutzi, A. and Rausch, B. (2016) Earnings management before bankruptcy: A review of the literature. *Journal of Accounting and Auditing: Research & Practice*, 2016, 1–21.

Elias, D. (2001) HIH auditors face scrutiny. *The Age*, 6 December.

Ettredge, M., Li, C. and Emeigh, E. (2011) *Auditor independence during the 'Great Recession' of 2007–2009*. Working paper, The University of Kansas, University of Pittsburgh.

Ettredge, M., Li, C. and Sun, L. (2006) The impact of SOX Section 404 internal control quality assessment on audit delay in the SOX era. *Auditing: A Journal of Practice and Theory*, 25 (2), 1–23.

Evaluation report: North Macedonia. (2019). [online] Available at: [Accessed 17 February, 2022].

Francis, J. R. (2011). A framework for understanding and researching audit quality. *Auditing: A Journal of Practice and Theory*, 30 (2), 125–152.

Francis, J. R. (2004) What do we know about audit quality? *British Accounting Review*, 36 (4), 345–368.

Francis, J. R. and Yu, M. D. (2009) Big 4 office size and audit quality. *Accounting Review*, 84 (5), 1521–1552.

Francis, J. R., Maydew, L. E. and Sparks, H. C. (1999) The role of Big 6 auditors in the credible reporting of accruals. *Auditing: A Journal of Practice and Theory*, 18 (2), 17–34.

Frederick, S., Loewenstein, G. and O'Donoghue, T. (2002) Time discounting and time preference: A critical review. *Journal of Economic Literature*, 40 (2), 351–401.

Freeman, R. E. (1984). *Strategic management: A stakeholder approach*. Boston: Pitman.

Gaeremynck, A., Van Der Meulen, S. and Willekens, M. (2008) Audit-firm portfolio characteristics and client financial reporting quality. *European Accounting Review*, 17 (2), 243–270, DOI: 10.1080/09638180701705932.

Garsombke, H. P. and Choi, S. (1992) The association between auditors' uncertainty opinions and business failures. *Advances in Accounting*, 10, 45–60.

Ge, W. and McVay, S. (2005) The disclosure of material weaknesses in internal control after the Sarbanes–Oxley Act. *Accounting Horizons*, 10 (September), 137–158.

Geiger, M. A. and Rama, D. V. (2006) Audit firm size and going-concern reporting accuracy. *Accounting Horizons*, 20 (1), 1–17.

Geiger M. A. and Rama, D. V. (2003) Audit fees, non-audit fees, and auditor reporting on stressed companies. *Auditing: A Journal of Practice and Theory*, 22 (2), 53–69.

Geiger, M. A. and Raghunandan, K. (2002) Auditor tenure and audit reporting failures. *Auditing*, 21 (1), 67–78.

Geiger, M. A., Raghunandan, K. and Rama, D. V. (2005) Recent changes in the association between bankruptcies and prior audit opinions. *Auditing: A Journal of Practice and Theory*, 24 (1), 21–35.

Geiger, M. A., Raghunandan, K. and Rama, D. V. (1998) Costs associated with going-concern modified audit opinions: An analysis of auditor changes, subsequent opinions, and client failures. *Advances in Accounting*, 16, 117–139.

George, J. M. and Jones, G. R. (2000) The role of time in theory and theory building. *Journal of Management*, 26 (4), 657–684.

Gul, F. A., Sun, S. Y. J. and Tsui, J. S. L. (2003) Audit quality, earnings, and the Shanghai stock market reaction. *Journal of Accounting, Auditing, and Finance*, 18 (3), 411–427.

Handoko, B. L., Sabrina, S. and Ayuanda, N. (2019, August). Admission of information technology in external audit profession: Impact of organizational, social and individual factors. *In 2019 International Conference on Information Management and Technology (ICIMTech)* pp. 36–41.

Healy, P. M. and Whalen, J. (1999) A review of the earnings management literature and its implications for standard setting. *Accounting Horizons*, 13 (4), 365–383.

Holstrum, G. L. and Messier, W. F. (1982) A review and integration of empirical research on materiality. *Auditing: A Journal of Practice and Theory*, 2 (2), 45–65.

International Standard on Auditing 320 materiality in planning and performing audit (2009). Available at: https://www.ifac.org/system/files/publications/files/A018%202013%20IAASB%20Handbook%20ISA%20320.pdf [Accessed: May 29, 2022].

International Standard on Auditing (ISA) 570 (revised) (2015). Available at: https://www.iaasb.org/publications/international-standard-auditing-isa-570-revised-going-concern-3 [Accessed 12 August, 2021].

International Standard on Auditing 705 (revised) (2015). Available at: https://www.ifac.org/system/files/publications/files/ISA-705-Revised_0.pdf [Accessed 10 August, 2021].

Janev, A. (2021). *Пандемијата ја влошила наплатата на побарувањата.* [online] Kapital.mk. Available at: [Accessed 10 March, 2022].

Jiang, W., Rupley, K. and Wu, J. (2010) Internal control deficiencies and the issuance of going concern opinions. *Research in Accounting Regulation*, 22 (1), 40–46.

Jiao, T., Mertens, G. M. H. and Roosenboom, P. G. J. (2007) *Industry valuation driven earnings management.* ERIM Report Series Research in Management ERS-2007-069-F&A, Erasmus Research Institute of Management (ERIM).

Jones, J. (1991) Earnings management during import relief investigation. *Journal of Accounting Research*, 29 (2), 193–228.

Kallunki, J.-P. and Martikainen, T. (1999) Financial failure and managers´ accounting responses: Finnish evidence. *Journal of Multinational Financial Management*, 9 (1), 15–26.

Kasznik, R. and Lev, B. (1995) To warn or not to warn: Management disclosures in the face of an earnings surprise. *Accounting Review*, 69 (January), 113–134.

Kida, T. (1980) An investigation into auditors' continuity and related qualification judgments. *Journal of Accounting Research*, 18 (2), 506–523.

Knechel, W. R. and Vanstraelen, A. (2007) The relationship between auditor tenure and audit quality implied by going concern opinions. *Auditing: A Journal of Practice and Theory*, 26 (1), 113–131.

Koh, H. C. (1991) Model predictions and auditor assessments of going concern status. *Accounting and Business Research*, 21 (84), 331–338.

Kothari, S. P., Leone, A. J. and Wasley, C. E. (2005). Performance matched discretionary accruals measures. *Journal of Accounting and Economics*, 39 (1), 163–197.

Krishnan, J. and Krishnan, J. (1996) The role of economic trade-offs in the audit opinion decision: An empirical analysis. *Journal of Accounting, Auditing and Finance*, 11 (4), 565–586.

Landau, S. and Everitt, B. (2004) *A handbook of statistical analyses using SPSS.* Boca Raton: Chapman and Hall/CRC.

Lara, J. M. G., Osma, B. G., and Neophytou, E. (2009) Earnings quality in ex-post failed firms. *Accounting and Business Research*, 39 (2), 119–138.

Larcker, D. F. and Richardson, S. A. (2004) Fees paid to audit firms, accrual choices and corporate governance. *Journal of Accounting Research*, 42 (3), 625–658.

Law on Securities, Закон за хартии од вредност. (2018) [online] Available at: [Accessed May 2, 2021].

Lee, P., Jiang, W. and Anandarajan. A. (2005) Going concern report modeling: A study of factors influencing the auditor's decision. *Journal of Forensic Accounting*, 6 (1), 55–76.

Lennox, C. (1999) Are large auditors more accurate than small auditors? *Accounting and Business Research*, 29 (3), 217–227.

Louwers, T. (1998) The relation between going-concern opinions and the auditors' loss function. *Journal of Accounting Research*, 36, 143–156.

Mareque, M., López-Corrales, F. and, Pedrosa, A. (2017) Audit reporting for going concern in Spain during the global financial crisis. *Economic Research-Ekonomska Istraživanja*, 30 (1), 154–183.

McKeown, J. C., Mutchler, J. F. and Hopwood, W. S. (1991) Towards an explanation of auditor failure to modify the audit opinions of bankrupt companies. *Auditing: A Journal of Practice and Theory*, 10 (Supplement), 1–13.

Menon, K. and Williams, D. D. (2010) Investor reaction to going concern audit reports. *Accounting Review*, 85 (6), 2075–2105.

Messier, W. F. (1983) The effect of experience and firm type on materiality/disclosure judgments. *Journal of Accounting Research*, 21 (2), 611–618.

Mutchler, J. F. (1985) A multivariate analysis of the auditor's going-concern opinion decision. *Journal of Accounting Research*, 23 (2), 668–682.

Mutchler, J. F. and Williams, D. D. (1990) The relationship between audit technology, client risk profiles, and the going-concern opinion decision. *Auditing: A Journal of Practice and Theory*, Fall, 39–54.

Mutchler, J. F., Hopwood, W. S. and McKeown, J. C. (1997) The influence of contrary information and mitigating factors on audit opinion decisions on bankrupt companies. *Journal of Accounting Research*, 35 (2), 295–310.

Myers, L. A., Schmidt, J. J. and Wilkins, M. S. (2014) An investigation of recent changes in going concern reporting decisions among big N and non-big N auditors. *Review of Quantitative Finance and Accounting*, 43 (1), 155–172.

Nogler, G. (1995) The resolution of auditor going-concern opinions. *Auditing: A Journal of Practice and Theory*, 15 (2), 54–73.

Numan, W. and Willekens, M. (2011) *Competitive pressure, audit quality and specialization.* Working paper, Katholieke Universiteit Leuven.

Raghunandan, K. and Rama, D. V. (1995) Audit reports for companies in financial distress: Before and after SAS No. 59. *Auditing: A Journal of Practice and Theory*, 14 (1), 50–63.

Rama, D. V., Raghunandan, K. and Geiger, M. A. (1997) The association between audit reports and bankruptcies: Further evidence. *Advances in Accounting*, 15, 1–15.

Reichelt, K. J. and Wang, D. (2010) National and office-specific measures of auditor industry expertise and effects on audit quality. *Journal of Accounting Research*, 48 (3), 647–686.

Reynolds, J. K. and Francis, J. R. (2001) Does size matter? The influence of large clients on office-level auditor reporting decisions. *Journal of Accounting and Economics*, 30 (3), 375–400.

Reynolds, J. K., Deis, D. R. and Francis, J. R. (2004) Professional service fees and auditor objectivity, *Auditing: A Journal of Practice and Theory*, 23 (1), 29–52.

Rosner, R. L. 2003. Earnings manipulations in failing firms. *Contemporary Accounting Research*, 20 (2), 361–408.

Ryu, T. G. and Roh, C. Y. (2007) The auditor's going-concern opinion decision. *International Journal of Business and Economics*, 6 (2), 89–101.

Schipper, K. (1989) Commentary on earnings management. *Accounting Horizons*, 3 (4), 91–102.

Smith, M., Kestel, J. and Robinson, P. (2001) Economic recession, corporate distress and income increasing accounting policy choice. *Accounting Forum*, 25 (4), 335–352.

Sovet za unapreduvanje I nadzor na revizijata na Republika Makedonija (2018). *Bilten*, Skopje: Magnasken.

Spathis, C. (2003) Audit qualification, firm litigation, and financial information: An empirical analysis in Greece. *International Journal of Auditing*, 7 (1), 71–85.

Tversky, A. and Kahneman, D. (1991) Loss aversion in riskless choice: A reference-dependent model. *Quarterly Journal of Economics*, 106 (4), 1039–1061.

____eer, T. E., Raghunandan, K. and Forgione, D. A. (2013) Going-concern modified audit opinions __ __ __ ___ rofit organizations. *Journal of Public Budgeting, Accounting and Financial Management*, 25 (1), __

Weber, J. and ____ ____ org, M. (2003) Do expert informational intermediaries add value? Evidence from auditors in micro___ IPOs. *Journal of Accounting Research*, 41 (4), 681–720.

Weil, J. (2001) *Going co....erns: Did accountants fail to flag problems at dot-com casualties? Wall Street Journal*, 9 February, C1–C2.

Weygandt, J. J., Kimmel, P. D. and Kieso, D. E. (2011) *Financial accounting.* New Jersey: John Wiley and Sons.

Wheeler, S., Pany, K. and Chewning, E. (1993) Inter-firm differences in propensities to modify audit opinions for pre-SAS no. 58 accounting principles changes. *Accounting Horizons*, 7, 46–54.

Zmijewski, M. E. (1984) Methodological issues related to the estimation of financial distress prediction models. *Journal of Accounting Research*, 22, 59–82.

12. Digital platforms in a hotel's performance measurement and management: a sociomateriality perspective

Sung Hwan Chai

12.1 INTRODUCTION

This chapter discusses how digital platforms, specifically TripAdvisor, can be reconfigured and become taken-for-granted as an important part of a hotel's performance measurement and management (PMM), from a sociomateriality perspective. Prior research in PMM has often viewed technology as an external factor that triggers a change to existing management accounting practice (Granlund and Malmi, 2002; Scapens and Jazayeri, 2003). From this view, research in digital platforms' influence on PMM practice would consider technology as an exogenous factor which is introduced into an organisation with a specific purpose. On the other hand, the sociomateriality perspective (for example, Orlikowski, 2007, 2010; Orlikowski and Scott, 2008; Leonardi, 2012; Jones, 2014) suggests that technologies are often more closely entangled with organisational practice often without recognition from the users. This study aims to adopt a sociomateriality perspective to provide an interpretation of the relationship between technology and PMM practice.

This chapter does not reject the potential purpose of adopting a digital platform into an existing PMM practice but instead argues that digital platforms are entangled with their users and can produce an alternative practice often without users' awareness. With this in mind, this chapter examines the following research question:

How does TripAdvisor and its user-generated information interact with existing performance measurement and management practices?

This question allows this study to consider how TripAdvisor interacts with existing PMM practices and becomes taken-for-granted by the users. This study explores the question by examining findings from a case study of a luxury resort hotel in Vietnam, where TripAdvisor is incorporated into different aspects of their PMM practices. Despite the resistance and distrust from different groups of users in the case organisation, for example, service employees, and the senior management team, this study identified that information from TripAdvisor was integrated into existing PMM practice, giving rise to alternative ways of interacting with hotel guests.

The remainder of this chapter is structured as follows. Section 12.2 presents the review of PMM literature to provide a background for this study. Section 12.3 discusses the sociomateriality perspective which enables this study to explore the process through which information from TripAdvisor interacts with its organisational users, in this case hotel employees. Section 12.4 outlines the research method. Section 12.5 presents the case description and findings.

Lastly, Section 12.6 presents an analysis and discussion. The chapter concludes with suggestions for future research and limitations.

12.2   PERFORMANCE MEASUREMENT AND MANAGEMENT

The importance of the strategic use of performance measures has been highlighted by a number of researchers (Merchant 1985; Kaplan and Norton 1992; Kaplan and Norton 1993; Otley 1999) as it ensures organisations maintain their competitive advantage in rapidly changing business environments. Instead of focusing on a few financial performance indicators, such as revenues and profit, prior literature highlights the importance of incorporating a broader view of performance (for example, Kaplan and Norton, 1996, Simons, 1995). For example, low revenue from a hotel's restaurant could be caused by the unsatisfactory quality of food or service, or simply because of a decrease in the number of hotel guests. If the fall in restaurant revenue is not due to a decrease in the number of hotel guests, the manager needs to find a way to make the restaurant more attractive. As such, a strategic performance management system enables managers to identify a specific problem area and manage the organisation's performance at both individual and organisational levels. This is especially important in the hotel industry, as the service delivery process involves a complex mix of retail and manufacturing and pure service elements (Atkinson and Brown, 2001; Harris and Mongiello, 2001).

In order to strengthen the link between strategy and performance management systems, management accounting researchers paid attention to the importance of flexible performance management systems and nonfinancial performance (Bhimani and Langfield-Smith, 2007; Bromwich, 1990; Kaplan and Norton, 1992; Kloot and Martin, 2000; Merchant, 1985). Mintzberg (1978, 1987) suggests that the strategies in practice often deviate from the original intended vision and new strategies emerge to keep the business on track. Therefore, in order to implement emergent strategies without delay, it is important to have a certain level of flexibility in a performance management system.

The importance of nonfinancial performance is even more crucial for organisations in the service industry as it is directly linked to the survival of the business (Atkinson and Brown, 2001). In order to maintain a competitive advantage in the hotel business, where customer satisfaction and quality of service are key success factors, an efficient strategic performance measurement system that can reflect the company's strategy accurately is crucial for success (Hoque, 1999). Despite the importance of nonfinancial performance, many hotel managers still put more emphasis on financial performance (Atkinson and Brown, 2001). This is mainly because managers' incentive schemes are designed according to the financial performance of the hotel, as nonfinancial performance is hard to quantify and often relies on managers' subjective interpretation. This suggests why researchers have tended to focus on the relationship between financial performance measures and hotel performance, rather than acknowledging the strategic importance of the nonfinancial measures. Such research focuses on either popular financial measures such as the economic value added (EVA) (Kim, 2006), or traditional financial performance measures in the hospitality industry, such as the occupancy rate, average daily rate or revenue per available room (Ciucă, 2009). However, neither of these can be used to measure the service performance of hotels (Atkinson and Brown, 2001). To manage the quality of service, hotels need to obtain other relevant data related to their service performance.

More recently, the growing influence of digital technologies in accounting practice has attracted the attention of researchers to user-generated content from various sources, such as social media and digital platforms in accounting practices. For example, studies have explored different hospitality and entertainment platforms such as TripAdvisor (for example, Jeacle and Carter, 2011; Scott and Orlikowski, 2012; Karunakaran et al., 2022), Airbnb and IMDb (Leoni and Parker, 2019; Bialecki et al., 2017). These studies have focused primarily on how user-generated ratings, rankings and reviews work as accounting practices and are used by consumers (or guests or users) in their decision-making process. The prior studies (Brivot et al., 2017; Bialecki et al., 2017) suggest that user-generated information on digital platforms is largely unpredictable and less controllable from the organisation's perspective, yet may still influence customer (and potential customers) behaviour, even if the information lacks expertise and objectivity (Bialecki et al., 2017). In this regard, Scott and Orlikowski's (2012) study on online accountability sheds light on how TripAdvisor users interact with each other to build a wisdom of the crowd that gives legitimacy to the information they created and consume. While these studies explored the role of preconstructed measures available on digital platforms, research on how the user-generated information influences organisations' existing PMM practices remains scarce. This study aims to fill this gap by exploring how TripAdvisor became entangled with a hotel's PMM practices by drawing on a sociomateriality perspective. This allows us to explore the role of TripAdvisor, not as an external factor, but at the interface of multiple actors involved in existing PMM practices.

12.3   SOCIOMATERIALITY

The term sociomateriality refers to the stream of research that has received great attention in organisation and information system studies since 2007. Jones' (2014) review of studies on sociomateriality points out that most of the literature in this area has either directly or indirectly cited the work of Orlikowski (2007, 2010) and Orlikowski and Scott (2008). This highlights the significant role of Orlikowski's work in the understanding of the concept of sociomateriality.

Orlikowski and Scott (2008) define sociomateriality as an 'umbrella term' for the research stream that draws attention to a number of pre-existing theoretical frameworks. The main body of literature that influenced the concept of sociomateriality draws on Actor–Network Theory (ANT) (Callon, 1984; Latour, 2005), post-humanist performativity (Barad, 2003), the notion of relationality and the concept of a mangle of practice[1] (Pickering, 1993, 1995), and the ethnographic study of the workplace (Suchman, 2007). As opposed to the traditional studies of technology in management practice, which often focus on the relationship between technology and management practice, by assuming them to be separate entities, sociomateriality suggests that technology and management practice are not separate, but are constitutively entangled and ontologically inseparable (Orlikowski and Scott, 2008).

As the concept of sociomateriality is constructed by combining a number of pre-existing theoretical frameworks, whether sociomateriality offers a new research perspective is often questioned (Kautz and Jensen, 2013). However, this could also suggest that sociomateriality recognises the insightful theoretical implications of various existing theories. Therefore, as long as the user of the sociomateriality perspective constructs their sociomateriality framework with coherent ontological and epistemological assumptions, sociomateriality could be viewed as a successful example of theoretical triangulation that can be used to explore an area of research that was previously neglected.

Jones (2014) points out that, although the sociomateriality research stream is still relatively new and has yet to establish a unified approach, there are common issues that feature in most sociomateriality studies: (i) an ontological assumption that views social and technical entities' properties as a product of their mutual entanglement; (ii) the notion of performativity which suggests how the description of phenomena (for example, technology in management practice) intervenes and contributes to the reality that it describes; and (iii) through performativity, how the social and the material entities interact and establish their relationships and boundaries.

Although sociomateriality is a complex term to understand, Jones' (2014) review of Orlikowski and Scott's work summarises the five main notions of this theoretical concept which makes it unique. They are as follows: (i) materiality; (ii) inseparability; (iii) relationality; (iv) performativity; and (v) practices. Sociomateriality, therefore, can be seen as an umbrella term for using all five of these theoretical notions to understand an ongoing relationship between social (often referred to as human actors) and material (such as technologies) factors. Using these notions separately does not justify the theoretical distinctiveness of sociomateriality (Jones, 2014).

12.3.1   Strong and Weak Sociomateriality

Despite the common research theme, variation exists within sociomateriality literature due to different ontological assumptions. Therefore, it is important to recognise the different ontological assumptions in sociomateriality studies and make it clear where this study stands in terms of philosophical assumptions. Jones (2014) suggests that there is either strong or weak sociomateriality based on the researcher's ontological assumption of the existence of sociomateriality.

First, there are sociomateriality researchers with a stricter assumption about the existence of sociomateriality, which Jones (2014) referred to as strong sociomateriality research. Strong sociomateriality proposes that entities only exist in their relationships with others (Barad, 2007), which suggests that there are no predefined characteristics of both social and technical entities. For example, strong sociomateriality research would not recognise the existence of a phenomenon unless it is observed. This ontological assumption is similar to the assumption of actor–network theorists (ANT) (Latour 1987, Callon 1984), but, unlike early ANT studies, sociomateriality studies focus on the conceptualisation of phenomena through performativity rather than the process of network stabilisation.

This strict ontological assumption makes it problematic for some information system and management accounting research grounded in a sociomateriality perspective, as it rejects the premise of pre-existing characteristics or roles of entities, and expected practice can no longer be taken for granted. This could be problematic when studying the influence of technology on existing accounting practices that have persisted and become automatically expected, i.e. doing things without questioning the reason (Burns and Scapens, 2000), such as the use of budgeting, performance measures and financial reporting. These accounting practices have been widely used by organisations, often without being questioned by the finance and accounting employees.

On the other hand, weak sociomateriality has a more relaxed ontological approach. Weak sociomateriality researchers reject the strong sociomaterialist's view on the existence of

Table 12.1   Summary of key concepts

Inseparability	Social (human) and material (technology) entities are not independent of each other, but are inextricably related
Materiality	Tangible and/or intangible properties that persist across time and place
Performativity	Actions produce realities in which the action is being performed
Sociomaterial property	Human and/or non-human actors' materiality emerges from their inseparable entanglement and performativity

entities and propose that phenomena can persist to become a norm (Leonardi, 2012; Leonardi and Barley, 2010). Expected practice can pre-exist under a weak sociomateriality perspective, but the pattern of sociomaterial relationality is open to revision at any instant. Leonardi and Barley (2010) argue that even the sociomaterial entanglement is in the process of continuous change, and there are generally accepted practices that often remain unchanged and unnoticed. This is similar to the idea of the expectations assumption embedded in management practice, as discussed in much management accounting research grounded in institutional theory (Burns and Scapens, 2000; Lukka, 2007; Scapens and Varoutsa, 2010). Therefore, a weak sociomateriality perspective would allow this study to recognise that some human and non-human properties can persist and become the norm, without drifting apart from the focal point of sociomateriality.

This study adopts the weak sociomateriality perspective and recognises that sociomaterial relationships can persist. As discussed earlier, a weak sociomateriality perspective will enable this study to look at technology, not as a tool that was introduced for a specific purpose, but as an actor that is closely entangled with management practice at both the individual and organisational levels. By relaxing strong sociomateriality's fully relational ontology, this study assumes that there can be institutionalised practices that are generally accepted by actors within an organisation. This would allow this study to analyse how the role of technology is shaped through interacting with different aspects of the case hotel's PMM practices and examine how the newly shaped role of technology persists within an organisation.

For this study, the relationality notion is relaxed to account for 'taken-for-granted' PMM practices that existed before TripAdvisor was introduced. Analysis of the findings will therefore focus on how the sociomaterial property emerges from the entanglement of technology and users by focusing on PMM practices entangled with TripAdvisor using the three notions of sociomateriality as an analytical lens: (i) inseparability; (ii) materiality; and (iii) performativity. The summary of key concepts is given in Table 12.1.

12.4   METHODOLOGY

This study adopts an interpretive case study approach (Golden-Biddle and Locke, 2007; Ryan et al., 2002) to explore how TripAdvisor and its user-generated information interact with the case hotel's existing PMM practices and become 'taken-for-granted'. The initial data was collected by interviewing owners, employees and managers from four different hotels located in three different countries (Switzerland, Vietnam, and South Korea) in 2014. This study draws on IC Resort (pseudonym) which is located in Da Nang, Vietnam as the main case to illustrate how TripAdvisor is entangled with the existing PMM practices. Table 12.2 summarises the interviewees.

Table 12.2   *Overview of the interviewees*

Case hotel	Interviewees	No. of Interviews
IC Resort	Resort Manager – 1	1
	2 Managers – 1	1
	2 Directors from the owner group – 1	1
VH	Owner – 1	1
	Service Employee – 1	1
SH	General Manager – 1	1
	2 Service Employees – 2	2
KH	Accounting Manager	1
	Service Employee	1
Total	12	10

Interviews with IC Resort were conducted in three separate semi-structured interviews with the hotel's resort manager, 2 employees, and 2 owners. Each interview lasted between half an hour and one hour. The interviews with some employees and owners were conducted with non-English speakers and, therefore, were conducted with the presence of a translator. The interview recordings and transcripts were kept together with observation notes to better record the context in which each interview was conducted. Additionally, the author collected secondary data in the form of reviews, training booklets, and information from hotel websites and TripAdvisor to gain a better understanding of the case hotel.

In addition to the interviews with the main case organisation, interviews were conducted with owners and managers from three other hotels located in three different countries (Switzerland, Vietnam, and South Korea). Although findings from these interviews are not directly mentioned in this study, these interviews were used to gain a better understanding of the influence of TripAdvisor in the hospitality sector, especially for hotels of different sizes.

The findings from the interviews were conducted in two phases. First, the author conducted initial thematic coding (Braun and Clark, 2006) by looking at the recurring themes in the empirical findings. The identified themes are as follows: (i) use of technology; (ii) managing external relationships; and (iii) data analytics. These themes were primarily related to the existing way in which the case organisation measures and manages its service performance. After the initial coding, the influence of TripAdvisor's user-generated information on the case organisation's existing PMM practice became evident, despite the doubts on the reliability and usefulness of TripAdvisor's information for PMM purposes raised by most of the interviewees. This contrasting attitude towards TripAdvisor's user-generated information prompted a reflection on the finding of the selected three notions of sociomateriality, to examine the relationship between the existing PMM practices and TripAdvisor.

12.5   CASE DESCRIPTION AND FINDINGS

Since the unification of the south and north in 1975, Vietnam has become one of the fastest-growing Asian countries. Vietnam's rapid economic growth and its geographic location, neighbouring China to the north and located parallel to the great sea trade routes of Asia, have attracted many international corporations over the years.[2] The hotel and tourism industry in Vietnam accounts for more than six million foreign visitors with 19.9 per cent growth year to year. The case hotel, IC Resort, is located in Da Nang City, which is one of the fastest-growing tourist destinations in Asia.[3]

IC Resort opened in June 2012 with the aim to be the best luxurious hotel resort in Asia. The resort was initially developed by a local hospitality developer SV (pseudonym), one of the largest investors in the tourism and entertainment industry in Vietnam. SV was in charge of capital investment and hardware maintenance of the IC Resort from the beginning of the project. However, as IC Resort was a 'first-of-its-kind' SV outsourced the hotel management to an international hotel management company (hereafter referred to as MIG) to achieve the highest possible quality of service. As a result, less than 2 years after its opening, IC Resort was recognised as the 'world's leading luxurious resort' from 2013 to 2015.

IC Resort is hugely important for both SV and MIG, due to its strategically important geographic location and growth potential. For SV, IC Resort is seen as an opportunity to establish itself as a successful hotel and resort developer; and for MIG, it is an opportunity to gain the title of the world's most luxurious hotel chain. Therefore, their primary goal was not to maximise revenue but to create prestige and a unique resort that will become a phenomenon in Asia. In order to achieve their goal, the management team from MIG brought in their established performance management system, known as the 'Winning Metrics', into IC Resort's management practice. As shown in Table 12.3, Winning Metrics is comprised of a set of Key Performance Indicators (KPIs) with a brief overview of the criteria. The target for each KPI is set at the beginning of the performance year by taking account of both previous performance and seasonal factors. Actual KPIs are calculated monthly and are compared to predetermined targets in order to assess the hotel's performance.

'Winning Metrics' is aimed at providing a visual representation of the hotel's performance by displaying the set of most important KPIs in one table. This table was placed in a number of different rooms, such as the meeting room, the manager's office, and the administrative employees' shared office. The list of KPIs on Winning Metrics consists of both financial performance measures (revenue per available room (RevPAR), Food and Beverage Revenue, gross operating profit (GOP), total gross operating profit (TGOP), and revenue generated index (RGI)), and nonfinancial performance measures (Standard, Loyalty Recognition, Problem Handling, Guest Engagement,[4] and Employee Engagement). All these KPIs are internally measured with the exception of RGI, which represents the hotel's market share against its comparable peers. IC Resort and MIG obtain this information through STR Report, provided by STR Global.[5] The outsourcing relationship with STR Global enables IC Resort to look at its current position in the market, without violating the anti-price-fixing regulations which prohibit hotels from sharing their pricing-related information.

Winning Metrics provides an effective framework for the visual presentation and constant reminder of the hotel's current performance position and targets. However, the measurement and management of these KPIs in the Winning Metrics are not possible without IC Resort's resources and information technology. During the data collection, the three most crucial components that enable the Winning Metrics to function as a performance management system with strategically linked performance measures were identified. They are (i) TripAdvisor; (ii) data analytics; and (iii) managing external relationships – outsourcing.

First, the significance of TripAdvisor in IC Resort's performance management practice is critical. According to the resort manager, a large part of the hotel's performance measurement practice is not possible without the Internet intermediaries, such as Trip Advisor and Booking. com. These websites contain millions of customers' opinions about IC Resort and its competi-

Table 12.3   *Example of the Winning Metrics in IC Resort[6]*

KPIs	Target	Measurement Method	January	February
Standard	X %	Brand Safety, Cleanliness and Condition Report	P	
Loyalty Recognition	X %	Guest Engagement Report	O	
Problem Handling	X %	Guest Engagement Report	P	
Guest Engagement	X %	Guest Engagement Report	O	
Employee Engagement	X	Employee Survey	P	
RevPar	X	Monthly P&L	O	
F&B Revenue	X	Monthly P&L	P	
GOP	X	Monthly P&L	P	
TGOP	X	Monthly P&L	P	
RGI	X	STR Report	P	
Score			7/10	

tors. This publicly available information is collected and evaluated alongside IC Resort's own online surveys and guest comment cards to measure IC Resort's service performance. This practice allows IC Resort to evaluate its service performance in a more accurate and detailed manner.

However, the Internet and digital platform do not only benefit the IC Resort. The Internet allows customers to gain access to information about substitutes and competitors (such as other hotels or Airbnb) easily. Therefore, IC Resort needs to ensure the highest service quality while offering acceptable prices for rooms to satisfy customers. Moreover, it is not uncommon for customers to recognise the significance of their online reviews to IC Resort's business and try to abuse the system. The resort manager points out,

> Sometimes, guests insist on getting upgrades or freebies because they know they can write bad reviews on TripAdvisor or Booking.com and which prove detrimental to our reputation.

Although not all negative reviews have a blackmail intent, TripAdvisor's reviews can be shared with the public instantly. Once the review goes public, the review will be visible to anyone who uses TripAdvisor and can begin to influence potential future guests' decisions even if the review is not based on truth. Such a characteristic of TripAdvisor reviews not only threatens hotels' practice to satisfy their customers but also implies that online customer reviews may be unreliable. The resort manager further explained how their customers' expectation differs from what they called a 'MIG standard', which is a long list of standardised practices and ways to manage service performance to ensure consistent service quality across MIG managed hotels and resorts. The resort manager claimed that TripAdvisor's reviews are not written by experts and therefore the employees do not use the reviews as a basis to measure their performance. Instead, they refer to their internally conducted PMM report which utilises data analytics. IC Resort uses data analytics mainly for the measurement of service performance and customer analysis. The resort manager gave an example to explain how they use this technology to enhance their service performance measurement practice.

> When you look at customer satisfaction and it shows a great result, it does not necessarily mean that the hotel's service is perfect. For example, when you filter the data according to customers' nationality, it could show very different results. Customers from countries with the highly developed service industry, like Singapore or Hong Kong, are often more difficult to please than customers from

countries with less developed service industries such as Vietnam. Therefore, we can identify the exact area that requires improvement while maintaining our strong points.

IC Resort relies on MIG's proprietary resource, HeartBeat, to analyse most of the nonfinancial KPIs in the Winning Metrics. HeartBeat provides a detailed analysis of the nonfinancial performance of the hotel (such as problem handling, customer satisfaction, and loyalty). This does not only provide IC Resort's service performance but also other hotels and resorts under the management of MIG. However, the HeartBeat report does not only draw on data collected through IC Resort's own survey questionnaires but also reviews from TripAdvisor. Even though IC Resort's management is sceptical about the quality of information generated on TripAdvisor, it is still incorporated into the HeartBeat report which they use on a daily basis to plan their activities. For example, the HeartBeat report can highlight a problem area by analysing patterns in customer/guest complaints. This process takes place through a formal system designed by MIG and is outside IC Resort's control. Once a problem area is identified, the hotel's management team would try to find out the underlying cause of the problem using various resources to identify where the problem starts. The resort manager of IC Resort refers to this approach as the 'Root Cause Analysis'. For example, as he explains,

> Customer satisfaction can be caused by various factors, let's say it was caused by a broken TV in the room. The TV might not have worked because of hardware problems or electricity, or even faulty cables. Sometimes the problem occurs during the installation phase due to a technician's careless mistake. It is, therefore, important to correctly identify where the true issues lie, instead of buying a new receiver or TV every time. The same logic applies to any other part of this business.

Lastly, the performance management practice of IC Resort cannot function without its outsourcing relationship. Oshri et al., (2015) define outsourcing as 'contracting with a third-party provider for the management and completion of a certain amount of work, for a specified length of time, cost, and level of service'. According to this definition, there are two outsourcing relationships involved in IC Resort's performance management practice, IG's management team and STR Global.

Due to anti-price discrimination regulations, hotels are not allowed to share their strategies or performance information that may be used for price-fixing. However, competitors' performance analysis is important for any organisation as it can highlight the competitive advantage of the organisation. IG's outsourcing relationship with STR Global enables both MIG and IC Resorts to obtain benchmark reports that rank their performance against their competitors. This allows IC Resort to evaluate its performance not only against its past performance but also against its competitors' current performance.

The finding shows how technology (TripAdvisor) and human activity (PMM) are closely entangled within the boundary of IC Resort's PMM practice, 'Winning Metrics'. The findings show that the user-generated information from online booking intermediaries in IC Resort's performance management system has deviated from its originally intended role of sharing travel information among people from different parts of the world, to an essential part of PMM practice despite the initial scepticism. The next section will discuss this deviation from the digital platform's role in IC Resort's PMM practices and how it persists to become taken-for-granted from a sociomateriality perspective.

12.6 ANALYSIS AND DISCUSSION

This research focuses on how digital platforms influence performance management systems in the hotel sector. Scott and Orlikowski (2012) explain how online accountability produced by social media in the travel sector, such as TripAdvisor, became part of hotels' management practice using the sociomateriality perspective. They argue that user-generated content, such as customer opinions from social media, often dominates the traditional forms of offline performance measures. However, the findings from this study show that in the case of a large hotel with substantial resources, both publicly available user-generated contents on social media and internally generated performance reviews are equally important in the measurement of service performance.

The findings from the case study also show that the role of digital platforms in IC Resort's performance management practice differs from one user to the other, for example, as a bargaining tool for customers and a source of service performance data for IC Resort. These different roles of digital platforms emerged through interaction between human and non-human actors and some of these roles persist longer than others and become part of institutionalised practices. This discussion aims to analyse the findings from a sociomaterial perspective by focusing on three key elements of sociomateriality: inseparability, materiality, and performativity, to explain how different roles of digital platforms emerge. Then, the discussion will explain how some of these roles can persist to become part of institutionalised performance management practice.

12.6.1 Inseparability

Prior to a discussion about materiality, it is important to establish the notion of inseparability. As argued by a number of sociomateriality researchers, social and material are not independent of each other (Jones, 2014; Leonardi, 2012; Orlikowski, 2007; Orlikowski and Scott, 2008). Therefore, the materiality of performance management practice and technology can only be considered after recognising their inseparability. The case of 'Winning Metrics' presents two notable forms of inseparability that shape different roles of TripAdvisor, the customers' different uses of online user-generated content and IC Resort's way of utilising online user-generated content. The different uses for user-generated content in online booking intermediaries cannot be understood without considering the users.

Pickering (1993, 1995) argues that the interaction or, as he puts it, 'mangle' of human and non-human actors is what creates their properties. For example, the online reviews on TripAdvisor can only be used by the customer either as a tool for blackmailing hotels for freebies or as a way to show their appreciation for good service. These different uses are often based on the morality of the users. If a morally questionable customer decided to use the online review system as a weapon for exploiting hotels, the digital platform can become a weapon and could be a very unreliable source of travel information. On the other hand, if these online customer reviews are used by hotels along with other technology, such as data analytics, digital platforms could become a vast pool of valuable data in the hotel's performance management. The customer reviews in online booking intermediaries can only be used as data for service performance management when there are sufficient resources, such as technology and human capital, to process them. Also, if the user does not have the intention to use these reviews as data for service performance management, they could just be other people's unprofessional subjective opinions that may or may not be 'true'.

Moreover, MIG's intention to use online customer reviews as a part of their data set for service performance measures is likely to be influenced by the increasing number of customers who actively use these reviews to plan their holidays. Scott and Orlikowski (2012) suggest that this substantial number of TripAdvisor users creates online accountability that controls and influences a hotel's practice, at both individual and organisational levels. The customer reviews on TripAdvisor can only have the online accountability property because there are a sufficient number of users who depend on it. These examples illustrate why human and non-human actors are inseparable in the discussion of different roles of digital platforms in the hotel's PMM practice.

12.6.2   Materiality

While sociomateriality researchers agree that materiality is important, the definition of materiality is inconsistent across different literature. For example, Leonardi (2012) argues some technologies, such as digital technology, do not have a physical existence, therefore, have no materiality in the traditional sense. However, taking account of the significance of intangible 'stuff', such as data, Leonardi (2012) proposes that technology's materiality should be equated with its physical and/or digital materials that persist across time and place. Therefore, following Leonardi's definition, digital platforms' materiality would be their constituent features that are available to all users, such as the feature that allows users to share their opinion online.

In the case of IC Resort, digital platforms and information technology have shifted the materiality of service performance data from physical to nonphysical materiality. Traditionally, service quality was measured by the hotel manager's report which was constructed by reviewing their notes on staff actions and the customer review cards, both of which have physical materiality. However, since MIG started to utilise user-generated information from Internet booking intermediaries, the service performance data can no longer be defined solely by the physical quality of the data. User-generated information, such as online customer reviews from TripAdvisor, provides the same feature to everyone regardless of their location. This not only enables IC Resort and MIG to gain access to large volumes of potentially valuable data but also enables customers to find out about the more detailed service performance of the hotel.

Although some features of customer reviews persist from one user to another (such as sharing information freely online in an interactive manner), their materiality is continuously reshaped by their 'intra-action' with social entities (Barad, 2003). Through intra-action with special users, online customer reviews can be combined with other service performance data, such as IC Resort's customer review cards, to form a service performance measurement system.

12.6.3   Performativity

From a sociomateriality perspective, the notion of performativity follows Barad's (2003, 2007) view of performativity which emphasises that actions are part of realities which they produce through a material-discursive process. This is an important notion of the sociomateriality perspective as technology researchers seek to understand the context of management

Table 12.4   *Sociomateriality of digital platform in the case of IC Resort*

Example	Inseparability	Materiality	Performativity
Customers using their online customer reviews to ask hotels for freebies	Customers' opportunistic behaviour and TripAdvisor are inseparable in the discussion of customers using the online review system to exploit hotels	'Bad' customer review, regardless of its existence on the Internet, can act as a weapon to threaten hotels	Untruthful and fake reviews become part of the online customer review and influence the way hotels process such information
IG using online customer reviews as part of data set for their service performance measures	In the discussion of online customer reviews' role as service performance data, IG's intention, big data analytics, and digital platform are inseparable	Online customer reviews can act as data for service performance measure	Online customer review enacts the hotel's performance management system, influencing the hotel's service performance which the reviews initially aim to describe

practice. It is often both an exogenous force that acts as a catalyst for change and a significant part of the changed system that feeds back to the technology.

The role of digital platforms in PMM practices far exceeds their original role as information sharing mechanisms, as their roles are actively and materially reshaped by interacting with different social entities. The findings from the case study show how TripAdvisor and the customers' online reviews influence the way IC Resort measures its service performance, and at the same time, it influences the way customers behave. The example of customers threatening the hotel with their ability to write bad reviews on the Internet shows how these technologies reshape both customers' and managers' behaviour. This shows how online customer reviews can be seen as performative, as maintaining good review records has become the focus of the hotel's service and a new performance management system that emphasises the importance of these reviews that emerged in the interaction between them.

Table 12.4 provides a summary of how different roles of TripAdvisor emerge in the case of IC Resort's performance management system. Different roles of online customer reviews emerge through their inseparable relationship with different users. Therefore, the materiality of the digital platform is shaped by its inseparable relationship with its users, and through its performativity, and it becomes closely entangled with IC Resort's performance management practice.

12.7   CONCLUSION

The study discusses how TripAdvisor has become an integral part of the hotel's PMM practices through a sociomateriality lens. This study's finding illustrates how the role of TripAdvisor deviates from its originally intended use through the sociomaterial entanglement of other human and non-human actors in the specific context of IC Resort. In contrast to prior studies which often view technology as an external factor that initiates changes in an organisation (for example, Grandlund and Malmi, 2002; Scapens and Jazayeri, 2003), this study focuses on how TripAdvisor and the hotel's PMM practices' materiality are performative and inseparable for both of their existence. The analysis of the findings demonstrates how TripAdvisor is closely entangled with various actors involved in the case hotel's PMM practices. The specific use of TripAdvisor in IC Resort's PMM can only persist through continuous interaction between related actors, i.e. guests, TripAdvisor users and the hotel's employees.

This study contributes to the growing accounting research on digital platforms by drawing attention to the complex relationship among digital platforms, user-generated information and PMM practices. Prior studies (for example, Bialecki et al., 2017; Scott and Orlikowski, 2012; Jeacle and Carter, 2011) have explored how accounting practices emerge from digital platforms. This study extends those prior studies by focusing on how user-generated information from digital platforms interacts with user organisations and becomes taken-for-granted. The sociomaterial perspectives used in this study are not limited to accounting research, but applicable to studies that seek to understand the relationship between technologies and other organisational practices.

As with any study, this study has some limitations. First, the study does not explore in detail the implications of data analytics in the hospitality industry. Although the case hotel claims to utilise publicly available information from TripAdvisor and other social media in their PMM practices, this study did not explore the detailed algorithmic practice hidden behind PMM practices. This opens new opportunities for future research to explore.

NOTES

1. A concept introduced by Pickering (1993) to highlight that both human and material agencies do not have an inherent property, but emerge temporally through their mutual entanglement. Pickering (1993, 1995) suggests any human or non-human agencies' properties 'mangle' with each other whenever there is interaction between them and through this entanglement their properties are continuously reconfigured.
2. Whitebridge Report: Hotel Beat Destination: Vietnam. November, 2012.
3. Grant Thornton Report: Vietnam Hotel Survey 2012.
4. A service performance measurement system developed by IG. The guest engagement report gathers service performance related data (such as customer satisfaction, problem handling efficiency, and loyalty) from various sources (social media, IG customer survey, etc) and processes this data with data analytics.
5. A data and bench marketing service provider for the hotel industry.
6. This table was recreated by the author with the actual figures removed for confidentiality. The actual table was given during the interview along with other IC Resorts strategic documents.

REFERENCES

Atkinson, H. and Brown, J.B. (2001). Rethinking performance measures: Assessing progress in UK hotels. *International Journal of Contemporary Hospitality Management*, 13(3), pp.128–136.

Barad, K. (2003). Posthumanist performativity: Toward an understanding of how matter comes to matter. *Journal of Women in Culture and Society*, 28(3), pp.801–831.

Barad, K. (2007). *Meeting the universe halfway: Quantum physics and the entanglement of matter and meaning*. Durham, North Carolina, USA: Duke University Press.

Bhimani, A. and Langfield-Smith, K. (2007). Structure, formality and the importance of financial and non-financial information in strategy development and implementation. *Management Accounting Research*, 18(1), pp.3–31.

Bialecki, M., O'Leary, S. and Smith, D. (2017). Judgement devices and the evaluation of singularities: The use of performance ratings and narrative information to guide film viewer choice. *Management Accounting Research*, 35, pp. 56–65.

Braun, V. and Clarke, V. (2006). Qualitative research in psychology: Using thematic analysis in psychology. *Qualitative Research in Psychology*, 3(2), pp.77–101.

Brivot, M., Gendron, Y. and Guenin, H. (2017). Reinventing organizational control. *Accounting, Auditing & Accountability Journal*, 30(4), pp.795–820.

Bromwich, M. (1990). The case for strategic management accounting: The role of accounting information for strategy in competitive markets. *Accounting, Organizations and Society*, 15(1–2), pp.27–46.

Burns, J. and Scapens, R.W. (2000). Conceptualizing management accounting change: An institutional framework. *Management Accounting Research*, 11(1), pp.3–25.

Callon, M. (1984). Some Elements of a Sociology of Translation: Domestication of the Scallops and the Fishermen. *The sociological review*, 32(1), pp. 196–233

Ciucă, N. (2009). Revenue generation indexes used in the lodging industry. Finance and economic stability in the context of financial crisis. *Theoretical and Applied Economics*, 12(541) pp. 557–564.

Golden-Biddle, K. and Locke, K. (2007). *Composing qualitative research*. Sage. [online].

Granlund, M. and Malmi, T. (2002). Moderate impact of ERPS on management accounting: A lag or permanent outcome? *Management Accounting Research*, 13(3), pp.299–321

Harris, P.J. and Mongiello, M. (2001). Key performance indicators in European hotel properties: General managers' choices and company profiles. *International Journal of Contemporary Hospitality Management*, 13(3), pp.120–128.

Hoque, K. (1999). Human resource management and performance in the UK hotel industry. *British Journal of Industrial Relations*, 37(3), pp.419–443.

Jeacle, I. and Carter, C. (2011). In TripAdvisor we trust: Rankings, calculative regimes and abstract systems. *Accounting, Organizations and Society*, 36(4–5), pp.293–309.

Jones, M. (2014). A matter of life and death: Exploring conceptualizations of sociomateriality in the context of critical care. *MIS Quarterly: Management Information Systems*, 38(3), pp.895–925.

Kaplan, R.S. and Norton, D.P. (1992). The Balanced Scorecard – measures that drive performance. *Harvard Business Review*, 70(1), pp.71–79.

Kaplan, R.S., & Norton, D.P, (1993). Putting the Balance Scorecard to Work. *Harvard Business Review*, 71(5), 134–147

Kaplan, R.S. and Norton, D.P. (1996). Using Balanced Scorecard as a strategic management system. *Harvard Business Review*, (January–February), pp.75–85.

Karunakaran, A., Orlikowski, W.J. and Scott, S.V. (2022). Crowd-based accountability: How social media commentary reconfigures organizational accountability. *Organization Science*, 33(1), pp.170–193.

Kautz, K. and Jensen, T.B. (2013). Sociomateriality at the royal court of IS. A jester's monologue. *Information and Organization*, 23(1), pp.15–27.

Kim, W.G. (2006). EVA and traditional accounting measures: Which metric is a better predictor of market value of hospitality companies? *Journal of Hospitality & Tourism Research*, 30(1), pp.34–49.

Kloot, L. and Martin, J. (2000). Strategic performance management: A balanced approach to performance management issues in local government. *Management Accounting Research*, 11(2), pp.231–251.

Latour, B. (1987). Science in action: How to follow scientists and engineers through society. Boston, Massachusetts. *Harvard Business School Press*.

Latour, B. (2005). *Reassembling the social – an introduction to actor-network-theory*. Oxford, UK: Oxford University Press.

Leonardi, P.M. (2012). Materiality, sociomateriality, and socio-technical systems: What do these terms means? How are they different? Do we need them? In P.M. Leonardi, B. A. Nardi, & J. Kallinikos (eds.), *Materiality and organizing: Social interaction in a technological world* (pp.25–48). Oxford: Oxford University Press, 2012.

Leonardi, P.M. and Barley, S.R. (2010). What's under construction here? Social action, materiality, and power in constructivist studies of technology and organizing. *Academy of Management Annals*, 4(1), pp.1–51.

Leonardi, P.M., Nardi, B.A. and Barley, S.R. (2012). *Materiality and organizing: Social interaction in a technological world*. Oxford: Oxford University Press, pp.25–48.

Leoni, G. and Parker, L.D. (2019). Governance and control of sharing economy platforms: Hosting on Airbnb. *British Accounting Review*, 51(1), pp.1–22.

Lukka, K. (2007). Management accounting change and stability: Loosely coupled rules and routines in action. *Management Accounting Research*, 18(1), pp.76–101.

Merchant, K.A. (1985). Organizational controls and discretionary program decision making: A field study. *Accounting, Organizations and Society*, 10(1), pp.67–85.

Mintzberg, H. (1978). Patterns in strategy formation. *Management Science*, 24(9), pp.934–948.

Mintzberg, H. (1987). Crafting strategy. *Harvard Business Review*, 65(4), pp.66–75.

Orlikowski, W.J. (2007). Sociomaterial practices: Exploring technology at work. *Organization Studies*, 28(9), pp.1435–1448.

Orlikowski, W.J. (2010). The sociomateriality of organisational life: Considering technology in management research. *Cambridge Journal of Economics*, 34(1), pp.125–141.

Orlikowski, W.J. and Scott, S.V. (2008). Sociomateriality: Challenging the separation of technology, work and organization. *Academy of Management Annals*, 2(1), pp.433–474.

Oshri, I., Kotlarsky, J., & Willcocks, L. (2015). *The Handbook of Global Outsourcing and Offshoring* (3rd ed.). London, UK. Palgrave Macmillan.

Otley, D.T. (1999). Performance management: A framework for management control systems research. *Management Accounting Research*, 10(4), pp. 363–382.

Pickering, A. (1993). The mangle of practice: Agency and emergence in the sociology of science. *American Journal of Sociology*, 99(3), pp.559–589.

Pickering, A. (1995). *The mangle of practice: Time, agency, and science.* Chicago, Illinois: The University of Chicago Press, p.281.

Ryan, B., Scapens, R.W. and Theobold, M. (2002). *Research methods and methodology in finance and accounting.* 2nd ed. Andover, UK: Cengage Learning EMEA.

Scapens, R.W. and Jazayeri, M. (2003). ERP systems and management accounting change: Opportunities or impacts? A research note. *European Accounting Review*, 12(1), pp.201–233.

Scapens, R.W. and Varoutsa, E. (2010). Accounting in inter-organizational relationships – the institutional theory perspective, in H. Håkansson, K. Kraus, and J. Lind (eds) *Accounting in Networks*. New York: Routledge, pp.314–341.

Scott, S.V. and Orlikowski, W.J. (2012). Reconfiguring relations of accountability: Materialization of social media in the travel sector. *Accounting, Organizations and Society*, 37(1), pp.26–40.

Simons, R. (1995). Control in an age of empowerment. *Harvard Business Review*, 73(2), pp.80–88.

Suchman, L. (2007). *Human-machine reconfigurations: Plans and situated actions.* Cambridge, UK: Cambridge University Press.

13. The relationship between accounting information systems and digital public services: the case of Croatia

Ana Novak, Ana Rep and Katarina Žager

13.1 INTRODUCTION

The intensive use of information technology in all aspects of business operations, as well as constant improvements in the field of information technology, has affected traditional ways of performing accounting tasks. Information technology affects accounting information systems as well as their users, who demand quality information, which includes, among other qualitative characteristics, information that is delivered on time and in a form that is useful to users. In this regard, the progress of digital technology has influenced the development of new products and services, which enables new ways of interaction between the company's accounting information system and interested users.

The importance of everyone's involvement in the digital transformation process is emphasised through the European Commission's 2030 Digital Compass for the EU's digital decade, in which the Commission presented a vision for Europe's digital transformation by 2030. The Digital Compass for the EU's digital decade consists of four main points: skills, digital transformation of businesses, secure and sustainable digital infrastructures, and digitalisation of public services (European Commission, 2021a). The Digital Compass for the EU's digital decade sets several targets to be reached by 2030, including 80 per cent of all adults having basic digital skills (European Commission, 2021b), all EU households having gigabit connectivity, all populated areas being covered by 5G (European Commission, 2021c), for 75 per cent of European enterprises to have adopted cloud computing services, big data, and artificial intelligence (AI), for more than 90 per cent of small and medium-sized enterprises to have reached at least a basic level of digital intensity (European Commission, 2021d) and for all key public services to be available online (European Commission, 2021e).

The impact of digital technology is reflected in all aspects of the activities of people and enterprises; accounting information systems are no exception. Information technology has impacted all steps of the accounting process, from collecting, processing, and storing data to producing and communicating information for different parties. To be useful to users in decision-making, information must have certain qualitative characteristics such as relevance and faithful representation (IASB, 2018). In this regard, information technology has contributed to enhancing qualitative characteristics of information, such as timeliness, comparability, and accessibility.

The accounting information system comprises interrelated elements to realise its organisational function and produce useful financial information that users may need to make decisions. The accounting information system includes people, procedures and instructions, data, software, information technology infrastructure, and internal controls and security measures

(Romney & Steinbart, 2018). The focus of this chapter is on information technology as one of the main drivers of change in accounting information systems (Mancini et al., 2013).

In light of digital transformation and new technological achievements and their integration into business processes and services, this chapter aims to examine the effects of digital technologies on accounting information systems and public services, focusing on financial and other administrative reporting. Thus, one of the goals is to investigate digitalisation in accounting and to analyse the impact of digitalisation in the accounting process on the accounting profession. In this context, the benefits of digitalisation in accounting are also explored.

Information technology affects both accounting information systems and their users' requirements. Digital technology advancements influence the development of new products and services that enable new means of interaction between companies and accounting information users, which will be analysed in the example of Croatia. The chapter will also examine the presence of digital public services of various accounting information users such as financial agencies, tax administration, commercial courts, and others. In order to analyse the current state of development of Croatian digital public services and their interaction with accounting information systems, the content and function analysis of selected digital public services was conducted. The rapid digitalisation of public services also influences accountants' daily activities. In that sense, one of the essential factors is the compatibility of the accounting information system with each public service. On the other hand, the accountant's familiarity with the systems' functionalities is no less important. Therefore, to research deeper such relations and the future of the accounting profession, the level of digitalisation of public services, their connection with accounting information systems, and implications on the profession itself are examined and described. We believe that research findings will contribute to understanding digitalisation's current state and perspectives in accounting and public services. These findings could interest accounting educators and students, accounting professionals, and regulators.

This chapter consists of five parts. The introduction is followed by a part that examines the effects of technology on accounting information systems. The central research part, which focuses on the relationship between digital public services and accounting information systems, comprises four subparts. This relationship is considered in the context of registering a business entity, tax-related public e-services, and annual financial reports submission. It ends with a focus on the contribution of EU funds to Croatian public e-services. Before the conclusion, the effects of digitalisation on the accounting profession are presented.

13.2   EFFECTS OF DIGITAL TECHNOLOGIES ON ACCOUNTING INFORMATION SYSTEMS

Over time, information technology has significantly impacted accounting and the accounting profession. In the literature, it is possible to identify three phases of technological advancement that have had a significant impact on accounting (Knudsen, 2020). The first phase occurred in the 1960s and 1970s and was characterised by the introduction of computerised information systems; the second phase was primarily characterised by the development of the World Wide Web and integrated information systems (Porter & Heppelmann, 2014, as cited in Knudsen, 2020); and the third phase, commonly known as 'digitalisation', is currently emerging (Knudsen, 2020). Big data and cloud computing mainly characterised the 2010s, while the 2020s began with automation and modernisation (Agarwal et al., 2020).

There are many definitions of digitalisation in the literature. According to Gartner, digitalisation is 'the use of digital technologies to change a business model and provide new revenue and value-producing opportunities; it is the process of moving to a digital business' (Gartner, n.d.; Gray & Rumpe, 2015 cited in Hellsten & Paun, 2020, p. 229). Digital technologies are 'a sub-term of information and communication technologies and refer to the most advanced technologies that today almost exclusively enable the digital transmission of content' (Spremić, 2017, p. 52). Digital technologies can be divided into primary or fundamental technologies, such as mobile, social, cloud, big data, and the Internet of Things, and secondary digital technologies, such as 3D printing, robotics, drones, virtual and augmented reality, and AI (Spremić, 2017).

Given the rapid development and increasing application of digital technologies in the company's operations and accounting, as well as among the stakeholders with whom the company cooperates and communicates, accountants are expected to accept digital technologies and recognise the advantages as well as the challenges of their application. According to the results of a study conducted by ACCA (2020), accounting and finance professionals are familiar with the traditional technologies they use in their daily work, such as spreadsheets and enterprise resource planning (ERP) applications, but they often lack an understanding of new technologies such as AI and machine learning. Schmidt et al. (2020) also noted that some accounting professionals are reluctant to move beyond Excel and adopt a new data analytics technology. According to FloQast's study (2018), proficiency in Excel remains a crucial skill for accountants despite the availability of sophisticated technologies.

With the application of new technologies, the need for new IT knowledge and skills of accountants is constantly growing. The results of the FloQast study (2018) show that the importance of technology, data, and systems skills for accountants has increased in today's environment compared to the previous decade. Looking ahead to the next decade, the accounting profession will experience significant changes in tasks and required skills due to some tasks being performed by digital technologies such as AI (Leitner-Hanetseder et al., 2021). Technological progress is changing the way work is done (Hajkowicz et al., 2016). Ten years ago, 75 per cent of a finance function's work consisted of repetitive processing, whereas today most organisations automate processes and systems (Institute of Financial Accountants, 2022). According to Ng and Alarcon (2021, p. 19), 'many of the current AI use cases automate traditional accounting functions'. In financial accounting, AI can be used, for example, to automate bank reconciliation processes, manage inventory levels in real time, and match invoices to supporting documents (Ng & Alarcon, 2021). Additionally, AI can be used for tax functions, such as extracting critical data from tax documents and classifying sensitive transactions (Van Volkenburgh, 2019 cited in Ng & Alarcon, 2021, p. 28). According to Gartner research, it is estimated that globally only about 10 per cent of businesses receive electronic invoices (Keck et al., 2019, as cieted in Ng & Alarcon, 2021), which presents an opportunity to increase the efficiency and effectiveness of the accounts payable process through the use of targeted AI applications (Ng & Alarcon, 2021). Despite the increase in digital payments during the pandemic, which has resulted in a higher demand for AI-based accounting software, payment processing remains time-consuming and manual (Institute of Financial Accountants, 2022). Organisations can benefit from automating rules-based business processes and tasks using software bots, and these benefits are seen through cost savings, lower error rates, and improved report quality (Kokina & Blanchette, 2019).

An important step towards paperless accounting is the application of cloud-based accounting software. Cloud computing is one of the digital technologies having a great impact on the way accounting is done. Cloud accounting, sometimes 'referred to as online accounting' (IFAC, 2021), has been particularly boosted by the pandemic that has forced many companies to work remotely. In 2021, 41 per cent of enterprises in the EU used cloud computing, of which 25 per cent accessed office software such as word processors and spreadsheets via the cloud, and 19 per cent accessed software applications for finance or accounting (Eurostat, 2021). There is a wide range of cloud financial applications in use, with no single type dominating, and the variety includes payroll, expense management, general ledger, reporting, invoicing and other financial cloud applications (FloQast, 2018). The main advantages of cloud accounting include increased security, reduction or even elimination of technology support staff cost, elimination of the capital cost for hardware, the elasticity of services provided, centrally installed and updated cloud software, flexible delivery of information that can be accessed from any location, at any time, and from any Internet-enabled device (CIMA, 2015). From the viewpoint of accountants, the positive effects of technology are enhanced work efficiency through automation, flexibility to work from any location, reduced paper management, and decreased training requirements as software has become easier to use (FloQast, 2018).

Technologies have transformed financial reporting from paper-based statements to digital formats, beginning with the adoption of PDF technology and further evolving with the introduction of the eXtensible Business Reporting Language (XBRL) standard (Alles et al., 2021). XBRL is the open international standard specifically designed for preparing, publishing, and automatically exchanging financial information (Hall, 2018). A significant difference between the earlier financial reports in PDF, HTML or Word and the new XBRL-based one lies in the fact that all versions before XBRL were only readable by humans, while the XBRL-based financial report is readable by humans as well as by computer software applications (Hoffman & Mora Rodríguez, 2013). XBRL is implemented in companies, public sector agencies, and a wide range of other organisations in numerous countries around the world, mainly for regulatory and supervisory purposes, and therefore 'millions of XBRL documents are created every year, replacing older, paper-based reports with more useful, more effective and more accurate digital versions' (XBRL, n.d.). Along with digital technologies, open data standards, such as the XBRL standard, have great potential to reduce delays in business reporting (Agarwal et al., 2020, p. 6) and offer a variety of different features that improve report quality, consistency and usability (XBRL, n.d.). Technologies have the potential to enhance corporate reporting by 'eliminating inefficient, inconsistent formatting and streamline the most informative data from source to user' (Agarwal et al., 2020, p. 4). In the future, reporting will likely be intelligent, interactive, and real time, and technology that can make this happen includes robotic process automation (RPA) software, chatbots, visualisation, predictive analytics, and AI (Morganti et al., 2018).

It is understood that the accounting information system exchanges information with numerous external users of the accounting information system, such as regulators, tax authorities, business partners, creditors, or statistical and monetary policy authorities. And for this purpose, numerous reports should be created, which often means 'the data from a regulated entity's enterprise resource planning (ERP) software needs to be compiled and repackaged in order to meet a regulator's "form:" and "data format" requirements for filing submissions' (Agarwal et al., 2020, p. 11). Around the world, regulated entities, governments, and regulatory authorities are recognising the necessity to move away from 'inflexible paper-based documents or proprietary digital data formats and embrace open data standards' (Agarwal et al., 2020, p. 15). By surveying 3,298 accountants worldwide, Sage (2020, p. 9) found that '79% of accountants agreed that regulations from government, industry, and international bodies are forcing changes to working practices'. Considering the rapid development and adoption of new information technologies and cooperation with different users that are also influenced by digital transformation, it is certain that professional accountants must continuously expand their IT knowledge and skills to be able to perform their roles.

13.3   CORRELATION OF DIGITAL PUBLIC SERVICES AND ACCOUNTING INFORMATION SYSTEMS: THE CASE OF CROATIA

It is well known that accounting is not a purpose for itself but for its stakeholders. Regarding external stakeholders, public sector bodies and independent administrative organisations (hereafter public authorities) are their representatives. Evidence and various reports as accounting outputs are inputs of several public services governed by public sector bodies and organisations. Some Croatian public authorities whose e-services will be analysed in this chapter are the Government of the Republic of Croatia, the Tax Administration, the Commercial Court, the Financial Agency (from now on: FINA), and the Croatian Bureau of Statistics. The mentioned bodies and institutions are essential when requesting various evidence and reports from business entities' accounting information systems. Public services from the said authorities and their connection and interaction with accounting information systems are described below.

At the end of the 20th century and the beginning of the 21st century, the majority of documentation required by the public authorities was delivered in hard-copy form, either by post or personally to the counter. Although some of the public services were already digitised, not all business entities used them. That is because existing accounting and other business information systems had to be upgraded or aligned with the formats required by digital public services. From the accounting perspective, accountants with very few clients or those not digitally literate and skilled at a high level thought that digital transformation causes more costs than benefits for them, and they were reluctant to leave their traditional business operations. Although they already used accounting information systems, they needed additional help from IT staff to align their accounting systems with the needs of digital public services and educate them on how to use and report via digital public services. Croatia entering the EU in 2013 was a watershed for the digital transformation of public services. Although Croatia had some funds through the pre-accession programme before its entrance to the EU, the 2014–2020 financial perspective was a turning point in the digitalisation of public services, i.e. e-services.

The Government of the Republic of Croatia cooperates with ministries and numerous partners to ease various tasks that business entities are required to deliver. One of the most outstanding achievements of the Croatian economy's digitalisation process, which provides digital services for both citizens and business entities, is the digital service e-Citizens. It was introduced in 2014 with 15 services available, while in 2022 it provided entry to more than 90 public e-services (Government of the Republic of Croatia, 2021).

Regarding registering a business entity, the Commercial Court was the first public institution that founders had to visit. Although it is still possible to register the business entity physically, the e-service of the Court register (START) enabled all the registering processes to be done digitally. That resulted in saving time and money for the founders of new entities. Furthermore, from the aspect of daily business activities, the digitalisation of the Croatian tax system by launching the e-Tax Administration system was a turning point in integrating and making available various tax data and reports. Since its launch, the data have been available to business entities, their accountants, and other authorised persons anywhere at any time with a proper means for authorisation. At the same time, a lot of paperwork has been replaced with direct access to data management via the system by the authorised person, most often by the accountant. Besides, many other daily activities of accountants are also digitised. For instance, they include the digital registration and deregistration of employees in the pension and health insurance system, which is then communicated to the Croatian Employment Service, then sending and receiving e-invoices, as well as monitoring the statuses of all sent requests. Another meaningful institution, which is indispensable when it comes to financial reporting, is FINA. 'FINA's information system connects all branches, even the farthest, guaranteeing fast and reliable processing of even the most complex and sophisticated requests, making each contact point in the system ready and capable to execute any order and meet any service request' (FINA, n.d.a). FINA actively participates in EU co-funded projects making a solid foundation for widening and improving public e-services. Hence, FINA has been a coordinator or partner in numerous projects which have resulted in a broad spectrum of digitalised public services. The functionalities of the e-services mentioned above are described in the following subchapters.

13.3.1   Registration of a Business Entity

Before the digitalisation of public services, to start a business, entrepreneurs had to collect a whole set of documentation, visit several public offices, and often deliver the same data to various public services. It was time-consuming, stressful, and strenuous. As a result of one of the EU projects, which was conducted in cooperation with eight partners (public authorities and Croatian banking association), called Electronic Identification Croatia (ePIC) and ended in 2019, an e-service named Registration of a Company via the Internet (START) started functioning. This service enables the submission of requests and documents for registering a limited liability company or craft but also necessary additional services related to establishing the business, such as:

- registration of the entity in the Court register,
- registration of the entity's business activities in the Register of Business Entities (governed by the Croatian Bureau of Statistics),
- electronic payment of the share capital,
- electronic payment of the Court fees,
- submitting a request for opening a transaction account in the selected bank,
- registration of the entity in the Register of the VAT Payers and/or allocation of a VAT ID number,
- registration in the Croatian Pension Insurance Institute (FINA, n.d.c; Government of the Republic of Croatia, n.d.; European Commission, 2021f).

START service provides entity founders with registration decisions and other documents in electronic form via a notice sent to the eCitizen Personal Mailbox or per e-mail (DPA European Commission 2021f). The registration process lasts up to a few days and requires the possession of FINA's digital certificate with a high level of security or electronic ID (eID). Finally, the administrative relief of the entrepreneurs using the START has been accomplished since it has decreased both public administrative fees and time spent registering a business entity.

13.3.2   Tax-Related Public e-Services

As some of the objectives of introducing public e-services have been to integrate and unite the data among the public authorities, decrease various fees, and save time, it was inevitable to digitalise the tax system since the business entities use it on a monthly or even daily basis. Business entities registered as VAT payers are obliged to prepare and submit the VAT monthly report (some may be registered as quarter obligators). It includes the VAT form and accompanying attachments, such as the incoming invoices form, collective application (for goods and services delivered to an entity registered in the EU), and acquiring form (for goods and services bought from an entity registered in the EU). To replace the physical submission of the mentioned but also all other documents related to the taxes, the Tax Administration, in collaboration with project partners, developed another public e-service, e-Tax Administration. The e-Tax Administration system is intended for all taxpayers in Croatia and is designed on the One-Stop-Shop principle (Ministry of Finance, n.d.). Access to services depends on the electric credential used for logging in. External accountants providing accounting services to their clients may have access to the e-Tax Administration throughout the given authorisation by their clients so that they can submit the documentation in their clients' names. Some of the functionalities of the e-Tax Administration system are:

- managing taxpayer data,
- reviewing tax and other data in the records of the Tax Administration,
- submitting forms,
- submitting requests,
- requesting a tax refund,
- asking for a transfer of funds,
- requesting the connection of unrelated payments of the JOPPD form (a form for reporting personal income taxes, local taxes and contributions calculated on receipts per individual taxpayer),
- carrying out electronic communication with the Tax Administration to fulfil tax obligations,
- receiving documents electronically,
- receiving notifications and information,
- and others (Ministry of Finance, n.d.).

The introduction of the e-Tax Administration system has increased data security and confidentiality, facilitating, simplifying, and accelerating the fulfilment of obligations towards the Tax Administration, as well as growing the informativeness of taxpayers. By generating the forms in the accounting information systems, accountants can submit them to the e-Tax Administration system directly from the accounting system or by exporting the documents in XML form from the accounting systems and simply uploading them to the e-Tax Administration system. The forms are generated automatically in the accounting information systems by posting a specific business event, such as payroll, or completing the posting of all incoming and outgoing invoices in a particular month. Most accounting information systems commonly generate the forms for submission to the e-Tax Administration system with 'one-click'.

13.3.3   Annual Financial Statements Submission

All business entities operating in Croatia that are obliged to prepare and publish the annual financial statements deliver the set of required financial and statistical reports and accompanying decisions to FINA. Afterwards, the financial statements and accompanying decisions are available publicly on the Internet through the Web Annual Financial Statements Registry, which FINA runs. Thus, the Registry is one of the public e-services since it stands for an electronic booklet. Business entities have four options for documentation delivery: through the web application of the Registry, through the online service for submitting documents, by post or at the counter at FINA's branches. For business entities to enter the Registry, sign and deliver the reports electronically, it is required to possess one of the following: FINA's e-card/ USB stick, FINA's business certificate issued by FINA's partner bank, eID or qualified certificates for electronic signatures of the EU issuers. In addition, business users holding FINA's digital certificate may apply for the Web e-Signature that 'enables electronic signature of documents and authentication of signatures on electronically signed documents' (FINA, n.d.b). There is no additional fee for those who deliver the reports electronically, while the hard copy and partly electronic reports deliveries are payable. The structure and content of financial statements, excluding the notes to the financial statements and the accompanying decisions, are prescribed by the Rulebook on the structure and content of annual financial statements (Official Gazette No 95/16, 144/20). After their submission, FINA prepares the digital format of financial statements (in a shortened form), which are publicly available free of charge to all who register, and the registration is also free. Accordingly, accounting information systems used by Croatian business entities are mostly adjusted to the prescribed reporting format, making the financial statements prepared in the accounting information system compatible for delivery through the available public e-services. It saves time and human resources for business entities, especially accounting services keeping the business ledgers to dozens of clients.

13.3.4   Contribution of EU Funds to Croatian Public e-Services

The cohesion policy of the EU has made additional funds available for Croatia to reform and improve its public services. E-Croatia 2020 Strategy set key goals to be achieved by using the EU funds, where the e-services were distinguished between those for citizens and businesses. One of the goals was to increase the number of business entities which use public administration e-services from 92.7 per cent in 2013 to 97 per cent in 2020 (Ministry of Public Administration, 2017). When it comes to the goals set for the current period, one of the strategic goals for Croatia set in The National Development Strategy 2030 of the Republic of Croatia refers to the digital transition of society and economy. Measured by the DESI (Digital Economy and Society Index) of economic and social digitisation, Croatia took 20th place in the EU in 2020 with a score of 47.6, while its goal by 2030 is to reach the EU average, which was 52.57 in 2020 (National Development Strategy of the Republic of Croatia until 2030, 2021). DESI represents 'a composite index that summarises relevant indicators on Europe's digital performance and tracks the evolution of EU Member States, across five main dimensions: Connectivity, Human Capital, Use of Internet, Integration of Digital Technology, Digital Public Services' (European Commission, n.d.a). Figure 13.1 presents the position of Croatia among the selected EU member states and the average for the whole EU. It was generated by considering the e-Government as an indicator and setting only one dimension,

the Digital Public Services for Businesses. For data clarity, not all the EU member states were taken into account, but only some from Eastern Europe since the Croatian economy is comparable to these selected countries.

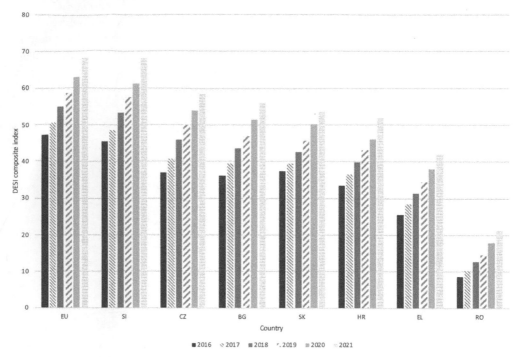

Source: Authors' work based on the EU data sets (European Commission, n.d.a).

Figure 13.1   *DESI composite index of selected Eastern Europe countries from 2016 to 2021: development of e-Government based on Digital Public Services for Businesses*

Before the analysis, it has to be mentioned that Croatia (HR) is the latest country to join the EU. Croatia joined in 2013. Bulgaria (BG) and Romania (RO) joined in 2007, Slovenia (SI), Czech Republic (CZ), and Slovakia (SK) joined in 2004, and Greece (EL) joined in 1981 (European Commission, n.d.b). The graph shows that all the analysed countries record continuous growth in the development of e-Government, taking into account the Digital Public Services for Businesses. Although Croatia shows better results only compared to Greece and Romania, one should keep in mind that the other four countries joined the EU up to nine years before Croatia, meaning they had the whole financial perspective funds available in addition to the funds Croatia had. Comparing the increase in 2021 with 2016 as a base, Croatia's DESI (in the mentioned field) increased by 55.42 per cent, while the EU average increased by 44.47 per cent. In addition, compared to 2020, Croatia shows an increase of 12.87 per cent, which is 4.61 percentage points greater than the increase on the level of the EU average.

Figure 13.2 considers only Croatian and average EU trends to evaluate that relationship more clearly. Each year shows a relative difference compared to the previous year. From this

perspective, although Croatia is under the absolute average of the EU, its relative changes exceed those of the EU average, except for 2020, compared with 2019. Considering relations from the graph showing the EU average and Croatia, Croatia should meet the EU average at a certain point in time. Furthermore, Croatia has great potential to even exceed the EU average from the perspective of e-Government development based on Digital Public Services for Businesses unless that trend slows down substantially. However, these results should be perceived in the context of Croatia's lower base compared to other countries exceeding the EU average.

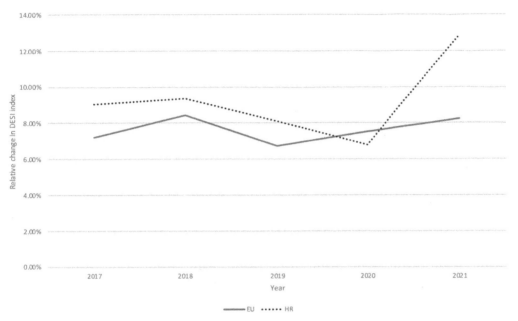

Source: Authors' work based on the EU data sets (European Commission, n.d.a).

Figure 13.2   *Comparison of the EU's and Croatian development of e-Government based on Digital Public Services for Businesses*

Finally, it should be noted that during the 2021–2027 financial perspective, Croatia has more than double the funds available compared to the previous financial perspective (2014–2020), and there should be no obstacles to continue with the development of e-Government based on Digital Public Services for Businesses.

13.4   EFFECTS OF DIGITALISATION ON THE ACCOUNTING PROFESSION

Digital technology advancements have significantly impacted accounting information systems. Digital technologies have enabled automating many accounting tasks, reducing the time and effort required to complete these tasks. That has allowed companies to speed up their account-

ing processes and improve accountants' effectiveness. Enhanced accuracy comes in line with improved efficiency, while implemented security measures have impacted greater transparency. Accounting information systems are flexible systems that can be customised based on users' or regulatory needs. Of course, that requires an engineer's intervention since accountants are the users of a final product. At the same time, accountants can use implemented performances to communicate directly or indirectly with colleagues, clients, and authorities through their digital systems.

The rapid digitalisation of public administration services also influences accountants' daily activities. That influence may be either positive or negative, depending primarily on the compatibility of each public e-service with the accounting information system and the accountant's familiarity with the systems' functionalities. Although Croatia has significantly improved in increasing the number of digital public services, most citizens still do not recognise their value. For instance, in 2021, only 37 per cent of labour-active citizens used the portal e-Citizens, which gathers more than 90 e-services for citizens and business entities (calculated as the number of e-Citizens users in 2021 over the number of labour-active citizens, 15+) (Government of the Republic of Croatia, 2021; Croatian Bureau of Statistics, 2022). These data fall in line with the fact that the majority of citizens (probably most of those who are older and those not educated at the secondary or tertiary level of education) are reluctant to change and are afraid of mistakes. On the other side, young generations are much more attached and somehow dependent on digital technology, and they are not scared of making a mistake because they know or can search for how to fix it.

Regarding accountants in Croatia, most of them are either highly educated, highly experienced, or both. Not all are educated at the university level because there are no barriers to entering the accounting profession in Croatia, and accountants do not have to hold a specific licence or certificate. But to do their job well, they must continuously invest in their education. In that sense, they can educate themselves in informal ways by reading professional literature, listening to specialised education, participating in accounting workshops, or through formal education in their area of interest. It should be emphasised that an accountant can specialise in various fields, from taxes and payroll to financial reporting and financial analysis. When an accountant is highly educated and continuously invests in professional development, he has no fear of digitalisation. Understanding the accounting process is indispensable for anybody who wants to do that job. As long as an accountant understands what he is doing and can think beyond that, he should not be afraid of 'massive' digitalisation. Good accountants favour digitising repetitive processes as much as possible to have more time for making advanced decisions that a machine cannot generate. In addition, automated processes result in fewer errors, require fewer resources, either time or human, and increase the efficiency of accountants. However, it should also be noted that there are older accountants and those not so skilled in using digital technology, some of whom still do not use public e-services when they have a choice not to, which is a reason for incomplete exploitation of possibilities of public e-services. Despite this, accountants working for large companies, especially young generations of accountants, must strive to improve their digital skills and develop them continuously. Professional development in accounting and information technologies will enable them to use integrated accounting information systems, various accounting tools, and other technologies that can make their job easier only if they have the required skills.

13.5   CONCLUSION

When considering the digitalisation of business processes, including accounting as a business function, it is no more a matter of the future but rather the deep present. Accounting does not stand alone; it depends on and is interrelated with numerous other functions and services inside and outside the organisation. One of the external connections is public services that mainly require various data from accounting, and connecting these two systems has primarily depended on digitalisation advancements.

Digital transformation has played a significant role in the modernisation of public services in Croatia, with the introduction of the e-Citizens system and the digitalisation of the Croatian tax system enabling easier access to information and streamlining processes for business entities. The START service has significantly improved the process of registering a business in Croatia by allowing entrepreneurs to submit requests and documents electronically and providing access to a range of additional services related to establishing a business. That has resulted in significant administrative relief for entrepreneurs but also accountants who often assist them, reducing both fees and the time required to register a company or craft. Access to the START service requires possessing a digital certificate or eID. Another valuable digital service refers to the e-Tax Administration system that has increased data security and confidentiality, simplifying and accelerating the process of fulfilling tax-related obligations. The e-Tax Administration system's introduction has also improved taxpayers' informativeness. Accountants can use the system to submit tax forms on behalf of their clients. They can either submit them directly from accounting information systems or export them from the accounting system and import them to the e-Tax Administration system. When it comes to the end of a reporting period, annual financial statements must be prepared and submitted for statistical purposes and public announcements. Electronic services of FINA have also saved time and resources for business entities by allowing for the electronic delivery of the whole set of financial reports to the Registry and reducing the need for hard-copy documentation. Overall, e-services have greatly improved the accessibility and efficiency of public services in Croatia and thus allowed accountants, other experts, and citizens to be more effective, professionally or privately.

To meet the EU average regarding digitalisation, one of the strategic goals for Croatia set in The National Development Strategy 2030 of the Republic of Croatia is the digital transition of society and economy. Croatia has consistently shown growth in e-Government services, considering the Digital Public Services for Businesses, from 2016 to 2021, as measured by the DESI. A significant contribution to Croatian public e-services development has been played by the EU funds that enabled the financing of all the improvements. Although Croatia is still below the EU average, its growth rate is greater than the EU's for the observed period. If the positive trend continues, Croatia should reach the EU's average.

It is known that the digitalisation of public administration services had more positive than adverse effects on the users of these services in Croatia, as is the case in other areas. Although automation has made some processes more efficient, not all citizens and accountants have accepted using digital services, which has prevented their full potential from being exploited. But highly educated and experienced accountants who are adept at using digital technology have embraced digitisation and are taking advantage of it to focus on those things that technology has not covered, such as providing informed advice and making decisions based on case analysis and the existing legal constraints. Ultimately, computers will not replace accountants but will improve their abilities as advisors and controllers within business entities. To make it that way, accountants must constantly invest in their knowledge and skills by educating themselves in areas of accounting but also innovative technologies to acquire skills necessary for implementing and using those technologies that facilitate their daily tasks.

REFERENCES

ACCA (2020) *The digital accountant: Digital skills in a transformed world.* Association of Chartered Certified Accountants. Available at: https://www.accaglobal.com/gb/en/professional-insights/technology/The_Digital_Accountant.html

Agarwal T., Leipziger, D., Mehta. U., Murray, D., Watson, L. A. and Wray, D. (2020) *A digital transformation brief: Business reporting in the fourth industrial revolution.* Institute of Management Accountants. Available at: https://www.imanet.org/insights-and-trends/external-reporting-and-disclosure-management/a-digital-transformation-brief-business-reporting-in-the-fourth-industrial-revolution?ssopc=1

Alles, M. G., Dai, J. and Vasarhelyi, M. A. (2021) Reporting 4.0: Business reporting for the age of mass customization, *Journal of Emerging Technologies in Accounting,* 18 (1), 1–15. DOI: 10.2308/jeta-10764

Croatian Bureau of Statistics (2022) *Aktivno stanovništvo u Republici Hrvatskoj u 2021 – prosjek godine* (*Active population in the Republic of Croatia in 2021 – a yearly averag*e). Available at: https://podaci.dzs.hr/2022/hr/29256

European Commission (2021a) *Europe's Digital Decade: Digital targets for 2030.* Available at: https://commission.europa.eu/strategy-and-policy/priorities-2019-2024/europe-fit-digital-age/europes-digital-decade-digital-targets-2030_en

European Commission (2021b) *Digital Skills Part of 2030 DIGITAL COMPASS: YOUR DIGITAL DECADE.* Available at: https://futurium.ec.europa.eu/en/digital-compass/digital-skills

European Commission (2021c) *Digital Infrastructures Part of 2030 DIGITAL COMPASS: YOUR DIGITAL DECADE.* Available at: https://futurium.ec.europa.eu/en/digital-compass/digital-infrastructures

European Commission (2021d) *Digital Businesses Part of 2030 DIGITAL COMPASS: YOUR DIGITAL DECADE.* Available at: https://futurium.ec.europa.eu/en/digital-compass/digital-businesses

European Commission (2021e) *Digital Public Services Part of 2030 DIGITAL COMPASS: YOUR DIGITAL DECADE.* Available at: https://futurium.ec.europa.eu/en/digital-compass/digital-public-services

European Commission (2021f) *Digital Public Administration Factsheet 2021 – Croatia.* Available at: https://joinup.ec.europa.eu/sites/default/files/inline-files/DPA_Factsheets 2021_Croatia_vFinal.pdf

European Commission (n.d.a) *Digital economy and society index.* Available at: https://digital-agenda-data.eu/datasets/desi

European Commission (n.d.b) *From 6 to 27 members.* Available at: https://ec.europa.eu/neighbourhood-enlargement/enlargement-policy/6-27-members_en

Eurostat (2021) *Digital economy and society statistics – enterprises.* Available at https://ec.europa.eu/eurostat/statistics-explained/index.php?title=Digital_economy_and_society_statistics_-_enterprises

FINA (n.d.a) *Who we are.* Available at: https://www.fina.hr/en/who-we-are

FINA (n.d.b) *e-business.* Available at: https://www.fina.hr/en/e-business

FINA (n.d.c) *START.* Available at: https://www.fina.hr/hr/start

FloQast, Inc. (2018) C*loud technology advances the accounting profession. A survey of accounting and financeprofessionals,*sponsoredbyFloQastandconductedbyDimensionalResearch.Availableat:https://floqast.com/wp-content/uploads/2019/01/Cloud-Technology-Advances-Accounting-Profession-Survey-FloQast-1.pdf

Gartner (n.d.) *Digitalization.* Gartner Glossary. Available at: https://www.gartner.com/en/information-technology/glossary/digitalization#:~:text=Digitalization%20is%20the%20use%20of,moving%20to%20a%20digital%20business

Government of the Republic of Croatia (2021) *Sedma obljetnica: e-Građani* (*Seventh anniversary: e-Citizens*). Available at: https://rdd.gov.hr/vijesti/sedma-obljetnica-e-gradjani/1840

Government of the Republic of Croatia (n.d.) *START*. Available at: https://start.gov.hr/st/o-startu.html

Hajkowicz, S. A., Reeson, A., Rudd, L., Bratanova, A., Hodgers, L., Mason, C. and Boughen, N. (2016) Tomorrow's digitally enabled workforce: Megatrends and scenarios for jobs and employment in Australia over the coming twenty years, *Australian Policy Online*, CSIRO, Brisbane. Available at: https://publications.csiro.au/rpr/download?pid=csiro:EP161054&dsid=DS1

Hall, J. A. (2018) *Accounting information systems.* Tenth Edition. Boston: Cengage.

Hellsten, P. and Paunu, A. (2020) Digitalization: A concept easier to talk about than to understand. *Proceedings of the 12th International Joint Conference on Knowledge Discovery, Knowledge Engineering and Knowledge Management (IC3K 2020)*, 3, 226–233.

Hoffman, C. and Mora Rodríguez, M. (2013) Digitizing financial reports – issues and insights: A viewpoint. *The International Journal of Digital Accounting Research*, 13, 73–98. DOI: 10.4192/1577-817/1577-8517-v13_3

IASB (2018) *Conceptual framework for financial reporting.* IFRS Foundation. Available at: https://www.ifrs.org/content/dam/ifrs/publications/pdf-standards/english/2021/issued/part-a/conceptual-framework-for-financial-reporting.pdf

IFAC (2021) *Why is a cloud-based accounting migration the right choice for PAOs?* Available at: https://www.ifac.org/knowledge-gateway/developing-accountancy-profession/discussion/why-cloud-based-accounting-migration-right-choice-paos

Institute of Financial Accountants (2022) *What does the future of accounting look like?* Available at: https://www.accountancyage.com/2022/08/01/what-does-the-future-of-accounting-look-like/

Keck, M., Sommers, K. and Abbabatulla, B. (2019) *Success with AP invoice automation requires more than paper to digital.* Available at: https://www.theshelbygroup.com/wp-content/uploads/2019/08/AP_Invoice_Automation_Gartner_Research_Note.pdf

Knudsen, D. R. (2020) Elusive boundaries, power relations, and knowledge production: A systematic review of the literature on digitalisation in accounting, *International Journal of Accounting Information Systems*, 36 (C), 1–22. DOI: 10.1016/j.accinf.2019.100441

Kokina, J. and Blanchette, S. (2019) Early evidence of digital labor in accounting: Innovation with robotic process automation, *International Journal of Accounting Information Systems*, 35, DOI: 10.1016/j.accinf.2019.100431

Leitner-Hanetseder, S., Lehner, O. M., Eisl, C. and Forstenlechner, C. (2021) A profession in transition: Actors, tasks and roles in AI-based accounting, *Journal of Applied Accounting Research*, 22 (3), 539–556. DOI: 10.1108/JAAR-10-2020-0201

Mancini, D., Vaassen, E. H. J. and Dameri, R. P. (2013) Trends in accounting information systems. In: Mancini, D., Vaassen, E. H. J., Dameri, R. P. (eds) *Accounting information systems for decision making. Lecture notes in information systems and organisation*, 3, 1–11. DOI: 10.1007/978-3-642-35761-9_1

Ministry of Finance (n.d.) ePorezna. Available at: https://e-porezna.porezna-uprava.hr/Pages/Ousluzi.aspx

Ministry of Public Administration (2017) e-CROATIA 2020 STRATEGY. Available at: https://rdd.gov.hr/strategija-e-hrvatska-2020/1577

Morganti, T., Schloemer, J. and Panth, A. (2018) *Crunch time 7: Reporting in a digital world.* Available at: https://www2.deloitte.com/content/dam/Deloitte/us/Documents/finance-transformation/us-crunch-time-seven-reporting-in-a-digital-world.pdf

National Development Strategy of the Republic of Croatia until 2030 (2021) Available at: https://hrvatska2030.hr/

Ng, C. and Alarcon, J. (2021) *Artificial Intelligence in Accounting: Practical Applications. Applications of AI in Accounting*, 19–34. Abingdon, Oxfordshire, UK: Routledge.

Official Gazette No 95/16, 144/20, Rulebook on the structure and content of annual financial reports.

Porter, M.E., Heppelmann, J.E. (2014). How smart, connected products are transforming competition. *Harvard Business Review* 92 (11), 64–88.

Romney, M. B. and John Steinbart, P. J. (2016) *Accounting information systems.* Fourteenth Edition. New York: Pearson

Sage UK (2020) *Report: The Practice of Now 2020: Insight and practical advice for today's accountants and bookkeepers based on the latest independent research*. Available at https://www.sage.com/en-gb/blog/wp-content/uploads/sites/10/2020/07/The-Practice-Of-Now-2020.pdf

Schmidt, P. J., Riley, J. and Church, K. S. (2020) Investigating accountants' resistance to move beyond Excel and adopt new data analytics technology, *Accounting Horizons*, 34 (4), 165–180. DOI: 10.2308/HORIZONS-19–154

Spremić, M. (2017) *Digitalna transformacija poslovanja*. Zagreb: Sveučilište u Zagrebu, Ekonomski fakultet.

The Chartered Institute of Management Accountants (CIMA) (2015) The effects of cloud technology on management accounting and decision making, *Research Executive Summary Series*, 10 (6). Available at: https://www.aicpa-cima.com/resources/download/the-effects-of-cloud-technology-on-management-accounting

XBRL (n.d.) *An introduction to XBRL*. Available at: https://www.xbrl.org/the-standard/what/an-introduction-to-xbrl/

14. Exploring accountability in an entrepreneurial firm

Jiafan Li, Julia A. Smith and Gavin C. Reid

14.1 INTRODUCTION

This chapter investigates the nature and efficacy of governance and accountability in a new entrepreneurial firm in China. We observe the actions of a single and dominant owner-manager, with a Westernised view of business, and explore how these influences impact upon his decision-making characteristics (cf. Lumpkin and Dess, 1996). Whilst previous studies of organisational control have often focused on financial reporting, directors' control strategies, and budgetary control in listed, large firms, there is little in the extant literature to provide insights into governance within smaller organisations, especially those in developing economies. With this focus on the balance of control between inside and outside shareholders (cf. Parker, 2008a), the issue of whether firms without boardrooms have an organisational advantage over larger firms has been somewhat overlooked. Aside from the firm's capital structure, authority and power also depend upon the ownership of tangible and intangible assets (cf. Willig and Schmalensee, 1989). Directors who own firms outright can carry out strategic control plans alone, using various control mechanisms, such as those embodied in the internal accounting system (cf. Parker, 2008b). This study therefore focuses on the significance of one sole director and the ways in which he exercises control to meet organisational goals.

As a corollary of this, we consider how accountability has developed beyond its original bookkeeping function to become an essential component of good governance (cf. Bovens, 2007; Joannides, 2012; Bovens et al., 2014). For instance, in its broadest sense, accountability measures and rewards good conduct (cf. Roberts and Scapens, 1985), as commonly acknowledged in accountability research (Sinclair, 1995; Ahrens, 1996; Mulgan, 2000; Messner, 2009; Joannides, 2012). This can be explored within a principal–agent framework that specifies the principal's distribution of power and agents' delegated behaviour (cf. Gibbins and Newton, 1994; Bovens, 2007, 2010; Joannides, 2012); with stress being placed on the importance of the principal in managing a hierarchical firm (Willig and Schmalensee, 1989). Furthermore, the accountability relationship can serve as a social relationship or an obligational mechanism for explaining and justifying accountable behaviour. As a result, such justification can lead to the final judgements of bonuses and rewards, or negative sanctions on agents' behaviour (Bovens, 2007; Joannides, 2012), which then become the foundation of various control and monitoring mechanisms in the principal's decision-making process.

Accounting information is not only a way of recording and defining the results of events, but it is also a means of expressing and enforcing expectations in power relations (Roberts, 1991, 2001). It is expressed financially and used more in formal meetings to report and discuss the results of a certain period, during which the values and relations of power, reflected by accounting, shape interactions in hierarchical structures (Roberts and Scapens, 1985). The ways in which daily communication and updated financial statements are passed around a firm are illustrated by the basic principal–agent framework.

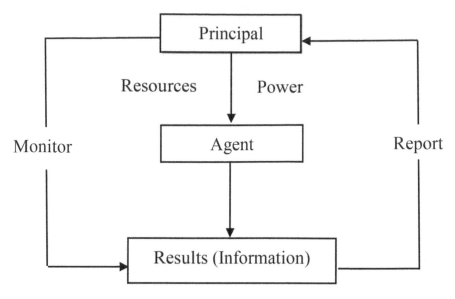

Figure 14.1   A single principal–agent relationship

As in Figure 14.1, the principal grants the agent power and resources, and the agent acts on behalf of the principal. In particular, principals monitor agents via information from various sources, such as accounting information, personal observation, and the voices of other employees. Accounting information can be favoured by the owner-manager of a small firm in carrying out monitoring and control activities for various reasons. First, when positioning accounting in a principal–agent relationship, it imposes an understanding by agents of what is required to explain and justify their actions. Combined with positive sanctions such as financial rewards or career promotion, or negative sanctions such as fines or punishment, accounting contributes to instrumental legitimacy and individual conformity in face-to-face contexts (Roberts and Scapens, 1985; Roberts, 1991).

Second, beyond formal talks, informal and random face-to-face chat in or after work can enhance loyalty and friendship, ease conflicts and misunderstanding, and add more humanity and sociability into work (Roberts and Scapens, 1985). On an equal setting, talks and negotiations can relax the nerves of defensive individuals and offer them a safe platform in which to gain deeper mutual understanding and recognition. This is in contrast to the indifferent values of an imposed hierarchy (Roberts, 1991). It further offers the owner-manager an implicit approach to collecting soft information when employees are unprepared, and can create a harmonious environment in the firm.

This chapter proceeds, first of all, by considering the literature surrounding the concept of hierarchical relationships within an agency setting. Here, good governance is influenced by the nature of the control environment, the ability to make relevant and useful assessments of risk, flows of information and communication, and the supporting activities of monitoring and control that facilitate organisational practice. We then move on to a discussion of our methodology, which employed ethnographic techniques of participant observation in the setting of a Chinese entrepreneurial firm, a few years into its existence, setting the scene for the context of accountability withing a developing nation.

We present our findings according to the structure set in the literature review, exploring aspects of control, risk assessment, communication and monitoring. We do this by providing qualitative evidence from a daily diary kept by the observer and presenting illustrative direct quotes from conversations with key players in the business. Our results reflect the cultural difficulties in adopting Western views of accountability; whilst this firm can be said to be a success, there remain difficulties in communication that only a strong owner-manager can overcome.

14.2   CONTEXT AND LITERATURE

Recent studies have paid increasing attention to the significance of capturing the 'tone from the top', in budgeting systems and performance measurement. For instance, this is exemplified in the top-down hierarchical approach to the communication of expectations, alongside the bottom-up approach for boosting the communication of risk identification and assessment (Braumann et al., 2020). Hence, this study also references the collection and use of both hard and soft information in corporate governance and accountability practice. In exploring the nature of work in this area, we structure our own discussion around the accepted framework devised by Jones (2008), and elaborated on below, viz. the control environment; risk assessment; information and communication; and monitoring and control activities.

14.2.1   Control Environment

Control refers to the behaviour that influences the probability of reaching organisational goals, and is created from the imbalance between these goals and the effort imparted by organisational members (Flamholtz, 1983). Jones (2008) argued that the control environment includes the owner's philosophy and management style, hierarchical organisational structure, control approaches, and the allocation of authority and resources. A dominant feature of hierarchical accountability is that the authorised delegation from principals to agents fosters the duties from agents to principals (Bovens et al., 2014), which in turn provides opportunities for principals to exercise the power of control (Cäker, 2007). In an SME (small-to-medium-sized enterprise) setting, where the principal (owner-manager) has direct influence over their agents (workforce), the nature and extent of hierarchical accountability is readily observable (cf. Mulgan, 2000; Koppell, 2005; Cäker, 2007). In addition, horizontal accountability is an interesting aspect for analysis, in that it considers the practice of control through indirect principal–agent relationships that develop naturally and equally, without formally designated obligations and rights (cf. Jansen, 2015). Horizontal accountability is manifest both in relationships within the same group, and between more 'distant' parties (Cäker, 2007, Schillemans, 2008). But the impact of horizontal accountability may not always have a positive effect on the interests of the group, and its impact in practice remains to be explored.

Combining an accounting ideology with control procedures is a widely used approach for exercising organisational control (cf. Otley and Berry, 1980), as accounting control lends itself well to a hierarchical structure with strict and clear responsibilities at different levels; but it also depends upon the principal's knowledge and control strategies (Mulgan, 2000; Koppell, 2005; Cäker, 2007). As hierarchical relationships are typically arm's-length principal–agent relationships, principals can exert control over agents to achieve their own expectations with designated rewards (Jansen, 2015). Therefore, how to ensure the effectiveness of incentivised controls under a hierarchical structure is a common concern for principals in organisations (Willig and Schmalensee, 1989).

14.2.2   Risk Assessment

Risk assessment refers to the identification, evaluation, and resolution of risks (Jones, 2008), which becomes all the more important when assessing new opportunities (cf. Battisti and Deakins, 2017). Within a principal–agent framework, the risks and information manipulation faced by a sole principal are mainly due to information asymmetry which arises through delegation. This may arise through concealment, distortion or ignorance. Further, coalitions are regarded as posing a common threat to firms' organisational objectives, as the actions of one or more parties might generate so-called 'favours' (Jean, 1986). A 'one-sided favour' refers to the phenomenon where one party benefits from manipulating information from others; whilst all parties would benefit from 'shared favours' (Jean, 1986). Therefore, the ways in which principals handle monitoring are paramount in reducing the risks caused by information asymmetry (cf. Guston, 1996; Day, 1999; Bushman and Smith, 2003).

Previous researchers have explored multiple ways of detecting and reducing risks, using a principal–agent framework. For instance, Braun and Guston (2003) suggested that using multiple agents would reduce the possibility of agents' self-interested behaviour; and Stevens and Thevaranjan (2010) suggested that the traditional way to resolve moral hazard issues is to provide financial incentives based on performance-related rewards. However, some scholars argued that the latter could be costly and that the practical incentives are too complicated to incorporate into contracts. Further, principals are not always helpless when faced with the types of risk mentioned above; another effective risk precaution is for principals to develop personal relationships with agents over a period of time. The embedded social networks (cf. Martiz et al., 2020) could then help principals to find the most effective methods for reducing agents' moral hazard behaviour, and would also offer agents opportunities to observe and capture principals' preferences (Shapiro, 2005). Overall, it is feasible for principals to use monitoring and control mechanisms to carry out risk assessments, based on their preferences, in order to achieve collectively organisational goals (Guston, 1996).

14.2.3   Information and Communication

The gathering of information incorporates the identification, selection, processing, and recording of material, whilst communication here focuses on face-to-face transmission of that information (Jones, 2008). Its significance has been explored by former researchers from various standpoints. For instance, information is particularly significant in decision-making, monitoring and control, from the perspective of organisational structure (Reid and Smith, 2009). Day (1999) argued that information is the key dimension for identifying and verifying accountability relationships. And Willig and Schmalensee (1989) found that information is both crucial and costly: organisations must pay for it to facilitate production and expansion;

and it takes time and effort to coordinate any individual interests that diverge from organisational objectives.

Willig and Schmalensee (1989) explored both hard and soft information in organisations, offering a broader view for evaluating the importance of information in enhancing corporate governance in organisations. Hard information refers to accounting-related information, such as accounting reports, performance evaluation standards and any other reports. For instance, the function of financial accounting information could assist stakeholders in identifying good investment opportunities (cf. Braun and Guston, 2003). It could also assist short-term objectives in achieving the owner's targets such as monthly sales benchmarks and profit targets across departments. Thus it serves as a tool for the exchange of implicit and explicit knowledge and signals by firm rules and regulations, performance measurements, and other targets (Jansen, 2015; Reid and Smith, 2009). Briefly, accounting information enhances corporate governance by assisting in appropriate resource allocation, thereby reducing information asymmetry, adverse selection, and moral hazard problems. Thus objective accounting information facilitates the principal's monitoring and subsequent control of agents' behaviour (Bushman and Smith, 2003).

Soft information is invisible, and resides in formal and informal conversations, facial expressions and tones (Willig and Schmalensee, 1989; Jansen, 2015). However, it might be challenging for principals to capture and validate agents' soft information, as agents could carry out moral hazard behaviour such as shirking or cheating (Willig and Schmalensee, 1989). To resolve this, owners might participate in nonsupervisory activities, for instance, using informal communication, coordination, and management, to observe their agents' comprehensive performance and to better inform subjective opinions. Therefore, detailed and specific information, such as the extension of accounting and other forms of information, is increasingly receiving more attention, and providing deeper insights into the implicit and complicated meanings of an individual's intentions (Jansen, 2015).

Moreover, Roberts and Scapens (1985) and Jean (1986) argued that regular face-to-face contexts can enhance trust and increase mutual knowledge through the interpretation and understanding of accounting information. Dialogue plays a key role in identifying and enhancing organisational and social affairs, first, by forming and enhancing accountability relationships, and fostering trust and cooperation (Mulgan, 2000; Schillemans, 2008). Second, it facilitates horizontal accountability, which can be manipulated by principals as a silent monitoring mechanism, thereby adding tension to relationships with agents (Schillemans, 2008). So face-to-face contexts do not always guarantee effective results: an individual's knowledge and resources might determine the significance of the negotiation and acknowledgement of specific responsibilities in practice; or the distrust and conflict of interests generated from hierarchical accountability might be more severe under face-to-face contexts (Roberts and Scapens, 1985), and further distorted or manipulated to reach an individual's goals (Bovens et al., 2014).

14.2.4   Monitoring and Control Activities

Monitoring consists of supervisory activities, including observation, inspection, enquiry, and performance evaluation. In other words, supervision is more about detection than prevention. And control activities relate to daily actions performed to achieve organisational goals, such as clarifying responsibilities, specifying the designated authority, formal recording, and independent checks on performance and assets (cf. Jones, 2008). A key aspect of control is found in the use of information to reduce moral hazard triggered by asymmetric information. Individuals with information expertise might have an edge over the organisation as a whole, and could use this advantage to prioritise their own interests to the detriment of organisational goal congruence (Willig and Schmalensee, 1989).

Monitoring activities can be more prevalent in a hierarchical structure where competition is introduced to boost agents' competence and confidence (Willig and Schmalensee, 1989). Three layers are typical of hierarchical accountability relationships: the principals, upper agents, and downward agents. Downward agents carry out most of the frontline work, which is observed by upper agents, but the final decisions about rewards and promotions are made by the principals. However, upper agents can be crucial in offering fair views on evaluation, and in reminding principals to be cautious of their significance in supervising, coordinating, and uniting organisations (Willig and Schmalensee, 1989). Jean (1986) argued that it can be hard for principals to collect information from upper agents, as coalitions or covert behaviour are typical ways for agents to protect their interests, for example, by exerting poor effort when facing threats or risks, or receiving inappropriate incentives. Thus it is important to build effective incentive schemes to reduce such information manipulation. One means of doing so is to encourage principals to collect information from all agents directly (Willig and Schmalensee, 1989). However, upper agents can have a negative effect on monitoring activities and can cause downward agents to perform less efficiently, if they are receiving inappropriate incentives from principals (Jean, 1986). Further, Philippe and Jean (1997) argued that intensive and strict monitoring with inappropriate incentives might cause employees' passion for work to diminish, and subsequently lead to low efficiency. Hence, it is crucial for principals to manage effectively the trade-off between initiatives and loss of control in managing accountability relationships.

14.3   RESEARCH DESIGN

14.3.1   Materials and Methods

The evidence for our study is drawn from an ethnographic case study, using immersion in the business through participant observation. Ethnography describes social complexities (Krefting, 1991) and interprets individuals' cognition and behaviour through the observer's immersive experience (Holloway et al., 2010; Smith and England, 2019). It is also recognised as a key approach in understanding the phenomenon behind the 'black box' of organisational and individual behaviour (Lee and Humphrey, 2006; Parker, 2014). Ethnography with a field-based case study can provide researchers with richer evidence about the relationships between the daily social interactions and organisational structures; for example, it can generate reflections on what happens in organisations; the reasons behind an individual's behaviour; or insights into unique and exceptional behaviour (Scapens, 1990; Parker, 2012; Smith and England, 2019). Further, researchers have moved from exploring shareholder accountability to stakeholder accountability, which includes corporate governance and stakeholder groups who affect or are affected by corporations' actions. This has coincided with a shift in interest from listed companies to private companies (including family businesses and SMEs), which require more qualitative methods to provide meaningful insight (Brennan and Solomon, 2008).

As a result, qualitative methods, such as interviews, case studies, questionnaires and surveys, and participant observation have become increasingly popular in corporate governance and accounting research (cf. Ahrens, 2022; Covaleski and Dirsmith, 1990; Himick et al., 2022).

Participant observation, an evidence collection approach (Vinten, 1994), is the most commonly used method in ethnographic research (Lee and Humphrey, 2006; Jaimangal-Jones, 2014). On the one hand, it provides observers with an insight into individual intentions, motivation, behaviours, and influence within an organisation, through attendance at meetings and particular events (Jaimangal-Jones, 2014). On the other hand, narrative data, discourse, or conversation analysis can be used with focus groups to provide novel insights or new discoveries, which provide a further explanation by story, metaphor, and other means (Frazier et al., 1984; Flick, 2002; Beattie, 2014). Finally, behavioural and verbal data from the observation is complementary to the single form of narrative data alone, which could also improve the efficiency of carrying out a large number of repeated interviews or content analysis, avoiding any misunderstandings (Friedrichs, 1975; Spradley, 1980).

However, participant observation has also been criticised, for instance, by being 'automatically less objective' or 'too narrow' (Friedrichs, 1975) because of the extended time and effort required, the lack of access to certain information, ethical issues, and/or personal bias (Scapens, 1990; Vinten, 1994); or through the trap of 'participant reactivity', which refers to the potential influence of researchers on participants' responses (Jaimangal-Jones, 2014). We acknowledge that a small sample poses difficulties in generalising the findings (Scapens, 1990) but note, however, that the results can contribute to hypothesis generation for future large sample tests (Spradley, 1980). Participant observation has also proved powerful for analysing complicated situations with various people and activities. In summary, the ethnographic method, represented by participant observation in this fieldwork study, offers more reliable and valid views of organisational practices compared with interviews alone, as the observer is able to learn about the social structure of the observed site by the embedded experience (Ahrens and Mollona, 2007).

Chinese SMEs and entrepreneurial firms have benefitted from greater access to financial resources since the strong and fast economic growth that followed the 'open-door' policy of 1978, leading to many new opportunities (Battisti and Deakins, 2017; Greene and Rosiello, 2020; Okura, 2008). However, previous research found that the challenges of the internal and external financial constraints (Li and Rowley, 2007), the heavy pressure from state-owned enterprises (Wu et al., 2008; Tsai, 2015), and information asymmetry in the banking sector (Hong and Zhou, 2013) put financial and political restrictions on the growth and expansion of Chinese SMEs (Ballou et al., 2012). And more importantly, owner-managers in Chinese SMEs seem to play a dominant role in dealing with the challenges above (Gibb, 2006; Lepoutre and Heene, 2006; Firth et al., 2009; Borgia and Newman, 2012). For instance, it is found that owner-managers' managerial characteristics and attitudes might influence the capital structure in firms. This includes their being risk-averse to external financial input or reluctant to lose flexibility and control over decision-making (Borgia and Newman, 2012). Moreover, due to owner-managers having limited negotiation power with markets and environmental forces, agency issues are less common in Chinese SMEs. Hence, the initial aim of the participant observation undertaken here was to understand how a small Chinese entrepreneurial firm would operate on a daily basis, using flows of information to enhance corporate governance and accountability. The observer took part in their work, listened and observed employees' conversations and facial expressions, and communicated with the owner-manager and employees informally. An Observation Journal was recorded after work every day, as such note-keeping is essential when recording details based on observations and feelings (Jaimangal-Jones, 2014).

14.3.2   Evidence

This study adopted Jones' (2008) framework of investigating internal control, as discussed above, to analyse corporate governance and accountability issues across four headings: control environment; risk assessment; information and communication; and monitoring and control. Before analysing the evidence, an introduction to the observation site is given below, in order to provide some background context to the setting.

14.3.2.1 Background

A two-week period of participant observation was carried out in December 2019 in a small Chinese entrepreneurial firm, using the researchers' networks to find a company willing to participate and provide our illustrative case. Given the notoriously private and secretive nature of Chinese firms, this was deemed to be the only way to gain such privileged access. Prior to the fieldwork, ethical approval was granted for the research by the researchers' university's Ethics Committee, and all participants gave fully informed consent, according to the university guidelines.[1] The firm was founded in 2017, as a seller of distillers for factory wine, homemade wine, and hydrosol for skincare. It launched on Alibaba, one of the key online shopping platforms in China. It was located inside a state-owned spinning mill in the suburb of Hangzhou city, Zhejiang Province, due to the low business unit rentals available there. The founding entrepreneurs started with ambitions of becoming a global business, and had grown reasonably to generate an average sales revenue of £2,500 per month (see Table 14.1). Both the owner-manager and senior manager had received university bachelor's degrees from a US–China collaboration. Their blended educational background made it easier for them to process modern Western ideas with an open mind (cf. Battisti and Deakins, 2017). Given its size, it provided an ideal setting for carrying out the observation within a limited time, enabling the observer to gain full oversight by getting closer to the daily operations.

The owner-manager had the dual responsibility of also being the internal accountant, dealing with all accounting responsibilities, such as invoicing and taxation, purchasing inventories, making budgets, etc. This organisation therefore provides a useful setting in which to explore how the internal accountant (owner-manager) exercised control through accounting practice, whilst dealing with multiple stakeholder demands and conflicts. In addition, an external accountant was hired to provide outsourced services for tax declarations and returns, tax avoidance, and to assist in interpreting up-to-date governmental policies and regulations. In short, this firm enabled the researchers to observe various accountability issues and control activities relating to the firm's internal practice.

In addition, three internal stakeholders were chosen as the focus of the observation, viz. the owner-manager, with internal accounting responsibility; the production and packing staff, led by the senior manager; and the sales staff, also controlled by the owner-manager. Their daily interactions seemed simple and clear; however, the implicit power relations and cultural differences provided rich opportunities to explore more closely their accountability in practice; including the influence of hierarchical accountability on agents' behaviour under a single principal; or issues of horizontal accountability among and between various relatively equal stakeholders.

14.3.2.2 Business strategy and shareholder structure

The firm was created by three unrelated final-year undergraduates, who each grew up in an entrepreneurial family setting (see Figure 14.2). One (the current owner-manager) gave up his plan to pursue further study in the US and instead invested the total amount of the education fund as the start-up capital for the firm instead. Inspired by this chief shareholder's determination, another (the current senior manager) also invested money in the firm, and the final partner (who subsequently left the firm one year later) decided to work as a sales and customer service manager. Thus, the young entrepreneurial firm was founded.

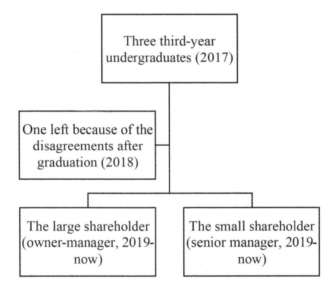

Figure 14.2   The historical development of shareholder structures

During phase one (see Table 14.1), as the chief shareholder's family had access to large sets of distillers they decided to act as a distributor and seller of this equipment to overseas bar owners and wine factories. They started to contact potential overseas buyers via email, Facebook, and Skype. During these interactions, they would introduce their products and build trust with their potential customers. After months of effort, they would get one or two orders if they were lucky, but sometimes had no success at all. Thus, they did not earn much profit compared to the effort put in of time and cost. They summarised their failure as being determined by the high costs of building trust with customers, as they had not set up a formal firm and had no official contract. So, they discussed adopting different strategies shortly after graduation; and because of disagreements over business strategy, one of the founding members left the company.

The remaining two founders started to build a formal firm in 2018. They began by purchasing finished distiller products from third party suppliers and sold them on Alibaba.[2] However, they barely earned a profit, as the purchase price of the finished products was unstable and they

Table 14.1   *The changing business model*

The development of an entrepreneur to a small firm (2017–2020)	Phase I: Sold whole large sets of distiller equipment (£11000–22000 per set) to customers overseas (2017)
	Phase II: Bought the distillers from a third party and then sold small distiller equipment (£1000–2000 per piece) on Alibaba (2018)
	Phase III: Invented, produced and sold their own distillers (£50–1000 per piece) on Alibaba (2019–present)

had little room to raise their own selling price due to fierce online market competition. Thus, they decided to change the business strategy again, a not uncommon practice in entrepreneurial firms (cf. Reid et al., 2020).

Moving to phase three in 2019, the owner-manager had moved up the learning curve and begun to understand how overseas distillers operated their business and advertised their products. They started to invent their own distillers to suit online customer needs by providing diverse functions at a low price. This involved the purchase of raw materials and production of their uniquely designed goods for the online international market. With good advertising and low-price products, they started to earn a profit and expanded the business quickly. After receiving a high volume of orders, the smaller shareholder became the senior manager, taking responsibility for focusing on the quality of the production and packaging line. Accordingly, the owner-manager became responsible for making every decision in the firm. The hierarchy structure of employees is shown in Figure 14.3. In sum, this remained their current business model in 2020.

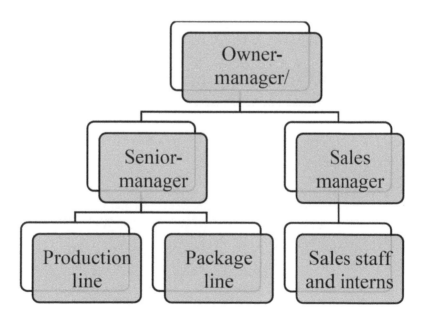

Figure 14.3   *The hierarchy of the firm*

Figure 14.3 presents the simple hierarchical structure of the firm. All employees were accountable to the owner-manager, who also acted as the internal accountant. The owner-manager controlled the sales team of five directly, and the senior manager was responsible for four people in the production and packing team. During the observation, the owner-manager was found to assign tasks and requirements to the sales manager to resolve sales issues and after-sales service from the perspective of a business leader; collecting online receipts of orders and preparing invoicing after double-checking with sales staff, from the perspective of being an accountant. In the meantime, the senior manager monitored carefully all orders and checked how production staff prepared specific products, and whether the package reached their transportation requirements. Although the owner-manager and senior manager were the shareholders and co-founders of the firm, the owner-manager would also make unilateral decisions without listening to others. The power distribution which had seemed equal at the start of the observation began to give rise to issues and concerns, as time went on. The following sections will list the evidence on corporate governance and hierarchical accountability relationships garnered from the observation.

14.4   RESULTS

14.4.1   Control Environment

The first few days of the observation were to gain a basic understanding of the operation of the firm and to become acquainted with the employees. The first and most striking impression of the firm was the open and transparent workplace, where all employees worked together in a dubious cargo house between mountains of stocks, and with very little privacy.

> I had not expected employees to be working between piles of stocks, and there is no personal space and privacy in the firm. There is only one tiny office, which is shared by the owner-manager and sales staff. And I was assigned to sit outside with the packing team and stocks. The owner-manager could monitor everyone easily by simply coming out of his office and taking walks around. And sometimes he might intrude in the conversation by silently listening to his employees' communications. *Observation Journal*, Day 1

The open workplace enabled the owner-manager to stay alert to the control environment and to shift strategies for managing employees, which may also have reflected his understanding of information manipulation and control strategies (cf. Reid et al., 2020). For example, the transparent working environment indicated that all productivity was visible to the principal and other agents, and most of their conversations were open and in public. This might have reduced the possibility of agents' moral hazard behaviour, such as shirking, cheating, or conspiring. Further, the owner-manager would frequently walk around the firm, exerting an effective monitoring mechanism across departments. In addition, the limited working space and conditions gave rise to opportunities for agents to develop close relationships, both formally and personally, which could increase the possibility of a coalition against the principal's will. Finally, the open space accelerated the flow of information through face-to-face contexts, as information on sales volume, costs of products, semimanufactured goods, inventories, transportation and packing fees was readily disseminated across departments, facilitating better decision-making. For instance, employees stressed the importance of timely accounting information in their daily work:

> We get a summary of sales volume and returns, transportation and packing fees, and stock updates, before finishing work every day, so that everyone can grasp the up-to-date information; and it is more efficient for the owner-manager to make decisions for the firm. *Senior Manager*

Hence, the highly transparent working environment for communication and appraisals enabled the owner-manager to carry out monitoring and control activities any time he was in the firm. However, the control environment became invalid in the absence of the owner-manager, which showed that too much emphasis on accountability and transparency could bring about inefficient and poorly considered decisions, rather than improve the overall performance (Bovens, 2007).

> I found the employees to be serious and focused (or apparently so) when the owner-manager is around in the firm, whilst, when the owner-manager was away for business, he left the senior manager in charge. However, some employees would check their phone more regularly, play around, and make jokes by acting just the opposite. And the senior manager seemed to be fine with that. *Observation Journal*, Day 9

An over-transparent environment could be considered as 'ethical violence' (Messner, 2009) towards employees, who value a certain degree of privacy, dignity, and freedom. This can lead to agents' behaviour of shirking, cheating, and responsibility avoidance, and might also explain why employees have two 'faces'; one for when the owner-manager is present, and one for when he is away from the firm. In summary, the open workplace enabled the owner-manager to manage the firm effectively and enforce employees to act diligently to please the owner-manager, but it also indicates that too much focus on accountability and openness could trigger the agents' coalition behaviour, thus weakening hierarchical power relationships.

14.4.2   Risk Assessment

From the owner-manager's standpoint, the evidence on risk assessment, observed in practice, covers three main aspects: the owner-manager's change of business model; precautionary measures taken again internal risks; and sensitivity to market pricing strategies. Figure 14.4 introduces the three phases of the business model, from receiving single large orders with a high cost of trust, through taking unstable online orders restricted by suppliers, to the current more mature online business model. Most of the vital decisions were made by the owner-manager alone, who we recall also acted as an internal accountant, in reacting to financial performance rapidly by processing first-hand resources and accounting information. One of the reasons why the owner-manager held on so tightly to the accounting role was that this shaped the control of organisational space, one of the most important boundaries defined by organisational accountability (Roberts and Scapens, 1985; Hopwood, 1990). The strict and disciplined order created by accounting ideology and practice offered the owner-manager effective tools, such as separating organisational life into accounting periods, requesting regular reports, creating budgets, and performance evaluation, for identifying potential risks and implementing procedures to suit different situations (Roberts and Scapens, 1985). For instance, the observer found that there were clear appraisal rules for bonuses and promotion for employees, to encourage cooperation and improve overall performance.

> There is a board next to the main gate with weekly and monthly rankings for the sales team, in terms of reaching their sales targets. The criteria are based on sales volume, sales returns, and customer service, in credits. And the statements of sales volume and returns are requested through the firm's group chat every day, before going home. There are bonuses for staff who resolve any return orders, quality or packing issues, or customer complaints of others' orders, which aims to improve the overall customer service and reputation. *Observation Journal*, Day 2

The specific firm rules reduced internal conflicts or avoidable competition amongst employees, to some degree, which in turn minimised the potential risks of harming the organisational benefits. However, the owner-manager, with only limited time and energy, could not dedicate enough time and attention to fulfilling the responsibility of being the management accountant, which meant that he could sometimes overlook the hidden risks from an accountant's point of view. For instance, what if the sales staff were to provide fake orders, or the packing staff sent products for their own self-interests? In general, the management accountant was responsible for checking sales orders and ensuring the accuracy of production and stocks. Hence, given this situation, the owner-manager came up with two strategies: one, to 'double-check the order'; and two, to 'track the order', in order to reduce coalition risks. These strategies proved to be efficient and effective during the observation.

> 'Double-check the order' was a procedure introduced because of the ambiguous accountability between stakeholder groups, which had created arguments and disputes that harmed internal relations. Nobody was willing to be fully responsible for the mistakes of others, so the owner-manager forced related employees to take part in the inspection and monitoring process of completing an order. First, the senior manager would look into the questionable order to decide who was to blame if the package was broken, due to transportation, since both logistics firms and packing staff were involved in this process. Second, if customer complaints were about wrong or missing products, the senior manager would investigate whether this was caused by wrong or incomplete orders placed by sales staff or by packing mistakes of the packing staff. Hence, the owner-manager would urge sales staff to double-check the order with the packing staff before the box was sealed.

> To eliminate operational risks, the owner-manager also proposed 'tracking the order', to urge the sales staff who took the order to regularly follow up during the whole process, by taking photos, checking the quality, and updating the transportation status, so that they could impart the latest information to both the firm and the customer. *Observation Journal*, Day 2

These two strategies are in line with Braun and Guston's (2003) suggestion to exploit multiple agents, in order to reduce the possibility of moral hazard and potential risks or threats to unity and harmony. In sum, the owner-manager carried out risk assessments and control by making individual observations, encouraging internal cooperation, and using external competition to help direct business strategies or support big decisions with impunity. However, the owner-manager's subjective opinions could cause bias, for instance, by forcing him to make incorrect judgements about inventories or poor decisions about launching new products, discussed below.

One example of bias in decision-making was highlighted by the fact that the owner-manager and sales staff did not always make correct judgements or predictions about markets; and this could occasionally mislead the production team and the purchase of inventories. For example, the company had two similar products, Alpha and Beta. Alpha was cheaper than Beta, and accordingly, Alpha sold more quickly than Beta. As a result, the production team often ran short of materials for Alpha, leading the senior manager to purchase more. However, for various reasons the owner-manager decided to raise the price of Alpha, meaning that Beta became the cheaper option. Due to the high similarity between both products, customers subsequently started to buy more Beta than Alpha and they only sold a few items of Alpha per month, leading to massive overstocking issues.

This example shows that incorrect decisions made because of avoidable internal competition could increase the risks of financial sustainability. It also highlights that the owner-manager made decisions without listening to the voices of different agents, which led to cash being tied up in stock, and wrong judgements made about the market. Despite the subjective mistakes, the owner-manager did make progress in clarifying responsibilities and avoiding disputes in complicated practices (cf. Roberts and Scapens, 1985; Roberts, 1991). This is common practice in modern organisations, where the principal defines what happens and who is responsible for what, according to consumed resources and related behaviour, rather than through negotiation or exploring the significance of events (Roberts and Scapens, 1985). Viewed in this way, a certain level of contingency is inevitable in daily interactions, discussed now below.

14.4.3   Information and Communication

This firm had created an open and transparent environment for the fast dissemination of information via face-to-face contexts across departments. The observed information could be hard information like accounting information, but it could equally be soft information such as facial expressions, tones and other social signals. This section focuses on the flows of information and how agents captured or interpreted the information that influenced their behaviour. Previous studies have stressed the significance of the flows of accounting information in hierarchical organisations. For instance, accounting information can make organisational activities visible (Roberts and Scapens, 1985; Robert, 1988) through mechanisms of transparency like financial reporting and related voluntary accounting disclosures (Brennan and Solomon, 2008). Accounting information could also be created through planning, budgeting, and costing, to facilitate organisational management and decision-making processes. Our case suggests that the owner-manager relied upon aggregated accounting information, from his role as the management accountant, to make financial decisions, such as purchasing inventories, launching new products, or carrying out performance evaluation.

Serving as a common language in organisations, accounting also gathers and translates competitive marketing pressures and production activities by calculation (Hopwood, 1990; Bushman and Smith, 2003). This is supported by the evidence above which describes how daily updated accounting reports were prepared and shared through both hierarchical and horizontal accountability relationships. Apart from hard information, soft information was also captured during the observation. For instance, the owner-manager's decision-making process was based on his own observations, feedback from his senior manager and other employees, accounting information and soft information (micro-expressions). Accordingly, the senior manager and other employees adopted different strategies, according to the owner-manager's attitude or reaction, in trying to meet the owner-manager's organisational goals. The following quote offers a vivid example of different perceptions of soft information from the observer's view:

> The owner decided to launch a new product, which was much simpler and cheaper than the current expensive ones, cutting the price from 7500 yuan (£833) to 3500 yuan (£416). However, the new product had a fatal defect: an important component would shake easily, and this would raise safety issues if the customer could not operate the distiller well. So the owner-manager, senior manager,

and one member of the production staff were undertaking the final test together. The owner-manager stressed (with a very enthusiastic and determined tone) that the most direct reason to launch this product was to cater to 'rich' and 'normal' customers' demands, as a low-price strategy always worked in online market competition.

However, the senior manager disagreed and argued that launching the cheaper product might create internal competition again, and that the safety issue with the product might hurt the customer or increase the returned orders, thereby pushing up the delivery costs.

Whilst this discussion was ongoing, the production employee was trying to stabilise the component, whilst listening to their argument and observing their facial expressions. When he realised this was a non-negotiable conflict, which created some awkward tensions, he remained silent and tried to fix the problem.

Of course, the owner-manager was unhappy and kept repeating how successful this product would be, and that the safety issue would not be a big problem for customers with a low budget. Then the senior manager became silent and stared at the owner-manager's face for a while. After realising that there was no room for negotiation, he gave up and left. *Observation Journal*, Day 5

Repeated dialogue between two parties can encourage trust and cooperation (Schillemans, 2008), as it uses face-to-face contacts and real-time interaction, which can in turn enhance mutual understanding and stimulate the learning process (Roberts, 1991, Cäker, 2007). However, the distrust and conflicts of interest generated from hierarchical accountability might also cause more serious distortion and suppression in face-to-face contexts. Hierarchy can inhibit discussion, as hierarchical power tends to solve problems by securing the dominant voices over others and determining subordinates' value based on the understanding of their superiors (Roberts, 1991). Such previous findings can help us to interpret the story above; agents interpreted the principal's facial expressions and tone to protect their interests and follow the principal's will, reluctantly, under this hierarchical power relationship.

Day (1999) pointed out that the reliability of information could be protected by audit, however, the understandability of information might depend on principals' abilities and agents' reporting techniques. Moreover, information is not restricted to flow within the hierarchy structure, instead, it also moves across in lateral relations (Hopwood, 1990), but it does not promise that all the horizontal communications will be successful. The following example aims to show a failed communication case across departments, which is affected by the agents' understanding and ability.

It was on a Sunday; the whole production team were off and the senior manager took a half-day off. However, there were two sales staff taking care of orders and dealing with customer complaints. The sales staff received several orders and they printed the delivery labels and packed the products themselves in the morning, without the production team being there. When the senior manager arrived in the afternoon, he got angry as the labels and the packages were all wrong. He complained to the employees: 'I told you several times how to follow the procedures to pack the products but you all still did it wrong.' Then the sales team members started to evade responsibility by claiming that it was not their fault.

When the senior manager had taken care of everything, he told me that it was not about who was to blame; it was just unprofessional: 'They have procedures to follow for online orders, printing labels, and packing, which has clarified everyone's responsibilities. However, the sales staff just don't put enough effort into learning it.' *Observation Journal*, Day 7

It is notable that accounting created a mutual language of rights and obligations for entities throughout the organisation, and was used for communication and evaluation (Roberts and Scapens, 1985; Dermer, 1990). However, the limitations of horizontal accountability often led to ineffective communication, as limited formal sanctioning power remains to maintain a formal principal–agent relationship (Schillemans, 2008). Therefore, agents were not necessarily motivated enough to put the effort into learning and evaluating the truthfulness of the information provided; most of them took for granted the information on which they depended, as they believed that they had formed good relationships and friendships with the information providers. On the other hand, harmonious relationships could enhance the trust and loyalty between them (Schillemans, 2008; Bovens et al., 2014), which might improve the efficiency of information sharing and dissemination across departments in this firm. But horizontal accountability could be manipulated and used as a monitoring mechanism by the principal. For instance, the open workplace in this firm enabled the owner-manager to be a silent listener of his agents' discussions; it is understandable that an individual might be afraid to report bad behaviour under certain circumstances. Hence, the ambiguity of possible consequences can add tension to the dialogue between principals and agents that could in turn reduce the risks of collusion (Schillemans, 2008).

14.4.4   Monitoring and Control Activities

Owners with heavy workloads might not have enough time to monitor the performance of all employees, which could lead to a loss of control and might harm organisational interests (Philippe and Jean, 1997). Moreover, social signalling can also increase difficulties for a single owner-manager in monitoring and controlling the whole firm. Therefore, covikep issues, collusion, or shirking behaviour is in evidence, as employees used these techniques to protect their own interests.

As the leader of the firm, the owner-manager here had to manage employees, make business decisions, carry out strategic plans, and enhance innovations (cf. Lumpkin and Dess, 1996; Maritz et al., 2020; Wenzel et al., 2020). However, as an internal accountant, he also had to prepare invoices and financial statements, make budgets and purchase inventories, cooperate with the external accountant for tax declarations and returns, deal with banks for reconciliation, and manage all other accounting services. A single person with multiple demands and a heavy workload could not possibly manage everything. Hence, the principal's subjective opinions or ideas sometimes created ambiguous and confusing signals for agents; and employees either took the blame or shirked on effort, to avoid punishments, leading to lower efficiency and lesser effectiveness at work.

> Sometimes he (the owner-manager) schedules some tasks for me without clear instructions. So I have to go over things again and again until he is satisfied, or I just cannot make his demands, and then things are postponed. But he brings it up again after a while, and then the same thing happens. This takes me more time and effort, without extra payment, and it also affects my initial work plan …
> *Senior Manager*

Imbued with power and other resources, a principal can force agents to act as they wish by the use of power domination. Consequently, agents are required to account for the principal, rather than the reverse (Bovens et al., 2014). However, under power dominance, agents might protect or expand their discretion, based on the resources they have to hand, due to information asymmetry as principals rely primarily on the information provided by agents. Figure 14.4 describes the story of a failure in power dominance, due to information asymmetry.

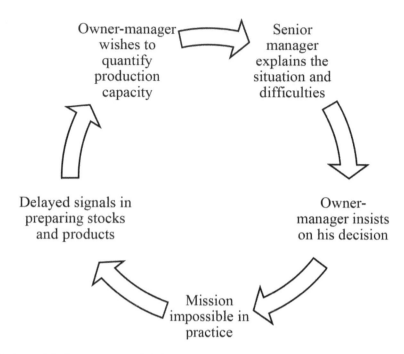

Figure 14.4   A failure to quantify labour

Figure 14.4 gives a real example that was encountered by the observer on several occasions, of an argument about how to predict and quantify labour precisely. Since online orders were less predictable, it quite often happened that they would stock excess raw materials or run out of special equipment at short notice, which restricted cash flows and led to losses in the financial statements; this had concerned the owner-manager for a long time. Thus, he wanted to quantify the ability of the production line, or its capacity, so that he could allocate the workload more flexibly. For instance, how many hours would staff require to finish assembling a distiller; or how many employees should be hired over different periods? They had this conversation several times, but without resolving the issue. Initially, the senior manager would argue about the difficulty of quantifying labour in practice, but he always received strict orders to comply from the owner-manager; so the senior manager just gave up on the issue. When the senior manager was asked why, he replied that they had no idea how to quantify labour and that the staff only wanted to finish their work and be paid for it, without worrying about how to improve production efficiency.

In another example, the principal is observed to listen and accept different stakeholders' voices without processing all of the information; as such, the effectiveness of accountability is affected. In this case, the observer noted that the company kept having new deliveries of inventories every two to three days; these were either the frozen flowers for their essential oil products, or components for their distiller products. However, there were tonnes of the same stocks in the fridge and stockroom. Hence, the observer asked the owner-manager and senior manager about their purchasing strategies, and received the following explanations:

We have a lot of stocks that really tie up our cash flow (87 per cent in a month). But the quality of the flowers was so good that I couldn't miss this opportunity ... Sometimes the senior manager and employees remind me to purchase stocks, and sometimes I will make predictions based on the market and our sales volume. The production staff always complain that they're running short of some components, which would affect their work efficiency and bonus. And there is always a time delay until the components arrived that can affect the completion of orders; and this makes the sales team complain about customer disputes, as well as affecting their bonus. Well, as you can see, I made some bad decisions; and that's why we have so much stock covered in dust. *Owner-Manager*

I will make predictions based on our sales and returns volume, and then remind our boss about preparing inventories in advance. But the manufacturing employees remind us more often when they need some key components urgently. However, it can happen that we overstock some components, due to changes in market preferences and to have extra safe guarantees. *Senior Manager*

Table 14.2   Stakeholder demands on inventories

Stakeholder	Stakeholder demands
Owner-manager/ Management accountant	Direct orders (e.g. good quality raw materials with reasonable price)
	Abundant cash flow
	Satisfy other employees' demands
Senior-manager	Personal judgement
	Manufacturing demands
Production team	Shortage of components
	Delayed orders
	Bonus
Sales team	Bonus
	Customer complaints

Table 14.2 presents different stakeholders' considerations regarding the purchasing of inventories. The owner-manager/internal accountant is seen to pay more attention to cash flow management and the long-term sustainability of the firm, as would be required by an owner-manager, although he presented his explanation for stock-building with an awkward smile, showing his conflicting thoughts about whether he had made the right decision. The demands of other stakeholder groups sometimes conflicted with the principal's interests in the hierarchical accountability relationship. If the agent were to prioritise the principal's interest, the use of cash flow would be mainly based on the principal's personal judgement. If the agent prioritised the manufacturing and sales team's demands, who might only pay attention to the current situation, the firm might suffer from a shortage of cash in the long run, which could restrict their future development. The internal accountant, influenced by his responsibility for controlling and managing the entire firm, as owner-manager, chose to satisfy all stakeholder demands. Hence, listening to the voices of different agents without prioritising them caused cash to be tied up, and wrong judgements made about the market.

14.5   DISCUSSION

This chapter has presented evidence on the use of information to enhance corporate governance and accountability. In particular, hard information (accounting information) and soft information (facial and tone expressions) in the accountability and accounting practices are considered within the hierarchical structure, to show how information is collected, evaluated, and used by the principal and multiple agents. Under simple hierarchical control, information should enhance control and monitoring, by the fast dissemination it offers through face-to-face contexts. However, power relations and information asymmetry might also trigger moral hazard and information manipulation behaviour that pose a threat to organisational interests.

Delegation in the principal–agent relationships further encourages adverse selection and moral hazard behaviour (Guston, 1996), which stresses the importance of monitoring and incentive compatibility to control agents' urges to act in a self-seeking manner (Stevens and Thevaranjan, 2010; Bovens et al., 2014). Another factor that can contribute to moral hazard is that when agents are offered only a basic salary they have an incentive to cheat or put less effort into work (Stevens and Thevaranjan, 2010). Moreover, there should be trade-offs for principals, as agents have options to misbehave, which explains how transaction costs are created (Bovens et al., 2014). Hence, Braun and Guston (2003) pointed out that it is important to admit that agents have incentives to be self-seeking, and might struggle to cooperate. An upgraded principal–agent framework is shown in Figure 14.5.

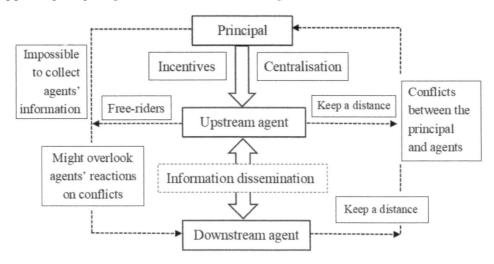

Figure 14.5   The flow of information in the single principal and multi-agent setting

Figure 14.5 shows that it is normal for principals and agents to have disagreements in various organisations (Newman and Kirill, 2009). For example, the production staff might disagree with the senior manager's requirements on the acceptable ratio of product defects. However, the senior manager just acts on behalf of the owner-manager, who might conflict with other agents' interests. In other words, it is the principal who has conflicts with the downward agent. Assigning multiple agents to work collectively could reduce the risk of moral hazard (Braun and Guston, 2003), but it also happens when agents have diverse or conflicting interests, some of whom might even be free-riders that harm the principal's benefits. Therefore, agents might start to keep their distance to observe the principal, which might be overlooked by the principal as it can be costly for them to collect productivity information directly in a multi-agent setting (Zhang, 2008). Above, we saw that a member of the production staff chose to remain silent to protect his own interests when he heard the owner-manager and senior manager disagreeing.

However, if the owner-manager had paid attention to the employee's facial expressions and silence, he might have hesitated about his timing in launching this product with defects.

Furthermore, the company's 'double-check the order' and 'tracking the order' strategies comply with the previous finding that performance-related rewards are more effective in stimulating agents than fixed-rewards (Shapiro, 2005; Dobbs and Miller, 2009; Stevens and Thevaranjan, 2010). They clarify the responsibility of each agent and reduce the accountability disputes that can trigger agents' shirking or cheating behaviour. The dissemination of information is via the accounting system and verified reports in firms (Rothenberg, 2015), and evidence shows that photos and physical inspection provide additional means of dissemination. The way information flows around the business shows that it can improve risk-sharing and increase agents' incentives at work (Feltham et al., 2016). Moreover, it encourages truthful reporting and signals trust, whilst also leaking some important information about social norms and the principal's preferences (Cardinaels and Yin, 2015); becoming the soft information of which agents might take advantage.

Overall, the principal's ultimate goal is to boost productivity and positivity in organisations (Christian and Naomi, 2013; Larmande and Ponssard, 2014; Rothenberg, 2015). On the one hand, the principal provides incentives for agents to be more productive (Robert, 1988); on the other hand, the lack of observability of agents' behaviour offers the principal a good opportunity to elicit information from one agent about the other, in order to enhance centralised power (Roberts, 2009; Zhang, 2008) as each agent can observe the others' work in a multi-agent setting (Zhang, 2008).

Cultural practice is also an important aspect of studying organisational control, and the dominant features in cultural practice are the intensive linguistics and practical knowledge, which can be captured more accurately by observation, in order to understand organisational members' ideas and understandings (Ahrens and Mollona, 2007). Under observation, the owner-manager put more effort into learning and understanding different stakeholders' needs and embedding them into organisational development to survive and grow, which complies with Lepoutre and Heene's (2006) argument that the personal characteristics of owner-managers influence accountability in small firms. And it also breaks down the old stereotype of owner-managers of small firms as being unprofessional, with insufficient time and knowledge to devote to business management. The owner-manager's highly responsible behaviour and management strategies prove the existence of the 'responsibility' feature of accountability in Chinese SMEs (Waldmann, 2000; Gibb, 2006; Parnell et al., 2015).

Chinese culture promotes cooperation, adaption, and harmony in developing social relationships (Liu et al., 2012). And Parnell et al. (2015) argued that Chinese culture appreciates thrift and productivity, which might explain why this firm's business model is cost-effective, in focusing on transparency, fast dissemination of information, and communication. Accordingly, a series of standards are created through the accountability mechanism, which becomes the general rules and principles to guide the firm to share expectations, be held answerable for their behaviour and outcomes, and pose sanctions or rewards to maintain and enhance coordination (Gelfand et al., 2004).

14.6   CONCLUSION

This study has investigated how flows of information can enhance corporate governance and accountability in a single owner-manager controlled firm in a developing economy. In sum, we find that Western views of accountability can overcome the inherent cultural differences and be incorporated into the management of an SME in China. This is brought to bear through the strong management imposed by an entrepreneur with a global outlook and international education. Our findings are based on the analysis of an Observation Journal and interview transcripts, gathered during an intense period of participant observation. We find that, under a single owner-manager dominated hierarchical structure, the owner-manager was able to exercise strong control over the entire firm, based on the individual observation, the extent of internal cooperation within the firm, and the degree of external competition. The setting also allowed the owner-manager to stay alert to the control environment and to shift business strategies over time. However, it was also found that his subjective opinions could cause bias in risk assessment, and needed the moderation of occasional inputs from his more junior partner.

Formal and informal information communicated through face-to-face contacts across departments was used to improve work efficiency, but it also allowed employees' coalition behaviour to undermine the owner-manager's decisions. Handling this complex organisational balancing act was seen to be difficult, and managing it was a key aspect of the effective monitoring undertaken by the owner-manager. Finally, the owner-manager's tone and facial expressions were key social signals for employees, in terms of carrying out tasks and reporting to superiors. Such social signalling can increase the difficulty of achieving monitoring and control targets, as employees can devise social counterstrategies, or even cover up issues to protect their own interests, rather than promote the interests of the owner-manager or the whole firm.

Our study provides unique empirical insight into the workings of an entrepreneurial firm in China. Given the difficulties inherent in gaining access to the secretive workings of such organisations, this crucial view of performance management is a significant contribution to our understanding of how they operate. Indeed, it is useful to understand how Western influences can impact upon the management of these types of firms. Our findings have implications for practical and theoretical understanding of decision-making, organisational control and small firm governance in family firms. Further, the use of accounting information in discharging accountability responsibilities is highlighted in this setting. Our case study shows how learning from Western experience can improve the flow of information across and around organisations, to the benefit of company performance. However, whilst our single case is illustrative of good performance, there remain research opportunities for larger scale studies and longitudinal assessment of these actions in practice. This we propose as a rich seam of potential for future research.

NOTES

1.   Ethical approval and funding were granted for the fieldwork by the host university. The participant information sheet and consent form were signed by the researchers and passed to interviewees in advance, to gain their permission to record and take notes during the meetings. All recordings and notes are stored locally and only accessible by the researchers. All interviewees were notified about the privacy of data collection and storage, their basic rights to stop or withdraw at any time,

and potential risks or hazards; and participant records were anonymised to protect privacy and confidentiality.

2. Alibaba is the largest online selling outlet in China.

REFERENCES

Ahrens, T. (1996) Styles of accountability. *Accounting, Organizations and Society,* 21 (2), pp. 139–173. http://dx.doi.org/10.1016/0361-3682(95)00052-6

Ahrens, T. (2022) Paper development in qualitative accounting research: Bringing social contexts to life. *Qualitative Research in Accounting & Management,* 19 (1), pp. 1–17. https://doi.org/10.1108/QRAM -03-2021-0044

Ahrens, T. and Mollona, M. (2007) Organisational control as cultural practice – a shop floor ethnography of a Sheffield steel mill. *Accounting, Organizations and Society,* 32 (4), pp. 305–331. http://dx.doi .org/10.1016/j.aos.2006.08.001

Ballou, B. et al. (2012) Exploring the strategic integration of sustainability initiatives: Opportunities for accounting research. (Report). *Accounting Horizons,* 26 (2), p. 265. http://dx.doi.org/10.2308/acch -50088

Battisti, M., & Deakins, D. (2017). The relationship between dynamic capabilities, the firm's resource base and performance in a post-disaster environment. *International Small Business Journal,* 35 (1), pp. 78–98. https://doi.org/10.1177/0266242615611471

Beattie, V. (2014) Accounting narratives and the narrative turn in accounting research: Issues, theory, methodology, methods and a research framework. *The British Accounting Review,* 46 (2), pp. 111–134. http://dx.doi.org/10.1016/j.bar.2014.05.001

Borgia, D. and Newman, A. (2012) The influence of managerial factors on the capital structure of small and medium-sized enterprises in emerging economies: Evidence from China. *Journal of Chinese Entrepreneurship,* 4 (3), pp. 180–205. http://dx.doi.org/10.1108/17561391211262148

Bovens, M. (2007) *Public accountability.* Oxford University Press. http://dx.doi.org/10.1093/oxfordhb/ 9780199226443.003.0009

Bovens, M. (2010) Two concepts of accountability: Accountability as a virtue and as a mechanism. *West European Politics,* 33 (5), pp. 946–967. http://dx.doi.org/10.1080/01402382.2010.486119

Bovens, M., Goodin, R.E. and Schillemans, T. (2014) *The Oxford handbook of public account-ability.* First edition. New York: Oxford University Press. http://dx.doi.org/10.1093/oxfordhb/ 9780199641253.013.0012

Braumann, E.C., Grabner, I. and Posch, A. (2020) Tone from the top in risk management: A complemen-tarity perspective on how control systems influence risk awareness. *Accounting, Organizations and Society,* 84, 101128. http://dx.doi.org/10.1016/j.aos.2020.101128

Braun, D. and Guston, D.H. (2003) Principal–agent theory and research policy: An introduction. *Science and Public Policy,* 30 (5), pp. 302–308. http://dx.doi.org/10.3152/147154303781780290

Brennan, N.M. and Solomon, J. (2008) Corporate governance, accountability and mechanisms of accountability: An overview. *Accounting, Auditing & Accountability Journal,* 21 (7), pp. 885–906. http://dx.doi.org/10.1108/09513570810907401

Bushman, R.M. and Smith, A.J. (2003) Transparency, financial accounting information, and corporate governance. (Part 1: A review of the literature on corporate governance). *Economic Policy Review (Federal Reserve Bank of New York),* 9 (1), p. 65.

Cardinaels, E. and Yin, H. (2015) Think twice before going for incentives: Social norms and the prin-cipal's decision on compensation contracts. *Journal of Accounting Research,* 53 (5), pp. 985–1015. http://dx.doi.org/10.1111/1475-679X.12093

Christian, H. and Naomi, R.R. (2013) Interim performance measures and private information. *The Accounting Review,* 88 (5), pp. 1683–1714. http://dx.doi.org/10.2308/accr-50484

Cäker, M. (2007) Customer focus – an accountability dilemma. *European Accounting Review,* 16 (1), pp. 143–171. http://dx.doi.org/10.1080/09638180701265911

Covaleski, M.A., and Dirsmith, M.W. (1990). Dialectic tension, double reflexivity and the everyday accounting researcher: On using qualitative methods. *Accounting, Organizations and Society*, 15 (6), 543–573. https://doi.org/10.1016/0361-3682(90)90034-R

Day, R. (1999) Accountability, accounting regulation and the Principal Agent Model. *Journal of Interdisciplinary Economics*, 10 (4), pp. 293–319. http://dx.doi.org/10.1177/02601079X99001000402

Dermer, J. (1990) The strategic agenda: Accounting for issues and support. *Accounting, Organizations and Society*, 15 (1), pp. 67–76. http://dx.doi.org/10.1016/0361-3682(90)90014-L

Dobbs, I.M. and Miller, A.D. (2009) Experimental evidence on financial incentives, information and decision-making. *The British Accounting Review*, 41 (2), pp. 71–89. http://dx.doi.org/10.1016/j.bar.2008.10.002

Feltham, G.A., Hofmann, C. and Indjejikian, R.J. (2016) Performance Aggregation and Decentralized Contracting. *The Accounting Review*, 91 (1), pp. 99–117. http://dx.doi.org/10.2308/accr-51111

Firth, M. et al. (2009) Inside the black box: Bank credit allocation in China's private sector. *Journal of Banking and Finance*, 33 (6), pp. 1144–1155. http://dx.doi.org/10.1016/j.jbankfin.2008.12.008

Flamholtz, E.G. (1983) Accounting, budgeting and control systems in their organizational context: Theoretical and empirical perspectives. *Accounting, Organizations and Society*, 8 (2), pp. 153–169. http://dx.doi.org/10.1016/0361-3682(83)90023-5

Flick, U. (2002) Qualitative research – state of the art. *Social Science Information*, 41 (1), pp. 5–24. http://dx.doi.org/10.1177/0539018402041001001

Frazier, K., Ingram, R. and Tennyson, B. (1984) A methodology for the analysis of narrative accounting disclosures. *Journal of Accounting Research*, 22 (1), pp. 318. http://dx.doi.org/10.2307/2490713

Friedrichs, J. (1975) *Participant observation: Theory and practice*. Farnborough, Hants.; Lexington, Mass.: Lexington Books.

Gelfand, M.J., Lim, B.-C. and Raver, J.L. (2004) Culture and accountability in organizations: Variations in forms of social control across cultures. *Human Resource Management Review*, 14 (1), pp. 135–160. http://dx.doi.org/10.1016/j.hrmr.2004.02.007

Gibb, A. (2006) Making markets in business development services for SMEs. *Journal of Small Business and Enterprise Development*, 13 (2), pp. 263–283. http://dx.doi.org/10.1108/14626000610665962

Gibbins, M. and Newton, J.D. (1994) An empirical exploration of complex accountability in public accounting. *Journal of Accounting Research*, 32 (2), p. 165. http://dx.doi.org/10.2307/2491280

Greene, F.J. and Rosiello, A. (2020). A commentary on the impacts of 'Great Lockdown'and its aftermath on scaling firms: What are the implications for entrepreneurial research? *International Small Business Journal*, 38 (7), pp.583–592. http://dx.doi.org/10.1177/0266242620961912

Guston, D.H. (1996). Principal–agent theory and the structure of science policy. *Science and Public Policy*, 23 (4), 229–240.

Himick, D., Johed, G. and Pelger, C. (2022), Qualitative research on financial accounting – an emerging field. *Qualitative Research in Accounting & Management*, 19 (4), pp. 373–385. https://doi.org/10.1108/QRAM-11-2021-0207

Holloway, I., Brown, L. and Shipway, R. (2010). Meaning not measurement: Using ethnography to bring a deeper understanding to the participant experience of festivals and events. *International Journal of Event and Festival Management* 1 (1), pp. 74–85. http://dx.doi.org/10.1108/17852951011029315

Hong, Z. and Zhou, Y. (2013) Can third party's collateral arrangements tackle the financing problem of small-medium enterprises? *China Finance Review International*, 3 (4), pp. 353–380. http://dx.doi.org/10.1108/CFRI-08-2012-0094

Hopwood, A.G. (1990) Accounting and organisation change. *Accounting, Auditing & Accountability Journal*, 3 (1). http://dx.doi.org/10.1108/09513579010145073

Jaimangal-Jones, D. (2014) Utilising ethnography and participant observation in festival and event research. *International Journal of Event and Festival Management*, 5 (1), pp. 39–55. http://dx.doi.org/10.1108/IJEFM-09-2012-0030

Jansen, E.P. (2015) Participation, accounting and learning how to implement a new vision. *Management Accounting Research*, 29, pp. 45–60. http://dx.doi.org/10.1016/j.mar.2015.07.003

Jean, T. (1986) Hierarchies and bureaucracies: On the role of collusion in organizations. *Journal of Law, Economics, & Organization*, 2 (2), pp. 181–214.

Joannides, V. (2012) Accounterability and the problematics of accountability. *Critical Perspectives on Accounting*, 23 (3), pp. 244–257. http://dx.doi.org/10.1016/j.cpa.2011.12.008

Jones, M.J. (2008) Internal control, accountability and corporate governance: Medieval and modern Britain compared. *Accounting, Auditing & Accountability Journal*, 21 (7), pp. 1052–1075. http://dx .doi.org/10.1108/09513570810907474

Koppell, J.G. (2005) Pathologies of accountability: ICANN and the challenge of Multiple Accountabilities Disorder. *Public Administration Review*, 65 (1), pp. 94–108. http://dx.doi.org/10.1111/j.1540-6210 .2005.00434.x

Krefting, L. (1991). Rigor in qualitative research: The assessment of trustworthiness. *American Journal of Occupational Therapy*, 45 (3), pp. 214–222. http://dx.doi.org/10.5014/ajot.45.3.214

Larmande, F. and Ponssard, J.P. (2014) Fishing for excuses and performance evaluation. *Rev Account Stud*, 19 (2), pp. 988–1008. http://dx.doi.org/10.1007/s11142-013-9268-1

Lee, B. and Humphrey, C. (2006) More than a numbers game: Qualitative research in accounting. *Management Decision*, 44 (2), pp. 180–197. http://dx.doi.org/10.1108/00251740610650184

Lepoutre, J. and Heene, A. (2006) Investigating the impact of firm size on small business social responsibility: A critical review. *Journal of Business Ethics*, 67 (3), pp. 257–273. http://dx.doi.org/10.1007/ s10551-006-9183-5

Li, X. and Rowley, C. (2007) Human resource management in Chinese small and medium enterprises. *Personnel Review*, 36 (3), pp. 415–439. http://dx.doi.org/10.1108/00483480710731356

Liu, W., Friedman, R. and Hong, Y.-Y. (2012) Culture and accountability in negotiation: Recognizing the importance of in-group relations. *Organizational Behavior and Human Decision Processes*, 117 (1), pp. 221–234. http://dx.doi.org/10.1016/j.obhdp.2011.11.001

Lumpkin, G.T. and Dess, G.G. (1996). Clarifying the entrepreneurial orientation construct and linking it to performance. *Academy of Management Review*, 21 (1), pp. 135–172. http://dx.doi.org/10.2307/258632

Maritz, A., Perenyi, A., De Waal, G. and Buck, C. (2020). Entrepreneurship as the unsung hero during the current COVID-19 economic crisis: Australian perspectives. *Sustainability*, 12 (11), p. 4612. http://dx.doi.org/10.3390/su12114612

Messner, M. (2009) The limits of accountability. *Accounting, Organizations and Society*, 34 (8), pp. 918–938. http://dx.doi.org/10.1016/j.aos.2009.07.003

Mulgan, R. (2000) 'Accountability': An ever-expanding concept? *Public Administration*, 78 (3), p. 555. http://dx.doi.org/10.1111/1467-9299.00218

Newman, D.P. and Kirill, E.N. (2009) Delegation to encourage communication of problems. *Journal of Accounting Research*, 47 (4), pp. 911–942. http://dx.doi.org/10.1111/j.1475-679X.2009.00339.x

Okura, M. (2008) Firm characteristics and access to bank loans: An empirical analysis of manufacturing SMEs in China. (Research Paper) (small and medium enterprises). *International Journal of Business and Management Science*, 1 (2), p. 165.

Otley, D.T. and Berry, A.J. (1980) Control, organisation and accounting. *Accounting, Organizations and Society*, 5 (2), pp. 231–244. http://dx.doi.org/10.1016/0361-3682(80)90012-4

Parker, L.D. (2008a) Boardroom operational and financial control: An insider view. *British Journal of Management*, 19 (1), pp. 65–88. http://dx.doi.org/10.1111/j.1467-8551.2006.00517.x

Parker, L.D. (2008b) Strategic management and accounting processes: Acknowledging gender'. *Accounting, Auditing & Accountability Journal*, 21 (4), pp. 611–631. http://dx.doi.org/10.1108/ 09513570810872941

Parker, L.D. (2012) Qualitative management accounting research: Assessing deliverables and relevance. *Critical Perspectives on Accounting*, 23 (1), pp. 54–70. http://dx.doi.org/10.1016/j.cpa.2011.06.002

Parker, L.D. (2014) Qualitative perspectives: Through a methodological lens. *Qualitative Research in Accounting & Management*, 11 (1), pp. 13–28. http://dx.doi.org/10.1108/QRAM-02-2014-0013

Parnell, J.A., Long, Z. and Lester, D. (2015) Competitive strategy, capabilities and uncertainty in small and medium sized enterprises (SMEs) in China and the United States. *Management Decision*, 53 (2), pp. 402–431. http://dx.doi.org/10.1108/MD-04-2014-0222

Philippe, A. and Jean, T. (1997) Formal and real authority in organizations. *The Journal of Political Economy*, 105 (1), pp. 1–29. http://dx.doi.org/10.1086/262063

Reid, G.C. and Smith, J.A. (2009). A coevolutionary analysis of organisational systems and processes: Quantitative applications to information system dynamics in small entrepreneurial firms. *Critical Perspectives on Accounting*, 20 (6), pp. 762–781. http://dx.doi.org/10.1016/j.cpa.2008.01.009

Reid, G.C., Smith, J.A. and Xu, Z. (2020). The impact of strategy, technology, size and business environment on the organizational form of small firms in China. *Asian Journal of Economics, Business and Accounting*, 20 (4), pp. 15–32. http://dx.doi.org/10.9734/ajeba/2020/v20i430330

Robert, P.M. (1988) Variable cost allocation in a principal/agent setting. *The Accounting Review*, 63 (1), pp. 42–54.

Roberts, J. (1991) The possibilities of accountability. *Accounting, Organizations and Society*, 16 (4), pp. 355–368. http://dx.doi.org/10.1016/0361-3682(91)90027-C

Roberts, J. (2001) Trust and control in Anglo-American systems of corporate governance: The individualizing and socializing effects of processes of accountability. *Human Relations*, 54 (12), pp. 1547–1572. http://dx.doi.org/10.1177/00187267015412001

Roberts, J. (2009) No one is perfect: The limits of transparency and an ethic for 'intelligent' accountability. *Accounting, Organizations and Society*, 34 (8), pp. 957–970. http://dx.doi.org/10.1016/j.aos.2009.04.005

Roberts, J. and Scapens, R.W. (1985) Accounting systems and systems of accountability – understanding accounting practices in their organisational contexts. *Accounting, Organizations and Society*, 10 (4), pp. 443–456. http://dx.doi.org/10.1016/0361-3682(85)90005-4

Rothenberg, N.R. (2015) Communication and information sharing in teams. *The Accounting Review*, 90 (2), pp. 761–784. http://dx.doi.org/10.2308/accr-50910

Scapens, R.W. (1990) Researching management accounting practice: The role of case study methods. *The British Accounting Review*, 22 (3), pp. 259–281. http://dx.doi.org/10.1016/0890-8389(90)90008-6

Schillemans, T. (2008) Accountability in the shadow of hierarchy: The horizontal accountability of agencies. *Public Organization Review*, 8 (2), pp. 175–194. http://dx.doi.org/10.1007/s11115-008-0053-8

Shapiro, S.P. (2005) Agency theory. *Annual Review of Sociology*, 31 (1), pp. 263–284. http://dx.doi.org/10.1146/annurev.soc.31.041304.122159

Sinclair, A. (1995) The chameleon of accountability: Forms and discourses. *Accounting, Organizations and Society*, 20 (2), pp. 219–237. http://dx.doi.org/10.1016/0361-3682(93)E0003-Y

Smith, J.A. and England, C. (2019). An ethnographic study of culture and performance in the UK lingerie industry. *The British Accounting Review*, 51 (3), pp. 241–258. http://dx.doi.org/10.1016/j.bar.2019.02.002

Spradley, J.P. (1980) *Participant observation*. New York: Wadsworth Thomson Learning.

Stevens, D.E. and Thevaranjan, A. (2010) A moral solution to the moral hazard problem. *Accounting, Organizations and Society*, 35 (1), pp. 125–139. http://dx.doi.org/10.1016/j.aos.2009.01.008

Tsai, K. (2015) Financing small and medium enterprises in China: Recent trends and prospects beyond shadow banking. *IDEAS Working Paper Series from RePEc*. http://dx.doi.org/10.2139/ssrn.2607792

Vinten, G. (1994) Participant observation: A model for organizational investigation? *Journal of Managerial Psychology*, 9 (2), pp. 30–38. http://dx.doi.org/10.1108/02683949410059299

Waldmann, E. (2000) Teaching ethics in accounting: A discussion of cross-cultural factors with a focus on Confucian and Western philosophy. *Accounting Education*, 9 (1), pp. 23–35. http://dx.doi.org/10.1080/096392800413636

Wenzel, M., Stanske, S. and Lieberman, M.B. (2020). Strategic responses to crisis. *Strategic Management Journal*, 41 (7/18).

Willig, R.D. and Schmalensee, R. (1989) *Handbook of industrial organization*. Amsterdam; North-Holland; New York: Elsevier Science Pub. Co.

Wu, J., Song, J. and Zeng, C. (2008) An empirical evidence of small business financing in China. *Management Research News*, 31 (12), pp. 959–975.

Zhang, Y. (2008) The effects of perceived fairness and communication on honesty and collusion in a multi-agent setting. *The Accounting Review*, 83 (4), pp. 1125–1146. http://dx.doi.org/10.2308/accr.2008.83.4.1125

PART VI

TECHNOLOGICAL DEVELOPMENTS

15. The role of artificial intelligence in accounting
Andrew Skidmore and Julia A. Smith

15.1 ARTIFICIAL INTELLIGENCE (AI) AND ACCOUNTING

This chapter heeds calls for further research into the impact of artificial intelligence (AI) on the accounting profession (Sutton et al., 2016; Moll and Yigitbasioglu, 2019; Kokina and Davenport, 2017). AI is significantly impacting and changing the accounting profession even though its development is still in its infancy (Kokina et al. 2021; Oesterreich et al., 2019). There is a lack of understanding as to how it can benefit the accountancy profession, the challenges it creates and how the profession will need to change to incorporate it. Since the development of AI within accounting is in its infancy, there is a need to assess and understand the impact of AI on the role of accounting as AI develops. This chapter seeks to explore these aspects, contributing to the existing literature surrounding the role of AI in accounting and providing support for future research on the role of AI in the accounting sector.

The structure of the chapter is as follows. First, a background to AI is discussed, considering different definitions of AI and the development of AI from its origin until now. Following this, the literature review addresses the application of AI in the accounting sector so far and considers the future of AI within the accounting sector. Then, the impact of AI on the role of the accountant is debated and accountants' perceptions of AI are considered. Subsequently, the implications of the impact of AI on accounting for accounting education are considered. Penultimately, the ethical considerations arising from the use of AI are discussed including biases, moral aspects and security issues. Finally, a summary of the literature review is presented, offering avenues for future research into the role of AI in accounting. From this a research plan is proposed for possible future work.

15.2 BACKGROUND TO ARTIFICIAL INTELLIGENCE

The term 'artificial intelligence' (AI) was coined in 1956 at a conference held at Dartmouth College, New Hampshire (Haenlein and Kaplan, 2019), and as of yet there is no singular agreed-upon definition for AI: the Oxford English Dictionary defines AI as 'the capacity of computers or other machines to exhibit or simulate intelligent behaviour' (OED Online, 2021); Nilsson (2009) defines AI as the 'activity devoted to making machines intelligent' (p.13); and Seshia et al. (2022) define AI as 'computational systems that attempt to mimic aspects of human intelligence' (p.1) What these definitions have in common is the notion that a machine has the ability to be 'intelligent', that is, to 'think' and mimic human behaviour as put by Turing (1950). In Turing's landmark paper 'Computing Machinery and Intelligence' (1950) he discusses the possibility of machines to 'think' like humans do and this lead to the creation of the Turing Test. The Turing Test proposed that if a machine is able to mimic human responses and behaviour under specific conditions such that it is indistinguishable from a human, then the machine is said to be 'intelligent' and to possess AI (Saygin et al., 2000).

From 1956 until the turn of the 21st century, the development of AI was sporadic with various advancements, such as the ELIZA computer program in the 1960s which was one of the first systems to pass the Turing Test, and setbacks, such as the ending of government support in AI research in both the UK and the US in the 1970s in response to negative reports about the capabilities of AI (Haenlein and Kaplan, 2019). At the turn of the 21st century the development of AI began to resurge and take off, following milestones in its development. For example, in 1997 IBM's Deep Blue became the first computer to beat a world chess champion. Nowadays, the applications of AI can be seen throughout the world from self-driven cars to digital personal assistants such as Apple's Siri (Hawking et al., 2014). One of the most notable achievements in the history of AI was when the AI platform IBM Watson won the game show 'Jeopardy!' against previous champions in 2011 (Mohammad et al., 2019).

Although there is significant interest and hype around AI and its capabilities, its adoption and development is still in infancy in businesses outside of the technology sector, including the accounting sector (Kokina et al., 2021; Kokina and Davenport, 2017).

15.3   APPLICATIONS OF AI IN ACCOUNTING

AI is part of Industry 4.0, also known as the digital revolution (Hoffman, 2017), which is used to label the current period where there have been and continue to be significant and rapid technological changes and developments (Kruskopf et al., 2020). Technological developments have impacted the accounting sector significantly, altering processes and the profession. Two recent technologies which are heavily impacting the accounting profession are big data and cloud computing. big data provides firms with vast quantities of data, both structured and unstructured, which aids firms in decision-making (Crookes and Conway, 2018). cloud computing allows accountants to store and access this data on the Internet through a server from anywhere instead of storing data on external hard-drives (Lim, 2013). Such technologies offer a competitive advantage which attracts many firms to adopt them, and firms must constantly strive to keep up with and maintain the latest technological developments or else they risk falling behind and losing business (Lim, 2013; Munoko et al., 2020). AI systems are developed from big data and there are various levels of sophistication in AI. Both Crookes and Conway (2018) and PwC (2017) identified three separate levels of AI in accounting, progressing with sophistication at each stage.

15.3.1   Assisted Intelligence

The first level is assisted intelligence as termed by PwC (2017), or process automation as described by Crookes and Conway (2018), whereby the entire process is in control of the human and what they require. The AI system supports the human in decision-making and has mechanical intelligence allowing it to perform repetitive and structured tasks. This is known as Robotic Process Automation (RPA).

RPA is one of the simplest forms of AI adopted in accounting so far. RPA describes an AI system which automates structured, repetitive and routine tasks. Recent research suggests the greatest benefit from employing RPA is the reduced costs: Cooper et al. (2019) found that the Big4 have seen large cost savings through implementing RPA in internal processes; one firm had implemented over one thousand bots by the end of 2017 which saved over one million human work hours a year; Kaya et al. (2019) report that RPA can create 25–50 per cent savings in costs. This is due to the increased productivity of RPA compared to humans as machines are able to work 24/7 and at a faster pace without reducing accuracy whereas humans must rest and make more errors as they tire (Losbichler and Lehner, 2021).

Whilst RPA is not intelligent in the sense that it cannot make decisions independently of a human, researchers argue that it is perfectly suited to accounting due to the many routine, repetitive and structured tasks involved (Kokina and Davenport, 2017; Kruskopf et al., 2020). Cooper et al.'s (2019) study on the adoption of RPA in Big4 firms supports this; they interviewed leaders of RPA from the Big4 accounting firms and found that these firms have been developing RPA since 2013 and the adoption of RPA is furthest along in tax services, advisory and assurance services. These three subsets of accounting have suitable structured tasks which RPA can take over. For example, within the tax service, RPA is used to automate the time-consuming and structured tasks such as extracting information for tax returns; within the advisory service Cooper et al. (2019) found that the Big4 firms use RPA to automate clients' business processes. However, Cooper et al.'s (2019) research only extends to the Big4 accounting firms as these firms have developed RPA the furthest, meaning it is difficult to apply findings to the wider accounting sector and highlighting that AI even in its simplest form in RPA is still to be rolled out industry wide. Despite this, the potential for RPA in the accounting sector is enormous: Cooper et al. (2019) estimate that 10–30 per cent of all accounting processes can be automated. The World Economic Forum (2015) found in a survey of 816 executives from the IT and communications sector that 75 per cent believe that by 2025 30 per cent of corporate audits will be automated.

The current research in RPA in accounting is limited to large organisations, especially the Big4 (see Cooper et al., 2019), as they are furthest along in the implementation and development of RPA. The significant costs involved in developing AI technology may provide a barrier to its uptake by smaller firms. However, there is a need to understand the adoption of AI technology across the whole accounting sector, not just the Big4 firms, and its subsequent impact. This warrants research exploring the use of AI throughout the accounting sector into smaller accounting firms.

15.3.2 Augmented Intelligence

The next level of AI is augmented intelligence (PwC, 2017), or cognitive insight as termed by Crookes and Conway (2018). Augmented intelligence describes AI technology where the machine has analytical intelligence and can learn from data and problem solve through detecting patterns in big data. Here the human and machine are co-decision-makers. Applications of augmented intelligence include machine learning and natural language processing. Machine learning describes an AI system that learns independently without intervention from a human – it uses algorithms and data to learn the same way that humans do (Dickey et al., 2019); natural language processing technology uses learning algorithms to generate speech and/or text from data (Gotthardt et al., 2020).

As well as accounting firms incorporating and developing RPA to streamline their internal processes, they are also investing heavily in technological innovation and are developing AI capabilities past that of RPA to systems with capabilities including machine learning and natural language processing. By conducting a content analysis, Ucoglu (2020) examined the machine learning technology being developed by the Big4 firms. Ucoglu found that Deloitte is furthest along in the development of machine learning technology, with platforms in each service of the business: Sonar in Tax, Argus among others in Audit, HR Agent Edgy in Consulting, Eagle Eye in Risk Advisory, and Brainspace in Financial Advisory services. The remaining three Big4 firms have developed machine learning technology within their auditing departments: PwC have developed Halo; KMPG has partnered with IBM Watson to help develop a platform called Clara; EY has developed Canvas and Helix. Moreover, EY employs natural language processing in reviewing lease accounting standards in cases when the US governing body issues new regulations, allowing tens of thousands of contracts to be analysed and have information extracted quickly (Kruskopf et al., 2020). Whilst these technologies are still in the early developing phase for the accounting sector, researchers claim they have the capability to transform the accounting sector further than RPA (Dickey et al., 2019; Kokina and Davenport, 2017). Cooper et al. (2019) found interviewees believe RPA to be a springboard to more advanced automation and reported that RPA vendors were already developing more sophisticated AI. Furthermore, Sun and Vasarhelyi (2017) and Dickey et al. (2019) predict that machine learning technology such as speed recognition will be able to be used to detect fraud in interviews carried out when auditing as it can identify deception and nervousness in speech and facial patterns. It is evident that AI has potential to develop beyond its current capabilities, and the more sophisticated it becomes the more benefits and greater impact it will have on accounting.

15.3.3 Autonomous Intelligence

The third level is autonomous intelligence as put by PwC (2017) and cognitive engagement as put by Crookes and Conway (2018). Autonomous intelligence describes the most sophisticated level of AI technology where the machine has intuitive and emotional intelligence giving the AI system the ability to understand human emotions, respond to them and make decisions independent of humans. In other words, the machine is able to 'think' (Crookes and Conway, 2018). This level of intelligence is not yet seen within the accounting sector but Lehner et al. (2020) report in their study on the future of accounting that ultimately there will be a 'Fully Autonomous Accounting System' (FAAS):

> FAAS is a firm-wide, fully autonomous, self-aware and self-improving accounting system. The centre of an FAAS is a state-based, multi-functional, deep-learning network as AI that is able to holistically simulate and potentially outpace human-cognition and decision-making processes. This AI manages structured and unstructured data and regulations from various sources and delivers timely and apt information to the right audience in the right format (Lehner et al., 2020, foreword, in Leitner-Hanetseder et al., 2021, p.540)

The adoption of AI in accounting is still in its infancy but its current impact on the accounting sector is undeniable and as technology advances further it will become more prominent and further change the accounting sector. Not only is AI changing accounting processes but AI has also improved the regulation of accounting. The accounting rule 'FAS133' regulates large hedging programmes of registrants of the US's SEC (US Securities and Exchange Commission) and is over 1800 pages making it very complex and difficult to implement. Only with AI was it able to be supported and implemented properly (Le Guyader, 2020). With AI capabilities already replacing many of the tasks previously done by accountants and being adopted in all facets of the industry, it is predicted to develop and impact greatly the accounting profession in the coming years, raising concerns the accounting profession may become obsolete (Shi, 2020; Cooper et al. 2019).

15.4   THE IMPACT OF AI ON THE ACCOUNTANT

15.4.1   The Demand for Accountants

Within the AI accounting literature, a substantial amount of research focuses on how AI systems in the accounting sector are impacting the role of accountants (see Kokina et al., 2021; Moll and Yigitbasioglu, 2019; Oesterreich et al., 2019; Kruskopf et al., 2020; Crookes and Conway, 2018; Kaya et al., 2019; Leitner-Hanetseder et al., 2021; Shi, 2020; Dickey et al., 2019).

There is a concern that accountants risk losing their jobs as AI is replacing the tasks once done by accountants and reducing the demand for them. Frey and Osborne (2017) developed a model to predict the potential for 702 professions to be taken over by automation and predicted that 94 per cent of accounting jobs could be replaced by AI technology by 2027 and that 99 per cent of tax accountants will be replaced by AI. However, Frey and Osborne's (2017) research is limited to investigating only the destructive effects of automation and does not consider any potential opportunities it may bring for workers. Whilst Dickey et al. (2019) argue that it is still too early in the development of AI in the accounting sector to determine the impact on the demand for accountants, there is widespread agreement among researchers that AI is not reducing the need for accountants but instead changing the tasks accountants will carry out (see Kokina et al., 2021; Moll and Yigitbasioglu, 2019; Leitner-Hanetseder et al., 2021). Through interviewing leaders of RPA in the Big4 accounting firms, Cooper et al. (2019) find that interviewees do not expect reductions in labour because of technology but instead that the tasks accountants perform will change as AI replaces the routine and repetitive tasks accountants have traditionally done.

15.4.2   The Role of the Accountant

Several researchers argue that the role of accountants will never go away because there are capabilities which technology does not have that humans do such as the skills of imagination and ability to improvise (Kruskopf et al., 2020), and accountants are needed to manage the AI systems (Moll and Yigitbasioglu, 2019; Leitner-Hanetseder et al., 2021). Leitner-Hanetseder et al. (2021) predict that in 2030, humans and AI will be working together, humans will train and monitor AI, ensuring they work effectively together. Kaya et al. (2019) report that accountants will be needed to audit AI systems as AI systems use learned algorithms which risk being faulty leading to potentially catastrophic outcomes if hundreds of bots are using the same algorithm.

Kokina et al. (2021) adapted Wilson et al.'s (2017) categorisation of human jobs using AI systems and applied it to the role of accountants as AI infiltrates the field of accounting. They presented four main roles accountants will have. First is the identifier role whereby accountants must have an ability to understand what business processes are appropriate to be automated; the second is the explainer role whereby accountants must be able to explain to bot developers and software designers the steps in a process for RPA; the third role is the sustainer role whereby accountants will need to work with the IT organisation to govern and manage the system; the fourth role is the analyser role whereby the accountant analyses the outcomes and makes sense of them. It is evident the role of accountants are changing and they will have to learn to work alongside AI systems. As AI becomes integrated into the accounting profession it is inevitable that at least some roles of the accountant will change. However, whilst Kokina et al.'s (2021) adapted model describes the role of the accountant in interacting with the AI system, it does not consider the impact on specific job roles within the accounting profession and so interpreting the model for specific jobs is difficult.

This is addressed by Leitner-Hanetseder et al. (2021) who conducted expert workshops with academics and practitioners of accounting to investigate the influence of AI on various professional occupations within accounting. They find that bookkeepers will have to acquire IT skills and a greater understanding of processes; business data analysts will be common among accounting firms; treasurers' and risk managers' roles will become more important to ensure efficient planning due to the emergence of new AI technologies; financial systems and process managers will play an important role in selecting and evaluating the effectiveness and efficiency of AI technologies. Leitner-Hanetseder (2021) also find that the role of financial accountants will be less focused on technical accounting tasks such as preparing financial reports and more on handling, making sense of, and translating data. Crookes and Conway (2018) also report that the role of the financial accountant is changing from gathering data to being able to handle and interpret large quantities of data generated by AI systems. Leitner-Hanetseder et al. (2021) and Crookes and Conway (2018) report that the role of management accounting is shifting from solely information providers to providing support for decision-making and becoming active business partners as AI systems take over tasks such as the production of standard reports. Management accountants will also acquire a more data centric role as they are expected to provide insight on financial and nonfinancial data to those within and outside the business. However, Oesterreich et al. (2019) found in their research analysing job advertisements for management accountants and member profiles on social networks that roles were not advertised specifying these new roles and skills. The contrast between Leitner-Hanetseder et al.'s (2021) and Crookes and Conway's (2018) studies reporting the role of the management accountant becoming more data focused compared with Oesterrich et al.'s (2019) finding that this new role is not reflected in job advertisements indicates that the transformation of AI in accounting firms may not be proceeding as expected. This implies that it may be too soon in the development of AI for job roles to be changing, yet more studies are required to assess this change in practice.

A change in the roles of the accountant to more data focused activities means accountants must acquire new skills in order to adapt to these new roles (Kruskopf et al., 2020; Kokina et al., 2021; Shi, 2020). Many researchers attempt to define the specific technical skills accountants will need to develop in order to interact with and manage AI systems (Kruskopf et al., 2020; Dickey et al., 2019; Crookes and Conway, 2018). They conclude such attributes as analytical skills, data security knowledge, understanding of software, coding knowledge amongst many others. From a literature review Kruskopf et al. (2020) predict that new job roles will arise as technology advances in the accounting sector. They predict job titles such as 'cloud accounting specialist', 'data security accountant' and 'strategic accounting analyst' will be seen in accounting firms, but from Oesterrich et al.'s (2019) findings such changes are yet to be seen.

Researchers also highlight that a broader skill set will be needed with the accountants' changing roles, not just technical skills to work with AI systems (Leitner-Hanetseder et al., 2021; Dickey et al., 2019; Kruskopf et al., 2020). Soft skills will gain increased importance as the accountant spends less time using technical accounting skills as tasks requiring these are replaced by AI, and more time interpreting and understanding the data to relay it to those inside and outside the business such as clients. Accountants need good communication and customer service skills in order to transfer their understanding of the AI systems and how they can benefit a client's business (Cooper et al., 2019; Kruskopf et al., 2020; Crookes and Conway, 2018). Overall, as AI progresses in the accounting sector, accountants will need to upskill to acquire a broader skill set including technical AI-based skills as well as social skills.

15.4.3   Accountants' Perceptions of AI

There is currently limited research which has investigated the impact of AI technology from the employees' perspective. AI replaces many of the tasks accountants have traditionally done. Researchers have found that this creates anxiety and a fear of job security among accountants leading to a reluctance to adapt and work with the new technology (Gotthardt et al., 2020; Fernandez and Aman, 2021). In contrast to Gotthardt et al. (2020) and Fernandez and Aman (2021), Cooper et al. (2021) found that employees believe that RPA is having a positive effect on them. Cooper et al. (2021), in addition to their research on the adoption of RPA in the Big4 (2019), interviewed leaders of RPA and surveyed low-level employees to investigate perceptions of RPA in the Big4 firms. The survey of low-level employees found that employees feel more valued and engaged in work and have higher job satisfaction as they are doing more interesting work because RPA has taken over the mundane tasks. In fact, employees report they are more likely to stay on in the company once RPA has been implemented. Furthermore, employees believe career prospects have improved with the implementation of RPA as employees do more value-adding activities and expand their skill sets; Fernandez and Aman (2021) also report that interviewees believe promotion opportunities have increased due to them carrying out more challenging tasks.

Cooper et al.'s (2021) study collects data from the Big4 accounting firms whereas Fernandez and Aman (2021) research the accounting and finance section of a large oil and gas company. The Big4 may be able to focus more resources into ensuring the implementation of RPA in accounting processes is a success with employees compared to a non-accounting organisation where the implementation of RPA in accounting processes may be less of a priority. More studies are required into non-accounting firms and smaller accounting firms to explore this and to gain a deeper understanding of accountants' perceptions of AI.

15.4.4   Organisational Structure

As the role and skills of accountants' change, the organisational structure of accounting firms will change as well. Kruskopf et al. (2020) and Losbichler and Lehner (2021) argue that the magnitude of change that technology is bringing in the accounting sector will force not only accountants to acquire new skills but companies to transform their organisational structure. Cooper et al.'s (2019) findings from interviewing the Big4 support this; they find that the Big4 firms are taking preventative measures to mitigate the risk of complete automation by changing their position as an accounting firm to be seen as a technology company which specialises in accounting knowledge. However, as of yet there is little research into how the influence of AI will change the structure of organisations, and it may be too early on in the evolution of AI in accounting to have had a measurable impact on organisational structure.

It is evident that the impact of AI is greatly impacting the role of accountants. The impact of AI on the demand for accountants is yet to be fully observed but it is evident the role of the accountant is changing as AI becomes part of the profession. Accountants in all job roles are experiencing a shift to acquiring AI-based skills to work alongside AI. Their skill set must expand as soft skills increase in importance as accountants become responsible for interpreting and relaying information from AI technology to others. However, as AI is still developing this research quickly becomes out-of-date and research is continually needed to assess and understand the impact of AI on the role of accountants as it progresses. A greater understanding of the effects of AI on accountants' perceptions and well being across various settings is required and further research into how AI will influence the structure of organisations is a pressing research area.

15.5   THE IMPACT OF AI ON THE EDUCATION OF ACCOUNTING

The skills accountants need to remain in the profession are changing, and so the skills required of accounting graduates by hiring accounting firms will too. However, the existing research considering the impact of the changing role of the accountant on the education of accounting is limited. PwC (2017) and Kruskopf et al. (2020) report that students must acquire advanced IT skills through their education such as with statistics, data analytics and basic machine learning skills or risk firms hiring non-accounting graduates instead who possess the necessary skills.

Qasim and Kharbat (2020) found through a theoretical study that accounting curriculums have been slow to change and that there is an imbalance between how fast the profession is changing with technology compared to the rate at which accounting curriculums are updating in line with the skills required of accountants, creating a shortage of the necessary skills in new graduates required by accounting firms (Pan and Seow, 2016; Kruskopf et al., 2020). Cooper et al. (2019) found in their interviews with the Big4 firms that students with technological and computer programming skills have an advantage over those without these skills, and the number of graduates who did not study accounting but have been hired into accounting roles rose by 11 per cent from 2016–2018 to just under a third (BusinessWire, 2019). This implies there is a need for accounting education curriculums to adapt to incorporate training so students have the necessary skills to be hired into accounting roles.

On the other hand, there is an argument that it is more important for professional firms to train their employees to keep up with the changing skills required of them and not as important for education to do so. Firms train employees when they first join the firm and carry out training throughout employees' careers to keep up with the skills required of them. For example, in 2018 PwC launched a 'Digital Accelerator' program to train employees in AI-based skills (Kruskopf et al., 2020). Furthermore, there is evidence that firms do not require profession specific skills and hire graduates from a range of degrees. Violette and Chene (2008) carried out a study interviewing accounting firms on their recruiting methods. They found that the most important characteristics in candidates were leadership potential, a motivation and enthusiasm for the profession and good interpersonal communication skills. It questions whether the call by researchers for curricula to incorporate more IT learning is as much of a necessity as it is often claimed to be. Nevertheless, there is ample research that accounting firms do require accounting knowledge of graduates; Clune and Gramling (2012) conducted a survey on internal auditors' recruiting methods and found that possessing an accounting degree or internal audit coursework was an important factor in the hiring decision.

There is a need to understand how education curricula should reform to support the changing requirements of accounting graduates by hiring firms, yet so far there is a lack of empirical research into this especially from the perspective of different stakeholders including education institutions and students (Qasim and Kharbat, 2020; Losbichler and Lehner, 2021; Sledgianowski et al., 2017).

15.6   ETHICAL CONSIDERATIONS

Whilst AI provides many benefits to organisations, researchers highlight the potential for biases to influence AI systems (see Munoko et al., 2020; Losbichler and Lehner, 2021; Kokina and Davenport, 2017; Kemper and Kolkman, 2019). AI uses existing data to learn meaning that the system's learning process can be influenced by biases in the data through humans who input the data and interact with it (Moll and Yigitbasioglu, 2019; Kemper and Kolkman, 2019). One bias Kokina and Davenport (2017) discuss is data-driven bias whereby the AI system generates biased outcomes because the data input by the human is flawed or skewed. This can lead to emergence bias, also known as confirmation bias, whereby the machine's outputs confirm a human's beliefs due to the bias in the data originally put in by the human (Kokina and Davenport, 2017). Munoko et al. (2020) found there is risk of human biases influencing the AI system in risk assessments. Researchers are widely in agreement that there must be enhanced transparency in the implementation and interaction of algorithms and accountants must have an understanding of potential biases in order to mitigate the potential for biases to influence AI systems (Dickey et al., 2019; Kemper and Kolkman, 2019; Kirkpatrick, 2016). However, how this transparency is materialised and who should be held accountable for biases in AI systems is still unclear and so research is needed in this area (Munoko et al, 2020). Biases must also be taught to accountants and accounting students, yet how accounting education should incorporate such adaptions has not yet been researched (Losbichler and Lehner, 2021).

Another ethical concern arising from the use of AI systems is the moral aspect of AI. The literature surrounding the potential for managers to abuse their use of AI systems is mixed. From carrying out a literature review, Moll and Yigitbasioglu (2019) argue that managers are able to blame poor decision-making on AI systems because the decisions are automatic and the manager argues they do not interfere with them. On the other hand, in an experiment conducted by Kipp et al. (2020) to investigate how AI influences managers' ethical reasoning, they find that managers engage in less aggressive financial reporting when interacting with AI systems than when interacting with human agents. This is because of the greater control and responsibility associated with the AI system than with human agents.

One of the largest risks of AI is that to the security of data. AI requires vast quantities of data to be stored, managed and transferred electronically which makes it vulnerable to cyber-attacks and hackers (Shi, 2020). Munoko et al. (2020) found that all the Big4 firms use AI for evaluating controls which they found to have cybersecurity risks, privacy risks and a lack of trust in the AI resulting from these security risks. EY (2019) also reported accountants had less trust in the quality of data produced by AI than from traditional finance systems due to data privacy and security risks. Furthermore, the infancy of AI development means that AI systems are even more vulnerable as they are not as secure as other established systems.

These ethical concerns bring about a need for regulation and effective governance mechanisms to be implemented to govern the use of AI systems, yet researchers find that the development and integration of AI systems are outpacing the systems in place to govern them (Cobey et al., 2018; Losbichler and Lehner, 2021). More research is therefore required into the governance of AI.

15.7   A CALL FOR FUTURE RESEARCH

The development of AI is still in its infancy in the accounting sector and so there is limited empirical research on AI in the accounting profession. Of the empirical research available, much is focused on one of the simplest forms of AI, RPA, as this AI system is the most developed in the accounting sector. Some research has explored the adoption of RPA in the Big4 firms (see Cooper et al., 2019) and how RPA is changing the role and skills required of accountants (see Kokina et al., 2021), but more is required. Prior researchers have drawn data from a small number of organisations meaning that the generalisation of findings to the wider accounting sector is difficult.

A large focus of the research conducted on AI in accounting is on the changing role of accountants and skills they will need to acquire to keep up with the rapidly developing profession (see Kokina et al., 2021; Moll and Yigitbasioglu, 2019; Oesterreich et al., 2019; Shi, 2020; Leitner-Hanetseder et al., 2021). Due to the infancy of AI in accounting much of the research reviews the existing literature to determine how the roles, tasks and skills required of accountants are changing (see Moll and Yigitbasioglu, 2019; Shi, 2020). Empirical research into the changing role of accountants is mostly qualitative based, using interviews (see Kokina et al., 2021; Leitner-Hanetseder et al., 2021), document analysis (see Mohammad et al., 2020), analysis of job advertisements and member profiles (see Oesterreich et al., 2019). A qualitative method is appropriate as it allows for a more detailed and in-depth understanding to be gained from the under-researched area of AI in the accounting sector. There is limited research exploring the perceptions of AI by accountants (see Fernandez and Aman, 2021; Cooper et al., 2021) and further research into smaller accounting organisations in this area is required to get a deeper understanding across the whole industry.

Research has also explored the impact of AI on specific aspects of accounting such as financial reporting (see Kipp et al., 2020), which provides a more thorough understanding of how AI is impacting the accounting profession. Furthermore, some researchers have focused their studies on providing research agendas to advise future researchers in the area (see Losbichler and Lehner, 2021). And some studies have considered the impact of the changing role of accountants on the education of accounting (see Kruskopf et al., 2020) but research here remains scarce, and there is a lack of understanding as to how accounting education can incorporate such changes into curricula. Qasim and Khabart (2020) proposed a model to incorporate education of IT skills into the curriculum but there is a lack of research from the perspectives of various stakeholders such as students and education providers (Losbichler and Lehner, 2021; Qasim and Khabart, 2020). Research has also considered the challenges brought about by AI, including biases which accountants must be aware of, moral aspects and security issues (see Kemper and Kolkman, 2019; Kipp et al., 2020), and this could prove a fruitful avenue for future work. Overall, researchers generally conclude that regulation is needed to mitigate these problems identified above, yet there remain gaps in our knowledge and a lack of understanding as to how regulation should be implemented.

Notably, the literature examined here is very recent, with the majority of the studies published in the last few years, indicating the infancy of research in AI in the accounting sector, but also that interest in this area is moving apace. This mirrors the speed at which AI is developing and changing the accounting sector, so more research is required to understand this field for accounting firms, institutional bodies and academics.

15.8   A POTENTIAL PLAN FOR FUTURE RESEARCH

Whilst we acknowledge that this is not a comprehensive way forward, we suggest a plan for future work, based on our analysis of the above literature. First, we consider that the questions to be addressed might include the following: what does the adoption of RPA technology within small-medium sized (SME) accounting firms look like; how is RPA impacting employees within SME accounting firms; and what are employees' perceptions of RPA within SME accounting firms?

From a methodological standpoint, it would make sense to gather information from interviews with the leaders of RPA technology in such firms, in order to gain a deep understanding of how well developed RPA is within them, to what processes it has been applied, and how effective it is. For data triangulation, this might be supplemented with surveys of low-level employees of SMEs, in order to gain an understanding of how RPA technology is also impacting employees, how they perceive the RPA technology and their attitudes towards it. A qualitative method is appropriate for such a study, as the research would be exploratory and inductive in nature, given the limited extant research on the adoption of AI in SME accounting firms. Furthermore, a qualitative methodology is suitable when the sample is small, which is appropriate due to the limited uptake of AI in the accounting sector so far.

We would expect to find that, where AI has been implemented, accounting processes should see an improvement in efficiency and effectiveness (see Cooper et al., 2019). As AI technology has been replacing the tasks undertaken by employees in the Big4 firms, thereby shifting the role of the accountant to more value-adding activities, the same should be observed in SMEs. The perception of AI technology by low-level employees in SME accounting firms is uncertain, but findings here may differ to that of Cooper et al. (2021), who found that low-level employees had positive attitudes towards AI. Instead, we might expect to see more negative attitudes and resistance towards AI technology within smaller firms, as they have fewer resources to ensure that the integration of AI is a success with employees than the Big4 firms.

This research would extend the existing research by Cooper et al. (2019, 2021), who studied the adoption of RPA and the employee perceptions of RPA within the Big4 accounting firms. Through extending the research to smaller accounting firms, we would expect to contribute an understanding of the adoption of AI-based technology and employee perceptions of AI-based technology to the wider accounting sector. Furthermore, such work would extend and enhance the existing literature investigating AI in accounting in general (see Kokina et al., 2021; Oesterreich et al., 2019; Leitner-Hanetseder et al., 2021). As we have seen from our understanding of the literature above, AI will not be going away, so increasing our understanding of how it works, and how we might nurture it within organisations, can only be beneficial.

15.9   SUMMARY

This chapter has provided support for research into the impact of AI in the accounting sector. The adoption of AI is still in its infancy in this area, but it is already having a substantial impact on the profession. RPA is replacing tasks once done by accountants, streamlining processes and enhancing efficiency, and as it develops this impact will intensify. Research into the adoption of RPA beyond the Big4 to include smaller companies is required to get a fuller understanding of its impact. The Big4 firms are already developing more advanced AI than RPA, including machine learning and natural language processing, which can further improve the efficiency of accounting processes. However, the impact of these technologies on accounting is still to be fully understood as it is still in early development in the Big4 firms.

The impact of AI on the role of accountants has been a significant focus for researchers (for example, Kokina et al., 2021; Kruskopf et al., 2020; Leitner-Hanetseder et al., 2021). Whilst there is a fear that AI will make the accounting profession obsolete, researchers argue that instead accountants' roles will change to work alongside AI and they must acquire new technical and social skills to adapt to these new roles. Nonetheless, since the development of AI in accounting is still in early development, research is continuously needed to assess and understand the impacts AI is having on the profession. Future work should aim at understanding the impact of AI in accounting across the accounting industry, beyond just the Big4 firms, and should include accountants' perceptions of AI, in order to understand their acceptance, or otherwise, and likely adherence to new developments.

The skills accountants need are changing and so too are the skills required of graduates. There is a need to understand how education curricula should adapt to incorporate the new skills hiring firms are requiring, and to consider a range of perspectives such as those of both students and educators. Finally, whilst AI has its benefits, this literature review has shown that it also presents challenges: biases can quickly become a significant problem in the use of AI; there are moral risks to using AI; and there are security and privacy risks arising from the use of AI. Regulation is needed to minimise the risk these problems propose and increase transparency, and accountants must be educated about these problems to help mitigate them, motivating research into this area. As AI becomes more sophisticated, developing from RPA to more autonomous AI, the more benefits it will bring about, but ethical problems will also become more severe. Therefore, as AI continues to develop, ongoing research is required to understand the impact it might have on accounting.

REFERENCES

BusinessWire. 2019. Public accounting hiring model shifts: AICPA 'Trends Report.' Available from https://www.businesswire.com/news/home/20190813005630/en/Public-Accounting-Firm-Hiring-Model-Shifts-AICPA [Accessed 20/07/21]
Clune, R.R. and Gramling, A.A. (2012). Hiring recent university graduates into internal audit positions: Insights from practicing internal auditors. *Current Issues in Auditing*, Vol. 6, No. 2, pp. A1–A14.

Cobey, C., Strier, K. and Boillet, J. (2018). How do you teach AI the value of trust? https://www.ey.com/en_gl/digital/how-do-you-teach-ai-the-value-of-trust [Accessed 20/07/21]

Cooper, L.A., Holderness Jr, D.K., Sorensen, T.L. and Wood, D.A. (2019). Robotic process automation in public accounting, *Accounting Horizons*, Vol. 33, No. 4, pp. 15–35.

Cooper, L.A., Holderness Jr, D.K., Sorensen, T.L. and Wood, D.A. (2021). Perceptions of robotic process automation in Big 4 public accounting firms: Do firm leaders and lower-level employees agree? *Journal of Emerging Technologies in Accounting*. Available from SSRN: https://ssrn.com/abstract=3445005or http://dx.doi.org/10.2139/ssrn.3445005

Crookes, L., Conway, E. (2018). Technology Challenges in Accounting and Finance. In: Conway, E., Byrne, D. (eds) *Contemporary Issues in Accounting*. Palgrave Macmillan, Cham. https://doi.org/10.1007/978-3-319-91113-7_4

Crookes, L. and Conway, E. (2018). Technology challenges in accounting and finance. *Contemporary Issues in Accounting*, Springer, pp. 61–83.

Dickey, G., Blanke, S. and Seaton, L. (2019). Machine learning in auditing, *The CPA Journal*, Vol. 89, pp. 16–21.

EY (2019) How a Quality Audit Enhances Trust, Ernst & Young. Available from http://www.ey.com/en_gl/audit-quality [Accessed 05/12/23]

Fernandez, D. and Aman, A. (2021). The influence of robotic process automation (RPA) towards employee acceptance, *International Journal of Recent Technology and Engineering*, Vol. 9, No. 5, pp. 295–299.

Frey, C.B. and Osborne, M.A. (2017). The future of employment: How susceptible are jobs to computerization? *Technological Forecasting and Social Change*, 114, pp. 254–280.

Gotthardt, M., Koivulaakso, D., Okyanus, P., Saramo, C., Martikainen, M. and Lehner, O.M. (2020). Current state and challenges in the implementation of smart robotic process automation in accounting and auditing, *ACRN Journal of Finance and Risk Perspectives*, Vol. 9, No. 1, pp. 90–102.

Haenlein, M. and Kaplan, A. (2019). A brief history of artificial intelligence: On the past, present, and future of artificial intelligence, *California Management Review*, Vol. 61, No. 4, pp. 5–14.

Hawking, S., Tegmark, M. and Wilczek, F. (2014). Stephen Hawking: 'Transcendence Looks at the Implications of Artifcial Intelligence – but Are We Taking AI Seriously Enough?' *The Independent*. http://www.independent.co.uk/news/science/stephen-hawking-transcendence-looks-at-the-implications-of-artifcial-intelligence-but-are-we-taking-9313474.html [Accessed 14/07/21]

Hoffman, C. (2017). *Accounting and auditing in the digital age*. http://xbrlsite.azurewebsites.net/2017/Library/AccountingAndAuditingInTheDigitalAge.pdf

Kaya, C.T., Türkyılmaz, M. and Birol, B. (2019). Impact of RPA technologies on accounting systems, *Muhasebe ve Finansman Dergisi*, 82.

Kemper, J. and Kolkman, D. (2019). Transparent to whom? No algorithmic accountability without a critical audience, *Information, Communication and Society*, Vol. 22, No. 14, pp. 2081–2096.

Kipp, P.C., Curtis, M.B. and Li, Z. (2020). The attenuating effect of intelligent agents and agent autonomy on managers' ability to diffuse responsibility for and engage in earnings management, *Accounting Horizons*, Vol. 34, No. 4, pp. 143–164.

Kirkpatrick, K. (2016). Battling algorithmic bias: How do we ensure algorithms treat us fairly? *Communications of the ACM*, Vol. 59, No. 10, pp. 16–17.

Kokina, J. and Davenport, T.H. (2017). The emergence of artificial intelligence: How automation is changing auditing, *Journal of Emerging Technologies in Accounting*, Vol. 14, No. 1, pp. 115–122.

Kokina, J. Gilleran, R., Blanchette, S. and Stoddard, D. (2021). Accountant as digital innovator: Roles and competencies in the age of automation, *Accounting Horizons*, Vol. 35, No. 1, pp. 153–184.

Kruskopf, S., Lobbas, C., Meinander, H., Soderling, K., Martikainen, M. and Lehner, O.M. (2020). Digital accounting and the human factor: Theory and practice, *ACRN Journal of Finance and Risk Perspectives*, Vol. 9, No. 1, pp. 78–89.

Le Guyader, L.P. (2020). Artificial intelligence in accounting: GAAP's 'FAS133', *Journal of Corporate Accounting & Finance*, Vol. 31. No. 3, pp. 185–189.

Lehner, O.M, Forstenlechner, C., Leitner-Hanetseder, S. and Eisl, C. (2020). The dynamics of artificial intelligence in accounting organisations: A structuration perspective, *Working Paper Series*, Hanken School of Economics, Helsinki.

Leitner-Hanetseder, S., Lehner, O.M., Eisl, C. and Forstenlechner, C. (2021). A profession in transition: Actors, tasks and roles in AI-based accounting, *Journal of Applied Accounting Research*, Vol. 22, No. 3, pp. 539–556.

Lim, F.P.C. (2013). Impact of information technology on accounting systems. *Asia-Pacific Journal of Multimedia Services Convergent with Art, Humanities, and Sociology*, Vol. 3, No. 2, pp. 93–106

Losbichler, H., and Lehner, O.M. (2021). Limits of artificial intelligence in controlling and the ways forward: A call for future accounting research, *Journal of Applied Accounting Research*, Vol. 22, No. 2, pp. 365–382.

Mohammad, J.S., Hamad, K.A., Borgi, H., Anh Thu, P., Sial, S.M. and Alhadidi, A.A. (2020). How artificial intelligence changes the future of accounting industry, *International Journal of Economics & Business Administration (IJEBA)*, Vol. 8, No. 3, pp. 478–488.

Moll, J. and Yigitbasioglu, O. (2019). The role of internet-related technologies in shaping the work of accountants: New directions for accounting research, *The British Accounting Review*, Vol. 51, No. 6, p. 100833.

Munoko, I., Brown-Liburd, H. L. and Vasarhelyi, M.A. (2020). The ethical implications of using artificial intelligence in auditing, *Journal of Business Ethics*, Vol. 167, No. 2, pp. 209–234.

Nilsson, N.J. (2009). *The quest for artificial intelligence*. Cambridge University Press.

OED Online. (2021). Oxford University Press. Available from https://www.oed.com/view/Entry/271625 ?redirectedFrom=artificial+intelligence#eid

Oesterreich, T.D., Teuteberg, F., Bensberg, F. and Buscher, G. (2019). The controlling profession in the digital age: Understanding the impact of digitisation on the controller's job roles, skills and competences, *International Journal of Accounting Information Systems*, Vol. 35, pp. 1–25.

Pan, G. and Seow, P.-S. (2016). Preparing accounting graduates for digital revolution: A critical review of information technology competencies and skills development, *The Journal of Education for Business*, Vol. 91, No. 3, pp. 166–175.

PwC. (2017). Sizing the prize. What's the real value of AI for your business and how can you capitalise? Available from https://www.pwc.com/gx/en/news-room/docs/report-pwc-ai-analysis-sizing-the-prize .pdf [Accessed 12/07/21]

Qasim, A. and Kharbat, F.F. (2020), Blockchain technology, business data analytics, and artificial intelligence: Use in the accounting profession and ideas for inclusion into the accounting curriculum, *Journal of Emerging Technologies in Accounting*, Vol. 17, No. 1, pp. 107–117.

Saygin, A.P., Cicekli, I. and Akman, V. (2000). Turing Test: 50 years later, *Minds and Machines*, Vol. 10, No. 4, pp. 463–518.

Seshia, S.A., Sadigh, D. and Sastry, S.S. (2022). Towards verified artificial intelligence, *Communications of the ACM*, 65(7), 46–55.

Shi Y. (2020). The impact of artificial intelligence on the accounting industry. In: Xu Z., Choo KK., Dehghantanha A., Parizi R. and Hammoudeh M. (eds) *Cyber security intelligence and analytics*. CSIA 2019. *Advances in Intelligent Systems and Computing*, 928. Springer, Cham. https://doi-org .proxy.lib.strath.ac.uk/10.1007/978-3-030-15235-2_129

Sledgianowski, D., Gomaa, M. and Tan, C. (2017). Toward integration of Big Data, technology and information systems competencies into the accounting curriculum, *Journal of Accounting Education*, Vol. 38, pp. 81–93.

Sun, T. and Vasarhelyi, M.A. (2017). Deep learning and the future of auditing: How an evolving technology could transform analysis and improve judgment, *The CPA Journal*, Vol. 87, No. 6.

Sutton, S.G., Holt, M. and Arnold, V. (2016). 'The reports of my death are greatly exaggerated' – artificial intelligence research in accounting, *International Journal of Accounting Information Systems*, Vol. 22, pp. 60–73.

Turing, A.M. (1950). Computing machinery and intelligence, *Mind*, Vol. 59, No. 236, pp. 433–460.

Ucoglu, D. (2020). Current machine learning applications in accounting and auditing, *PressAcademia Procedia*, Vol. 12, No. 1, pp. 1–7.

Violette, G. and Chene, D. (2008). Campus recruiting: What local and regional accounting firms look for in new hires. *The CPA Journal*, Vol. 78, No. 12, p. 66.

Wilson, H.J., Daugherty, P. and Bianzino, N. (2017). "The jobs that artificial intelligence will create." *MIT Sloan Management Review* 58(4): p. 14.

World Economic Forum. (2015). Deep shift: Technology tipping points and societal impact. Available from http://www3.weforum.org/docs/WEF_GAC15_Technological_Tipping_Points_report_2015.pdf

16. Internet-based technologies, accounting processes, and management control systems

Vikash Kumar Sinha, David Derichs and Teemu Malmi

16.1 INTRODUCTION

Several Internet-based Technologies (IBTs),[1] including Cloud Computing, Big Data & Data Analytics (BDDA), Artificial Intelligence (AI), Internet of Things (IoT), and Blockchain, are rapidly revolutionising new modes of automation, facilitating faster analysis and exchange of data, enabling seamless transactions between humans and machines, and transforming web-connected business models. Many scholars have dubbed these IBT-driven technological transformations as the Fourth Industrial Revolution (Industry 4.0) (Stein, Campitelli and Mezzio, 2020). The sheer pace of such IBT-driven technological transformation is creating challenges as well as opportunities for Management Control Systems (MCS)[2] (Bhimani and Willcocks, 2014; Quattrone, 2016; Arnaboldi, Busco and Cuganesan, 2017; Moll and Yigitbasioglu, 2019; Möller, Schäffer and Verbeeten, 2020). For example, IBTs are creating opportunities for 'outside' experts in marketing, Human Resources (HR), and Information Technology (IT) to contribute to the development of innovative MCS by enabling decentralisation of information and effortless transformation of data into relevant and meaningful business information (Arnaboldi, Azzone and Sidorova, 2017). However, such participation of 'outside' experts in MCS development can also create tensions between the accounting function and these 'outside' experts (Arnaboldi, Busco and Cuganesan, 2017; Power, 2022). Many experts also point out that IBTs can pose grave threats to the personal freedom of employees (for example, through surveillance) (Zuboff, 2015, 2019; Kellogg, Valentine and Christin, 2020) and may increase information security risks through the deployment of remote and algorithmic control technologies (Moll and Yigitbasioglu, 2019). In doing so, experts have also raised fundamental questions on the hyper-rationalisation promoted by IBT-driven MCS approaches that can dehumanise the modern organisational 'work' by reducing the scope for emotional fulfilment, judgement-based decision-making, and ritualisation (Quattrone, 2016; Kellogg, Valentine and Christin, 2020). As pointed out by psychologists, emotions, rituals, and judgements are important for the well-being of individuals and society at large (Zapf, 2002; Hobson et al., 2018).

The threats and opportunities mentioned in the paragraph above highlight just a narrow selection of possible scenarios. To systematically understand how deploying IBTs can create threats and opportunities for MCS, we analysed academic and practitioner-oriented literature to propose a framework. We have deployed a staged approach to elaborate on our framework and its different elements. In the next section, we first describe the most influential digital technologies. Then we focus on identifying how different digital strategies of firms influence the choices of IBTs. Finally, we focus on identifying threats and opportunities to different MCS. We close the chapter with a discussion and future research opportunities.

16.2   EMERGING INTERNET-BASED TECHNOLOGIES

In selecting the prominent IBTs that present threats and opportunities for MCS, reports and white papers from professional bodies such as the Chartered Institute of Management Accountants (CIMA), the Association of International Certified Professional Accountants (AICPA), Chartered Global Management Accountant (CGMA), the Institute of Management Accountants (IMA), and the professional services firms (PSFs) such as Big 4 were relied upon. These professional bodies and PSFs were chosen since they not only set the agenda for management accounting practices and technologies but also contribute to their diffusion (Cooper and Robson, 2006). Our review identified five prominent IBTs that were recognised by the professional bodies and PSFs as particularly relevant to management accounting practices: Cloud Computing, BDDA, AI, IoT, and Blockchain. In the next paragraphs, we briefly highlight data on the adoption of these IBTs in firms and accounting processes to highlight their rising prominence.

According to a survey by Eurostat, 41 per cent of firms in the EU area used Cloud Computing (Eurostat, 2021). According to the same survey, 73 per cent of the cloud-adopting firms in the EU area indicated the use of sophisticated cloud services such as security software applications, hosting enterprise databases, or computing platforms for application development, testing, or deployment (Eurostat, 2021). When it comes to larger firms (more than 250 employees), more than 72 per cent report using cloud services in the EU (Eurostat, 2021). Cloud Computing is one of the most adopted IBTs in the accounting domain. Indeed, 54 per cent[3] of accounting firms worldwide (Farrar, 2019), 48 per cent[4] (2014) of accounting firms in the USA (Drew, 2015), and 40 per cent (2021) of the administrative/accounting firms in Europe indicate the use of cloud applications (Eurostat, 2021).

According to a forecast from the CIMA, BDDA and AI technologies will lead to massive automation of data gathering/transaction processing and dissemination/reporting processes, allowing controllers to devote 50 per cent of their time to strategic decision-making (CIMA, 2022). In a study conducted by the accounting software firm Sage in 2018, 42 per cent and 66 per cent of the 3000 participating accounting professionals suggested demand for strategic advice and BDDA and AI, respectively, from their clients and business leaders (Sage, 2018). In a CGMA and AICPA-sponsored survey of 5500 finance professionals (representing 2000 firms in 150 countries), 11 per cent and 18 per cent of respondents indicated using BDDA technology for automation and visualisation, respectively (Farrar, 2019). In the same CGMA and AICPA-sponsored survey, 25 per cent and 5 per cent of the respondents indicated using AI and cognitive computing (AI designed to interact with and help humans in their tasks), respectively (Farrar, 2019).

While demand for Cloud Computing, BDDA, and AI has been rising steadily, Blockchain and IoT-related technologies are still in their infancy. Nevertheless, these two technologies have been considered important by academics and practitioners alike (Böhme et al., 2015; Forbes, 2017; Chanson et al., 2019; Moll and Yigitbasioglu, 2019; Möller, Schäffer and Verbeeten, 2020; Lumineau, Wang and Schilke, 2021; Garanina, Ranta and Dumay, 2022). While only 2 per cent of the respondents in the CGMA and AICPA survey suggested the use of Blockchain in current accounting practices, 9 per cent of the participants indicated that their firm plans to use Blockchain for accounting purposes in 3–5 years (Farrar, 2019). Blockchain technology has recently gone through a hype phase, but there has been disillusionment and a lukewarm response from firms in adopting it (CPA.com, 2022).

When it comes to IoT, the potential of the technology can be gauged by understanding the number of devices that are connected or are projected to be connected by the technology. In 2021, there were 11.3 billion devices connected through IoT, but the number of such devices is projected to grow to 30 billion by 2030 (Statista, 2021). In 2017, 29 per cent of firms worldwide had adopted IoT and 82 per cent of adopting firms had declared its synergy with integrating BDDA, AI, and key digital initiatives (Forbes, 2017). While IoT's direct role in accounting has not yet been explored extensively, given its synergy with integrating data analytics and AI, it is expected to play a significant role in the digital strategy of accounting functions (Bullington, 2022).

16.3   IMPACT OF IBTS ON ACCOUNTING PROCESSES

Once we had identified the five prominent IBTs, we searched accounting journals by inputting each of the IBTs as a keyword. After, a quick reading of abstracts allowed us to include relevant academic papers that shed light on the threats and opportunities the selected IBTs posed to MCS. Before we elaborate on the threats and opportunities to MCS, in this section, we highlight how IBTs influence the accounting processes (i.e. gathering, analysis, and dissemination of financial and nonfinancial information), ultimately influencing measurement systems and posing different threats and opportunities for different MCS (Chenhall, 2003; Malmi and Brown, 2008; Chenhall and Moers, 2015). It is imperative to note here that accounting processes have been shown to be lagging behind in the use of IBTs in particular (Moll and Yigitbasioglu, 2019; Möller, Schäffer and Verbeeten, 2020) and technologies in general (Granlund and Malmi, 2002). Several studies have attributed such lagging behind not only to poor training and knowledge of accounting employees (Caglio, 2003; Arnaboldi, Busco and Cuganesan, 2017) but also to the inertia/resistance of accounting functions in upgrading their knowledge (Dechow and Mouritsen, 2005; Quattrone and Hopper, 2005; Korhonen et al., 2020).

Cloud Computing allows the on-demand deployment of computing resources such as data storage and computing power (Buyya, Broberg and Goscinski, 2010). There are four cloud deployment models: private, public, community, and hybrid cloud. Since firms have shown the most interest in public clouds, our discussion is more focused on public clouds (Moll and Yigitbasioglu, 2019). Many public Cloud Computing platforms such as Amazon Web Services (AWS) and Microsoft Azure allow firms to pay for their data storage, (customisable) applications, and computing power based on utilisation, for example, gigabytes of data storage firms need, the number of users accessing specific applications, and the amount of computing power consumed (Bharadwaj et al., 2013; Jain and Hazra, 2019). This pay-as-you-go model can play a prominent role in transforming all steps of the accounting processes, i.e. gathering, analysing, and disseminating financial and nonfinancial information, in various ways.

First, the setup and scaleup of accounting operations become less time and cost-intensive since firms do not need to invest time and capital in setting up IT infrastructure and specialised IT services. Cloud Computing platform providers such as Amazon and Microsoft take care of both infrastructure and specialised IT services (Jain and Hazra, 2019). Second, the rollout of accounting operations for multiple subsidiaries becomes faster since the environment for one subsidiary can be quickly cloned for the other subsidiaries (Carlsson-Wall et al., 2022). Firms can deploy and customise their proprietary accounting processes on such platforms as well since proprietary applications can also be easily rolled out for subsidiaries through cloning (Carlsson-Wall et al., 2022). Third, integrating accounting operations and information sharing with upstream and downstream supply chain partners becomes easier (Moll and Yigitbasioglu, 2019). While small and medium-sized enterprises benefit more in the way described above, Cloud Computing platforms also present information security challenges such as loss or theft of proprietary information. Because Cloud Computing platforms run over the Internet, firms have to put their information on the Internet including their proprietary data (although secured by firewalls), thereby making them accessible to hacker attacks (Strauss, Kristandl and Quinn, 2015). Certainly, at some level, Cloud Computing platforms do contribute to more rigorous and standardised information security processes since platform providers heavily invest in making their servers more secure (Moll and Yigitbasioglu, 2019). However, the standardised nature of information security processes can also allow hackers to find and exploit security vulnerabilities for multiple firms at the same time (Bhimani and Willcocks, 2014).

BDDA technologies allow firms to gather and analyse what experts dub 'high-volume, high velocity and/or high-variety data' to extract and disseminate insightful accounting information that humans cannot easily identify due to their cognitive limitations (Bhimani and Willcocks, 2014). It could be argued that BDDA technologies can significantly transform all steps of the accounting processes, i.e. gathering, analysis, and dissemination of financial and nonfinancial information. More specifically, BDDA technologies are enabling accounting processes to include not only a variety of nonfinancial data (for example, customer ratings concerning their products on e-commerce websites or suppliers' use of child labour in local newspapers published in local languages) but also unstructured data (for example, feedback from customers on both e-commerce websites and social media) to extract and disseminate business-relevant insights (Bhimani and Willcocks, 2014; Arnaboldi, Busco and Cuganesan, 2017). While BDDA technologies have a lot of potential, their usage is currently limited in accounting processes and their deployment by marketing and R&D teams has created tension between management accountants and other functional experts (Arnaboldi, Azzone and Sidorova, 2017). The most promising BDDA tools implemented in management accounting processes are related to the visualisation and summarising of vast amounts of information (Farrar, 2019; Moll and Yigitbasioglu, 2019). Such visualisation and summarising facilitate easy dissemination of business-relevant insights. BDDA approaches have prompted significant investments from firms in creating centralised data warehousing solutions (consisting of decentralised data access and management yet centralised storage of data).

Still, many experts have claimed that investments in data warehousing solutions have not benefitted companies due to a lack of agility, flexibility, and growing system complexity (Herden, 2020). Since data warehousing relies on extracting, transferring, and loading data into one centralised data repository before processing and analysing data, it poses several challenges. First, building centralised repositories imposes hefty upfront investments. Second, adding additional data sources or changing data formats in later stages becomes difficult due to formatting constraints introduced during the initial phases of database designs (O'Leary, 2014). Third, the centralised nature of data warehousing solutions makes them vulnerable to hacker attacks. Fourth, the response times of applications become larger if many user applications are built around the centralised data repository (O'Leary, 2014). To overcome the above-mentioned problems, approaches called data lakes are being promoted by experts. Data lake-based approaches rely on keeping data sources distributed while developing processing and analysis applications that can draw data from multiple sources to generate relevant insights. Since many current data analytics technologies rely on single sources of data, data lake approaches require additional resources and applications to develop appropriate data preprocessing modules (O'Leary, 2014; Herden, 2020).

AI includes innovations such as machine learning, natural language processing and well-known statistical techniques for analysing data for predictive or prescriptive purposes. In stark contrast to traditional expert and intelligence systems that rely upon hard-coded steps for arriving at answers, AI takes input and output variables and finds the logic of association between them (Martin, 2019). AI technologies can play an important role in transforming two steps of the accounting processes: the analysis and dissemination of financial and nonfinancial information. AI can find patterns in large amounts of structured and unstructured data that accountants cannot identify due to cognitive limitations (Lindebaum, Vesa and den Hond, 2020). In this sense, AI can help accountants overcome the limitations of their bounded rationality by helping them process large amounts and varieties of data to gain relevant insights (Davenport and Kirby, 2016; Holm, 2019).

AI can also be used to automate routine tasks of accountants, such as reading and recording different formats of supplier invoices and recording useful information in structured databases (such AI solutions are popularly referred to as Robotic Process Automation – RPA) (Rechtman, 2021). Through RPA, AI can also automate tasks that rely on complex calculation logic and formal inference (Ng, 2016; Fountaine, McCarthy and Saleh, 2019). AI can support accounting tasks of classifying data, determining effect sizes, anomaly/fraud detection, and decision recommendations (Raisch and Krakowski, 2020). AI technologies focusing on natural language processing can enable chatbot implementations that can be useful for helping managers with accounting and information-related issues through queries in plain language (Moll and Yigitbasioglu, 2019). Unstructured data analysis through AI can facilitate the measurement of sentiments and extraction of actionable insights from large amounts of unstructured data such as texts (Li, 2008). Deep learning algorithms and Q learning algorithms can use neural network and stochastic approaches, respectively, to make decisions in conditions involving more uncertainty (Li, 2010). AI can process audio-visual data (for example, videos, images, and speeches) to extract information on the personality and motivation of executives and managers during fraud investigations (Asay, Libby and Rennekamp, 2018a, 2018b). AI can also determine the best possible visualisation of multidimensional data that can provide useful insights to decision-makers and make communications more effective (Moll and Yigitbasioglu, 2019; Tsamados et al., 2022).

Blockchain and Distributed Ledger Technologies (DLTs) enable sharing of multiple copies of accounting ledgers among the members of a peer-to-peer network (Yermack, 2017). There are three modes through which Blockchain technology is deployed: Public, Private, and Consortium models (Tyma et al., 2022). Public Blockchain technologies have been used for payments, fungible cryptocurrencies, tokenisation of non-fungible assets (such as art), and smart contracting (automatic transactions between parties when conditions are met). Examples of public Blockchains include Bitcoin (payment), BNB (Binance-supported cryptocurrency), OpenSea (NFT marketplace), and Ethereum (supporting various smart contracts). Most public Blockchains are permissionless systems where users can easily join the Blockchain as a node. Permissionless public Blockchains use GitHub-like open-source platforms to manage their code (Böhme et al., 2015). Private Blockchains are owned by a centralised firm and require permissioned enrolment of users. One example of a private Blockchain is the Australian Stock Exchange (ASX) DLT system. It replaces the existing Clearing House Electronic Subregister

Table 16.1   Impact of IBTs on accounting processes

Internet-based technologies	Inter-organisational accounting			Intra-organisational accounting
	Information gathering and transaction processing	Information analysis and processing	Information dissemination and reporting	
Cloud Computing	++	++	++	++
Big Data and Data Analytics	++	++	++	
Artificial Intelligence		++	++	
Blockchain	++	+	++	++
Internet-of-things	++			++

Note: + Less prominent influence, ++ More prominent influence.

System (CHESS) used to record share-related transactions (Tyma et al., 2022). Consortium models of Blockchains are permissioned Blockchains where governance and updating of DLT require consensus from consortium participants (Lumineau, Wang and Schilke, 2021; Tyma et al., 2022).

One prominent example of a consortium Blockchain is the DIAS digital apartment buying platform in Finland. Blockchains can play a big role in transforming all steps of inter-organisational accounting processes, i.e. gathering, analysis, and dissemination of financial and nonfinancial information among the supply chain members. For example, Blockchain can gather information from every member of the supply chain to disseminate information on the origin of products or the carbon footprint of products to customers (Gaur and Gaiha, 2020; Garanina, Ranta and Dumay, 2022). While Blockchain technology is about storing information in distributed nodes, BDDA and AI technologies can be used to analyse the information stored on chains (Moll and Yigitbasioglu, 2019). Blockchain can also facilitate inter-organisational accounting through smart contracting where simple contracts can be executed automatically without much human intervention, for example, payment can be automatically sent to the supplier when goods are received at the client end (notified by the GPS technology embedded in the product) (Iansiti and Lakhani, 2017).

IoT and allied technologies (such as 5G) will enable machine-to-machine communication without human intervention (Forbes, 2017). IoT is essentially a global dynamic network facility with self-configuring capabilities that are based on standard and interoperable communication protocols. In this network, all substantial and virtual items have specific coding and physical features that can be seamlessly linked through smart interfaces to achieve the sharing of information (Wu, Xiong and Li, 2019). In essence, IoT can play a big role in both inter- and intra-organisational transaction processing and therefore influence the data-gathering step of the accounting process (Wu, Xiong and Li, 2019). IoT can allow direct and automatic transaction processing between machines without human intervention. Several scholars have argued that IoT, along with Blockchain/DLT technology, can change the way contracts between firms are executed (Chanson et al., 2019). Again, BDDA and AI technologies could be integrated with IoT to carry out real-time analysis of transaction data generated and stored by IoT.

Our discussion in this sub-section on how different IBTs affect inter- and intra-organisational accounting processes is summarised in Table 16.1.

16.4 DIFFERENT DIGITAL STRATEGIES OF FIRMS

While the IBTs discussed in the previous subsection can transform business models and the value creation of firms, in general, and accounting processes, in particular, it is important to note that a firm's digital strategy plays an important role in deciding which technologies to adopt. A firm's digital strategy depends on both external factors (for example, maturity of IBTs, customer adoption and attitude towards IBTs, competitors adoption and attitude towards IBTs) as well as on firms' internal capabilities (for example, available expertise, the attitude of top management team, digital culture) (Barney, 2001; Barney, Wright and Ketchen Jr., 2001; Saarikko, Westergren and Blomquist, 2020; Verhoef et al., 2021). In this subsection, we focus on three digital implementation strategies identified and documented in prior literature.

A number of academic and practitioner-oriented literature points towards three phases/ types of digitalisation strategy that firms pursue: Digitisation, Digitalisation, and Digital transformation (Saarikko, Westergren and Blomquist, 2020; Verhoef et al., 2021). Digitisation is linked to the encoding of analogue information into digital formats. Digitisation is primarily focused on transforming tasks performed by individuals through automation of data storage (for example, using a database for storing customer information, using digital tools for documenting processes), processing (for example, using Excel and other programs for calculating net present value), and exchange/reporting/communication (for example, using email for exchange of information). In essence, digitisation is primarily concerned with the automation of tasks performed by individuals (such as order processing, the use of digital surveys for data collection, use of Excel for calculating payback periods) and not processes. Consequently, digitisation does not change the way firms create value but rather focuses on the use of technologies to reduce costs (Verhoef et al., 2021).

From an accounting perspective, digitisation focuses on improvement in data gathering in digital forms, localised (team or function-specific) data analysis through standalone tools, and discontinuous dissemination through email and other mechanisms. In terms of IBTs, the digitisation strategy does not require any of the five IBTs discussed in the previous section. It is important to highlight that most firms in developed countries have moved beyond the digitisation phase when it comes to their digital strategies. And given the propensity and widespread usage of digital technologies, newer firms established by entrepreneurs are getting more digitally savvy and sometimes even founded as digital native firms (where business models extensively rely on digital technologies).

In contrast to digitisation, the digitalisation strategy is linked to the alteration of existing business processes, such as communication with stakeholders (for example, mobile and web communication with suppliers and customers), distribution of goods and services (for example, offering real-time information on traffic congestion) or business relationship management (for example, integrating all suppliers and customers to offer a shorter time of delivery to customers). In doing so, firms focusing on digitalisation bank on optimising business processes through efficient coordination of tasks. Such optimisations are obtained by integrating data storage (for example, data warehousing), business-focused data processing improvements, and integrated communication and coordination. Moreover, digitalisation is not about saving costs but focuses on process improvements that enhance customer experiences. From an accounting perspective, digitalisation focuses on gathering process-specific data, process-specific data analysis, and process-specific continuous dissemination of data within the firm (Verhoef et al., 2021). Given the focus on process-specific data analysis and continuous dissemination of data, the digitalisation strategy can benefit from the deployment of three IBTs: Cloud Computing, BDDA, as well as AI technologies.

Digital transformation is linked to strategies where firms introduce IT-based business model innovations to transform how they create and capture customer value. Digital transformation is not about changing or integrating a few processes and tasks; rather, it is about reorganising the way a firm does business and eventually recoding a firm's business logic. Digital transformation is achieved by deploying IT technologies that transform a firm's business model. While some digital transformations focus on the intra-organisational level, advanced digital transformations require inter-organisational synergies where firms cooperate and create a networked business model built around information sharing and transaction processing (Kostić and Sedej, 2022). From an accounting perspective, digital transformation focuses on improvements in intra-organisational accounting processes while advanced digital transformation focuses on improving both inter- and intra-organisational accounting processes (Saarikko, Westergren and Blomquist, 2020). Given the focus on inter- and intra-organisational accounting processes, digital and advanced digital transformations can benefit from deploying all five IBTs discussed in the previous section. Of course, advanced digitalisation strategy can leverage more on technologies that facilitate inter-organisational integration of accounting processes, viz. Blockchain, Cloud Computing and IoT.

Our findings have been summarised in Figure 16.1. If we take a look at firms today in developed countries, we find that the digital strategies of most firms can be categorised either into the digitalisation or digital transformation phase. Again, it is important to note two important aspects here. First, early studies on digitalisation and accounting suggest that accounting processes in most firms lag behind in the extent of digitalisation (Granlund and Malmi, 2002; Granlund and Mouritsen, 2003; Dechow and Mouritsen, 2005). Several studies have attributed such lagging behind not only to poor training and knowledge of accounting employees but also to the scepticism and inertia of accountants and accounting functions in upgrading their knowledge (Caglio, 2003; Arnaboldi, Azzone and Sidorova, 2017; Arnaboldi, Busco and Cuganesan, 2017). Second, several studies have also highlighted that the digitalisation and digital transformation of accounting processes are hampered by a lack of guidance from regulators (Salijeni, Samsonova-Taddei and Turley, 2019, 2021). In recent years, many firms have created hybrid accounting teams comprising both accounting and IT expertise to promote digitalisation and digital transformation of accounting processes (Salijeni, Samsonova-Taddei and Turley, 2019, 2021; Eilifsen et al., 2020). However, such hybrid team formations also have impediments in terms of resistance from traditional accountants and dysfunction arising due to conflict between the two expert groups.

16.5   POTENTIAL INFLUENCE, OPPORTUNITIES AND CHALLENGES TO MCS

In the previous two subsections, we focused on understanding how IBTs and digital strategies of firms affect accounting processes, specifically transaction processing and information gathering, data processing and analysis, and data dissemination and reporting. The changes in the accounting processes ultimately impact the MCS since such systems are affected by different steps of the accounting processes. From a broader perspective, IBTs affect MCS directly by influencing the way employees perform their tasks or respond to IBTs. IBTs also facilitate

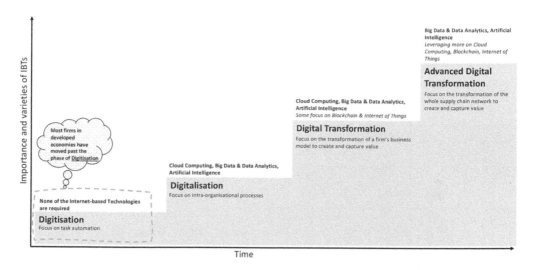

Figure 16.1 Firms' digital strategies and IBTs

new forms of observations (Flyverbom, 2022) and tracing of activities (Power, 2022), thereby directly influencing the development of new control technologies (for example, algorithmic control). IBTs indirectly affect MCS as well by changes in broader accounting processes where they enable inclusion of varieties of data (for example, financial and nonfinancial, structured and nonstructured) and deployment of advanced data processing and analysis for developing (new) control measures and real-time control of employee behaviour (see Figure 16.2). Building on how IBTs affect accounting processes, in this subsection, we focus on how different IBTs can influence different elements of the MCS, viz. cultural, planning, cybernetic, rewards/compensation, and administrative controls. We use the framework Malmi and Brown (2008) developed to structure our discussion.

16.5.1 Cultural Controls

Cultural controls refer to the values, beliefs, and social norms established in an organisation to impact/direct employee behaviour (Birnberg and Snodgrass, 1988; Dent, 1991; Pratt and Beaulieu, 1992). Value-based controls (Simons, 1995a, 1995b), Clan controls (Ouchi, 1979), and Symbols (Schein, 1997) form three important components of cultural controls.

16.5.1.1 Opportunities

IBTs can enable more transparency through easier and quicker access to decision-relevant information. Consequently, they can help implement value-based control that promotes transparency and open organisational cultures. IBTs can lower information asymmetry between different organisational units and hierarchies and thus also strengthen value-based controls focusing on flat or less-hierarchical organisations. IBTs can also facilitate the reengineering towards more responsive and autonomous organisational cultures such as 'agile' transformations. However, in professional expertise-oriented environments (for example, consisting of experts and professionals in healthcare, auditing, and law firms) where clan control (mutual monitoring) is the dominant approach to direct behaviour, managers (principals) often face

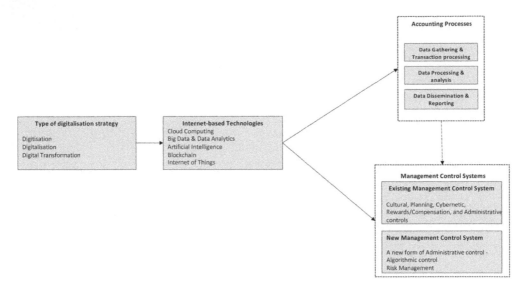

Figure 16.2   Impact of IBTs and firms' digital strategies on management control systems

legitimacy issues in exerting control over their subordinates – agents (Ouchi, 1979; Lebovitz, Lifshitz-Assaf and Levina, 2022). More often than not, managers' lack of legitimacy extends to the data, firms' information systems, or data-analysis approaches (Lebovitz, Lifshitz-Assaf and Levina, 2022). However, Kohli and Kettinger (2004) showed that the principal (manager) can influence the clan in such a situation. This is especially the case when the principal can improve the legitimacy of the information system through several processes: (a) by promoting influential agents to adopt the IBTs and then promote their usage among others; (b) by making IBT-enabled systems easily accessible and understandable to agents; and (c) by facilitating informed conversations among agents (Kohli and Kettinger, 2004). Deployment of the above-mentioned processes can transform clan control in clan-based environments to include data-driven and evidence-based reasoning facilitated by IBTs (Flyverbom, 2022).

16.5.1.2 Threats

IBTs can also create threats to cultural controls. Automation promoted by IBTs can negatively impact cultural control by threatening employees' jobs and/or identities. Employees' perceptions of threat can create anxiety and a breakdown of value-based controls around openness in favour of opacity and risk avoidance. Moreover, IBTs can instil a surveillance mindset among employees leading to a breakdown of communication between members of a group (Zuboff, 2015, 2019). Several studies have shown that employees perceived monitoring efforts by their superiors as stifling (Jensen and Raver, 2012; Martin, Wellen and Grimmer, 2016). A prominent example in this context is Amazon, where employees have complained that camera-based surveillance makes them feel dehumanised (Greene, 2021). While IBTs increasingly enable remote work, i.e. work from locations other than the office, remote work can create challenges for cultural controls. Remote work can create physical distances between employees which may reduce feelings of belongingness and emotional association with the team and organisation. It may also undermine common organisational values and norms, and reduce the impact of efforts to engineer values and symbols.

16.5.2   Planning Controls

Planning is an *ex ante* form of control (Flamholtz, Das and Tsui, 1985) that can allow different functional units of a firm to create long-term strategic plans as well as short-term and mid-term action plans (Malmi and Brown, 2008). Planning controls rely on directing employees' efforts and behaviour by setting goals for different functional areas as well as by establishing standards to be achieved in relation to the goals. Planning controls also facilitate the direction of employees' efforts and behaviour by highlighting the level of required efforts, and goal congruence through aligning goals across the functional areas of an organisation.

16.5.2.1 Opportunities

IBTs can help improve long-range (strategic and tactical) planning through enhanced strategic analysis by automating the financial evaluation of strategic options and facilitating quick and improved access to different strategic alternatives or scenarios. Strategic planning can benefit from the data-driven model of all five IBTs since they can provide detailed information on past actions and their impact on business goals (Möller, Schäffer and Verbeeten, 2020). Strategic planning can also benefit from understanding the future macroeconomic and socio-political environments (Merchant and Van der Stede, 2017). In this regard, IBTs can provide access to a variety of data – especially external to the firm (for example, forecasted political regime changes, market sentiment, customer reactions to newly launched products, or economic forecasts based on expert opinions collected through web crawling) – for informing the strategic planning processes. As a result, IBTs can improve goal setting, goal adjustments and variance analysis elements of strategic planning through automation.

Similarly, short-term action planning, especially in the production environment, can benefit from IBT-driven improved information flow within the firm as well as along the whole supply chain (both upstream suppliers and downstream buyers) (Slack, Chambers and Johnston, 2013). Again, since Cloud Computing, Blockchain, and IoT can promote both inter- and intra-organisational information sharing along the whole supply chain, they can create opportunities for improving action planning in firms (Kostić and Sedej, 2022). IoT through automatic transactions between machines and Blockchain/DLT through smart contracting can also streamline inter-organisational contracting and accounting processes, thereby creating opportunities for improvement in action planning across the supply chain (Iansiti and Lakhani, 2017; Garanina, Ranta and Dumay, 2022; Tyma et al., 2022). IBTs can also reduce efforts for data collection and processing of planning tasks by automatically filling in or suggesting prescribed scenarios and plans using driver-based model logic.

Automation, promoted by IBTs, can provide free time to employees, thereby directing employees' attention to tasks requiring human judgement and eventually facilitating more time to improve the planning processes (Raisch and Krakowski, 2020). Moreover, IBTs can also facilitate effective communication during the planning processes through various digital systems by enhancing representational clarity and increasing the access and availability of information. As a result, IBTs can facilitate goal congruence during the planning process by enhancing communicative efforts and participation.

16.5.2.2 Threats

On the negative side, IBTs, especially technologies such as AI and machine learning, can reduce employees' participation and understanding of the planning models by black-boxing the forecasting and other calculative techniques. Furthermore, automatic filling in of data and black-boxing in planning processes can also create risks linked to the quality of data and models (Anthony, Bechky and Fayard, 2023). Planning data autonomously collected and processed by IBTs from multiple sources can also make it difficult for employees to verify them independently. This can lead to inaccurate and ineffective plans if the input data is of low quality or the model logic is faulty (for example, mistaking correlation for causation or building a wrong forecast based on biased input data). Planning processes based on low-quality data and biased model logic can lead to faulty goal setting and variance analysis. Moreover, if the planning processes cannot be adequately understood by employees, IBTs can also lead to a breakdown of communication between different stakeholders during planning processes, thereby adversely affecting goal congruence.

16.5.3　Cybernetic Controls

Cybernetic controls are essential in creating accountability in most contemporary organisations. Green and Welsh (1988) note that cybernetic controls possess several elements: cybernetic controls allow for the measurement of a phenomenon; there are standards or targets attached to a phenomenon; there is feedback about whether targets have been achieved and there is the possibility to modify behaviour based on feedback. Cybernetic controls are closely linked to planning (target definition) as well as rewards and compensation (effects of feedback). Cybernetics control can be set up to work with financial performances, nonfinancial performances, as well as hybrid performance measurements comprising both financial and nonfinancial measures (for example, Balanced Scorecard). Budgets are one prominent cybernetic control mechanism that relies on financial measures of costs, profits, or investments.

16.5.3.1 Opportunities

The data-driven environment promoted by all five IBTs can improve the cybernetic controls in organisations where real-time information can be used to facilitate realistic target setting and continuous performance evaluations. IBTs can enhance the measurability of a phenomenon by making several difficult aspects measurable. In doing so, IBTs may allow measurements of aspects that may be difficult to measure and are more closely related to the impact employees are supposed to produce. This would create accountability measures that are 'accepted' as meaningful by employees. For example, some BDDA as well as AI technologies can help include advanced nonfinancial measures for cybernetic control purposes, such as employee or customer sentiment based on employees' or customers' posts on social media. Customer sentiments can be a direct and meaningful nonfinancial measure of customer satisfaction that can be gathered without asking customers to fill in surveys. Similarly, employee sentiments can be a direct and meaningful nonfinancial measure of managers' team management skills. It could be argued that IBTs can be especially powerful for nonfinancial and hybrid measurement systems because of their capability to access data available on the Internet/intranet and create non-standard measures (such as sentiments) for cybernetic control purposes. IBTs (especially AI and machine learning) can also support the design of complex measurement-oriented cybernetic controls (such as Balanced Scorecards) by identifying and testing for linkages amongst different goals and drivers.[5] These technologies can further help create more customer-driven nonfinancial measures (such as customer reaction to product launches, customer reaction to both positive and negative news concerning a firm's sustainability and corporate social responsibility initiative, etc.) to monitor and adjust firms' financial and nonfinancial goals (Möller, Schäffer and Verbeeten, 2020).

Including different nonfinancial measures can facilitate a holistic strategy for firms by enabling the monitoring and adjustment of firms' sustainability indicators (Kostić and Sedej, 2022). As discussed in the planning controls section, more data and better logics allow for improved target setting by providing improved feedforward information for decision-making and feedback information for accountability allocation (Power, 2022). This point will be further discussed in the Reward and Compensation Controls section. BDDA can also help in real time as well as improved visualisation of performance-related information dashboards (in Balanced Scorecards (BSCs)) through technologies such as Power BI (Bhimani and Willcocks, 2014). Real-time access to performance-related information can allow for quick reactions to potential deviations. Another example from the production context is also noteworthy. IoT technology can help implement better cybernetic control in production and inventory management through monitoring of machines' health on the production lines and automatic recording of inventory items. IoT technology can also help firms in improving customer services for heavy machinery since heavy machinery can be monitored through real-time information gathered by firms.

16.5.3.2 Threats
By giving more information control to IBTs, however, the risk of biased information and, eventually, biased target setting increases. As previously discussed, faulty input data and faulty model logic (correlation vs. causation) can misdirect employees' efforts by distorting the cybernetic control process. This problem is further exacerbated by the black-boxing of the analysis process, preventing employees from evaluating and validating their behaviour and efforts. Furthermore, if employees' trust in the data and information provided through IBT-enabled systems is lost, the cybernetic control process can break down entirely and trust in future IBT-based implementations can be reduced.

16.5.4   Reward and Compensation Controls

Reward and compensation controls are closely linked to cybernetic and planning controls by attaching rewards and or compensation to the achievement of goals (Flamholtz, Das and Tsui, 1985; Bonner and Sprinkle, 2002). They allow for the control of individuals' and groups' direction, duration, and intensity of efforts through monetary and nonmonetary rewards and compensation (Malmi and Brown, 2008). Generally, this control mechanism works in tandem with the target-setting process of planning and cybernetic controls. The targets set in planning and cybernetic controls are linked to financial and nonfinancial rewards and compensation. Furthermore, the feedback part of the cybernetic control systems informs the reward and compensation controls on the target achievement level. In summary, financial and nonfinancial rewards and compensation motivate people to achieve the targets set in planning and cybernetic controls. IBTs can impact the setting of rewards and compensation through similar mechanisms as discussed above in the planning and cybernetic controls section.

16.5.4.1 Opportunities
IBTs can improve the accuracy of reward and compensation setting by supporting improved planning and cybernetic measurement models, especially regarding the accuracy of target

setting (planning models) and timely measurement of target achievement (feedback of cybernetic control). Furthermore, by enhancing the understanding of what activities drive the target achievement (through monitoring) and whether those activities lie within the span of control of the employees (agents), IBTs can enhance the effectiveness of reward and compensation systems in steering the direction, duration, and intensity of employees efforts. BDDA and AI technologies can also help design better reward and compensation measures, both financial and nonfinancial, that can direct employees' behaviour (Möller, Schäffer and Verbeeten, 2020). This, in turn, can enhance employees' motivation and efforts in achieving their stipulated goals. In addition, IBTs can facilitate better variance analysis during target achievement evaluation by disentangling the antecedents for deviations. This can enhance transparency and accuracy in the reward process, allowing employees to better direct their efforts towards the stipulated goal.

One important way to reward employees nonmonetarily is by providing them with additional information. Such information provision, especially about employees' relative performance with respect to their peer groups, can also influence their efforts. For example, relative performance information (RPI) can affect effort by leading to positive and negative effects on employees' self-esteem. If one performs worse than one's peers, one can experience negative feelings, which one tries to avoid by performing better next time. Moreover, people try to manage their impressions in the eyes of their colleagues and therefore try to be seen as high performers. However, such positive effects of RPIs can only be achieved if the data is accurate and relevant for the employees. In this regard, IBTs can enhance data accuracy by giving access to more customisable data and better reference points. Finally, yet importantly, speedy access to real-time performance data can enable employees to take corrective action continuously, leading to more timely effort adjustments.

16.5.4.2 Threats

On the negative side, however, IBTs can lead to effort distortion if targets linked to rewards and compensation are set based on biased data or a biased prediction logic. This can be a grave problem, especially when the targets are complex and the process of achieving the target is not understood (for example, customer sentiment as a target for production employees) and hence cannot be challenged. As a result, employees cannot direct their efforts and can feel demotivated since the target is not within the span of their control. Finally, higher data transparency, especially in the context of RPI, can lead to toxic competition, sabotage of colleagues, and outright demotivation. As a result, higher transparency by IBTs can lead to unintentional effort misdirection. It is important to note that RPI provision can be unintentional as employees can seek data on their performance even without management's action, as it is human nature to judge one's competence and improve on it.

16.5.5   Administrative Controls

Administrative controls are controls geared towards directing employees' behaviour through organisational structures (Otley and Berry, 1980) such as functional specialisation or matrix structure; governance procedures (Abernethy and Chua, 1996) such as line of authority and reporting, coordination mechanisms; and policies and standards (Macintosh and Daft, 1987) (including action controls: standard operating procedures, physical and digital action constraints, manual and automatic pre-action reviews, and action accountability) (Malmi and Brown, 2008).

16.5.5.1 Opportunities

The data-driven approach and connectivity through the network (Internet) promoted by all five IBTs could definitely allow firms to manage dispersed teams in different geographies and therefore provide opportunities for creating more innovative and flat organisational structures and digitalised governance and coordination mechanisms. As highlighted previously (in the Cultural Controls section), IBTs can provide the basis for employee empowerment through flat hierarchies and reduced information asymmetries. According to self-determination theory, more autonomy can elicit higher motivation among employees, leading to effort enhancement. Organisational setups, such as those based on agile approaches, can be more effective when informational barriers are low, and management can commit to a coaching role rather than an effort-directing role. Moreover, automation of tasks and transactions promoted by the IBTs, such as Blockchain, IoT, and AI, could reduce the need for human intervention and action controls.

Furthermore, automation can also provide more free time to employees in accounting departments as well as other functional units to focus on complex tasks and problems requiring human judgement, eventually creating a 'virtuous cycle' for further innovation and improvement in MCS (Raisch and Krakowski, 2020). AI coupled with IoT can also be used for 'algorithmic control' to monitor, restrict, guide, and check employees' actions through cameras, other sensors, and digital access solutions (Kellogg, Valentine and Christin, 2020). Algorithmic control can facilitate the effective implementation of policies and procedures by preventing misadventures from employees. More effective preventive controls enabled by IBTs can also operationalise policies and procedures more efficiently and effectively.

16.5.5.2 Threats

On the negative side, excess algorithmic control, commonly dubbed 'surveillance' of employees (Zuboff, 2015, 2019), can also lead to tight control over employee behaviour, thereby demotivating employees and reducing productivity (Buhmann, Paßmann and Fieseler, 2020). Excessive controls can further reduce room for behavioural manoeuvrability, leading to inertia in the organisation and a lower propensity for employee-initiated innovation. Allowing for flat hierarchies and more employee autonomy can also lead to the breakdown of incumbent management practices and especially lead to the demotivation of middle management roles. Demotivation of middle managers, in turn, can lead to adverse behavioural consequences, such as reduced effort levels. Higher informational transparency can shift the power balance in the organisation from incumbent owners of information (for example, the finance and accounting function) to more data-driven organisational units such as data analytics or similar units (Power, 2022). Such shifts in the power balance could unintentionally change the effective organisational setup, threaten employees' identities, and eventually impact their motivation. IBTs have helped create flexible organisational structures dubbed the Gig Economy, where the mode of employment is purely contractual and transaction-based. While the Gig Economy can offer independence and flexibility to workers, it can also deprive them of 'economic rights' such as pension benefits (Vallas and Schor, 2020).

16.6   CONCLUSION AND FUTURE RESEARCH OPPORTUNITIES

In summary, the IBTs create opportunities by including different types of data for control purposes, viz. financial and nonfinancial, structured and nonstructured, interfirm, as well as data from the public domain. Data-driven control facilitates improvements in various MCS by including a number of nonfinancial indicators (for example, customer sentiment) during goal setting to direct employees' efforts. It also allows for timely effort and goal adjustment by facilitating real-time monitoring and feedback, and facilitating goal congruence through sharing of information. On the flip side, including various kinds of data creates issues with control over data and model quality (Möller, Schäffer and Verbeeten, 2020). MCS based on bad quality of data and models can misdirect employees' efforts and lead to bad consequences (financial as well as nonfinancial such as reputation loss) for organisations (Mittelstadt et al., 2016; Tsamados et al., 2022).

IBTs also pose threats to MCS since they pose a big challenge in terms of data governance and security (Möller, Schäffer and Verbeeten, 2020). Real-time connectivity makes IBTs vulnerable to hacker attacks (Cockcroft and Russell, 2018; Moll and Yigitbasioglu, 2019; Tsamados et al., 2022; CIMA, 2022). The hacking of personal data creates privacy concerns for both employees and customers. Hacking of personal data can also expose firms to legal risks under the EU's General Data Protection Regulation (GDPR) (Sørum and Presthus, 2020). Finally, IBTs enable machines to make autonomous decisions and thus create problems with determining who should be held ethically and legally responsible and liable for problematic decision-making – the firm using the machines or the firm developing the machine.

While we have discussed the impact of IBTs on MCS, primarily focusing on human agency, IBTs are also taking tasks away from humans. In doing so, IBTs are also creating problems with controlling tasks autonomously executed by them (Mittelstadt et al., 2016; Mokander et al., 2021; Power, 2022). AI (especially self-learning algorithms) may utilise data that contain existing societal biases for decision-making, leading to unethical decisions and ultimately resulting in bad consequences for organisations. For example, let us suppose a bank uses existing data on loan portfolios to train self-learning algorithms to decide the interest rate and risk for mortgages. If existing loan portfolio data reflect systemic biases present in a society, such as higher loan rates for marginalised and racialised sections of societies who live in poor neighbourhoods, then the self-learning algorithm will not be able to discern and remove these biases when trained using existing data. More specifically, since algorithms just use the correlation between input (factors such as income, existing debt, loan default rate, and so on) and output (interest rate, risk of clients) variables, they are unable to identify ethical biases. On the contrary, a self-learning algorithm may amplify such biases. Biased decision-making where banks discriminate against racialised and marginalised groups could fuel reputational loss and could also potentially result in legal penalties (Pager and Shepherd, 2008).[6]

Apart from traditional MCS, the five IBTs can also influence other control processes within firms (for example, risk management) (Mikes, 2009; Power, 2009; Soin and Collier, 2013). BDDA along with AI can be used to analyse and represent risks faced by organisations. Again, all kinds of financial and nonfinancial information, internal and external to the firm, can be used to understand the risks organisations face (for example, the sentiment of customers towards newly launched products such as vaccines or recall of faulty products, the level of societal outrage against firm's unethical practices). AI and BDDA technologies can also be used to detect fraud in real time (Sánchez-Medina, Blázquez-Santana and Alonso,

2017; PwC, 2021). Furthermore, advanced AI, such as machine learning, can help create new algorithms and methods for fraud detection. In addition, AI with advanced image and video processing capabilities can also help internal and external auditors in analysing recorded interviews for psychological clues that can help establish the veracity of accounts presented by the interviewees. Visualisation tools coupled with continuous updating features can help create self-updating real-time risk maps (two-by-two matrix heatmap representations of risks). Blockchain-based technologies can help understand the environmental risks of products (Iansiti and Lakhani, 2017; Gaur and Gaiha, 2020). For example, IBM Blockchain solutions have enabled identifying the sources of seafood and whether the seafood comes from a sustainable farming practice by bringing supply chain transparency.[7] Systemic risks of financial markets can also be continuously monitored by advanced AI and BDDA technologies.

Our approach presented in this chapter can be summed up in Figure 16.2. In this chapter, we offer an analytical approach that can help guide prudential digital approaches for accounting processes and MCS. In the chapter, we have focused on specific digital strategies of firms and five prominent IBTs that have been considered important by many academic and practitioner works. The approach adopted in this chapter has some limitations. Therefore, we propose further research on several aspects that can illuminate our understanding of the impact of IBTs on accounting processes and MCS. First, we promote further research on digital resources, digital capabilities, and implementation approaches that can play a significant role in chalking out a successful strategy for enabling the digital transformation of accounting processes and MCS. Second, since this chapter does not deal with role and identity changes for accountants, sources of inertia in accounting departments, and prioritisation approaches to successfully implement digital approaches in accounting processes and MCS, we promote further research on such topics. Third, we have primarily focused on traditional MCS, but IBTs also facilitate new forms of algorithmic control (Elmholdt, Elmholdt and Haahr, 2021) and measurements (Power, 2022) – we promote further research on such new forms of data-driven control. Fourth, since IBT-driven autonomous decision-making by machines and programs create challenges for controlling algorithmic behaviour and the agency of machines (Power, 2022), we promote further research on such topics.

NOTES

1. By IBTs, we mean all technologies that allow creating, storing, exchanging, analysing, and using information over the Internet in its various forms (Moll and Yigitbasioglu, 2019). The most notable advanced IBTs affecting management control systems are Cloud Computing, Big Data and Data Analytics, Artificial Intelligence, Internet of Things, and Blockchain.
2. By MCS, we mean cultural, planning, cybernetic, rewards/compensation, and administrative controls that guide and direct the behaviour of employees towards the strategic objectives, mission, and vision of a firm (Malmi and Brown, 2008). MCS rely on accounting processes, i.e. financial and nonfinancial information gathering, analysing, and dissemination to guide employees' behaviour (Bhimani and Willcocks, 2014).
3. A CGMA & AICPA sponsored survey of 5500 finance professionals representing 2000 firms in 150 countries conducted online in 2019.
4. 1750 US firms participated in the Management of an Accounting Practice (MAP) survey conducted by the AICPA in 2014.
5. Note also that self-learning algorithms may also create explainability problems in the sense that they just use correlations to create complex multi-level and multi-layered linkages between input (for example, activities drivers) and output variables (for example, firm's goals). Such linkages often

lack theoretical connections and can merely represent peculiar connections in the empirical data used in developing algorithms (Tsamados et al., 2022). Therefore, it is important to apply common sense and expert knowledge for scrutinising connections amongst goals and drivers of a BSC suggested by AI. This scrutinising can not only improve the explainaibility of BSCs but also make it easier to communicate the measure to employees, ultimately improving employees' acceptance of such hybrid measures.

6. Several studies in the USA in the aftermath of the Equal Credit Opportunity Act (1974) and the Community Reinvestment Act (1977) have found evidence of lesser discrimination against marginalised and racialised groups by banks and credit providers (Pager and Shepherd, 2008).

7. https://www.ibm.com/blockchain/resources/food-trust/seafood/.

REFERENCES

Abernethy, M.A. and Chua, W.F. (1996) A field study of control system "redesign": The impact of institutional processes on strategic choice, *Contemporary Accounting Research*, 13(2), pp. 569–606. Available at: https://doi.org/10.1111/j.1911-3846.1996.tb00515.x.

Anthony, C., Bechky, B.A. and Fayard, A.-L. (2023), "Collaborating" with AI: Taking a system view to explore the future of work, *Organization Science*, 34(5), 1672–1694. Available at: https://doi.org/10.1287/orsc.2022.1651.

Arnaboldi, M., Azzone, G. and Sidorova, Y. (2017) Governing social media: The emergence of hybridised boundary objects, *Accounting, Auditing & Accountability Journal*, 30(4), pp. 821–849. Available at: https://doi.org/10.1108/AAAJ-07-2015-2132.

Arnaboldi, M., Busco, C. and Cuganesan, S. (2017) Accounting, accountability, social media and big data: Revolution or hype?, *Accounting, Auditing & Accountability Journal*, 30(4), pp. 762–776.

Asay, H.S., Libby, R. and Rennekamp, K.M. (2018a) Do features that associate managers with a message magnify investors' reactions to narrative disclosures?, *Accounting, Organizations and Society*, 68–69, pp. 1–14. Available at: https://doi.org/10.1016/j.aos.2018.02.003.

Asay, H.S., Libby, R. and Rennekamp, K.M. (2018b) Firm performance, reporting goals, and language choices in narrative disclosures, *Journal of Accounting and Economics*, 65(2–3), pp. 380–398. Available at: https://doi.org/10.1016/j.jacceco.2018.02.002.

Barney, J.B. (2001) Resource-based theories of competitive advantage: A ten-year retrospective on the resource-based view, *Journal of Management*, 27(6), pp. 643–650. Available at: https://doi.org/10.1177/014920630102700602.

Barney, J.B., Wright, M. and Ketchen Jr, D.J. (2001) The resource-based view of the firm: Ten years after 1991, *Journal of Management*, 27(6), pp. 625–641. Available at: https://doi.org/10.1016/S0149-2063(01)00114-3.

Bharadwaj, A. et al. (2013) Digital business strategy: Toward a next generation of insights, *MIS Quarterly*, 37(2), pp. 471–482. Available at: https://doi.org/10.25300/MISQ/2013/37:2.3.

Bhimani, A. and Willcocks, L. (2014) Digitisation, "Big Data" and the transformation of accounting information, *Accounting and Business Research*, 44(4), pp. 469–490. Available at: https://doi.org/10.1080/00014788.2014.910051.

Birnberg, J.G. and Snodgrass, C. (1988) Culture and control: A field study, *Accounting, Organizations and Society*, 13(5), pp. 447–464. Available at: https://doi.org/10.1016/0361-3682(88)90016-5.

Böhme, R. et al. (2015) Bitcoin: Economics, technology, and governance, *Journal of Economic Perspectives*, 29(2), pp. 213–238. Available at: https://doi.org/10.1257/jep.29.2.213.

Bonner, S.E. and Sprinkle, G.B. (2002) The effects of monetary incentives on effort and task performance: Theories, evidence, and a framework for research, *Accounting, Organizations and Society*, 27(4–5), pp. 303–345. Available at: https://doi.org/10.1016/S0361-3682(01)00052-6.

Buhmann, A., Paßmann, J. and Fieseler, C. (2020) Managing algorithmic accountability: Balancing reputational concerns, engagement strategies, and the potential of rational discourse, *Journal of Business Ethics*, 163(2), pp. 265–280. Available at: https://doi.org/10.1007/s10551-019-04226-4.

Bullington, J. (2022) *Five technologies you need to explore to be employable.* Available at: https://mycareer.aicpa-cima.com/article/five-technologies-you-need-to-explore-to-be-employable-in-2020 (Accessed: 31 October 2022).

Buyya, R., Broberg, J. and Goscinski, A. (2010) *Cloud Computing: Principles and paradigms.* John New Jersey, US: Wiley and Sons.

Caglio, A. (2003) Enterprise resource planning systems and accountants: Towards hybridization?, *European Accounting Review*, 12(1), pp. 123–153. Available at: https://doi.org/10.1080/0963818031000087853.

Carlsson-Wall, M. et al. (2022) Exploring the implications of cloud-based enterprise resource planning systems for public sector management accountants, *Financial Accountability & Management*, 38(2), pp. 177–201. Available at: https://doi.org/10.1111/faam.12300.

Chanson, M. et al. (2019) Blockchain for the IoT: Privacy-preserving protection of sensor data, *Journal of the Association for Information Systems*, 20(9), pp. 1272–1307. Available at: https://doi.org/10.17705/1jais.00567.

Chenhall, R.H. (2003) Management control systems design within its organizational context: Findings from contingency-based research and directions for the future, *Accounting, Organizations and Society*, 28(2–3), pp. 127–168. Available at: https://doi.org/10.1016/S0361-3682(01)00027-7.

Chenhall, R.H. and Moers, F. (2015) The role of innovation in the evolution of management accounting and its integration into management control, *Accounting, Organizations and Society*, 47, pp. 1–13. Available at: https://doi.org/10.1016/j.aos.2015.10.002.

CIMA (2022) *What Big Data and AI mean for the finance professional.* Available at: https://www.cimaglobal.com/CGMA-Store/Finance-Futurist-Blogs/Blog-What-Big-Data-and-AI-mean-for-the-Finance-Professional/ (Accessed: 31 October 2022).

Cockcroft, S. and Russell, M. (2018) Big Data opportunities for accounting and finance practice and research, *Australian Accounting Review*, 28(3), pp. 323–333. Available at: https://doi.org/10.1111/auar.12218.

Cooper, D.J. and Robson, K. (2006) Accounting, professions and regulation: Locating the sites of professionalization, *Accounting, Organizations and Society*, 31(4–5), pp. 415–444. Available at: https://doi.org/10.1016/j.aos.2006.03.003.

CPA.com (2022) *The great accelerant: Thriving in the new 2025.* Available at: https://www.cpa.com/sites/cpa/files/2021-08/The-Great-Accelerant-Thriving-in-the-New-2025-cpacom-report.pdf.

Davenport, T.H. and Kirby, J. (2016) *Only humans need apply: Winners and losers in the age of smart machines.* New York, NY: Harper Business.

Dechow, N. and Mouritsen, J. (2005) Enterprise resource planning systems, management control and the quest for integration, *Accounting, Organizations and Society*, 30(7–8), pp. 691–733. Available at: https://doi.org/10.1016/j.aos.2004.11.004.

Dent, J.F. (1991) Accounting and organizational cultures: A field study of the emergence of a new organizational reality, *Accounting, Organizations and Society*, 16(8), pp. 705–732. Available at: https://doi.org/10.1016/0361-3682(91)90021-6.

Drew, J. (2015) *2014 MAP survey: Firms tech it up a notch.* Available at: https://www.journalofaccountancy.com/issues/2015/jan/2014-map-survey-cpa-firm-tech.html (Accessed: 31 October 2022).

Eilifsen, A. et al. (2020) An exploratory study into the use of audit data analytics on audit engagements, *Accounting Horizons*, 34(4), pp. 75–103. Available at: https://doi.org/10.2308/horizons-19-121.

Elmholdt, K.T., Elmholdt, C. and Haahr, L. (2021) Counting sleep: Ambiguity, aspirational control and the politics of digital self-tracking at work, *Organization*, 28(1), pp. 164–185. Available at: https://doi.org/Artn 135050842097047510.1177/1350508420970475.

Eurostat (2021) *Cloud Computing – statistics on the use by enterprises.* Available at: https://ec.europa.eu/eurostat/statistics-explained/index.php?title=Cloud_computing_-_statistics_on_the_use_by_enterprises#Use_of_cloud_computing_highlights.

Farrar, M. (2019) *Re-inventing finance for a digital world.* Available at: https://www.cimaglobal.com/Documents/Future of Finance/future-re-inventing-finance-for-a-digital-world.pdf.

Flamholtz, E.G. Das, T.K. and Tsui, A.S. (1985) Toward an integrative framework of organizational control, *Accounting, Organizations and Society*, 10(1), pp. 35–50. Available at: https://doi.org/10.1016/0361-3682(85)90030-3.

Flyverbom, M. (2022) Overlit: Digital architectures of visibility, *Organization Theory*, 3(3), 263178772210903. Available at: https://doi.org/10.1177/26317877221090314.

Forbes (2017) *The era of integrated IoT has arrived in the enterprise* Available at: https://www.forbes.com/sites/louiscolumbus/2017/09/29/the-era-of-integrated-iot-has-arrived-in-the-enterprise/ (Accessed: 31 October 2022).

Fountaine, T., McCarthy, B. and Saleh, T. (2019) Building the AI-powered organization, *Harvard Business Review*, 97(4), pp. 63–73.

Garanina, T., Ranta, M. and Dumay, J. (2022) Blockchain in accounting research: Current trends and emerging topics, *Accounting, Auditing & Accountability Journal*, 35(7), pp. 1507–1533. Available at: https://doi.org/10.1108/AAAJ-10-2020-4991.

Gaur, V. and Gaiha, A. (2020) Building a transparent supply chain: Blockchain can enhance trust, efficiency, and speed, *Harvard Business Review* [Digital article].

Granlund, M. and Malmi, T. (2002) Moderate impact of ERPS on management accounting: A lag or permanent outcome?, *Management Accounting Research*, 13(3), pp. 299–321. Available at: https://doi.org/10.1006/mare.2002.0189.

Granlund, M. and Mouritsen, J. (2003) Special section on management control and new information technologies, *European Accounting Review*, 12(1), pp. 77–83. Available at: https://doi.org/10.1080/0963818031000087925.

Green, S.G. and Welsh, M.A. (1988) Cybernetics and dependence: Reframing the control concept, *Academy of Management Review*, 13(2), p. 287. Available at: https://doi.org/10.2307/258578.

Greene, J. (2021) *Amazon's employee surveillance fuels unionization efforts: 'It's not prison, it's work'*, *Wsj.com*. Available at: https://www.washingtonpost.com/technology/2021/12/02/amazon-workplace-monitoring-unions/ (Accessed: 27 November 2022).

Herden, O. (2020) Architectural patterns for integrating data lakes into data warehouse architectures, pp. 12–27. Available at: https://doi.org/10.1007/978-3-030-66665-1_2.

Hobson, N.M. et al. (2018) The psychology of rituals: An integrative review and process-based framework, *Personality and Social Psychology Review*, 22(3), pp. 260–284. Available at: https://doi.org/10.1177/1088868317734944.

Holm, E.A. (2019) In defense of the black box, *Science*, 364(6435), pp. 26–27. Available at: https://doi.org/10.1126/science.aax0162.

Iansiti, M. and Lakhani, K.R. (2017) The truth about blockchain, *Harvard Business Review*, 95(1), pp. 118–127.

Jain, T. and Hazra, J. (2019) Hybrid cloud computing investment strategies, *Production and Operations Management*, 28(5), pp. 1272–1284. Available at: https://doi.org/10.1111/poms.12991.

Jensen, J.M. and Raver, J.L. (2012) When self-management and surveillance collide, *Group & Organization Management*, 37(3), pp. 308–346. Available at: https://doi.org/10.1177/1059601112445804.

Kellogg, K.C., Valentine, M.A. and Christin, A. (2020) Algorithms at work: The new contested terrain of control, *Academy of Management Annals*, 14(1), pp. 366–410. Available at: https://doi.org/10.5465/annals.2018.0174.

Kohli, R. and Kettinger, W.J. (2004) Informating the clan: Controlling physicians' costs and outcomes, *MIS Quarterly: Management Information Systems* 28(3), pp. 363–394. Available at: https://doi.org/10.2307/25148644.

Korhonen, T. et al. (2020) Exploring the programmability of management accounting work for increasing automation: An interventionist case study, *Accounting, Auditing & Accountability Journal*, 34(2), pp. 253–280. Available at: https://doi.org/10.1108/AAAJ-12-2016-2809.

Kostić, N. and Sedej, T. (2022) Blockchain technology, inter-organizational relationships, and management accounting: A synthesis and a research agenda, *Accounting Horizons*, 36(2), pp. 123–141. Available at: https://doi.org/10.2308/HORIZONS-19-147.

Lebovitz, S., Lifshitz-Assaf, H. and Levina, N. (2022) To engage or not to engage with AI for critical judgements: How professionals deal with opacity when using AI for medical diagnosis, *Organization Science*, 33(1), pp. 126–148. Available at: https://doi.org/10.1287/orsc.2021.1549

Li, F. (2008) Annual report readability, current earnings, and earnings persistence, *Journal of Accounting and Economics*, 45(2–3), pp. 221–247. Available at: https://doi.org/10.1016/j.jacceco.2008.02.003.

Li, F. (2010) The information content of forward-looking statements in corporate filings–a naïve Bayesian machine learning approach, *Journal of Accounting Research*, 48(5), pp. 1049–1102. Available at: https://doi.org/10.1111/j.1475-679X.2010.00382.x.

Lindebaum, D., Vesa, M. and den Hond, F. (2020) Insights from "the machine stops" to better understand rational assumptions in algorithmic decision making and its implications for organizations, *Academy of Management Review*, 45(1), pp. 247–263. Available at: https://doi.org/10.5465/amr.2018.0181.

Lumineau, F., Wang, W. and Schilke, O. (2021) Blockchain governance – a new way of organizing collaborations?, *Organization Science*, 32(2), pp. 500–521. Available at: https://doi.org/10.1287/orsc.2020.1379.

Macintosh, N.B. and Daft, R.L. (1987) Management control systems and departmental interdependencies: An empirical study, *Accounting, Organizations and Society*, 12(1), pp. 49–61. Available at: https://doi.org/10.1016/0361-3682(87)90015-8.

Malmi, T. and Brown, D.A. (2008) Management control systems as a package – Opportunities, challenges and research directions, *Management Accounting Research*, 19(4), pp. 287–300. Available at: https://doi.org/10.1016/j.mar.2008.09.003.

Martin, A.J., Wellen, J.M. and Grimmer, M.R. (2016) An eye on your work: How empowerment affects the relationship between electronic surveillance and counterproductive work behaviours, *The International Journal of Human Resource Management*, 27(21), pp. 2635–2651. Available at: https://doi.org/10.1080/09585192.2016.1225313.

Martin, K. (2019) Ethical implications and accountability of algorithms, *Journal of Business Ethics*, 160(4), pp. 835–850.

Merchant, K. and Van der Stede, W. (2017) *Management control systems: Performance measurement, evaluation and incentives*. Pearson.

Mikes, A. (2009) Risk management and calculative cultures, *Management Accounting Research*, 20(1), pp. 18–40. Available at: https://doi.org/10.1016/j.mar.2008.10.005.

Mittelstadt, B.D. et al. (2016) The ethics of algorithms: Mapping the debate, *Big Data & Society*, 3(2), p. 205395171667967. Available at: https://doi.org/10.1177/2053951716679679.

Mokander, J. et al. (2021) Ethics-based auditing of automated decision-making systems: Nature, scope, and limitations, *Science and Engineering Ethics*. 2021/07/08, 27(4), p. 44. Available at: https://doi.org/10.1007/s11948-021-00319-4.

Moll, J. and Yigitbasioglu, O. (2019) The role of internet-related technologies in shaping the work of accountants: New directions for accounting research, *The British Accounting Review*, 51(6), p. 100833. Available at: https://doi.org/10.1016/j.bar.2019.04.002.

Möller, K., Schäffer, U. and Verbeeten, F. (2020) Digitalization in management accounting and control: An editorial, *Journal of Management Control*, 31(1–2), pp. 1–8. Available at: https://doi.org/10.1007/s00187-020-00300-5.

Ng, A. (2016) What artificial intelligence can and can't do right now, *Harvard Business Review*, 9.

O'Leary, D.E. (2014) Embedding AI and crowdsourcing in the Big Data Lake, *IEEE Intelligent Systems*, 29(5), pp. 70–73. Available at: https://doi.org/10.1109/MIS.2014.82.

Otley, D.T. and Berry, A.J. (1980) Control, organisation and accounting, *Accounting, Organizations and Society*, 5(2), pp. 231–244. Available at: https://doi.org/10.1016/0361-3682(80)90012-4.

Ouchi, W.G. (1979) A conceptual framework for the design of organizational control mechanisms, *Management Science*, 25(9), pp. 833–848. Available at: https://doi.org/10.1287/mnsc.25.9.833.

Pager, D. and Shepherd, H. (2008) The sociology of discrimination: Racial discrimination in employment, housing, credit, and consumer markets, *Annual Review of Sociology*, 34(1), pp. 181–209. Available at: https://doi.org/10.1146/annurev.soc.33.040406.131740.

Power, M. (2009) The risk management of nothing, *Accounting, Organizations and Society*, 34(6–7), pp. 849–855. Available at: https://doi.org/10.1016/j.aos.2009.06.001.

Power, M. (2022) Theorizing the economy of traces: From audit society to surveillance capitalism, *Organization Theory*, 3(3), p. 263178772110522. Available at: https://doi.org/10.1177/26317877211052296.

Pratt, J. and Beaulieu, P. (1992) Organizational culture in public accounting: Size, technology, rank, and functional area, *Accounting, Organizations and Society*, 17(7), pp. 667–684. Available at: https://doi.org/10.1016/0361-3682(92)90018-N.

PwC (2021) *Harnessing the power of AI to transform the detection of fraud and error.* Available at: https://www.pwc.com/gx/en/about/stories-from-across-the-world/harnessing-the-power-of-ai-to-transform-the-detection-of-fraud-and-error.html.

Quattrone, P. (2016) Management accounting goes digital: Will the move make it wiser?, *Management Accounting Research*, 31, pp. 118–122. Available at: https://doi.org/10.1016/j.mar.2016.01.003.

Quattrone, P. and Hopper, T. (2005) A "time–space odyssey": Management control systems in two multinational organisations, *Accounting, Organizations and Society*, 30(7–8), pp. 735–764. Available at: https://doi.org/10.1016/j.aos.2003.10.006.

Raisch, S. and Krakowski, S. (2020) Artificial intelligence and management: The automation-augmentation paradox, *Academy of Management Review*. Available at: https://doi.org/10.5465/2018.0072.

Rechtman, Y.M. (2021) Can Robotic Process Automation improve quality control in audits?, *The CPA Journal*, August/September, pp. 69–72.

Saarikko, T., Westergren, U.H. and Blomquist, T. (2020) Digital transformation: Five recommendations for the digitally conscious firm, *Business Horizons*, 63(6), pp. 825–839. Available at: https://doi.org/10.1016/j.bushor.2020.07.005.

Sage (2018) *Accountants adoption of Artificial Intelligence expected to increase as clients' expectations shift.* Available at: https://www.sage.com/en-us/news/press-releases/2018/03/accountants-adoption-of-ai-expected-to-increase/ (Accessed: 31 October 2022).

Salijeni, G., Samsonova-Taddei, A. and Turley, S. (2019) Big Data and changes in audit technology: Contemplating a research agenda, *Accounting and Business Research*, 49(1), pp. 95–119. Available at: https://doi.org/10.1080/00014788.2018.1459458.

Salijeni, G., Samsonova-Taddei, A. and Turley, S. (2021) Understanding how big data technologies reconfigure the nature and organization of financial statement audits: A sociomaterial analysis, *European Accounting Review*, 30(3), pp. 531–555. Available at: https://doi.org/10.1080/09638180.2021.1882320.

Sánchez-Medina, A.J., Blázquez-Santana, F. and Alonso, J.B. (2017) Do auditors reflect the true image of the company contrary to the clients' interests? An artificial intelligence approach, *Journal of Business Ethics*, 155(2), pp. 529–545. Available at: https://doi.org/10.1007/s10551-017-3496-4.

Schein, E.H. (1997) Organizational culture and leadership (2nd ed.). San Francisco: Jossey-Bass.

Simons, R. (1995a) Control in an age of empowerment, *Harvard Business Review*, 73(2), pp. 80–88. Available at: https://doi.org/10.1016/0024-6301(95)91624-5.

Simons, R. (1995b) *Levers of control: How managers use innovative control systems to drive strategic renewal.* Boston: Harvard Business School Press.

Slack, N., Chambers, S., and Johnston, R. (2013). Operations Management. Harlow, England: Pearson Education Limited.

Soin, K. and Collier, P. (2013) Risk and risk management in management accounting and control, *Management Accounting Research*, 24(2), pp. 82–87. Available at: https://doi.org/10.1016/j.mar.2013.04.003.

Sørum, H. and Presthus, W. (2020) Dude, where's my data? The GDPR in practice, from a consumer's point of view, *Information Technology & People*, (ahead-of-print). Available at: https://doi.org/10.1108/ITP-08-2019-0433.

Statista (2021) *Number of Internet of Things (IoT) connected devices worldwide from 2019 to 2021, with forecasts from 2022 to 2030.* Available at: https://www.statista.com/statistics/1183457/iot-connected-devices-worldwide/ (Accessed: 31 October 2022).

Stein, M., Campitelli, V. and Mezzio, S. (2020) Managing the impact of Cloud Computing perspectives on vulnerabilities, ERM, and audit services, *CPA Journal*. Available at: https://www.cpajournal.com/2020/07/13/managing-the-impact-of-cloud-computing/.

Strauss, E., Kristandl, G. and Quinn, M. (2015) *The effects of cloud technology on management accounting and decision-making.* Available at: https://www.cimaglobal.com/Documents/Thought_leadership_docs/Management and financial accounting/effects-of-cloud-technology-on-management-accounting.pdf.

Tsamados, A. et al. (2022) The ethics of algorithms: Key problems and solutions, *AI & Society*, 37(1), pp. 215–230. Available at: https://doi.org/10.1007/s00146-021-01154-8.

Tyma, B. et al. (2022) Understanding accountability in blockchain systems, *Accounting, Auditing & Accountability Journal*, 35(7), pp. 1625–1655. Available at: https://doi.org/10.1108/AAAJ-07-2020-4713.

Vallas, S. and Schor, J.B. (2020) What do platforms do? Understanding the gig economy, *Annual Review of Sociology*, 46(1), pp. 273–294. Available at: https://doi.org/10.1146/annurev-soc-121919-054857.

Verhoef, P.C. et al. (2021) Digital transformation: A multidisciplinary reflection and research agenda, *Journal of Business Research*, 122, pp. 889–901. Available at: https://doi.org/10.1016/j.jbusres.2019.09.022.

Wu, J., Xiong, F. and Li, C. (2019) Application of Internet of Things and Blockchain Technologies to improve accounting information quality, *IEEE Access*, 7, pp. 100090–100098. Available at: https://doi.org/10.1109/ACCESS.2019.2930637.

Yermack, D. (2017) Corporate governance and blockchains, *Review of Finance*, 21(1), pp. 7–31. Available at: https://doi.org/10.1093/rof/rfw074.

Zapf, D. (2002) Emotion work and psychological well-being, *Human Resource Management Review*, 12(2), pp. 237–268. Available at: https://doi.org/10.1016/S1053-4822(02)00048-7.

Zuboff, S. (2015) Big other: Surveillance capitalism and the prospects of an information civilization, *Journal of Information Technology*, 30(1), pp. 75–89. Available at: https://doi.org/10.1057/jit.2015.5.

Zuboff, S. (2019) *The age of surveillance capitalism*. London, United Kingdom: Profile Books.

17. The impact of advancing technologies on the requirement for a human workforce in accounting

Victoria McKinlay and Julia A. Smith

17.1 AI AND ACCOUNTING

Technology is at the forefront of all businesses, generating new prospects and demanding superior technological skills from employees (Greenman, 2017). Therefore, it is crucial that business professionals are capable of working with and adapting to new technology. Artificial Intelligence (AI) and process automation are replacing the repetitive and redundant jobs carried out by accounting professionals (Stancu and Duțescu, 2021), allowing room to focus on more complex activities such as business advisory and analysis (Rîndașu, 2017). A study by ACCA (Association of Chartered Certified Accountants) and IMA (Institute of Management Accountants) (2015) concluded that new jobs are being created in the profession that will focus on information technologies, as well as accounting and finance. By evaluating and implementing controls involving systems and applications, accountants and auditors are expected to exhibit satisfactory skills for guarding sensitive information (Chorafas, 2008).

Although technology offers numerous benefits to organisations, it also poses threats to the requirement for a human workforce within businesses. AI is able to gather information and process data instantaneously, allowing information to be at our fingertips. With the constant developments of technology, this has resulted in fear that robots could, at one point, substitute the requirement for a human workforce. This is relevant, in particular, to the accounting industry, where the profession is now completely different to when the first computer was introduced. For this reason, this raises the question: will AI become so advanced that it will eliminate the requirement for a human workforce within the accounting profession?

There is great uncertainty about the potential of new technologies and whether or not they will have the capabilities to remove or reduce the workforce. A paper by Sion (2018) highlights that there is large concern amongst upcoming professionals, who are looking to proceed in a career as an accountant, as the level of employment may be at threat, due to the rise in the implementation of technologies. The current skills trainee accountants are being taught are likely not to match the desired skills that employers will be looking for in the future (Daylor and St. Amant, 2017), so the profession must keep up-to-date with the changes that are occurring, in order to achieve job security. Humans will need to be flexible and adapt to the changes, to ensure that there will always be requirement for them; if they fail to do so, the human race will fall behind technology. This research therefore aims to investigate the potential impact of AI and advancing technologies, by evaluating the relevant costs and benefits.

Accounting is viewed as being an artificial science due to its human activity and AI is connected with human activity. Accounting can be viewed as a perception of reality, which can explain the fact that it aligns symmetrically with AI being incorporated in the processes

(Johnston et al., 2021). The advancement of AI has progressed rapidly within our society over the past one hundred years and continues to challenge the limits of human creation. In businesses, accounting departments were the initial ones to significantly implement IT (Damasiotis et al., 2015) and they were the advocates behind the computerisation of workplaces. When new disruptive inventions arise in accounting, the Big4 accounting firms are normally the first adopters. Current studies have found that this is also the case surrounding AI, as the Big4 have been seen to implement AI to aid in the completion of audits and they also offer, through their consulting services, AI advice to their clients (Dowling and Leach 2014, KPMG 2017). Gray et al. (2014) showed that, since the 1990s, research on the use of AI in accounting has declined, and that there should be more research carried out on the use of AI techniques in the industry.

However, Sutton, et al. (2016) challenge this as they believe the application of AI remains predominant in accounting research and practice (cf. Johnson et al., 2021). The digital evolution within the accountancy profession has developed over time starting with accounting information systems (Ye and Hu, 2020), followed by ERP (Enterprise Resource Planning) systems, Big Data and cloud computing platforms (cf. Huttunen et al., 2019). Accounting tasks that, at one point in time, took hours or even days to complete, are now being completed with greater accuracy and speed, with the help of AI. Paper journals and ledgers as accounting information systems have been replaced by computer-based set-ups. Although this allowed for greater efficiency surrounding calculations, these accounting databases were solely used to store accounting transaction information and did not meet the requirements of decision-makers. To solve this difficulty, AI was introduced in order to work and react like humans. This included adding learning, planning, problem-solving and speech recognition into the existing accounting databases and making them intelligent machines. An aspect of AI that was developed in 1970 to perform expert human tasks and seize human knowledge is known as knowledge-based expert systems or expert systems (Thomas and Kleiner, 1995).

These expert technological systems enable computers to contribute to tasks that require human experts, for example, complicated planning and scheduling. They were made to solve complex problems and to offer the ability to make decisions, like a human expert. Expert systems are thought to be the most developed fragment of AI in accounting, which were made with the aim of advising the accountant on numerous matters (Emetaram and Uchime, 2021). They are predicted to completely alter the way in which humans contemplate problem-solving, as they now have access to up-to-the-minute data about any organisation. An expert system has the capability to replicate human activity and, over time, these systems are able to become more educated by learning more efficient ways to display information and a wide variety of processes (Moudud-Ul-Huq, 2014). They also improve decision-making, as the systems incorporate knowledge from more than one human expert (Emetaram and Uchime, 2021). Yang and Vasarhelyi (2008), for example, found that expert systems have a crucial role in financial accounting, for example, for cash-flow evaluations. Furthermore, O'Leary (2013) confirmed the use of these systems in taxation (for example, corporate tax accruals), showing they are a vital function in a variety of aspects in accounting.

In the late 1990s, the development of cloud computing platforms arose, with the central idea of allowing 'unlimited technological access to data', first mentioned in 1997 in a study by Giordanelli and Mastroianni (2010). The main idea behind these platforms was about keeping the organisation's confidential data in an external data storage centre, as a means of keeping data secure through a single platform and without the requirement of investing and installing further equipment. These platforms were seen to bring numerous benefits for companies who adopted them, generating competitive advantages. Along with large companies, smaller companies also need to contemplate transferring to the cloud in order to keep up with competitors and trade as efficiently as possible (Caldarelli et al., 2017). Benefits are seen to arise from an increased flexibility and mobility level within the company and economies of scale. As speed is now a crucial component of success for companies, the cloud computing platforms contribute by allowing real-time reporting and analyses. However, research has suggested that this leads to a potential loss of control of data (Marston et al., 2011; Armbrust et al., 2010), resulting in data privacy and security issues (cf. Badger et al., 2011; Caldarelli et al., 2017).

Cloud computing can increase a firm's competitive advantage, as it allows more flexibility, reliability and more available data. However, the reliability of cloud computing platforms depends on the hardware and software given by the provider (Marston et al., 2011; Fanning et al., 2012). The provider's reputation could also bring risks to the organisation as, if the provider has a bad reputation and the organisation is seen to be working with them, clients may move their business elsewhere (Almulla and Yeun, 2010). It is also seen that by moving to the cloud, organisations get benefits from the opportunity costs of freeing up IT admin time, which can be used to focus on core principals and helping to grow the business (Creeger, 2009). Although the adoption of cloud computing platforms can bring a variety of benefits to firms, there remain risks and disadvantages that could arise from implementation. Brender and Markov (2013) advise that firms consider these risks and disadvantages prior to any sensitive data being transferred to the cloud.

ERP systems were introduced to allow companies to streamline their operations, by integrating business data from different departments and functions within an organisation, for example, supply chain and financial data (Karsak and Özogul, 2009). These systems increased efficiency within organisations as all aspects of the organisation were integrated into one system that had centralised control. Financial reports were automatically created, using all the integrated information, as opposed to being created by groups of accountants, saving huge amounts of time (Sutton and Pfeffer, 2006). ERPs enabled accounting transactions to be traced to individual employees, helping to reduce error.

Although these systems allowed efficiency, they also needed to be connected to other applications, within the business. To solve this problem and eradicate the need to modify existing software, Robotic Process Automation (RPA), was created (cf. IBM, 2018), with the capability of carrying out various accounting procedures, for example, matching transactions to invoices, bank reconciliation and billing responsibilities. These robots can be programmed easily to complete repetitive, rule-based, large-volume jobs, the same way in which humans would, when analysing numerous documents, applications and systems (Cohen and Rozario, 2019; Emetaram and Uchime, 2021). By automating processes, efficiency within the accounting profession was increased, as accuracy was also dramatically increased. Thus more time could be spent on strategic tasks, alongside cost reduction. RPA has improved cycle time, increased productivity, regarding transaction processing, and has also elevated the workload by eliminating receptive tasks from employees (Kaya et al., 2019).

Within the accountancy profession, particularly in audit, one of the main technological developments that has been seen is the use of Big Data. This can provide reliable and efficient audit evidence, as it has the ability to search and integrate large sets of data (Andrew and Baker, 2019). It is categorised by volume, velocity, veracity and variety, complementing the traditional audit evidence from the past and allowing data to be handled efficiently, which is crucial in gathering audit evidence (Yoon et al., 2015). Big Data has transformed the value of the audit, with its use of population data (as opposed to sample testing) and its exploitation of real time data (ICAEW, 2017). Yoon, et al. (2015) also find that costs have been reduced within businesses as documents are being summarised automatically and showing more information than manual summaries would. However, Rouvroy (2016) argues that the production and application of Big Data creates new ethical and legal risks, along with privacy risks.

The process of decision-making is enhanced through AI by using decision support systems (DSS), which are prevalent in the auditing profession (Brown and Murphy, 1990). These improve the amount of data available, due to the fact that DSS have greater accuracy, are not biased and are objective. Hunton and Rose (2010) find DSS have become a crucial component of the audit procedure in the 21st century as they are able to provide numerous outcomes quickly, offering optimum proposals. In accounting firms, auditors employ DSS (for example, automated decision aids, electronic work-papers, predefined audit tests, expert systems) with the aim of sharing knowledge with trainee auditors (Hunton and Rose, 2010), as they allow novices to be trained to make expert-like judgements (Barrick and Spilker, 2003). They also use DSS to carry out tasks by identifying risks, evaluating red flags, planning the audit and determining which audit strategies to use (Dowling and Leech, 2014), and utilising data mining to discover patterns in large sets of data and turning raw data into useful information (Twin, 2019). However, Hunton and Rose (2010) explain that they can only discover problems that have been specifically programmed for detection; therefore, they can only identify irregularities that the auditor has predicted, and not what actually caused them (Yoon et al., 2015).

One of the clear benefits brought by AI is that computers are able to process information at a faster speed than humans, resulting in tasks being carried out quicker (Smigel, 2021). However, as seen in Moudud-Ul-Huq (2014), it is not always easy to use AI or expert systems in accounting databases, showing that training is crucial in allowing the benefits to be seen. The decisions made by AI are more reliable than those made by humans as they integrate a wider range of data sets and variables. Although, as discussed by Solaimani et al. (2020), this is only the case if the programmers are able to programme the machines correctly, without bias and errors. The decisions are also made much quicker than if humans made them, leading to greater efficiency within organisations (Solaimani et al., 2020). Zemánková (2019) questions whether this will reduce the requirement for labour in the industry. Machines are created to conduce monotonous activities and, compared to humans, they do not get distracted from their tasks. As seen in Jaslove (2017), the chief limitation of the human brain surrounds its processing speeds for data, which directly impacts its analysing abilities. However, these machines do not hold this limitation and can therefore deliver the company with analyses that are generally free of bias and error (cf. Solaimani et al., 2020; Janvrin et al., 2008). But contrast this with the view of Elon Musk that AI poses a greater danger than nuclear weapons, and that there needs to be a regulatory body assessing it (Zemánková, 2019).

Mukti and Yuniati (2021) discuss how the adoption of technology is crucial for the prevention of fraud. Further, Carpenter and Mahoney (2001) show that organisations employ software technologies as a fraud detection and prevention method. An example of this is explored by Bierstaker et al. (2006), who analyse the use of firewalls within software that can control unauthorised access to data, preventing hackers from discovering a company's Internet connection and accessing their data. Reepu (2020) suggests that AI can check public databases, in order to verify employee details, whilst also carrying out fraud detection. Shaikh (2004) discusses that not only does advanced IT help prevent external frauds, but it also helps to protect the systems from internal fraud. And PwC invested a significant amount of money into implementing AI for their audit that analyses every user, transaction, account and amounts entered, in order to detect any abnormal transactions (PwC, 2017). By not having any bias or variability, these systems are able to indicate possible fraud that has occurred.

This is also seen in Stancheva-Todorova (2018), where machines are found not to be influenced by power or money, unlike humans, who make decisions based on these factors. Marr (2022) finds that fraud costs organisations billions of dollars per year and organisations in financial services have costs of $2.92 for every dollar of fraud. However, with the implementation of AI, a large amount of the accounting work is carried out by computers, meaning employees only have to code in the instructions and evaluate it. And Jędrzejka (2009) discusses the fact that digital footprints can be monitored and traced, as a result of AI. Therefore, despite the fact that accounting systems cannot completely prevent financial fraud, as the systems still require humans to control them, AI allows it to be monitored to a degree.

Li (2020) discusses how, with the use of AI, workload may be eased and repetitive tasks are alleviated. This allows employees to focus on other activities that need greater human attention. Kaya, et al. (2019) adds that AI can improve the service offered by firms, as it enables production and accuracy to be increased, reduces the need for ongoing training and also decreases cycle times. AI therefore enables organising and gathering data to be easier, allowing businesses to forecast upcoming results and enhance their processes. This generates more precise data, resulting in improved operations and increased efficiency levels. Jędrzejka (2019) finds that recording accounting transactions demands consistency, great accuracy and, in some cases, manual handling of transactions that are repetitive. Prior to saving information into an accounting system, an employee is required to manually gather this data from various systems and then has to process all the data, which is open to errors, manipulation and is also extremely time consuming (Tucker, 2017). There could also be mistakes made due to fatigue; therefore, using AI systems, for accounting procedures, will dramatically save time and reduce human errors, resulting in the organisation becoming more efficient in their work (Chui et al., 2016). Although, if AI can carry out tasks free of error and fatigue, it creates a sense of worry that humans will no longer be needed.

In order to avoid audit failure and material misstatement, auditors are becoming more thorough and varied when collecting audit evidence (Yoon et al., 2015; Bell et al., 2005). New technologies allow audits to include a wider variety of data, both financial and nonfinancial, and have allowed enhanced audit efficiency, due to the automation of the audit process (Trompeter and Wright, 2010). It is crucial for accounting firms to utilise these advancements in technology, as if they do not, they could lose their customers to competitors who are providing more efficient and higher quality services. KPMG have been seen to invest in AI data analytics technologies, from IBM Watson, that are capable of increasing productivity, especially in their audit and assurance tasks (KPMG, 2017). The computers are programmed to draw conclusions from a large amount of financial and nonfinancial data, in order to communicate more effectively and deliver insights more quickly.

Data analytics is extremely important for auditors, as it allows them to easily establish the scope of the audit and perform a risk assessment. By digitalising the audit process, it has also allowed the security level to be improved, as the auditor can trace every file that was accessed using a digital tracker. Jędrzejka (2019) states that this ensures integrity and allows the requirements of the audit to be met. However, a member of the Public Company Accounting Oversight Board (PCAOB) suggested that there should not be an overreliance from auditors on AI technology, as it is not a substitute for the professional judgement, scepticism and knowledge of the auditor (Harris, 2017). Audit quality demonstrates the auditor's credibility and objectivity and is thought to be the foundation of auditing standards that govern the audit's engagements (FRC, 2020; Fanani et al., 2020). However, due to coding, on which basis AI is programmed, there is concern that bias may be introduced (Solaimani et al., 2020; Janvrin et al., 2008). However, Albawwat and Frijat (2021) found that auditors perceived all types of AI to considerably contribute to the audit quality, but that quality varies according to the type of AI.

As well as the profound benefits brought by the evolution in emerging technologies and AI, the Big4 companies have also highlighted the risks that could arise from the adoption of these technologies (Rîndaşu, 2017). For this reason, the professional bodies, such as, ACCA and IMA, released guidelines and other tools, like Terrain Intelligence, based on centralised platforms including Big Data, which enable organisations to evaluate and monitor their cyber-security risks (PwC, 2016). Along with cybersecurity risks, there are also risks surrounding the reputation of a firm, which could be exceptionally damaged if AI is not used in the correct way.

AI may harm the firm's reputation if not used appropriately. Jędrzejka (2019) points out that there are no regulatory standards for automated robots, which may lead to them inadvertently disrespecting laws. If it was seen that a firm was engaging in fraudulent practices, this would have a direct impact on the way their clients would view them, leading to the firm losing the trust of these clients and also the public. Yoon (2020) shows that human beings are able to make judgements that are ethically correct and can take full responsibility for the consequences of their decisions; however, this cannot be anticipated from machines. However, Wynsberghe and Robbins (2019), assume that, in some cases, machines are able to be ethical agents, who are accountable for the actions they take. Luo et al. (2018) states that there must be relevant policies and regulations put in place in order to guide and encourage the use of AI in the accounting profession. Both sides of the argument are extremely relevant, and despite the fact technology is advancing at an uncontrollable pace, it may be seen in future years that a regulatory framework will be developed surrounding the ethics of AI (cf. Stavrakakis et al., 2021).

McCarthy and Outslay (1989) highlight the challenge of implementing advanced technologies, including investments in research and development; hardware and software; cybersecurity; and renewing original systems to keep up-to-date with current legislation. Stancheva-Todorova (2018) state that businesses have to be persuaded that using this technology will improve the performance of the work and the quality of it. Luo et al. (2018) also discuss the fact that due to the personalised structures of AI, organisations require an immense number of recourses, in the preliminary implementation of the systems, creating high costs for the business. Richard Anning, Head of the Tech Faculty at ICAEW, states that there is a challenge surrounding the immense rise in the level of supplies needed to implement AI, regarding individuals with applicable experience (ICAEW, 2021).

A prediction by the Boston Consulting Group forecasts that up to 25 per cent of jobs will be substituted by robots or software by 2025, with accounting professionals being included in the top 10 per cent of occupations that are most likely to be computerised (Peccarelli, 2017). AI can work faster, longer and smarter than humans. It can automatically process a large number of transactions, which, in turn, saves employees time for simple day-to-day tasks like billing, reconciliation processes and processing transactions (PwC, 2018). Jaslove (2017) states that computers can understand information in a superior way compared to humans and make predictions that are usually unnoticed or disregarded by the human eye.

Jędrzejka (2019) believes that the accountant's role in the future will be shaped by two key matters: working alongside automation and having more time. The accountant's biggest asset will become their professional expertise, for example, applying their knowledge to meet the obligations of disclosure practice. ICAEW (2017) believes the future will consist of an integration of technology and humans, as it is thought that RPA is not substituting the accountant, but rather, progressively modifying the job (Kaya et al., 2019). Smigel (2021), does not believe AI will replace human intelligence, but does agree that it is best used in repetitive tasks and allows accountants to focus on activities that require creativity and problem-solving.

Rîndaşu (2017) and Sion (2018) back the idea that robots will, in the future, substitute the accounting professional's role through the use of their cognitive superior memory, entirely eliminating numerous responsibilities from the profession. However, although these technologies have effective control procedures, to suggest that AI provides good judgement over humans is debatable. Machines make decisions on exclusively data alone (Jaslove, 2017). However, Parcells (2016) believes that if robots were to take over another aspect of accounting, accountants would transform themselves into fraud and compliance experts, business advisors or technology leaders, showing that the role of the accountant would not be lost, but rather, adapted. Jędrzejka (2019) agrees that the accountant's role will focus more on data interpretation and analysis, to make better decisions, as opposed to focusing on audits, preparing reports and accounting operations.

We have seen that AI has already been introduced in auditing, with high accuracy and speeds, for example, to test revenue and payroll (ICAEW, 2017). RPA has been seen to independently lead internal audits, which could result in auditing becoming commoditised (Cohen and Rozario, 2019). A report published in 2016 by McKinsey concluded that AI could automate 86 per cent of accountants, bookkeepers and auditing clerks' tasks (Mohammad et al., 2020). However, although AI can be effective, humans are still required for the remaining 14 per cent, showing that humans are still important and needed within the profession.

A British company, Engineered Arts, developed a human robot, known as 'Ameca', the most advanced human-shaped robot in the world (engineeredarts.co.uk, 2022). It has cameras in its eyes for face detection, can perform facial movements and can speak back to you. It was designed in order to be a platform for development into robotic technologies in the future. Engineered Arts have stated that 'robots aren't AI and AI isn't only about robots' (engineeredarts.co.uk, 2021). Although AI is used within the robots, for speech recognition and facial recognition, it is just computer code and is not as intense as the robot. While the robot can speak back to humans, Engineered Arts have stated that 'you were speaking to a human through a telepresence software', showing human intelligence will always be ahead of AI. As the robots cannot actually think or reply for themselves, we can hope that accountants are safe within the profession, as technology has not yet been developed to the extent that robots can think for themselves.

17.2   DATA AND ANALYSIS

In order to explore the issues raised in the review of the literature above, we utilised interview-based techniques to gather our data (Yin, 2003) from meetings at Johnston

Carmichael and PwC. Johnston Carmichael is the biggest independent accountancy firm in Scotland. It is a well-established mid-tier firm that has rapidly developed over the past years, with anticipated future growth. As it develops, Johnston Carmichael has been adopting new approaches and processes, in particular AI and advancing technologies. PwC is one of the Big4 leading accountancy firms within the industry. Due to their immense size and multinational operations, they need to ensure they have the most efficient but effective processes implemented. These require a large degree of technology and AI, in order to trade at a high level and offer the best services to their clients. A questionnaire was developed to interview individuals at different hierarchy levels in each organisation about their thoughts on AI and its impact on the accounting profession. The issues of research were raised by asking open-ended questions, which were easily comprehended to prevent misunderstandings (Ryan et al., 2002). Their roles include: Audit Manager (AM), Audit Senior (AS) and an IT Expert (IT). Through limitations of space, illustrative quotes have been selected for presentation, and are included in Tables 17.1 to 17.5, with associated discussion in the narrative.

17.2.1   Ethics and Judgement

Compared to a human workforce, there is a lack of consciousness and awareness within technology. Humans are able to make fair and justified judgements, however, the same cannot be said for machinery. As seen in the response of the Audit Manager (cf. Table 17.1), judgements require experience and knowledge, which cannot be formulated into a machine. They also make the point that computers cannot observe behaviour, which is important within the industry, as the way someone behaves when being questioned about discrepancies within the accounts can uncover fraudulent behaviour. From the Audit Senior's response, this is exemplified by the fact that, as an auditor, you are constantly seeing new problems and situations, showing that AI and advancing technologies would not be able to handle this; they are not programmed to be able to deal with new situations. It can be said that technology is capable, when it comes to making decisions, however, it lacks ethical values that professionals have. The decision to eliminate the human workforce from advisory roles may be reconsidered if there is a progression in the ethical and moral values; however, even if this occurred, it still does not seem ethical to completely remove human interaction from advisory roles and enable computers to finalise documents and decisions. Adoption of these technologies would be self-fulfilling, from a cost-benefit evaluation, offering a motivation for governing entities to deliberate the operation of unethical technologies due to institutional theory. However, as seen from the responses, it is not believed that sentient machinery will ever reach the point where the requirement for humans is not needed. This type of machinery is regarded as being theoretical, rather than possible. Society has a rigid and narrow perspective on the possibilities for developments and research in the future.

It is also apparent that the responsibility for AI making errors is considered to be the fault of humans, as humans were the initial programmers of the machines, so the technology is only as smart as the humans who were responsible for the initial programming of it (Allen et al., 2005). From the Audit Senior's response, it is clear that humans are using AI at their own risk and need to check for errors when using it, and that it is the responsibility of humans to prevent misuse. The respondents, who work within the industry, do not believe that AI and advancing technologies can completely eliminate the accounting professional; human judgement and experience are crucial within the profession to ensure the most informed and

Table 17.1   Evidence on ethics and judgement

Q1. Do you think there are any ethical issues surrounding AI and humans being the programmers?	
"I don't see ethical issues as such – the only real ethical issues I think are around AI taking over the job of an accountant and making people redundant, however I do not see this happening to a large degree".	AM
"Not generally, unless software/programming was made to record false information and not operate in the way it was supposed to".	AS
"If we are referring to the machine learning subset of AI then yes. As the rules are presented by humans for the machine learning process then it would be unethical if this was a machine leaning code which monitored the human who programmed it. If we are referring to a true AI, then yes but for a different reason. The amount of data needed to train an AI is vast so manipulating it is difficult. However, the goals of the AI are still set by the user who may have a cognitive bias for what is expected of the AI and misses an independent view of what is expected. Therefore the AI simply follows their flawed logic from the start. Again, I suppose the ethical issue is one of independence."	IT
Q2. Do you think AI is capable of making reasonable and justified judgements?	
"No – judgements require experience and background knowledge around information. This is something which cannot be formulated. A computer will never be able to pick up on personal behaviours that a human can (such as a shifty, uncomfortable client when questioned about how they have incorrectly accounted for something.)".	AM
"Only to a certain level relating to how they have been programmed. The issue is that with the nature of different clients and audit work, you are always faced with new situations and problems. It is uncertain how AI would cope with unique situations to be able to provide a reasonable and justified judgement each time".	AS
"Well, that is the definition of AI, so yes i.e. if you have AI then you have a system which is capable of making reasonable and justified judgements. Whether we ever achieve AI in accounting is another question. There are already AI's for other non-accounting processes which do give reasonable and justified judgements. Machine learning is readily available for accounting, but this doesn't make judgements as such, only obeys rules and cannot readily deal with something it doesn't have a rule for. A true AI requires a lot of processes to train it to interpret what it should do and there simply may not be enough transactional information, even in the biggest company, to train an AI to cover all aspects of its accounting processes. Having said that, some aspects … may be focused enough with enough data to create a true AI to … judge if an action is a fraud or not".	IT
Q3. Do you think the responsibility of AI making errors is on humans?	
"AI is only as smart as the person/people responsible in using it, and as such it is susceptible to making mistakes like humans can. It is on humans if they use AI without carefully monitoring and checking for mistakes".	AM
"AI would still require human interception for controls and to monitor the use of it to ensure it is operating effectively. Therefore, such errors could be considered responsibility of humans if they fail to intercept and involve themselves with AI and instead rely on it too much".	AS
"Yes – this is why all AI's and machine learning tools still require human interpretation – especially when training the AI. After that the AI may make decisions with 99 per cent confidence or maybe just 50 per cent confidence which should require review. The more training the AI gets the less prone to error it would become but if the scope of its environment changes then this error margin would also change. Machine learning similarly would require the human user/programmer to make the right initial interpretations and properly define the scope of its actions (note – there is some excellent reading from Arthur C Clark's I Robot (not the film) which looks at how AI can go wrong by simply following the rules as defined)".	IT

ethical decisions are being made. Humans have responsibility for the initial programming of rules-based systems and inputting data in machines. Therefore, mistakes, handwritten data and misinterpretations are down to the relevant personnel ensuring the machines have the correct information programmed into them.

17.2.2 Fraud Reduction and Security Risks

Overall, it is clear the respondents believe that AI and technologies will help reduce the number of fraud cases and help detect numerous scandals (cf. Table 17.2). This is done through the capability for eliminating human interaction, enhancing time efficiency, enabling transactions to be audited and using pattern recognition, which in turn helps to uncover suspicious and unusual transactions, using data mining. Access can be restricted through the use of technology and extra monitoring can be implemented for security, in order to decrease fraud cases. Technology can also be used to enable a segregation of duties leading to individual access restriction in order to reduce financial fraud, as everyone has their own distinct privileges to specific areas (Emetaram and Uchime, 2021). Testing has progressed from sample testing to population testing (ICAEW, 2017). This enhances the reliability of testing and, from the IT Expert's response, it can be seen that if individuals know that machines are able to check every transaction, this will prevent them from carrying out fraud.

The Audit Manager mentions Blockchain technology as a way of preventing hacking which is also seen in Bierstaker et al. (2006). Implementing these firewalls allows unauthorised access to data to be controlled, along with preventing hackers from uncovering a business's Internet connection and accessing data. Although technology can help prevent fraud, it will not be completely mitigated. This shows that technology should not be fully relied upon in firms, as discussed by the IT Expert, where it is stated that there will also be a human required to intervene in order to confirm the conclusion.

Hackers are attracted to cloud computing platforms, as immense amounts of data are being stored in one place. From the respondents, it is seen that this is a big threat and if the hackers were able to get access to these platforms, this would cause numerous problems for a firm.

Table 17.2   Evidence on fraud and security

Q4. Do you believe that AI will reduce the number of fraud cases and help uncover the number of scandals?	
"Yes – In my line of work we can use AI to process large amounts of data at one time. This means that AI can scan systems and search for irregular reporting, e.g. entries posted outside normal working hours; journals to accounts not normally used; round numbers etc. There will still be a human element involved in uncovering fraud however AI can help us get there".	AM
"From my experience in audit, one of the main fraud risks is management override with the risk that employees and management manipulate financial information. If AI replaced all manual input by humans for e.g. year-end processing of journals, this could potentially reduce the threat of fraud. AI can help identify unusual transactions or journals with specific criteria e.g. rounded amounts or journals with amounts over materiality threshold. Another main risk is where a business is heavily cash based or have assets which provide opportunity for theft. AI will not necessarily reduce these risks".	AS
"Yes, there are some sort-of-AI programs in place which monitor and learn standard transactional patterns and, based on various factors, can detect and sometimes predict when an event is likely related to fraud. They always require a human intervention to confirm the conclusion and only really work on large scale scenarios (like point of sale transactions on tills across multiple stores over a year rather than a small business doing a few transactions a year). In many ways the main benefit will be prevention, as if people know they are faced with the possibility of a machine reviewing their every transaction looking for fraud they are less likely to try to fool it".	IT
Q5. Do you think there are any security or confidentiality risks attached to Big Data or Cloud Computing Platforms?	
"Yes – given the large amounts of data now stored online through maintaining AI there are increased risks of people trying to steal this data. This can be helped through technologies such as Blockchain".	AM
"Potentially, given the large volumes of data and information requested and obtained as part of our audits".	AS
"Yes – definitely yes. There are whole standards and certifications which exist just to address these issues. It's a huge industry in its own right".	IT

These include issues that would impact the company's future and reputation (Addis and Kutar, 2018). It is clear Big Data enhances the reliability and efficiency of practices within the profession, but it does come attached to risks, for example, data leakage, which can also be extremely damaging for a firm.

17.2.3   Recruitment and Employment

Grossmann (2005) discusses the fact that the adoption of RPA has a strong connection with the rate of unemployment, as tedious tasks are being replaced with automation. This also creates an aspect of inequality as the highly paid jobs, which have a high degree of responsibility, are not threatened, at the moment, by technology. However, there is a declining need for individuals to carry out repetitive tasks like bookkeeping and journal entries, as seen by the Audit Manager's response (cf. Table 17.3). This removal of menial tasks could result in more focus on human evolution, showing that the employees who are adaptive will benefit the most. Within the hierarchy of a business, the lower levels will be the first to become obsolete due to AI and advancing technology. It has already been seen that automation has taken over standard tasks, but lacks the ability to undertake more complex tasks at the other end of the hierarchy, due to the sentient component.

From the responses, it can be seen there is a common opinion that the more day-to-day and repetitive jobs are the most likely to become obsolete. Although these jobs can be replaced, the role of managers, for example, cannot yet be replaced by automation, as technology has not been developed to the extent of having brain intelligence, which is current within a human workforce (Huimin et al., 2018). Human input is still necessary within the accounting profession, as machinery is not yet sentient and is incapable of making reliable and justified decisions. The Audit Senior highlights the requirement for human interaction to still be present within the profession, which could explain why the more 'superior' individuals in companies are not worried about their job becoming obsolete. In positions of lower power, it can be seen that one-sided information is being received and managers express biased understandings, enabling technology to decentralise procedures that are established. Management do this out of self-interest and are motivated by greed and money. This enables technology to eliminate standard jobs, presenting the power that technology has. However, from the answers above, it is apparent that the participants are aware of the threats that are attached to AI and technologies, which should be the case for all existing and upcoming professionals.

In line with the IT Expert's answer, it can be seen that the accounting role is adapting in line with the developments in technology. In those jobs that cannot be replaced, it will be seen that the individuals within these roles will have to learn to adapt and keep up with changes, as opposed to being replaced by the advancements. Those who excel at problem-solving and data analytics, for example, will be attractive to employers as they will be needed to ensure that the cloud and other software is running efficiently. The Audit Manager has already seen a decline in the number of individuals in audit jobs, but has seen an increase in the number of jobs in technology fields, like data audit. Although there has already been a decline in jobs in the industry, there has also been an opening for new opportunities, that include the use of technology. This develops the argument that the professional will be required to adapt with the changes, if they want job security. All participants agree that the role is adapting rather than becoming obsolete. The IT Expert highlights that there will be a change in skill set required from accountants, as opposed to the number of accounts needed. The Audit Senior also builds

Table 17.3   Evidence on recruitment and employment

Q6. How will AI impact the upcoming jobs for accountants and have you seen a decline in your workforce due to AI?	
"AI has led to slightly less jobs in the audit sector, and more jobs in technology fields such as Data audit".	AM
"Eventually the number of jobs may reduce; however, at present, there has not been a significant decline in number of employees. There has however been more of a shift towards focus on data and revised ISA requirements and focus on quality".	AS
"It will change the skill sets required for accountants rather than the amount of accountants required. With advances in technology, businesses are becoming more complex which require more accountants in general to deal with the workload. Machine learning and process automation can address this increase in workload but the supervisory nature of these technologies still require knowledgeable people to operate and interpret them. To date, there is some machine learning and automation in accounting practices but next to no proper AI systems in operation, so we've seen no reducing in workforce for this reason (yet)".	IT
Q7. Do you think the requirement for a solid understanding and skills surrounding AI will become a necessity in the recruitment process?	
"Not a necessity just now – although a basic knowledge of Excel, simple accounting softwares will still help candidates in the recruitment process".	AM
"[I've] been seeing lots of people coming in who lack basic computer skills and due to systems for audit being electronic rather than paper files this is key for the efficiency and smooth running of the audit. When AI becomes more prominent in the industry, this could be more linked with recruitment and candidate requirements".	AS
"I think they will only need a high-level understanding – in the same way that we would expect accountants to be able to use Excel, not program their own spreadsheet software (although it would be nice if they could too). Any AI tools or machine learning used which are advanced enough to use yet secure enough to rely on will be so tightly wrapped up in IP that the average user will be a front-end operator only. They will need some basic understanding of training an AI/ Machine learning tool within given parameters, but the intricacies will still be in the control of dedicated specialists and programmers. "Rogue" AI or machine learning programs (those developed in-house) will be unlikely to be seen as independently reliable and secure".	IT
Q8. Do you think the need for accountants is under threat due to the rise of artificial intelligence?	
"Generally, yes there will be a less of a need for the more day-to-day accountants, such as bookkeepers and accounts assistants due to the repetitiveness of the tasks involved, such as putting through simple journal entries etc".	AM
"While over time as AI develops and its presence increases in the profession, it will never entirely replace the need for accountants. AI is programmed whereas humans have the creativity and can provide adaptability to solve problems and new challenges".	AS
"Machine learning is having an impact on the role of the accountant, but as every business is different, every code will need to be adapted to suit that business and the supervision of this will need to be the responsibility of the accountant (including adaption of new accounting regulations as well as how unusual exceptions should be dealt with)".	IT
Q9. Do you think repetitive, but, critical roles within organisations, for example, bookkeeping, will be obsolete, due to AI doing it in a more efficient way?	
"Where there are similar patterns in the way a company records transactions, such as recording sales or expenses then yes these will (if not have) become obsolete. Artificial intelligence has led to accounting systems learning a company's more regular transactions and knows how to record them. This means that the majority of businesses can purchase software allowing a reviewer to go onto the system and change any entries which are outwith the normal course of business. This removes the need for old fashion bookkeeping methods of using physical 'sales books' or 'purchase books'".	AM
"For standard processes such as bookkeeping, there has already been a change in the industry as this has been computerised. However, there is still some manual input required for controls to ensure these are working correctly".	AS
"It's more likely these minor repetitive tasks will be obsolete due to process automation rather than machine learning or AI. Mobile phones scanning invoices and the process automation applying the correct accounting treatment automatically is possible now and is fully rule-based rather than requiring any complex (and comparatively very expensive) AI to make a decision or judgement call. Using machine learning in such cases may seem like overkill to apply a complex solution to a simple process which can be solved through basic automation".	IT

on the argument, discussed in the literature review, that there will be more focus on the quality of service provided and also a greater focus in areas that generate more value for the business.

It is also clear that the need for upcoming accountants to understand AI and technologies will be beneficial and desirable. From the Audit Supervisor's answer, where it is discussed that due to the audit being electronic rather than paper files, there is already a need for a basic understanding of computer skills. This is essential for the audit to be as efficient as possible, and if individuals do not hold a basic understanding, this can hold up the process. A predominant issue is that trainees lack basic computer skills. This leads to the question of how these trainees can gain underlying skills and a solid understanding of these processes. For this reason, there should be a requirement for the education system to adapt with the changes in the nature within the profession. It may be that universities will start to implement more AI and technology learning into their curriculum, in the future. As AI becomes more predominant in the upcoming years, the requirement for skills in this area will become more desirable. By including this in the curriculum, this will not only allow students a better chance of a job but will enable students to gain confidence within this area, resulting in them knowing what to do when they start in a firm.

17.2.4   Potential Threats

All respondents believe that smaller accounting firms are not under threat of going out of business due to AI (see Table 17.4). One could argue there is a barrier between the success of medium/large firms and smaller firms, due to the high costs of implementing new machinery, which might be a constraint to smaller companies. However, this could be viewed as an opportunity, as technology will enable them to be more competitive and offer a more efficient and higher quality service. There is also potential for small firms to merge and invest with collective funds to guarantee that the service they are offering is comparable with AI. A common theme is that there is still a need for accountants and that AI and technology cannot communicate or compare to humans. Although machinery is efficient in processing data, for example, it is still unable to interpret the true meaning behind the results, showing the advantage humans have (Andrew and Baker, 2019).

The respondents highlight the risk of the loss of staff due to technology and the threat of obsolescence. Both the Audit Manager and Audit Senior consider the lack of human interaction, leading to a poorer service, to be a main threat. The requirement for human interaction is extremely important within organisations, in order to build trust and relationships. That respondents observe this first hand, therefore, emphasises the true importance of this. At the moment, it can be seen, from professionals, there is no serious threat of complete obsolescence within the industry. Although, with the speed at which technology is developing, it could be the case in the future that there is a high threat of complete obsolescence, unless there is appropriate action in place to resist a complete technological takeover.

There are also numerous risks associated with cybersecurity, which have also been highlighted. External hacking is much more prevalent now and unauthorised access is a major concern to firms within the industry. As well as firms taking advantage of the developments in technology, hackers are also doing so and utilising it to act unethically and acquiring access to unauthorised data. Addis and Kutar (2018) emphasise that organisations are facing fines, due to data leakage and losing clients, as a result of a damaged reputation and, therefore, trust. It is important for firms and individuals to acknowledge these threats, which is clear, within the

Table 17.4   *Evidence on potential threats*

Q10. Do you think smaller accounting firms will be impacted by AI and go out of business?	
"No – there will always be a need for smaller firms. These smaller firms will still need humans to navigate software, collate information from clients, communicate with clients and also provide professional support on different accounting treatments for the clients of the firm. AI cannot communicate with clients who do not have accounting knowledge".	AM
"Not largely as there will always be a requirement and place for smaller firms. A lot of these firms will also still likely invest in such software where possible".	AS
"Potentially, if the AI industry is able to tailor the programming/machine learning software to the client needs then they can bring their accounting back in-house and the need for an accounting firm would be reduced to oversight of the AI and review of output".	IT
Q11. Can you think of any new threats brought to companies due to the advancements in technology?	
"Cyber threats/ loss of staff due to not having enough jobs/ too much reliance placed on it meaning not enough human involvement which could lead to a lesser of a service being provided".	AM
"The lack of human interaction and creativity. Also becoming too reliant on AI and the processes it involves that it impacts the service being provided e.g. audit quality".	AS
"Main threats are obsolescence. Failure to adopt new technologies might result in competitors gaining a significant edge which clients flock to. There's a similar risk for those who do adopt early but end up over-investing in something that just doesn't do what's needed and is quickly bypassed. The more complex a system is, the more removed from it the user becomes so there is an increased risk that if something goes wrong, it goes wrong BIG and recovery is much more difficult. It also becomes easier to hide fraudulent activity in more complex technology systems. Hacking and malware are advancing fast (and are one of the main drivers of AI technologies. Some computer viruses are the best examples of independent machine learning programs – not quite full AI but it's getting closer to this.)".	IT
Q12. Why do you think machinery is welcomed so easily, despite the fact it could eventually make the accountant's role obsolete?	
"There are massive costs savings from using AI compared to hiring employees. There also aren't HR conflicts with AI whereas there are with employees. AI don't take holidays or sick days; employees do".	AM
"The idea of processes booming faster and more efficient to help with time pressures and to make the jobs easier I think currently outweighs the potential negatives. Also would result in less staff required therefore cutting costs".	AS
"Machinery (computers and automation) make day to day activities easier. They do not replace the need to perform the activity and it still needs to be reviewed, processed and reported on. Automation means we can do more but doesn't mean we can stop doing it so we will still need the accountants to run and interpret these processes. The advances of AI technologies and machine learning will be welcomed by accounting firms as it will make them more competitive and give them an edge (at least for the early adopters) but it will still be within their control until such times as it becomes so cheap that anyone can buy them, after which the accountant role will likely evolve to be more supervisory in nature over the exceptions presented in each AI and challenge the judgements and assumptions".	IT
Q13. What do you think the most predominant problem is in accounting as a result of AI?	
"Too much reliance placed on it. At the end of the day a client wants to talk to a human and not a computer. If there is too much work getting completed by AI then there could be less human input and ideas being created. As above, this could lead to a poorer service being provided".	AM
"The lack of human interaction and creativity. Also becoming too reliant on AI and the processes it involves that it impacts the service being provided e.g. audit quality".	AS
"The lack of understanding of how it can be effectively used to benefit them and the inherent limitations it has".	IT

responses. The professionals within the industry are aware of these cyber threats, as if they were to occur this could be detrimental to the firm.

The IT Expert highlights the risk of adopting automation too early and overinvesting in technology that is quickly bypassed, which is discussed within the literature review. Although this threat is not widely considered, it is extremely detrimental within firms. Literature suggests that firms need to put immense consideration into what type of technology to invest in, so they are certain that the most appropriate technology is being chosen for their organisation (McCarthy and Outslay, 1989; Stancheva-Todorova, 2018). Technology prevents competitors providing a cheaper service as there is less labour and other expenses. Therefore, although there is a high initial investment, technology does not impose additional costs after it has been implemented, facilitating competition from smaller organisations.

17.2.5   Efficiency and Overall Service

Overall, the respondents have not yet seen a reduction in human interaction with clients (cf. Table 17.5). The Audit Manager and IT Expert both discuss how they are able to complete testing without constantly asking the client questions, which they view as an advantage, as opposed to being a threat. By shifting the human mindset, this has turned a potential threat to the accountant's job into an advantage that benefits both the client and the auditor. The auditor can carry out their role more efficiently and quickly and the client does not have to continually provide answers and data. The Audit Senior highlights that communicating with clients is at the forefront of the service they provide. This demonstrates how crucial human interaction is within auditing and is a large part of the job, meaning that the auditor's role is not currently at risk of fully being replaced by automation. Technology enables data to be handled extremely efficiently and humans provide interaction with clients, showing that the best service is provided when the two work alongside each other.

It is clear from the responses that AI has not solved any problems that were unsolvable by humans, but it has helped to advance the profession (cf. Gordon, 2018). Technology has meant that the accountant needs to adapt to the resources accessible to them, in order to benefit from the efficiencies, for example, being able to process large amounts of data quickly, as highlighted by the Audit Manager. The capabilities and impact technology has had were created by humans and, for this reason, it can also be resisted by adapting the dominating attitude to stop viewing technology as a superior, but instead viewing it as an assistant (Kaya et al., 2019).

All respondents agree that AI and advancing technologies have freed up more time for accountants to focus on value-adding tasks, by carrying out repetitive jobs. The Audit Manager discusses how this, in turn, enables a better service to be provided to clients as there is more time spent on problem-solving and analysis (Li, 2020). As employees have more time to spend on value-adding tasks, this will increase the competitiveness of the firm. However, as highlighted by the Audit Manager, this could widen the gap between smaller firms and larger firms, if the smaller firms cannot afford the technology.

17.3   CONCLUSION

Our study has explored why AI and advancing technologies are so readily implemented, despite the potential negative consequences of doing so. Our proposition implies that, if the rate at which technology is advancing continues, then the need for a human workforce, within the accountancy profession, will be eliminated in years to come. The main research objective was to evaluate the impact of technology on the requirement for a human workforce, enabling a clear and justified conclusion on the reasoning behind the adoption of technology. The research employed a subjective approach, using qualitative research methods by studying individual perspectives of those in the industry, within the framework of overarching opinion

Table 17.5   *Evidence on efficiency and service*

Q14. Do you think human interaction has been lost as a result of AI and has impacted on relationships with clients and/or employees?

"There has been a reduction in communication with clients around obtaining information from them, as we are able to complete testing using their data sets without communication with them. This reduces the amount of information we request from them which leads to them being less annoyed with us as auditors constantly asking them for information".	AM
"In my experience with audit and dealing with clients, communicating with them and maintaining sound relationships is still at the forefront of the service we provide. We are still requesting information and data from them and even where software carries out some of our work for example journals testing as noted above, we are still then following up on outliers and any queries with the client. So at this stage, no I don't think it has impacted relationships and communication, however may be potential for this in future".	AS
"No – because to date there is no AI or machine learning based process which has taken the place of human interaction. There are some automated processes implemented which have meant that there are less human interactions required but the interactions were quite mechanical in nature to begin with and, if anything, it's improved relations as these annoying mechanical processes are no longer required (for example, oh no, the accountant's coming again so I have to sit with them and go through every invoice one by one and then wait for them to check it all and give me advice based on some of the bigger ones. VS Accountants coming again. Cause all invoices are automated they've got the info, ran it through some analytics and can give me advice on the biggest issues facing me right away – yippee!)".	IT

Q15. As AI can complete various tasks within a business, do you believe this has allowed employees to focus on more complex areas that produce more value for the organisation?

"Definitely – by getting rid of the more repetitive tasks this frees up more time to focus on the more complex areas. This means that more time is spent on problem-solving and analysis meaning that we provide a better and more detailed service".	AM
"Yes to a certain extent this could be one of the major benefits. AI and automating some of the standard processes and transactions, therefore frees up time for accountants to spend on other areas which are more value adding or maybe require more judgement for example auditing accounting estimates".	AS
"It will if true AI is ever used. Machine Learning to date has removed some of the repetitive tasks which in turn has freed up time to focus on other areas but it's still very much in its infancy. Process Automation is the one which has removed the most mundane tasks''.	IT

Q16. Do you think AI has allowed firms to advance and provide a better service to their clients, resulting in them becoming more competitive within the industry?

"Yes however for smaller firms who cannot afford the technology of the big firms then this will make them less competitive. This will increase the gap in competition between large and small firms which is not necessarily a good thing".	AM
"I don't think it has got to this stage yet, however that may just be my lack of exposure to the extent of AI. In terms of competition, if all firms do not or cannot invest in AI then this could change the market in terms of competition and some firms having a competitive advantage to win over clients".	AS
"Again, the machine learning aspect has allowed a better and faster service, with a more consistent quality and definitely more competitive but I wouldn't refer to it as AI in this regard as there is no judgement taken, only rules followed".	IT

Q17. Have you seen any problems being solved by AI, within accounting, that were previously unable to be solved by humans?

"AI hasn't solved many problems in the auditing world. Typically areas where there are problems require judgement and skill which aren't characteristics of AI. It does help accountants solve problems by processing large amounts of data quickly".	AM
"Not in my experience, journals testing we perform through use of data analytics but this deals with finding patterns in data whereas AI involves data analysis and making assumptions beyond capabilities of humans".	AS
"Not in accounting. We've seen computers solve problems that we couldn't simply due to scale but not through machine learning or AI. Outside accounting I've seen machine learning review network traffic and predict when a member of staff is thinking of leaving a business, simply due to the volume changes in data across the network and emailsystems".	IT

of academic literature (Ryan et al., 2002). Technology has been welcomed into the accounting profession, despite the potential threats to the accountant's role. For this reason, this study aimed to uncover the influential factors of the adoption of technologies within the industry.

It is clear that AI and advancing technologies have brought numerous benefits to the profession, transforming it in many ways; however, these do not come without significant consequences (Jędrzejka, 2019). The profession has gained much from the implementation of technology, for example, it has resulted in an improvement in the quality and efficiency of the work carried out (Chui et al., 2016; Smigel, 2021; Shaikh, 2004). However, there are also many new concerns. One is unemployment, but there are numerous others, including cybersecurity threats, unethical usage, expectations gap widening, inequality and the requirement for a completely new skill set (Neely and Cook, 2011; Spafford,1992; PwC, 2016; Luo et al., 2018).

There is pressure on smaller accounting firms to keep up with the constant progress of automation, due partly to monetary constraints and the development of new accounting software. For this reason, it is anticipated that smaller organisations will not be able to survive the loss of business from clients buying their own AI software (for example, Sage Accounting), as they allow a more efficient and cheaper service. There is a belief that technology can provide a better, more efficient and cheaper service to their clients. But although technology can outperform humans in areas such as efficiency, speed and accuracy, it is clear from the respondents in this study, that the need for human interaction and creativity is still crucial. Humans remain a necessity within the profession and are required to monitor the work of machines. The greatest advantage humans hold over machines is in the personal aspect, as human interaction is a major feature within the profession. Humans have ethics, which cannot be said about machines and the development of sentient machines was found to be more of a theory than a likelihood (however, it could be possible as technology is developing at an immense speed). To completely remove human interaction from roles, like advisory roles, would be unethical and it does not seem possible to respondents, as it is such a crucial aspect of the profession.

The most influential factor of the implementation of AI and advancing technologies was thought to be efficiency, which enables organisations to meet objectives through enhanced productivity (Kaya et al., 2019). There has already been a decline in the human workforce, due to technology taking over repetitive and menial tasks, showing society needs to be more prepared for what is to come. This decline will continue in the future if the lack of awareness surrounding the consequences continues. Instead of completely taking over the role of the accountant, it is predicted that the accountant and technology will work together.

The dominating view within existing literature is that there will be an integration of humans and technology, as it is seen that technology is not replacing the accountant, but instead the accountant's role is evolving (Kaya et al., 2019; ICAEW, 2017). This will enable professionals to concentrate on more value-adding tasks, in order to improve the organisation and enhance the quality of work and service offered to clients. Accountants will have to adapt and transform into fraud experts, business advisors or technology leaders (Parcells, 2016). Although AI and advancing technology has replaced established jobs within the profession, it has also created new options and presented opportunities for accountants that allow focus on more complex areas within a firm.

Although there is no clear answer as to what the future of the accountancy profession holds, it is clear that humans need to adapt with the advancements in technology. Humans need to constantly question how they can differentiate themselves from the robots within the profession, to show their value (Schmitt, 2016). Emetaram and Uchime (2021) observed that AI is still in its early stages of use by wider society, due to the cost of adoption and lack of knowledge within businesses; but in years to come we may see a takeover. The most probable outcome is that humans and robots will work alongside each other, showing there is still a need for humans. Therefore, a continued presence by humans in the workforce, especially in the accountancy profession, is crucial, due to the qualities of instinct and judgement that cannot be provided through AI.

REFERENCES

ACCA & IMA. (2015). SoMoClo 'technologies: Transforming how and where business takes place'. *The Future Today*. London/Montvale, New Jersey: ACCA/IMA.

Addis, M. and Kutar, M. (2018). The General Data Protection Regulation (GDPR), Emerging Technologies and UK Organisations: Awareness, Implementation and Readiness. UK Academy for Information Systems Conference Proceedings, 29.

Albawwat, I. and Frijat, Y.A. (2021). An analysis of Aaditors' perceptions towards artificial intelligence and its contribution to audit quality. *Accounting*, 7, pp.755–762.

Allen, C., Smit, I. and Wallach, W. (2005). Artificial morality: Top-down, bottom-up, and hybrid approaches. *Ethics and Information Technology*, 7(3), pp.149–155.

Almulla, S.A. and Yeun, C.Y.(2010). Cloud computing security management. Proceeding of 2010 Second International Conference on Engineering Systems Management and Its Applications (ICESMA), 1(1), pp.1–7. Analysis. *Health Psychology and Behavioral Medicine*, 6(1), pp.245–261.

Andrew, J. and Baker, M. (2021). The general data protection regulation in the age of surveillance capitalism. *Journal of Business Ethics*, 168, pp.565–578. DOI: https://doi.org/10.1007/s10551-019-04239-z

Armbrust, M. et al. (2010). A view of cloud computing. *Communications of the ACM*, 53(4), pp.50–58.

Badger, L., Grance, T., Patt-Corner, R. and Voas, J. (2011). Cloud computing synopsis and recommendations (Special publication 800–146). *National Institute of Standards and Technology*.

Barrick, J. and Spilker, B. (2003). The relations between knowledge, search strategy, and performance in unaided and aided information search. *Organizational Behavior and Human Decision Processes*, 90(1), pp.1–18.

Bell, T.B., Peecher, M.E. and Solomon, I. (2005). The 21st century public company audit: Conceptual elements of KPMG's global audit methodology. New York: KPMG International.

Bierstaker, J.L., Brody, R.G. and Pacini, C. (2006). Accountants' perceptions regarding fraud detection and prevention methods. *Managerial Auditing Journal*, 21(5), pp.520–535.

Brender, N. and Markov, I. (2013). Risk perception and risk management in cloud computing: Results from a case study of Swiss firms. *International Journal of Information Management*, 33(5), pp.726–733.

Brown, C. and Murphy, D.S. (1990). The use of auditing expert systems in public accounting. *Journal of Information Systems*, 3(Fall), pp.63–72.

Caldarelli, A., Ferri, L. and Maffei, M. (2017). Cloud computing adoption in Italian SMEs: A focus on decision-making and post-implementation processes. In *Lecture Notes in Information Systems and Organisation*, pp.53–76. Springer International Publishing.

Carpenter, B.W. & Mahoney, D.P. (2001). Analyzing organizational fraud. *Internal Auditor*, 58(2), p.33.

Chorafas, D.N. (2008). *IT auditing and Sarbanes–Oxley compliance: Key strategies*. Florida, US: Auerbach Publications.

Chui, M., Manyika, J. and Miremadi, M. (2016).Where machines could replace humans – and where they can't (yet), *McKinsey Quarterly*, July 2016. https://www.mckinsey.com/businessfunctions/digital -mckinsey/our-insights/where-machines-could-replace-humans-and-wherethey-cant-yet

Cohen, M. and Rozario, A. (2019). Exploring the use of robotic process automation (RPA) in substantive audit procedures. *The CPA Journal*, 89(7), pp.49–53.

Creeger, M. (2009). CTO Roundtable. *Communications of the ACM*, 52(8), pp.50–56.

Damasiotis, V. et al. (2015). IT competences for professional accountants. A Review. *Procedia – Social and Behavioral Sciences*, 175, pp.537–545.

Daylor, J. and St. Amant, S. (2017). Education, preparation and training of young professionals. *The CPA Journal*, 1(1), pp.12–14.

Dowling, C. and Leech, S. (2014). A Big 4 firm's use of information technology to control the audit process: How an audit support system is changing auditor behavior. *Contemporary Accounting Research*, 31(1), pp.230–252. DOI: https://doi.org/10.1111/1911-3846.12010

Emetaram, E. and Uchime, H. (2021). Impact of artificial intelligence (AI) on accountancy profession. *Journal of Accounting and Financial Management*, 7(2), pp.15–25.

Engineered Arts. (2022). State-of-the-art wonder. Available at www.engineeredarts.co.uk [Accessed: 6 December, 2023].

Fanani, Z., Budi, V. and Utama, A. (2020). Specialist tenure of audit partner and audit quality. *Accounting*, 7(3), 573–580.

Fanning, K. and Centers, D.P. (2012). Platform as a service: Is it time to switch? *The Journal of Corporate Accounting and Finance*, 23(5), 21–25.

FRC. (2020). AQR. The Use of Technology in the Audit of Financial Statements March 2020. Retrieved from Financial Reporting Council.

Giordanelli, R. & Mastroianni C. (2010) The cloud computing paradigm: Characteristics, opportunities and research issues, Istituto di Calcolo e Reti ad Alte Prestazioni (ICAR)

Gordon, L.A. (2018). The impact of technology on contemporary accounting: An ABCD perspective. *Transactions on Machine Learning and Artificial Intelligence*, 6(5).

Gray, G., Chiu, V., Liu, Q. and Li, P. (2014). The expert systems life cycle in AIS research: What does it mean for future AIS research? *International Journal Accounting Information Systems*, 15(4), pp.423–451.

Greenman, C. (2017). Exploring the impact of artificial intelligence on the accounting profession. *Journal of Research in Business, Economics and Management* (JRBEM), 8(3), pp.1451–1454.

Grossmann, V. (2005). White-collar employment, inequality, and technological change. *Journal of Economics*, 10(1), pp.119–142.

Harris, S.B. (2017). Technology and the audit of today and tomorrow. *Hentet*, 5, 2018.

Huimin, L. et al. (2018). Brain intelligence: Go beyond artificial intelligence. *Mobile Networks & Applications*, 23(2), pp.368–375.

Hunton, J.E. and Rose, J.M. (2010). 21st century auditing: Advancing decision support systems to achieve continuous auditing. *Accounting Horizons*, 24(2), pp.297–312.

Huttunen, J, et al. (2019). Big Data, cloud computing and data science applications in finance and accounting. *ACRN Journal of Finance and Risk Perspectives*, 8, pp.16–30.

IBM. (2018). Robotic process automation (2018), IBM Corporation, https://www.ibm.com/downloads/cas/VYBGVKGL [Accessed January 26, 2022].

ICAEW. (2017). Understanding the impact of technology in audit and finance. Dubai: Dsfa.

ICAEW. (2021). The risks of AI and how to mitigate them. [online] Available at: https://www .icaew.com/insights/features/2020/mar-2020/the-risks-of-ai-and-how-tomitigate-them [Accessed 22 November, 2021].

Janvrin, D., Bierstaker, J.L. and Lowe, D.J. (2008). An examination of audit information technology use and perceived importance. *Accounting Horizons*, 22(1), pp.1–21.

Jaslove, C. (2017). The rise of artificial intelligence: An analysis on the future of accountancy. *Psychology* 18. https://scholarsarchive.library.albany.edu/honorscollege_psych/18, provided by University at Albany, State University of New York (SUNY): Scholars Archive.

Jędrzejka, D. (2019). Robotic process automation and its impact on accounting. *Zeszyty Teoretyczne Rachunkowości*, 105(161), pp.137–166.

Johnson, E., Petersen, M., Sloan, J. and Valencia, A. (2021). The interest, knowledge, and usage of artificial intelligence in accounting: Evidence from accounting professionals. *Accounting & Taxation*, 13(1), pp.45–58.

Karsak, E.E. & Özogul, C.O. (2009). An integrated decision making approach for ERP system selection. *Expert Systems with Applications*, 36(1), pp.660–667.

Kaya, C.T., Türkyilmaz, M. and Birol, B. (2019). Impact of RPA technologies on accounting systems. *Journal of Accounting and Finance*, 85(1), pp.235–250.

KPMG. (2017). KPMG Invests in Game-changing Cognitive Technologies for Professional Services, 28 June.

Li, Z. (2020). Analysis on the influence of artificial intelligence development on accounting. 2020 International Conference on Big Data, Artificial Intelligence and Internet of Things Engineering (ICBAIE)

Luo, J., Meng, Q. and Cai, Y. (2018). Analysis of the impact of artificial intelligence application on the development of accounting industry. *Open Journal of Business and Management*, 06(04), pp.850–856.

Marr, B. (2022). Artificial Intelligence in accounting and finance [online] Bernard Marr. Available at: https://bernardmarr.com/artificial-intelligence-in-accountingand-finance/ [Accessed 18 January, 2022].

Marston, S., Li, Z., Bandyopadhyay, S., Zhang, J. and Ghalsasi, A. (2011). Cloud computing – the business perspective. *Decision Support Systems*, 51(1), pp.176–189

Mccarthy, W.E. and Outslay, E. (1989). An analysis of the applicability of artificial intelligence techniques to problem-solving in taxation domains. *Accounting Horizons*, 3(2), pp.14-27.

Mohammad, S.J., Hamad, A.K., Borgi, H., Thu, P.A., Sial, M.S. and Alhadidi, A.A. (2020). How artificial intelligence changes the future of accounting industry. *International Journal of Economics and Business Administration*, 8(3), pp.478–488.

Moudud-Ul-Huq, S. (2014). The role of artificial intelligence in the development of accounting systems: A review. *IUP Journal of Accounting Research & Audit*, 13(2), pp.7–19.

Mukti, A.H. and Yuniati, T. (2021). How accounting artificial intelligence can prevent fraud. Conference on Management, Business, Innovation, Education and Social Science, 1(1).

Neely, M. and Cook, J. (2011). Fifteen years of data and information quality literature: Developing a research agenda for accounting. *Journal of Information Systems*, 25(1), pp.79–108.

O'Leary, D.E. (2013). Expert Systems. In *Wiley Encyclopedia of Computer Science and Engineering*, Forthcoming. Available at SSRN: https://ssrn.com/abstract=2349274.

O'Leary, D. (2013). Expert systems in accounting. In *Wiley Encyclopedia of Computer Science and Engineering*. John Wiley & Sons, Inc.

Parcells S. (2016). The power of finance automation. *Strategic Finance*, December, pp.40–45.

Peccarelli, B. (2017) The robo-accountants are coming. CFO. CFO, 9 May, 2016. Web, 27 March.

PwC. (2016). Toward new possibilities in threat management, privacy-possibilities.pdf (online access: 2 March, 2017)

PwC. (2017). Harnessing the power of AI to transform the detection of fraud and error. Available at: https://www.pwc.com/gx/en/about/stories-from-across-theworld/harnessing-the-power-of-ai-to-transform-the-detection-of-fraud-and-error.html

PwC. (2018). PwC AI predictions: How artificial intelligence is getting to work. Available at: https://blogs.oracle.com/modernfinance/how-artificial-intelligence-is-getting-towork [Accessed 23 November, 2021].

Reepu. (2020). Role of artificial intelligence in finance and accounting. *International Journal of Advanced Science and Technology*, 29(4s), pp.2275–2281.

Rîndaşu, S.-M. (2017). Emerging information technologies in accounting and related security risks – what is the impact on the Romanian accounting profession. *Accounting and Management Information Systems*, 16(4), pp.581–609.

Rouvroy, A. (2016). 'Of Data and Men'. Fundamental rights and freedoms in a world of Big Data. Belgium: University of Namur.

Ryan, B., Scapens, R.W. and Theobald, M. (2002) *Research method and methodology in finance and accounting*. 2nd Edition. Thomson: London.

Schmitt, B. (2016). Are you ready for robot colleagues? *MIT Sloan Management Review*, 6 July.

Shaikh, J.M. (2004). E-commerce impact: Emerging technology – electronic auditing. *Managerial Auditing Journal*, 20(4), pp.408–421.

Sion, G. (2018). How artificial intelligence is transforming the economy. Will cognitively enhanced machines decrease and eliminate tasks from human workers through automation? *Journal of Self-Governance and Management Economics*, 6(4), pp.31–36.

Smigel, L. (2021). History of AI in Finance. Analyzing Alpha. Available at: https://analyzingalpha.com/history-of-ai-in-finance#ai-benefits [Accessed January 31, 2022].

Solaimani, R., Mohammed, S., Rashed, F. and Elkelish, W. (2020). The impact of artificial intelligence on corporate control. *Corporate Ownership & Control*, 17(3), pp.171–178.

Spafford, E.H. (1992). Are computer hacker break-ins ethical? *Journal of Systems and Software*, 17(1), pp.41–47.

Stancheva-Todorova, E.P. (2018). How artificial intelligence is challenging accounting profession. *Journal of International Scientific Publications*, 12(1), pp.126–141.

Stancu, M.S. and Duțescu, A. (2021). The impact of the artificial intelligence on the accounting profession, a literature's assessment. *Proceedings of the International Conference on Business Excellence*, 15(1), pp.749–758.

Stavrakakis, I. et al. (2021). The teaching of computer ethics on computer science and related degree programmes. A European survey. *International Journal of Ethics Education*, 7, pp.101–129.

Sutton, R. and Pfeffer, J. (2006). Evidence-based management. [online] *Harvard Business Review*. Available at: https://hbr.org/2006/01/evidence-based-management [Accessed 13 March, 2022].

Sutton, S.G., Holt, M. and Arnold, V. (2016). 'The reports of my death are greatly exaggerated' – artificial intelligence research in accounting. *International Journal of Accounting Information Systems*, 22, pp.60–73.

Thomas, V. and Kleiner, B.H. (1995). New developments in computer software. *Industrial Management and Data Systems*, 95(6), pp.22–26.

Trompeter, G. and Wright, A. (2010). The world has changed – Have analytical procedure practices? *Contemporary Accounting Research*, 27(2), pp.669–700.

Tucker, I. (2017). Are you ready for your Robots? *Strategic Finance*, 99(5), pp.48–53.

Twin, A.(2019). Investopedia [online]. Available at: https://www.Investopedia.Com/Terms/D/Datamining .Asp

van Wynsberghe, A. and Robbins, S. (2019) Critiquing the reasons for making artificial moral agents. *Science and Engineering Ethics*, 25(3), pp.719–735.

Yang, D.C. and Vasarhelyi, M.A. (2008). *The Application Of Expert Systems In Accounting*. Available at: https://raw.rutgers.edu/MiklosVasarhelyi/Resume%20Articles/CHAPTERS%20IN%20BOOKS/ C10.%20expert%20systems%20app%20in%20act.pdf

Ye, Z. and Hu, J. (2020). Internal control of enterprise computer accounting information system in the age of Big Data. *Cyber Security Intelligence and Analytics*, 1147, pp.315–321.

Yin, R.K. (2003). Design and methods. *Case Study Research*, 3(9.2), p.84.

Yoon, K., Hoogduin, L. and Zhang, L. (2015). Big Data as complementary audit evidence. *American Accounting Association*, 29(2), pp.431–438.

Yoon, S. (2020). The impact of new technology on ethics in accounting: Opportunities, threats, and ethical concerns. *Korean Management Review*, 49(4), pp.983–1010.

Zemánková, A. (2019). Artificial intelligence in audit and accounting: Development, current trends, opportunities and threats – literature review. 2019 International Conference on Control, Artificial Intelligence, Robotics & Optimization (ICCAIRO).

Index